Within
Our Reach

Within
Our Reach

Breaking the Cycle of Disadvantage

LISBETH B. SCHORR
With Daniel Schorr

ANCHOR BOOKS
DOUBLEDAY
NEW YORK · LONDON · TORONTO · SYDNEY · AUCKLAND

An Anchor Book
Published by Doubleday, a division of
Bantam Doubleday Dell Publishing Group, Inc.
666 Fifth Avenue, New York, New York 10103

Anchor Books, Doubleday, and the portrayal of an anchor
are trademarks of Doubleday, a division of
Bantam Doubleday Dell Publishing Group, Inc.

Within Our Reach: Breaking the Cycle of Disadvantage
was originally published in hardcover
by Anchor Press/Doubleday in 1988.

Library of Congress Cataloging-in-Publication Data

Schorr, Lisbeth B.
  Within our reach: breaking the cycle of disadvantage
Lisbeth B. Schorr with Daniel Schorr.
    p. cm.
  Bibliography: p.
  Includes index.
  ISBN 0-385-24244-1
    1. United States—Social policy. 2. United States—Social
conditions—1945–   3. Family policy—United States. 4. Poor—United
States. 5. Problem families—United States. I. Schorr, Daniel,
1916–   . II. Title.
HN65.S423   1989
361.6′1′0973—dc19
                                                                89-82
                                                                 CIP

WKO

For Jonathan, our son, and Lisa, our daughter,
Who already understand the distinction between the world that is
and the one that might be, and who are blessed—amid much else—
with the capacity to act on that understanding.

Contents

Foreword

In the 1960s only a hard-core group of conservative observers would have endorsed the view that social programs to help the truly disadvantaged inevitably fail. In more recent times, and especially during the years of the Reagan presidency, this view has been adopted by many who represent the political mainstream.

The current negative sentiment toward programs targeted to less fortunate Americans has been enhanced, I believe, by the widely held belief that antipoverty and antidiscrimination programs have not only failed to alleviate social problems in the inner city, but that in some cases they have actually aggravated them. By the early 1980s even many liberal advocates of social justice, including those who had been deeply involved in either the civil rights movement or the War on Poverty, had become puzzled by the sharp increase in rates of social dislocation in America's ghetto neighborhoods. It seemed ironic that in the period following the passage of antidiscrimination legislation and the creation of Great Society programs, rates of inner-city poverty, joblessness, never-married parenthood, and welfare receipt had increased precipitously, and those of inner-city crime and victims of crime had remained at disturbingly high levels.

Civil rights and antipoverty advocates reacted to these developments with visible signs of demoralization, and the view that "nothing really works" began to compete with the belief that meaningful change is possible through progressive social programs. However, I believe that if the vulnerability of ghetto residents to changes in the economy throughout the 1970s and early 1980s had been sufficiently recognized and emphasized, the view that "nothing really works" would have less likely taken hold in liberal quarters.

Starting in 1973, recessions occurred every few years, and each cycle of boom and bust created higher levels of joblessness, which depressed wages. Low wages and high joblessness increased poverty and related problems, such as family dissolution and welfare receipt. Moreover, minority workers, especially in the rust-belt cities, have been particularly vulnerable to the structural economic changes of the past two decades because of their disproportionate concentration in industries with the largest number of layoffs due to economic cutbacks, plant closings, and the relocation of firms to cheaper labor sites and to the suburbs.

The comprehensive antidiscrimination and War on Poverty programs were not sufficient to overcome the profound effects of changes in the broader economy on disadvantaged minority citizens. By not recognizing the importance of these events, supporters of civil rights and antipoverty programs failed to challenge effectively conservative arguments that liberal programs only exacerbate the social conditions in the inner city, and that the problems of the ghetto underclass are intractable.

In the last two years, however, several influential publications have provided arguments that refute these assumptions, including Lisbeth B. Schorr's stimulating book, *Within Our Reach: Breaking the Cycle of Disadvantage,* which, in my judgment, offers the most unique and helpful critique of the conservative vision.

Ms. Schorr is fully aware of the "paramount importance" of policies to "promote economic growth, create more jobs and expand job training, and to assure that people who work can earn enough to support a family," but she also recognizes that noneconomic strategies are important for changing the future of "America's most vulnerable children." Indeed, one of the important contributions of *Within Our Reach* is that Ms. Schorr's detailed discussion of several highly successful local or community interventions in the areas of education, health, social services, and family support dramatically contradict conservative assumptions about the intractability of the problems of the truly disadvantaged.

All of the social interventions described in *Within Our Reach* are grounded on theoretical assumptions about ways to improve the life chances of high-risk children. They represent model programs that, in the words of Ms. Schorr, "provide a vision of what can be achieved, a benchmark for judging other efforts, and—at a minimum—a takeoff point in the search for better understanding of the elements of intervention worthy of widespread implementation."

Ms. Schorr acknowledges that her assessment of the effectiveness of these programs is not based on highly quantitative evaluation research. Indeed, as she so insightfully points out, there is good reason to question whether highly quantitative program evaluations can "capture the essential extra dimensions that characterized" effective interventions. Many of the most successful programs for high-risk families, she argues, "are inherently unstandardized and idiosyncratic." Decisions and judgments about any particular intervention should be based on an accumulation of information that includes the "experiences of committed practitioners" and that shows how findings from program evaluations relate to other relevant knowledge about human behavior and social interaction. To my knowledge nowhere is this argument more convincingly demonstrated and supported than in *Within Our Reach.*

Ms. Schorr challenges us both to expand our vision of ways to attack poverty, class subordination, racial isolation and their deleterious consequences, and to think more creatively about how and why certain interventions successfully break the cycle of disadvantage. Her message is potent and persuasive because it superbly highlights concrete examples of thoughtful programs that have positively shaped the lives of poor children.

However, Ms. Schorr is fully aware that although such interventions are essential in a serious attack on persistent poverty and related problems they are not sufficient. She appropriately argues that, in the final analysis, they ought to be combined with a comprehensive economic policy to enhance employment opportunities for disadvantaged Americans and to raise incomes. I fully agree, and I believe that if this policy prescription, calling for the integration of thoughtful noneconomic and economic strategies, were adopted in our country we would eliminate the problems of persistent poverty in a relatively short period of time. And the life chances of high-risk children and their families would noticeably improve.

—WILLIAM JULIUS WILSON,
University of Chicago

Acknowledgments

Because this book covers such a broad range of knowledge and experience, I accumulated an enormous burden of debt in the course of writing it.

The book would not exist without the encouragement, from beginning to end, of my longtime mentor, collaborator, and friend Julius B. Richmond. His faith in the power of knowledge to shape action not only is responsible for many of his own lasting achievements, but has been a strong influence on many of his colleagues, and I am fortunate to be among them.

I am grateful for the confidence of David Hamburg and his associates at the Carnegie Corporation of New York in supporting my crucial first year of full-time work on the book; also to the Rockefeller Foundation, which, for one unforgettable month at the Villa Serbelloni in Bellagio, provided as idyllic a setting for work as nature and human grace could together create.

I have been unusually fortunate in my professional and personal associations, which enabled me to obtain, from some of the most eminent persons in their fields, what amounts to a continuing postgraduate education. I am thankful particularly for the opportunities to learn that have come with participation in the Harvard University Working Group on Early Life, the Institute of Medicine of the National Academy of Sciences, and the boards of the Foundation for Child Development, the Alan Guttmacher Institute, the American Board of Pediatrics, and the National Center for Clinical Infant Programs.

I am grateful to Irving Harris, who at meetings formal and frivolous provided the impetus of frequent reminders that more Americans must come to understand the great stake that all of us have in changing outcomes for the most disadvantaged.

The enduring dedication—and the accomplishments—of Marian Wright Edelman and other friends at the Children's Defense Fund have been a constant inspiration.

An old friend, Beverly Gordey, and a new friend—who ultimately became my valued editor—Sally Arteseros, joined in helping me to imagine that the "project" I began working on in 1982 could actually become a book. Robert Lescher has been, throughout, a source of wise counsel.

Members of the Harvard Working Group on Early Life, over a period of five years, were unstinting in their willingness to read and comment on drafts, exchange ideas, and help me to puzzle out what worked and why. I am particularly indebted to Lorraine Klerman and Leon Eisenberg, who carefully read the entire manuscript, putting their vast range of knowledge at my disposal, and to Beatrix Hamburg, Jerome Kagan, George Lamb, Martha Minow, Elena Nightingale, Deborah Walker, and Paul Wise. Their suggestions and wisdom are reflected at many points throughout the book.

Other friends and colleagues who read and thoughtfully commented on parts of the manuscript were John Butler, Bettye Caldwell, Ruth Caplin, Steven Davidson, Rashi Fein, Amy Fine, Mitchell Ginsberg, Douglas Kirby, Jane Knitzer, Wendy Lazarus, Sara Lawrence Lightfoot, Richard Lincoln, Fitzhugh Mullan, James Perrin, Sally Provence, Sara Rosenbaum, Alvin Schorr, Judith Tolmach Silber, Vivien Stewart, Eleanor Szanton, Heather Weiss, Bernice Weissbourd, Michael Yogman, and Edward Zigler. Each helped in some significant way to raise the level of accuracy, readability, and insight.

Sarah Brown of the Institute of Medicine allowed me to draw on her extensive understanding of prenatal care and outreach and gathered the material on the Resource Mothers Program in South Carolina. Jonathan Schorr, as part of his high school senior project, visited a number of troubled families in Washington, D.C., to help me describe some of the details of their daily lives. Peter Edelman of Georgetown University Law School helped me think through many of the knottiest questions and contributed material directly to Chapter 10 from his rich knowledge of the practical politics of program implementation. William Julius Wilson was kind enough to let me work with the manuscript of his book *The Truly Disadvantaged* prior to its 1987 publication.

To say that despite the wealth of help I received, I alone am responsible for any errors that remain, and for all of the conclusions, is more than the customary disclaimer. Most of those who read parts of the manuscript did not see my final conclusions, and it is safe to assume that not all my colleagues share all of my perceptions, interpretations, and judgments.

I am indebted to Barbara Morse, Steven Buka, Monique Currie, Victoria Mitchell, Marlena Dasbach, and Lisa Mihaly for providing a rare kind of research assistance. Their competence and perseverance were always accompanied by flexibility in adapting to frequent and unpredictable changes in my needs for help.

I owe more than I can say to Judith Viorst, whose stores of friendship, wisdom, and balm for a novice writer are apparently inexhaustible.

I could not have undertaken this book without the willingness of my husband, Dan, to use his golden pen to sharpen my prose and to make the book accessible to a broad audience. He also visited and wrote about several of the programs described in the book, unhesitatingly subsidized my work for three of the last four years, and —along with our children—ungrumblingly learned the truth of Ann Tyler's observation that her family can always tell when she is well into a book "because the meals get very crummy." When gridlock occurred—in the household, amid the voluminous source material, or in the computer—our son, Jonathan, and daughter, Lisa, came through with breathtaking organizational, culinary, and electronic rescues. I am immensely grateful for their talents, and for their willingness to put them to use on behalf of book and family. And when I needed to be alone with my manuscript, everyone understood, and Don and Ann Brown warmly invited me to hide out at their Virginia country farmhouse. When the writing was over, my mother, Lotte Bamberger, contributed her awesome proofreading skills.

Lastly, my profound thanks to Kathryn Barnard, Ronald Bloom, Evan Charney, James Comer, Jean Ekins, Peter Forsythe, Sharon Glynne, Patricia Green, Stanley Greenspan, David Haapala, Janet Hardy, Lyn Headley, Barbara Howard, Jill Kinney, Marie Meglen, Deborah Meyer, David Olds, Sister Mary Paul, Sally Provence, John Rivera, Robert Schlegel, Aaron Shirley, Rosemary Streett,

David Tobis, David Weikart, and Laurie Zabin, all of whom were extremely generous in helping me to understand their work—the successful programs that are the core of this book.

—L.B.S.

Introduction

Many Americans have soured on "throwing money" at human problems that seem only to get worse. They are not hard-hearted, but don't want to be soft-headed either. Even when their compassion is aroused by moving stories of desperate families or neglected children, they feel helpless and are convinced that nothing can be done. Fear of actually doing harm while trying to do good, together with the threat of unmanageable costs, have paralyzed national policy-making.

It is a strange and tragic paradox that confidence in our collective ability to alter the destinies of vulnerable children has hit bottom just as scientific understanding of the processes of human development and the rich evidence of success in helping such children have reached a new high.

These were my thoughts on July 8, 1981, at the end of a Harvard seminar at which I listened to Mary Jo Bane, of the Kennedy School of Government, urging that we pay more attention to American adolescents who are afflicted with what she called "rotten outcomes"—the youngsters who are having children too soon, leaving school illiterate and unemployable, and committing violent crimes.

Professor Bane explained to our group, the newly created Harvard University Working Group on Early Life and Adolescence, that information just becoming available made it possible to identify what proportion of these young people came from single-parent families, how many were temporarily and how many persistently poor, and what fraction came from minority backgrounds, from urban slums, and even from given census tracts.

My colleagues encouraged Professor Bane's intention to investigate in depth the "epidemiology of adolescent rotten outcomes." I too thought it would be useful to know more about who was destined for serious trouble before the trouble became serious. But what really intrigued me was that we might already know enough to keep many of the "rotten outcomes" from happening.

My hunch was that if we could put together what we already knew about the early precursors of adolescent rotten outcomes and —even more to the point—about interventions that could prevent such damaging outcomes, we would have a solid foundation on which to build a strong network of preventive programs and policies, by governmental as well as private agencies. In conversations over the weeks that followed, Dr. Julius Richmond, chairman of the Working Group, encouraged me to pursue this hypothesis.

Because I had been working for much of the previous thirty years at trying, in one way or another, to improve the health and well-being of people left out of America's prosperity, I had a sense of where to look for evidence to test my hypothesis. And all my Working Group colleagues, even those who were dubious about my quest, were willing to provide me with leads to the newest and best information. So was just about every pediatrician, social worker, epidemiologist, child development expert, public policy analyst, and child advocate with whom I had ever worked.

No one I approached for help questioned the gravity of the problem: increasing numbers of American children growing up in surroundings that put them at high risk of adverse outcomes when they become adolescents. No one questioned the urgency of finding new ways of breaking the cycle of disadvantage.

As I read academic journals and government reports, learned the results of new studies which had followed children's development from earliest infancy to adulthood, and talked with researchers and the people who work on the front lines with families in trouble, I was astonished to find how much we knew. And I was dismayed at how little of this knowledge was being utilized to change the prospects for the children growing up in the shadows, the children most at risk.

Part of this gap between knowledge and action springs from traditions which segregate bodies of information by professional, academic, political, and bureaucratic boundaries. Complex, intertwined problems are sliced into manageable but trivial parts. Efforts to reduce juvenile delinquency operate in isolation from programs to prevent early childbearing or school failure. Academics burrow for what remains unknown but often fail to herald what is known.

Evaluators assess the impact of narrowly defined services and miss the powerful effects of a broad combination of interventions. Successes achieved by health centers, schools, and family service agencies have common characteristics which form patterns that are rarely perceived.

The more I looked, the clearer it became that in the last two decades we have accumulated a critical mass of information that totally transforms the nation's capacity to improve outcomes for vulnerable children.* The knowledge necessary to reduce the growing toll of damaged lives is now available. But many administrators, academics, practitioners, and public policy analysts are not aware of newly emerging insights, especially from outside their own fields.

As important, many thoughtful citizens are deeply skeptical about the value of trying systematically to change the conditions in which disadvantaged children grow up.

I came to believe that if current knowledge is to be harnessed to change outcomes for children growing up at risk, more Americans must become aware of the high stake that all of us have in what happens to these children, and more Americans must become convinced that we know what needs to be done and how to do it.

That is why I wrote this book.

SOCIETY'S STAKE AND SOCIETY'S CHANCE

High rates of violent juvenile crime, school failure, and adolescent childbearing add up to an enormous public burden, as well as widespread private pain. Our common stake in preventing these damaging outcomes of adolescence is immense. We all pay to support the unproductive and incarcerate the violent. We are all economically weakened by lost productivity. We all live with fear of crime in our homes and on the streets. We are all diminished when large numbers of parents are incapable of nurturing their dependent young, and when pervasive alienation erodes the national sense of community.

Because the antecedents of rotten outcomes are numerous and interrelated, not every factor that contributes must be changed before their incidence can be reduced. The correction of a vision prob-

* To make this information easily accessible to the general reader, references to sources and other elaborations usually do not appear as part of the text, but can be found in the Notes at the back of the book.

lem or a good preschool experience, for example, will improve the prospects of school success even for a child growing up in a single-parent home.

We can now identify the risk factors that we know are associated with later damaging outcomes and that we know we can change. And we are able to identify the interventions that can remove some of these risk factors. This new knowledge can become the foundation of new action to radically reduce the occurrence of adverse outcomes.

Throughout this country there are programs that have changed outcomes for high-risk youngsters. The programs described in this book serve families whose children are vulnerable because they are growing up in poverty or with other environmental handicaps. All offer hard evidence that systematic intervention and support from outside the family early in the life cycle can improve the lifetime prospects of children growing up at risk.

The drama of success chronicled in this book is not the drama of *beating* the odds, but the drama of *changing* the odds. While there are heroes and heroines whose life stories stir us because, as a result of extraordinary individual endowment, they have been able to triumph over adversity that would cripple more ordinary youngsters, this book is not their story. Rather, it is the story of how our society can raise the chances that millions of ordinary children, growing up in circumstances that make them vulnerable, will develop into healthy and productive adults.

We may not have all the information we might want, but we have enough to design powerful new social policies. By moving beyond isolated assessments of program effectiveness and applying imagination and intelligence to understanding the relationships among diverse findings, we can make rigorous judgments about what has worked in the past and what is likely to work in the future.

In judging what works, we cannot screen out human values. "A 'disinterested' social science is pure nonsense," wrote the late Gunnar Myrdal. "It never existed and it will never exist." To know what is worth investing in, we must include in our calculations enduring human values such as altruism, community, and justice. These values will aid us in discovering new connections and breaking out of disciplinary straitjackets.

The programs described in this book should inspire confidence that we have the knowledge to change outcomes for children at greatest risk so that fewer of them will come into adulthood seriously damaged and unequipped for a productive life.

Every program portrayed in the book has demonstrated, in some way, a favorable impact on key risk factors or outcomes. All employ methods shown at a theoretical level to be promising in improving the futures of high-risk children—additional corroboration that their successes are not flukes, but an important guide to action.

So much more is now known than we are now acting on; the lessons of research and experience combine to explode the myth that nothing works. We can do what needs to be done at a price we can afford; prevention is a bargain compared to the current cost of our failures.

Of course it is no coincidence that the programs that have proven successful with high-risk populations are and remain exceptions rather than the norm. I am aware that what works well on a small scale may not work equally well on a large scale, and that exotic hothouse flowers often do not survive when transplanted into the cold real world. However, programs may be complex, fragile, and even costly, but if they effectively address a previously intractable problem, they are, at the very least, an important starting point for further action. Careful planning based on a thorough understanding of political, bureaucratic, and professional realities can often clear the way to successful replication, even of programs established in unusual circumstances and run by extraordinary individuals.

THE SUBPLOT: HIGH-RISK FAMILIES NEED HIGH-INTENSITY SERVICES

The story I have described so far is the story I set out to tell. In going after it, I stumbled on an unexpected subplot.

I found my original hypothesis repeatedly confirmed: We can significantly change the odds for youngsters growing up in environments that threaten healthy development by building on programs that have already proven successful. I also found myself in the middle of a whole other story: Wherever I looked, in health, social services, family support, or education, the programs that worked for families and children living in concentrated poverty and social dislocation differed in fundamental ways from traditional programs that seemed to work for those in less devastating circumstances.

The programs that work best for children and families in high-risk environments typically offer comprehensive and intensive services. Whether they are part of the health, mental health, social service, or educational systems, they are able to respond flexibly to a wide variety of needs. In their wakes they often pull in other kinds of services, unrelated in narrowly bureaucratic terms but inseparable in the broad framework of human misery. These programs approach children not with bureaucratic or professional blinders, but open-eyed to their needs in a family and community context. Interventions that are successful with high-risk populations all seem to have staffs with the time and skill to establish relationships based on mutual respect and trust.

These findings about the attributes of successful programs are not novel, but their convergence is striking. Their empirical support is now sturdy because similar patterns emerge from so many different arenas.

These findings shed new light on the frequent observation that available services aren't much help to families mired in multiple problems. Too many observers have concluded that these families just can't be helped, that the so-called "underclass" is beyond the reach of well-intentioned organized services.

The evidence in this book suggests the opposite: Help from outside *is* possible for children growing up in persistent and concentrated poverty, with parents ill equipped for parenthood, isolated from the support of extended family, close friends, and sheltering surroundings. These families *can* be helped from the outside. Help for these families may be ineffective as provided by prevailing, rigidly circumscribed programs. But where programs are especially attuned to the distinct needs of high-risk families, these children *are* being helped from the outside, and this book tells how.

THE ROLE OF ECONOMIC POLICY AND WELFARE REFORM

Poverty is the greatest risk factor of all. Family poverty is relentlessly correlated with high rates of school-age childbearing, school failure, and violent crime—and with all their antecedents. Low income is an important risk factor in itself, and so is relative poverty —having significantly less income than the norm, especially in a society that places such a high value on economic success. Virtually all the other risk factors that make rotten outcomes more likely are also found disproportionately among poor children: bad health in infancy and childhood, malnutrition, having an isolated or impaired mother, being abused or neglected, not having a decent place to live, and lacking access to the services that would protect against the effects of these conditions.

Although economic policy and welfare reform, as conventionally considered, lie outside the purview of this book, they are, needless to say, of paramount importance in breaking the cycle of disadvantage. A better future for the families most disconnected from the nation's prosperity would require not only the kind of programs described in this book; equally essential are policies to promote economic growth, to create more jobs and expand job training, and to assure that people who work can earn enough to support a family.

If the nation adopted these economic policies, fewer families would be dependent on public assistance. Effective welfare reform would be more feasible. More jobs at better pay, expanded job training, and a welfare system that helped more recipients to become productively employed and provided effective income supports would significantly reduce the incidence of poverty—and therefore of rotten outcomes. The frequent concomitants of inadequate income—homelessness, hunger, family stress, and despair—would not continue, in such large measure, to add to the destructive legacy of the next generation.

But noneconomic strategies are as essential as economic strategies if the future is to change for America's most vulnerable children. Just as high school graduates who are competent and willing to work can't support a family if there are no jobs to be had at a decent wage, so expanded economic opportunities cannot be seized by young people whose health has been neglected, whose education has failed to equip them with the skills they need, and whose early lives have left them without the capacity to persevere and devoid of hope.

Economic strategies, even when coupled with welfare reform, will not eliminate the need for more effective services for high-risk children and their families. To reduce the incidence of rotten outcomes, we desperately need both. This nation is unlikely to redistribute its wealth so equitably in the foreseeable future as to obviate the need for services to deal with the consequences of poverty. For those living in persistent and concentrated poverty, it is reformed services and institutions that will furnish the essential footholds for the climb out of poverty. Yet in the legislative, academic, and political forums where antipoverty strategies and welfare reform are debated, the spotlight is only on short-term measures to reduce the numbers now on welfare, now unable to work productively. The shocking deficiencies in the health, welfare, and education of poor children, the long-term investments that could help the vulnerable children of today to become the productive and contributing adults of tomorrow, are rarely on the agenda. (The futures of children are, in fact, often blatantly shoved aside in the interest of short-term cost savings, as when welfare reform proposals would require mothers receiving assistance to work in the absence of a guarantee of high-quality child care.)

Children and families have needs that cannot be met by economic measures alone, and that cannot be met by individual families alone. This book focuses on those needs.

DOING GOOD, NOT HARM

Anyone proposing new or expanded social programs today must be prepared to respond to concerns that well-intentioned efforts to make things better could actually make them worse. The specter of investments in human services actually doing harm is given an air of reality because so many people are in fact worse off—after twenty years of vastly increased social spending. More children are poor, more children are growing up without stable families, and more young people are out of work.

Of the many possible explanations, perhaps the most influential—as well as the most irresponsible—was proposed by Charles Murray in his 1984 book, *Losing Ground.* Murray provided intellectual underpinnings to taxpayer reluctance to invest in social programs by contending that Great Society social policies changed the rewards and penalties that govern human behavior, and thereby brought about increasing rates of joblessness, crime, out-of-wedlock births, female-headed families, and welfare dependency. Murray argues that, faced with the choice between an unattractive job and a welfare check, it is "rational on grounds of dollars and cents" for poor unmarried women to decide to have babies. Only the elimination of support from outside the family would discourage young women from pregnancy and encourage both young men and young women to work for low wages and accept the discipline of the workplace—because the alternative would be so grim.

The evidence does not sustain Murray's contentions. First, countries with far more generous social welfare programs than the United States—Germany, Denmark, France, Sweden, and Great Britain—all have sharply lower rates of teenage births and teenage crime.

Second, if welfare benefits figured in the decision to have a baby, more babies would be born in states with relatively high levels of welfare payments. But careful state-by-state comparisons show no evidence that Aid to Families with Dependent Children (AFDC) influences childbearing decisions; sex and childbearing among teenagers do not seem to be a product of careful economic analysis.

The recent increase in childhood poverty and single-parent households has been, instead, the result of economic stagnation and high unemployment. The unemployment rate alone was twice as high in 1980 as in 1968. Without the antipoverty programs of the 1960s, it might have been higher, considering the 40 percent increase in the size of the American work force between 1965 and 1980. Far from governmental efforts being the cause of our troubles, Georgetown University Law School Professor Peter Edelman points out, the poor would be still worse off without such programs as Social Security, AFDC, Medicaid, and food stamps. "The government's specific efforts to alleviate poverty have not been counterproductive, only gravely insufficient."

A comparison between the deteriorating position of American children and the improved position of the aged also illuminates the difficulties in helping children through governmental income policies. In the last twenty years, this nation has been remarkably successful in reducing poverty among the aged. Despite the increase in the number and proportion of the aged, the United States has, through Social Security retirement and survivors' benefits and Supplemental Security Income, together with Medicare, food stamps, and Medicaid, managed to lift almost all the aged out of poverty. The steep rise in social spending between 1960 and 1980 was concentrated primarily on the aged and disabled, the so-called "deserving" or "lucky" poor. For them, income transfer programs have worked, doing exactly what they were supposed to do.

Why have we not been able to make similar gains in reducing childhood poverty? Why, as Senator Daniel Patrick Moynihan has asked, are we the first industrial nation in the world in which children are the poorest age group? Why, in 1974, did children replace the aged as the poorest group in the nation? Why, by 1980, had the poverty rate among preschool children become six times that of the aged?

National efforts to abolish poverty among the aged have been politically more attractive than those directed toward children—not, in my view, simply because we all have old age but not childhood ahead of us, or because we care only about our individual futures rather than the common good. Nor is it just that the aged vote and children don't. I believe that programs to assist the aged are politically more successful than programs for children, in part because it is almost impossible to help poor children without helping their families, and we worry that support to young families—especially with financial assistance—will rob them of their incentive to work, sap their motivation to be responsible parents, and encourage casual sex, early and multiple childbearing, and endless cycles of dependency.

But careful research has shown that public assistance has not had this effect, and, equally important, that many kinds of support have just the opposite effect. It is quite possible to avoid the negative and unintended consequences of efforts to help. By building on what has recently been learned, we can supplement economic policies and income support with more effective, timely services, thereby strengthening the capacity of families at risk to raise children who will become self-sufficient adults.

EARLY INTERVENTION TO PREVENT ROTTEN OUTCOMES

By the time adolescents actually drop out of school, become pregnant too soon, or are in serious trouble with the law, helping them to change course is a formidable, though not impossible, task. Adolescents in trouble can be effectively helped to make a successful transition to adulthood. Many need skills training coupled with intensive health, mental health, and other supportive services, interventions that are scandalously underfunded, even though we now know they are effective. There is no excuse for neglecting these youngsters, even after they have gotten into trouble. But we must recognize that earlier help would have been better help. The more long-standing the neglect, deprivation, and failure, the more difficult and costly the remedies.

Help early in the life cycle is likely to be more economical and more effective. Failure and despair don't have as firm a grip early as later. Life trajectories are more easily altered.

The great promise that early interventions hold for the prevention of later damaging outcomes is best recognized by those working on the front lines with youngsters in trouble.

"The determinants of early maternity are operative long before the onset of sexual intercourse," says Judith Jones of the National Resource Center for Children in Poverty, in describing the program she set up at a Manhattan junior high school. "How much more do we need to know to design interventions?"

A juvenile court judge asks the social worker accompanying a twelve-year-old boy charged with violent assault why it wasn't obvious that the family needed help ten years earlier—when his mother was admitted to the state psychiatric hospital and the family began to fall apart.

The New York superintendent of schools, Anthony Alvarado, testified to the Senate Children's Caucus that schools have to start their dropout prevention efforts much earlier. "It's strange," he said. "We know what to do, we just don't do it."

Many seasoned veterans share the feeling that they know what to do, that intervening early is at least part of what needs to be done, but that they lack the public support to do it.

Early interventions present the problem of all investments in growth—the dividends come later. Not only does a long time elapse between intervention and payoff, which makes prompt demonstration of effectiveness impossible, but the "profits" are likely to end up on a different agency's ledger than the expenditure. (There may be a threefold return on every dollar spent to prevent elementary school failure, but the prevention dollar comes from a budget that is rarely, if ever, part of the budget that realizes the later saving.)

Furthermore, many thoughtful Americans are uneasy about the idea that expanded social programs could lower rates of early childbearing, school failure, and juvenile crime, because they see these outcomes as matters of character and values, and childhood as a time when character and values should be formed within the family.

To view family matters as private matters, on which government and professionals should not trespass, is not unreasonable. If the development of a warm, secure, and trusting relationship between young child and adult is the beginning of conscience and character, where, one may ask, does social policy come in?

Perhaps in *The Little House on the Prairie,* in pastoral, rural, long-gone days, children's characters developed independently of influences outside the family. But no longer. Not today, in an age of economic uncertainty, working mothers, shrinking families, protective services and foster care, high teenage unemployment, and ubiquitous street drugs.

In today's world, social policy can significantly strengthen or weaken a family's ability to instill virtue in its children.

The public role in developing children's values and behavior is attracting the attention of an increasing number of conservative thinkers. James Q. Wilson, the Harvard criminologist, once of the opinion that the only public policy that could deter crime was severe punishment, has become convinced that the key to reducing crime is the improvement of character. He now writes that the problems of family disruption, welfare dependency, educational inadequacy, and crime in the streets require the federal government to take a role in "strengthening the formation of character among the very young" by supporting programs to better prepare children for school entry and to help parents cope with difficult children.

Liberals and conservatives used to talk about values and character in very different ways. Conservatives would extol their singular importance, and liberals would worry that rhetoric about values and character was being used as a cop-out by those who would not acknowledge the need for government programs. Today people with widely divergent ideologies can meet on the common ground that the family is central, but, to assure that children grow into sturdy adults, the family needs to be buttressed by social institutions, including churches, schools, community agencies—and government.

All families need help from beyond the family, in the form of health services, social support, and education. But for the families whose children are growing up at risk, effective services are even more crucial.

If the superb health, education, and social services described in this book, now provided to a fraction of those who need them, were more widely available, fewer children would come into adulthood unschooled and unskilled, committing violent crimes, and bearing children as unmarried teenagers. Fewer of today's vulnerable children would tomorrow swell the welfare rolls and the prisons. Many more would grow into responsible and productive adults, able to form stable families and contributing to, rather than depleting, America's prosperity and sense of community.

Utility and self-interest, as well as humanity, should move us to apply what we have learned to change the futures of the vulnerable children growing up in society's shadows, and thereby to break the cycle of disadvantage.

Within
Our Reach

The High Cost
of Rotten Outcomes

In the crossing zone between childhood and adulthood stands adolescence, with its many celebrated troubles. Most of these troubles are, happily, transient. But not all. Adolescents in trouble because they drop out of school, engage in criminal acts, or have children too soon are embarked on a rocky life course. Their troubles are a source of pain for themselves and their families, and often a burden for the rest of us. But much of that private pain and public cost can be prevented. With knowledge now at hand, society could improve the childhood experiences of those at greatest risk, and thereby reduce the incidence of school failure, juvenile crime, and teenage childbearing—and some of their most serious consequences.

As I gathered the information to support this proposition, I visited libraries and experts, and observed successful programs in operation. I also caught occasional glimpses of the faces behind the numbers of adolescents in trouble. It was on a visit to a murder trial in the District of Columbia Superior Court that I became involved in the story of seventeen-year-old Carrie Eleby, eyewitness to a particularly savage killing. Mrs. Catherine Fuller, a diminutive black ninety-nine-pound mother of six, had been attacked while walking home in a poor Washington, D.C., neighborhood. When she resisted attempts to grab her coin purse, a dozen young men mutilated her and beat her to death. One of the accused, later convicted with the help of Carrie Eleby's testimony, was the father of Carrie's second child, Tamika.

Carrie sat in the witness stand, responding in barely audible tones to questions about her activities on the day of the murder. She told of having been hanging out and smoking "loveboat," or PCP, of hearing a scream from the alley, and seeing "they was beating on a lady." She identified several of the defendants, including her former boyfriend. Suddenly, in the midst of her listless recital, she erupted in anger. The defense lawyer had asked her to read from the transcript of her previous testimony. The reason for the outburst, the Assistant U.S. Attorney explained to me later, was that Carrie had trouble reading.

In Carrie Eleby I could see a textbook case of the clustering and intertwining of rotten outcomes I was probing in my research. She was a school-age mother of two children, a high school dropout, barely literate, and lived surrounded by violent crime.

The story that began for me that day in the courtroom continued seven months later. Carrie Eleby, still seventeen, had just had her third child. A visitor who saw her soon after she came home from the hospital with the new baby said that Carrie seemed to be bored by the infant and never touched or held her while he was there. Carrie said she was scared to pick up the baby, because "when you pick it up, it's grunting all the time." Both Carrie and her mother seemed relieved that the baby lay quietly in the crib and exasperated by the constant activity of the two toddlers, whom they tried periodically to control with cries of "Shut up!" and "You hateful!"

The first time Carrie became pregnant, she was an eighth-grader. She made a brief attempt to return to school after her first child was born, but it didn't work out; she had had trouble with her schoolwork since early in elementary school. Then, in quick succession, two more children. Throughout each of her pregnancies she smoked PCP. During her last pregnancy she made only one prenatal care visit. Leaving her mother and sister to care for her three children, she was now spending most of her time at her new boyfriend's house. Her mother said she didn't understand why Carrie didn't either go back to school or stay home with her children. Mrs. Eleby thought her daughter needed psychiatric care or at least "mother training."

Mrs. Eleby said things had not really gone right for Carrie ever since she had been hit by a car when she was six. Her legs ached constantly, and she couldn't sleep. But Mrs. Eleby had not taken Carrie back to the doctor since they had been told, immediately after the accident, that nothing was wrong.

As I thought about Carrie, it seemed clear that the adult world had already failed her, and was in the process of failing her children. We can choose to attribute the failure to a weak economy or to weak individual character, to an unjust society or to a society lacking the political will to apply its accumulated wisdom. But whatever causal theories our ideological preferences lead us to, we can agree that life's cards are stacked against Carrie and her children and that they, and the rest of us, will likely pay a heavy price.

That price can be measured in the dollar costs of long-term dependency, prisons, and lost productivity. It can be measured in the human costs of children growing up in families unable to nurture their young, and of hunger, homelessness, and hostility amidst America's wealth and splendor.

But if we cannot quantify all the costs, we can seek to understand the stake that society has in reducing the numbers of adolescents who commit crimes, drop out of school, and bear children. For only by confronting fully the magnitude of our current failures and their consequences, can we develop the impetus to take the actions that can change the future.

ADOLESCENT VIOLENT CRIME

Americans murder, assault, rape, and rob one another at a greater rate than citizens of any other industrialized country. Fear pervades American cities, especially after dark. Fear of violent crime (homicide, rape, assault, and robbery) has changed the way we think and the way we live. According to a *USA Today* poll, most

American adults consider personal safety the single greatest factor in determining their "quality of life." Their physical safety looms more important than job satisfaction, financial security, marriage, or health. Crime, say 49 percent of New Yorkers, is the single worst thing about living in the city.

My friends and contemporaries, who remember never carrying a house key as children because the door was always unlocked, now install three kinds of locks and animatedly compare security systems. "Personal security" has become one of the nation's fastest-growing industries, with Americans spending $4.7 billion annually to protect themselves.

The nation's other massive—and considerably more expensive—response to high crime rates has been to put more criminals behind bars. Although increasing numbers of scholars agree that the limits of imprisonment may have been reached and that preventing people from becoming criminals is probably a more effective crime control strategy, our largest investment in crime control by far is the construction and operation of prisons. Prison construction costs over $50,000 a bed, and keeping a person in prison for a year in 1985 cost $14,600.

In the 1980s, the number of persons in federal and state prisons grew at a higher annual rate than at any time since the government began keeping statistics in 1926. Between 1972 and 1983 the U.S. prison population more than doubled, and by the end of 1985 the proportion of the population behind bars was the highest ever recorded. Only the Soviet Union and South Africa have higher rates of incarceration than the United States.

The United States pays for its high crime rates not only in dollars. Fear of crime breeds suspicion and distrust and perpetuates segregation and racism. The fearful elderly stay at home. City dwellers of all ages restrict their activities and learn to move with caution. All of us can identify with Ronald White of the Washington *Post* editorial page staff, who wrote that he trusts no one he passes on the street at night. "Every time I realize that I have not enjoyed the cool night air nor marveled at a full moon, I know that one does not have to be robbed at gunpoint to be a victim of crime."

Blacks and the poor remain the most frequent victims of crime, but since World War II, the geographical spread of serious crime has made it harder for everyone to avoid. It is no longer confined to a few parts of a city where "gangsters" and others with "evil reputations" hang out, or where the poor and minorities live. Jan and Marcia Chaiken, experts on crime for the Rand Corporation, write, "Crime, like television, has come into the living room—and into the church, the lobbies of public buildings, the parks, the shopping malls, the bus stations, the airport parking lots, the subways, the schools. . . . Crime and the fear of crime have spread from 'traditional' high crime areas into once-serene urban neighborhoods, from the central city to outlying suburbs and towns, and into summer resorts and college campuses."

Still, the victims of murder remain disproportionately black. Homicide is the leading cause of death among young black men. While blacks have the highest rates of committing violent crimes of all kinds, rapes and assaults by strangers are most frequently committed by lone white males.

But age is a more consistent factor in street crime than race. "Crime is a young man's game," says Welsley Skogan, Northwestern University sociologist. So much so that the peak age for arrests for property crimes is sixteen, and for violent crime, eighteen.

Violent juvenile offenders not only wreak a lot of damage while young, but they are likely soon to become career criminals. The typical violent adult criminal has committed his first crime before age sixteen, and most have spent considerable time in state juvenile institutions. Although most juvenile delinquents do not become adult criminals, virtually all adult chronic offenders were once juvenile offenders.

When people worry about crime as a threat to family and property, they worry most about the random murder, the unforeseen and unprovoked attack, or robbery by a stranger. While fear has increased, crime by strangers, violent crime, and overall crime rates have not changed much in recent years and have probably been in a slight decline. Although homicides rose as the number of young people—the most crime-prone population group—increased in the 1960s and 1970s, the homicide rate peaked in 1980 and has been decreasing slightly since then.

Recent minor fluctuations and even declines in crime rates pale into insignificance in the face of the starkly consistent high level of violent crime in the United States. The risk of being the victim of a violent crime is higher for an American than the risk of being divorced, being injured in a car accident, or dying of cancer. The risk of being robbed is 208 times greater in the United States than in

Japan. Homicide rates among young adults in the United States are 36 times as high as in Great Britain and 29 times as high as in Japan.

Japanese authorities recently expressed alarm about a rise in senseless street murders, which had brought the national total for the year to thirteen—about the total for a bad weekend in New York City, observed the New York *Times*. Baltimore, Maryland, with less than 1 percent of the population of Japan, had five "senseless killings" of young boys between the ages of fourteen and seventeen, just between April and October 1985. One, Craig Cromwell, was shot outside a public housing project by a seventeen-year-old who told a friend he "just wanted to shoot someone." Another seventeen-year-old, Kevin Diggs, the son of a thirty-one-year-old mother and himself the father of a nine-month-old daughter, was killed in a schoolyard argument.

In Detroit, emergency room physicians say they cannot take all the gunshot victims on the busiest nights. In 1986 Detroit had 646 homicides. Forty-three of the victims were less than seventeen years old. "Sometimes it seems all I do is children's funerals," said Detroit florist Denise Robinson.

The biggest recent change in patterns of criminal behavior is the sharp increase in vicious, senseless crime. University of Pennsylvania criminologist Marvin E. Wolfgang says that robbery victims who might previously have escaped with slight injuries are ending up dead or in the hospital. "People are getting their heads bashed in and seriously hurt in ways that didn't happen before."

To learn more about the changes in juvenile crime, Professor Wolfgang compared 10,000 children born in Philadelphia in 1945 with a similar group born in 1958. He found that about 6 percent of both groups were "hard-core" delinquents, responsible for more than half of all the offenses committed by their respective groups. The differences between the two groups, however, were startling. Those who were born in 1958 and became adolescents in the 1970s committed crimes far more serious and more violent than the youngsters who had come of age thirteen years earlier. The 1970s adolescents committed twice as many aggravated assaults and burglaries, five times as many robberies, and three times as many murders.

The Philadelphia findings resonate with those of other observers. The widespread availability of street drugs and a much more pervasive sense of hostility seem to distinguish the present from earlier times. Wanton violence, says writer Claude Brown, is the biggest difference between the Harlem of today and that of the generation in which he came of age and about which he wrote in *Manchild in the Promised Land*. Brown returned to the neighborhood where he had grown up, trying to understand the "senseless, often maniacal, rampant killings of mugging and robbery victims." A sixteen-year-old explained to him, "That's what they do now. . . . You know, you take their stuff and you pop 'em." Brown wrote it was too ghastly to understand, but what he was hearing from the young teenagers he talked to was that "murder is in style now."

LEAVING SCHOOL UNEDUCATED

In today's world, a youngster who leaves school unable to read, write, and do simple arithmetic faces a bleak future. When a substantial proportion of boys and girls leave school uneducated, the rest of us face a bleak future.

Americans have always seen education as the best route to individual achievement—and as being necessary to the maintenance of democracy, the softening of class lines, and the operation of a productive and profitable economy. Today, a good education is far more necessary than ever before.

In 1900, nine out of ten youngsters did not graduate from high school, but there was no high school dropout problem. At midcentury, when as many dropped out as graduated, there was no reason for public concern. The avenues to self-sufficiency, indeed to prosperity, were still many and varied. A young person could become a successful, participating adult by quitting school and going to work, as easily as by remaining in school until graduation.

But all that has changed in the high-tech last quarter of the century. Today there is only one way to adult self-sufficiency—the school way.

The need for unskilled workers has plummeted, both on farms and in the cities. There is little room left for pushcarts and family stores in an economy dominated by conglomerates. There is little call for just brawn when "any job that can be done by an illiterate can be done better and cheaper by a machine."

The impact on young people of not succeeding in school can be devastating. "Labor market problems of teenagers result largely from doing poorly in school," said the General Accounting Office, Congress's watchdog, in a report responding to Congressman Charles Rangel's questions about the extent and severity of teenage unemployment.

If nothing is done to change the prospects of the 13 million school-age children currently at serious risk of school failure, says a coalition of eleven education organizations, these children will grow up to become adults who will "drain the economy in welfare and social service costs and seriously hamper the nation's ability to compete internationally." The Committee on Economic Development states that in 1987, the one million youngsters who leave high school without graduating will be "marginally literate and virtually unemployable."

The consequences of dropping out of school are not confined to the economic sphere. Dropouts are three and a half times as likely as high school graduates to be arrested and six times as likely to be unwed parents.

The school dropout's future is bleak not only because employers need better-educated workers, but also because employers use the high school diploma as a screening device for almost any job—whether or not the job requires a high school education.

So it is not surprising that dropouts are seven and a half times as likely as graduates to be dependent on welfare, or that dropouts are twice as likely to be unemployed and to live in poverty. The disparity in income between dropouts and graduates increases each year. Between 1973 and 1984, not completing high school meant a 42 percent reduction in what a young man in his early twenties could expect to earn. An additional fact highlights how employers use school completion as symbolic reassurance: The lack of a high school diploma increases the chances of being unemployed twice as much for blacks as for whites.

Given such high penalties, the fact that about one in every seven young people today fails to complete high school is alarming. Dropout rates—which had been decreasing steadily throughout this century—stopped going down in 1972 and have held fairly steady since then. In forty of the fifty states, a smaller proportion of ninth-grade students finished high school in 1982 than in 1972. Black and Hispanic students and students from poor families drop out at higher-than-average rates, so where there are high concentrations of people in poverty and from minority backgrounds, dropout rates are enormous. Officials estimate that about half of all students in New York City, Chicago, and Detroit drop out before graduation.

As damaging to the nation as the high dropout rate is the fact that so many youngsters leave school with low levels of competence and skill. In Chicago, for example, of the 25,500 black and Hispanic students enrolled in nonselective inner city high schools, 63 percent did not graduate. Of the 9,500 who did, *only 2,000 read at or above the national average.* Schools and teachers with low expectations of inner city youngsters become silent partners with students who are not interested in school. Educator Gary Sykes calls it "The Deal" and says it can be struck with a few disruptive students or with a whole class. It can pervade an entire school. Its essence is "You don't bother me and I won't bother you. You can do only token work. You can spend the hour daydreaming. But do so quietly. So long as you stifle your heartfelt desire to spread disorder, I will give you a passing grade."

So whether they quit of their own volition, are suspended, or stay and remain uneducated, youngsters by the tens of thousands leave school unable to read a package label, follow an instruction manual, fill out a form, read a newspaper, calculate a percentage, or write an understandable letter. Even when they do find jobs, they produce less and produce it less efficiently.

"We've had thousands of dollars of inventory that has been wasted because somebody didn't know how to read a ruler," says John Dashler, the president of Unituft. The business executives of the prestigious Committee for Economic Development concluded that even many high school graduates have not learned how to solve problems and make decisions, and lack the most fundamental skills and attitudes to make them employable.

The great fright of 1957 over the Soviet launching of Sputnik has now been replaced, noted Harvard Professor Nathan Glazer, by the more acute fear that "American soldiers would not be competent enough to know how to use and repair [the products of American military technology, and that] American workers did not seem able to turn out a bus that did not fall apart, a subway car that did not malfunction, automobiles that could compete with those from Japan and Germany."

Concerned that not only our economy but our national security might be threatened, the Department of Defense in 1980 commissioned a nationwide assessment of the abilities of current and potential armed services recruits. They asked the National Opinion Research Center to test a national sample of 12,000 Americans sixteen to twenty-three years of age. The results were reassuring to the department only in the narrow sense that new recruits scored well above their civilian counterparts. But they cannot be reassuring to anyone concerned with the long-term economic prospects of the nation. Thirty-one percent of the young men and women scored so low that they would be ineligible or only conditionally eligible for military service. A shocking 72 percent of blacks and 59 percent of Hispanics fell into these two bottom categories.

Such gross racial and ethnic disparities denote serious failures in the nation's progress toward equality of opportunity, as well as an increasing mismatch between current job requirements and available skills. Both threaten our collective future.

New jobs being created daily in American cities require skills that increasing numbers of city residents don't have, while enterprises that require blue-collar skills are declining. The gulf between the help-wanted columns and the people looking for work continues to widen.

Youngsters who leave school without basic skills pay a high price in self-esteem, face radically curtailed economic prospects, and will have a hard time raising children whose lives will be better than theirs. Young people with weak reading and math skills are four times as likely to be dependent on public assistance as those with strong basic skills, and eight times as likely to have children out of wedlock. Children of parents without a high school education are twice as likely as their schoolmates to be nonreaders. Writer/teacher Jonathan Kozol quotes a despairing illiterate father: "My son was supposed to repeat ninth grade for the third time this year. He finally said he wanted to drop out. I see my handicap being passed on to my son. I tell you, it scares me."

The personal and individual pain that results from not having acquired an education has its counterpart in the damage inflicted on the society as a whole.

Data General Corporation warns that we face "a massive shortage of human resources . . . that will dwarf all other obstacles to our company's growth and could topple the U.S. high technology and computer industry." J. Richard Munro, chief executive officer of *Time* magazine, concludes that there will not be "enough new, skilled workers to go around," with costs to the economy that will soon be "staggering."

The proportion of the population that is younger than twenty-five is shrinking; it is now at its lowest point in the history of the nation, and is projected to go down still further. Dreams of a rising standard of living for all Americans, and of a nation that can compete in international markets, will go unrealized if a significant proportion of young people continue to come into adulthood unschooled and unskilled.

The prestigious Carnegie Forum on Education and the Economy declared that the cost of our present failure to educate all American children will be "a steady erosion in the American standard of living," with a growing number of permanently unemployed people seriously straining our social fabric. The Council warned that as the world economy changes shape, "it would be fatal to assume that America can succeed if only a portion of our schoolchildren succeed."

The prospect of a new age of American affluence will evaporate unless a much greater proportion of this shrinking pool of young people can enter the labor market with a high level of literacy and the ability to perform sophisticated technical and managerial tasks —and with the kind of education that equips them to continue learning and relearning throughout their lives.

Once the state of technology and the state of demographics were such that the economy could flourish with only a fraction of the total work force well educated and skilled. Writing off the youngsters who were least promising might not have been a moral or compassionate option, but the economy could run without them. It no longer can.

SCHOOL-AGE CHILDBEARING

When a baby is born to a mother who has not yet grown up herself, both mother and baby are likely to have a limited future and to place a substantial burden on society.

The alarms now being sounded about "children having children" are the response not to increasing rates of early births, but to the increasingly serious *consequences* of early births. Teenage childbearing has not risen—birthrates among American teenagers have been declining steadily since 1957. But the burdens borne by the young mother, her child, and the rest of us have become far greater.

First, the mother is likely to drop out of high school. (Of all the girls who drop out of high school, more than one fifth do so because they are pregnant.) Forty-seven percent of the girls who drop out of school because they are pregnant don't ever return to school. The dropout rates are similar for pregnant blacks and whites (45 percent) but considerably higher for Hispanics (67 percent).

Dropping out of high school, as we saw in the last section, has disastrous effects on a young person's long-term income and employment opportunities. The school-age mother, who has to cope with one or more babies in addition to her inadequate education, will earn less than half the income of women who become mothers later. Her chances of earning enough to support herself and her child are slim. If she works, her job is likely not only to pay less, but to carry less prestige and less satisfaction than it does for her childless counterpart. In part because of the sorry economic prospects of most of the men she knows, she is unlikely to be married.

So it is no wonder that most teenage mothers turn to public assistance for support, or that more than half of all women on welfare today began receiving Aid to Families with Dependent Children (AFDC) when they became teenage mothers. And it is no wonder that more than half of the total AFDC budget goes to families in which the mother was a teenager when she had her first child. Young, never-married mothers are the population group at highest risk of long-term welfare dependency. In fact, of all mothers under the age of thirty receiving AFDC, 71 percent began their childbearing as teenagers. Annual public expenditures for these families through AFDC, food stamps, and Medicaid were estimated in 1985 to be $16.65 billion.

The burdens for mother, child, and society are all compounded by the fact that women who have their first child as teenagers end up having a higher-than-average number of children. Their children are also spaced more closely together, and by the time the teenage mothers are twenty-nine, they are likely to have more children than they want, though their classmates do not.

The baby of an adolescent mother is born into peril. It is more likely than other babies to have physical problems at birth—to be born prematurely, at low birthweight, in generally fragile health, in need of expensive neonatal intensive care, and at risk of cerebral palsy, epilepsy, mental retardation, and other handicaps. This is less often the result of physiological immaturity than of inadequate prenatal care and the lack of social and economic support characteristic of most teenage pregnancies.

In the last decade or so, professionals have come to believe that, at least for teenagers over the age of fifteen, the threat of having a physically damaged, premature, or low-birthweight baby can be markedly lessened, if not removed, by prompt, comprehensive prenatal care and appropriate supportive services.

However, the risks of physical problems are only the beginning. More damaging consequences for the child of a teenager flow from the high chance of being raised by a single mother who is poor and unready for parenthood.

The percentage of unmarried teenage mothers has risen steadily over the past several decades. In 1984 it was more than triple what it was twenty-five years ago.

Children of unmarried teenagers are four times as likely as children in other families to be poor, and the child of a poor teenage mother is likely to remain poor for a long time. This is not only because of the mother's own dim economic prospects but also because, in most cases, she will be raising her child alone. Even if the young woman marries, her chances of a stable marriage are small.

Before they reach the age of nine, 70 percent of children born to mothers under eighteen have spent part of their childhoods in single-parent households.

But not just any single-parent household. The single-parent household at issue here is one headed by someone whose preparation for adult life has been rudely interrupted.

In modern industrial society, the educational and social maturation process that prepares young people to become independent extends well into their twenties. The adolescent has important psychological and practical tasks to accomplish between puberty and adulthood.

If the normal transition to adulthood is halted before the individual has reached a reasonable degree of maturity, there is likely to be trouble. Adolescence, after all, is a time of trying out different kinds of roles, different ways of behaving. It is a time of unpredictable swings between dependence and independence. Egocentrism, impulsiveness, exploitativeness, risk taking, and the need for immediate gratification are at their peak, even in well-integrated young people.

As psychiatrist Beatrix A. Hamburg points out, when adolescents grow up in a supportive school and family environment and the process is neither rushed nor interrupted, youngsters can experiment, learn from their mistakes, and build a solid foundation of self-esteem and independence. If parenthood, with its preemptive demands, intervenes, it can prevent the young mothers, and sometimes fathers as well, not only from completing school and finding work, but also from completing the personal maturation that would prepare them for adult responsibilities in the world of work, in their intimate personal relationships, and in caring for the next generation.

Researchers disagree about whether immaturity, poverty, or isolated parenting is the most destructive aspect of teenage childbearing, but they agree that children born to teenage mothers are more likely to be handicapped in their cognitive, social, and emotional development, are at greater risk of neglect, and are less likely to do well at school.

Teenage childbearing may impose its heaviest burden on the next generation when it comes of age. Although there is enormous diversity in how the children of school-age mothers turn out, as a group they are in substantially worse shape—academically, emotionally, and socially—than the children born to otherwise similar women in their twenties. They are more likely to have children themselves while still adolescents, their school dropout rates are higher, their achievement is lower, and they are more frequently retained in grade. The children of teenage mothers also start sexual activity earlier than their peers, are more frequently suspended from school, and more often run away from home, get drunk, and hurt someone seriously.

The rate of births among American teenagers is unparalleled in the industrialized world. American girls under the age of eighteen have proportionately twice as many babies as British and Canadian girls, more than three times as many as the French, more than four times as many as the Swedish and the Dutch. Among youngsters under the age of fifteen, the contrasts with other countries are still greater. And although the figures are higher for black than for white Americans, those who would attribute our high rates to the fact that ours is such a heterogeneous society should note that U.S. birthrates for whites alone are also higher than those of teenagers in any other Western country.

The outcomes of adolescent childbearing are by no means uniform, but—with heartwarming exceptions—they are depressing. Most of the nearly half million teenagers having babies every year have meager economic and emotional resources and are without support from family, friends, and social institutions. The consequences are wrenching. Public costs—especially for neonatal intensive care and many years of dependency—are high, but so is private pain. Many of the babies are frail and difficult; many of the mothers and babies never become part of a stable family that could give the children a decent start on life and reason to hope for a bright future.

Damage That Reaches into the Next Generation

Adolescent crime, dropouts, school-age childbearing. Each can be studied separately, but in the real world they interact, reinforce one another, and often cluster together in the same individuals. Increasingly, the individuals also cluster, and the damage that begins in childhood and becomes so visible in adolescence reverberates throughout a neighborhood as part of an intergenerational cycle of social devastation.

Some of the adolescents who leave school early and have babies too soon—and even some who commit serious crimes—will ultimately become self-supporting, responsible, and productive adults. But many will be trapped by the interwoven strands of men without jobs, women without husbands, children without fathers, and families without money, hope, skills, opportunities—or effective supports and services that might help them escape. These young people will become the long-term welfare dependent, the unemployed and unemployable, and the parents who are unable to form stable families of their own.

In the absence of a means of breaking the grim cycle, many of their children will grow up in poverty and in isolated single-parent families. Many will join the ranks of the hungry and homeless. Surrounded by despair, neglect, and violence, these children are unlikely to be given—from inside or outside the family—any vision of the future which would inspire present sacrifice. They are unlikely to get the extra boost of nurturance and encouragement that the children of disadvantage especially need to succeed. They will lack, as many of their parents did, the kind of schools, health care, and social services that might protect them from the worst consequences of their living conditions.

And ultimately, as these children themselves grow into adolescence, many will have their own turn at perpetuating the cycle by leaving school unskilled, having children as teenagers, or becoming delinquent. Disconnected from the mainstream of American society, unable to make the transition to productive adulthood, they too will be stuck in what has come to be called the "underclass."

I am aware that the term "underclass" has been shunned by many lest the label be seized on to blame the poor for their poverty or to mark off a small minority with problems that seem so intractable that they will be dismissed as impossible to help. I agree with the contention of William J. Wilson, chairman of the University of Chicago Department of Sociology, that the liberal reluctance to address candidly the clustering and concentration of social casualties has ceded the territory to conservatives, who see both causes and remedies in exclusively individualistic terms and cannot imagine a successful response through societal intervention and support.

The evidence I have compiled demonstrates decisively that intensive societal efforts can reach and help even those stuck at the bottom—and that the rest of us have a high stake in seeing to it that they are reached and helped. The successful programs I describe in this book are not aimed exclusively at an underclass, however defined. But these programs can prevent some of the disasters that ultimately ensnare people in deep and lasting poverty and despair. They have the capacity to reach those who are not only poor, but who also live in neighborhoods which lack the supports essential to children's healthy growth.

Many attempts have been made to estimate the number of individuals and families whose lives are pervaded by combinations of persistently low income, inadequate education, long-term unemployment, unstable family relationships (including teenage childbearing and single parenting), and behavior patterns and norms deviating from those of mainstream populations.

Until quite recently, mainly because income measures were most readily available, estimates of the size of this population at multiple disadvantage were based exclusively on income, and ranged from about two to about eight million persons.

But in 1986 sociologist-demographer Erol R. Ricketts and economist Isabel V. Sawhill of the Urban Institute, a Washington, D.C.,

think tank, began making estimates which incorporated several of
the most commonly accepted social and behavioral attributes of the
population they classify as underclass. They imaginatively put together 1980 census data to produce what are probably the best nationwide estimates. They identified every census tract (the statistical
equivalent of a neighborhood, with a generally homogeneous population of 2,500 to 8,000 people) that had unusually high proportions
of high school dropouts, welfare recipients, female heads of household, or working-age males not regularly attached to the labor
force. Not sure how much overlap they would actually find, they
then looked to see how many census tracts had high proportions
(one standard deviation above the mean) of several of these indicators.

They found 880 tracts (about 2 percent of urban census tracts)
which had *all four of these characteristics at once.* These they classified as underclass areas.

In 1980 these areas contained a total of 2.5 million people, or
about 1 percent of the U.S. population. In these areas, more than
half of the men had worked less than twenty-six weeks the previous
year, more than a third of men and women between the ages of
sixteen and nineteen had dropped out of school, more than a third
of the households received welfare assistance, and well over half (57
percent) of the families were headed by women. (If one added a fifth
criterion, that at least 20 percent of the population of the census
tract had incomes below the poverty line, one would have to eliminate only six census tracts.)

As one might expect, most of these underclass census tracts are in
the inner city—99 percent of the identified neighborhoods are urban. Geographically, the largest concentration is in the Northeast.
The six cities with the highest number of underclass areas are New
York, Chicago, Detroit, Newark, Philadelphia, and Baltimore.

In the 880 census tracts, 58 percent of the population were black,
11 percent Hispanic, and 28 percent white. Thirty-six percent were
children. The inclusion in the estimates of nonurban areas of great
poverty, like some in Appalachia and along the United States–Mex-
ican border, would somewhat increase the totals. But the estimates
need not be more precise to make the crucial point that the number
of children growing up in the midst of dense concentrations of poverty and social dislocation is small enough that intensive efforts to

serve these children and their families would be manageable—and high enough that inaction is intolerable.

Earlier in this century, the routes up and out of poverty were imperfect, and they worked less well for blacks than for whites, but they were plentiful. Most poor and otherwise disadvantaged families lived in an environment that provided day-to-day evidence that hard work, ambition, and perseverance brought rewards—reflecting in large part the expanding demands for unskilled labor. Moving up from disadvantage did not require either the personal heroism or intensive help from outside it does now. Today, escape has become harder and happens less often. "It was difficult for me and my generation [to escape the ghetto]," says Claude Brown. "It's almost impossible now."

One long-term study of white men born in the late 1920s found that those who came from chronically dependent, multiproblem families were indistinguishable, by the age of forty-seven, from men of more favored family backgrounds. But these men belonged to a historical cohort that entered the work force in the late 1940s, when high employment levels, a steady demand and good pay for unskilled workers, and outside support of higher education through the G.I. Bill offered escape routes unavailable to those who came of age in the next generation.

Forces largely beyónd individual control, particularly the slowdown in economic growth and the shift to service and high-technology occupations, now propel families into the underclass and keep them there. Young men who cannot earn a decent living are less likely to marry and create stable families. (Regardless of race or level of education, young men between the ages of twenty and twenty-four whose earnings are above the poverty level are three times as likely to marry as those with lesser earnings.) But between 1973 and 1984, the ability of young men to support a family plummeted. Sixty percent were able to earn enough to keep a family of three out of poverty in 1973, but only 42 percent were in 1984. The marriage rate of the men in this age group fell by half during this period, and the number of female-headed families doubled. Considering that the longest spells of poverty for children are those that begin with a child being born into a single-parent family and the most frequent long-lasting way out of poverty for children is when their mother marries, the drop in the number of young men who earn enough to support a family is a crucial factor in explaining what is keeping so many children in environments that undermine healthy development.

Economic changes have had an especially devastating effect on black family life. Having migrated in large numbers from the rural South after World War II, predominantly unskilled black males bore the brunt of the decline in the steel, auto, rubber, and textile industries. Even as legal barriers of racial discrimination came down, new technological barriers for the less skilled went up. By 1984, almost half of the 8.8 million black men of working age were out of work.

Bleak employment and earnings prospects for so many black men contribute to the bleak marriage prospects for black women. By 1986 one of every two black families was headed by a woman. The Center for the Study of Social Policy has projected that by the year 2000, in the absence of intervention, 70 percent of black families will be headed by single women and fewer than 30 percent of black men will be employed.

As economic opportunity shrank for the less skilled of all races and backgrounds, the many blacks who were in a position to take advantage of expanded opportunities to obtain higher education and enter the professions, business, or the skilled trades moved up and out, with devastating effects on many inner city areas. Professor William J. Wilson calls it "one of the most important social transformations in recent U.S. history."

Professor Wilson's recent book *The Truly Disadvantaged* dramatically describes and carefully documents how the inner city ghettos became "a social milieu significantly different from the environment that existed in these communities several decades ago." Buoyed by receding discrimination, outlawed restrictive covenants, and their improving economic position, steadily employed and middle-class blacks moved to safer and more comfortable surroundings in other areas of the city and the suburbs, leaving the urban ghettos to the most disadvantaged segments of the urban black community. Although there are still plenty of people in these neighborhoods who work very hard, there is no longer the critical mass of stable, achievement-oriented families that once provided neighborhood cohesion, sanctions against aberrant behavior, and support for churches and other basic community institutions. Missing are the essential practical connections to mainstream society, the informal ties to the world of work that provide models of conventional roles and behavior and could alert youngsters to job openings and help them obtain employment.

Rare in the ghetto today are neighbors whose lives demonstrate that education is meaningful, that steady employment is a viable alternative to welfare and illegal pursuits, and that a stable family is an aspect of normalcy. The vacuum is being filled, says Yale University psychiatrist James Comer, by drug pushers, pimps, and prostitutes. "They're often the only successful people that the kids see."

In depressed neighborhoods of all kinds, drugs have vastly exacerbated other social dislocations, from robbery to personal violence, adding an element of pathology that earlier generations did not have to cope with.

More and more families, stressed and depleted, are surrounded by others in similar straits. This concentration of the persistently poor, unskilled, alienated, unemployed, and unmarried is central to the development of children who grow up in such a setting. These children are isolated from many essential socializing influences and supports. It is hard for the head of a family, male or female, black or white, who cannot support the family, to rear children to conform to cultural expectations and to contribute constructively to society. "In neighborhoods in which most families do not have a steadily employed breadwinner, the norms associated with steady work (e.g., the habit of waking up early in the morning to a ringing alarm clock) are absent. The combination of unattractive jobs and lack of community norms to reinforce work increase the likelihood that individuals will turn to either underground illegal activity or idleness or both."

A boy being brought up by a mother alone, even a poor mother alone, need not necessarily suffer damaging effects. In fact, a British study showed that growing up in a female-headed household is not in itself damaging. But when single parenting is not only a family fact but a community fact, the effect—especially on boys—can be highly disruptive of normal development. When the whole neighborhood is made up of families without fathers or a consistent male presence, not only the income but also the discipline and role models that fathers traditionally have provided are missing. Boys are left to learn about manhood on the streets, where the temptation is strong to demonstrate prowess through lawbreaking, violence, and fathering a child.

Husband-and-wife families constituted only 8 percent of the more than twenty-seven thousand families with children living in Chicago Housing Authority dwellings in 1985. Mrs. Robertus Coleman, president of a block association on Harlem's 114th Street, says, "We have 454 families on this block, 600 children, and I don't think there's more than 10 or 15 men."

Since the *concentration* of misery and social dislocation is so clearly implicated in its perpetuation, the growth in the population living in areas of concentrated poverty is alarming. In only ten years, between 1970 and 1980, in the nation's five largest cities, the number of poor people living in poverty areas increased by 58 percent, and the number living in *areas of extreme poverty* went up by a shocking 182 percent!

Despite the evidence of worsening conditions, the services which could buffer high-risk children against the impact of their harsh surroundings and strengthen families in their efforts to improve the odds for these children remain painfully inadequate. Many services have been reduced as a result of budget cuts, but their weaknesses go deeper than budgets. The kind of schools, preschools, day care, health clinics, and social services that might help are, with a few stellar exceptions, simply not reaching those who need them most. Cost constraints, market pressures, and bureaucratic rigidities operate to make services too narrow, too fragmented, too hard to obtain, and out of synch with the needs of traumatized families. So, instead of protecting against the destructive impact of the concentration of devastation, our social institutions often contribute to it.

The crisis of the underclass did not burst suddenly upon America. Already in 1978, Senator Edward Kennedy called attention to "the great unmentioned problem of America today . . . a group that threatens to become what America has never known—a permanent underclass in our society." In 1979, the Ford Foundation's vice president and expert on poverty, Mitchell Sviridoff, stated, "There is a segment of the nation's poor that does not seem to be touched by . . . any traditional sort of outreach. . . . Their isolation and concentration has only exacerbated the frustration and hopelessness of their life and made their condition the most dangerous and intractable problem facing the cities in which they live."

Projections for the future sound grim. In 1985 Eleanor Holmes Norton, former chairman of the Equal Employment Opportunity Commission, wrote of her fear that if nothing was done, a new group "without work and without hope, existing at the margins of society, could bring down the great cities, sap resources and strength from the entire society and, lacking the usual means to survive, prey upon those who possess them." In 1986 Congressman William H. Gray III, of Pennsylvania, warned that time was running out for the nation to respond to the needs of the underclass. "We're building social nitroglycerin that is going to explode, and the country is going to pay for it one way or another." In 1987 Professor Norval Morris, distinguished criminologist and former dean of the Chicago Law School, said that except for nuclear war, there is no more urgent problem than America's "locked-in underclass."

If we fail to respond, much that we care about will get worse. We have an enormous common stake in undoing the bonds that keep children mired in misery today and threaten to keep the next generation even more tightly locked out of America's mainstream.

But the prospects of even the most vulnerable children can be changed. Even for the children growing up in neighborhoods where poverty, social dislocation, and other deterrents to healthy development are concentrated, there is reason to hope that much of the gravest and most lasting harm can indeed be prevented. We begin to see why as we look at the interacting risk factors that precede adolescent damage.

The Risk Factors

Upon this gifted age, in its dark hour,
Falls from the sky a meteoric shower
Of facts . . . they lie unquestioned, uncombined.
Wisdom enough to leech us of our ill
Is daily spun; but there exists no loom
To weave it into fabric. . . .

EDNA ST. VINCENT MILLAY

Enough is now known about the risk factors that foretell many damaging outcomes in adolescence to provide the foundation for effective action to reduce their incidence. We may lack definitive causal theories, but the information now available about risk factors is enough to build on.

Solutions have been devised for many ills, social and biological, in the absence of a full understanding of causes. Dr. Joseph Goldberger, U.S. Public Health Service epidemiologist, was able to prevent pellagra among the children of the Methodist Orphanage in Jackson, Mississippi, in 1910 by enriching their diet—a decade before the cause of pellagra was understood. The information required for the design of social policy, as John W. Gardner, the psychologist who became Secretary of Health, Education and Welfare, has observed, need not attain the same level of precision as the behavioral theorists hope for and often demand.

An understanding of risk factors can, if necessary, substitute for a full understanding of causes as a basis for formulating social policy. Risk factors have been used for centuries to predict the probability of damage—first by shipowners and insurers figuring the chances of losing precious cargo in unexplored waters. Risk is a statistical concept. An understanding of risk factors does not lead to reliable predictions about individuals or single events, but does lead to accurate assessments of probabilities.

The seventeenth-century maritime insurers knew that the risk factors of a winter sailing presaged a more likely loss, as today's life insurance companies know that a high cholesterol level and little exercise raise the risk of premature death. In the same way we know that a child with school problems in third grade is at risk of dropping out of high school and becoming a teenage parent. The experts may not be able to forecast which of seven youngsters is most likely to commit a heinous crime on being released from detention, and which will henceforth lead a life of virtue. But great strides have been made in identifying the factors that place whole categories of children at risk of disastrous outcomes and in determining which of these factors are most amenable to intervention.

We now have proof that disastrous outcomes are much more likely when several risk factors interact. This is a critical finding, for it means that rotten outcomes can be changed through action on several fronts. Not everything must be changed for something to be accomplished. Not every factor that causes adverse outcomes must be removed before their incidence can be reduced.

THE INTERACTION OF RISK FACTORS

During the last twenty years, our understanding of how risk factors in childhood are related to destructive adult outcomes has taken a quantum leap, in large part as a result of several landmark studies of groups of children—and animals—over time.

These studies demonstrate that it takes more than a single risk factor to elicit an adverse outcome. They have rendered moot earlier controversies over nature versus nurture, by showing that the interplay between constitution and environment is far more decisive in shaping an individual than either alone.

A remarkable animal study provides dramatic evidence of how constitutional vulnerability and environmental insult can interact to produce adverse outcomes.

Anxious rhesus monkeys were the subjects of psychologist Stephen Suomi's investigation at the University of Wisconsin in Madison. Dr. Suomi monitored several physiological indicators to identify certain newborn monkeys as genetically or constitutionally anxious and fearful. These monkeys reacted with an unusually high degree of fear from birth until at least adolescence. But when these high-risk, high-strung monkeys were cared for in "socially rich and stable environmental settings," they grew up to be perfectly normal, often highly successful members of complex social groups.

Having established that the anxious temperament of the monkeys did not substantially affect their later behavior when they were reared in a propitious environment, Dr. Suomi separated some of the physiologically at-risk female monkeys from their mothers during several brief but critical periods. When the separated monkeys matured and gave birth, Dr. Suomi found that *80 percent of them neglected or abused their first offspring.* By contrast, when low-risk female baby monkeys were separated from their mothers, they remained unaffected and turned out to be perfectly good mothers—just as did the high-risk females who had not been separated.

A similar interaction between constitutional and environmental factors was found in human infants by New York psychiatrist Sibylle Escalona. She was one of the first to collect extensive physiological and social data on a population she called "babies at double hazard," in order to explore the combined effects of prematurity and poor environmental circumstances. Dr. Escalona chose a group of infants who had been low-birthweight patients in the neonatal intensive care unit of the Albert Einstein College of Medicine in New York and followed them from birth to age three and a half. She found the premature infants to be far more vulnerable than the full-term babies to damage as a result of "environmental insufficiencies" such as living in slums or deteriorated housing projects, ethnic minority status, and low income. Her study was one of the first to show that it was the combination of low birthweight and social and economic deprivation that accounted for high rates of later cognitive and social impairment among the low-birthweight children. She also demonstrated that the converse was true: for babies as well as for monkeys, favorable environments provide effective buffers to constitutional vulnerabilities.

Dr. Escalona's research provides careful documentation for the repeated observations of parents and clinicians that middle-class status protects against the effects of fragile constitutions as well as a host of environmental stresses.

Focusing even more precisely on the specific components of the interplay between constitutional and environmental factors, psychologist Leila Beckwith collaborated with pediatrician Arthur Parmelee at the University of California at Los Angeles, to study babies with an easy-to-measure neurological problem called "immature sleep organization." What was remarkable was that only the babies who had the "immature sleep" condition as newborns *and* who were also reared with "less responsive" caregivers later had IQ scores significantly lower than average. The children with the physiological vulnerability at birth who were reared in consistently responsive homes scored no differently on performance tests at the age of four than the average. Here, too, the investigators conclude that "only an accumulation of risk factors—which include not only biological vulnerabilities but enduring adverse environments—interferes with development of most infants."

Precisely the same conclusions emerged from a remarkable longitudinal study done in a totally different context—probably the largest, most thorough, and longest-term study of child development ever undertaken. On Hawaii's "garden island" of Kauai, clinical psychologists Ruth Smith and Emmy Werner followed all of the 698 babies born on the island in 1955 from before birth to adulthood.

The people of Kauai are descendants of Orientals, Polynesians, and Europeans who found their way to this island, off the beaten tourist track, to work on its fertile sugar and pineapple plantations. Among the elements that make this study so special is the combination of stability in this population—88 percent of the original sample were still study participants at the age of eighteen—and diversity. The racial, ethnic, and class backgrounds of the children cover a wide spectrum. More than half of the study children grew up in families with mothers who had not completed high school and fathers who were poorly paid semiskilled or unskilled laborers. Others came from middle-class and professional families.

A multidisciplinary team headed by Dr. Smith and Professor Werner charted the lives of these families beginning early in the mother's pregnancy and continuing through the first twenty years of the children's lives. Physical and mental health, experiences at home, school, and in the community, and developmental ups and downs were faithfully assessed and recorded at regular intervals.

The portrait of youthful development that emerges is highlighted by the youngsters' adaptability. When they could draw strength or support from elsewhere, they were able to compensate for a variety of constitutional and environmental misfortunes. Among the middle-class children, neurological problems during their first year, for example, did not mean later trouble at school. The opposite was true for the socially disadvantaged children. Early biological problems disappeared in the children growing up in stable and supportive environments by the time they were ten but were exacerbated in the children from families that were unstable, poorly educated, or very low income. Stimulating and supportive environments seemed to be what enabled a child to make up for moderate central nervous system abnormalities, while the stress of an impoverished home led minor defects to become major problems.

The experience of pediatrician Melvin D. Levine at Children's Hospital in Boston provides one more piece of corroboration for the importance of interaction among risk factors. Dr. Levine and his colleagues were asked to look into the hypothesis that there were an unusual number of neurological problems in the backgrounds of young delinquents. They failed to find a clear connection. Central nervous system deficits and later delinquent behavior showed no statistically significant correlation—until they analyzed their data in clusters. Then a pattern began to emerge. The child with neurological damage and no other risk factors emerged unscathed. It was only when the health problems occurred together with socioeconomic disadvantage or other risks that the chances of later delinquency did, in fact, increase.

It is striking that every study designed to allow for the possibility of finding that it takes multiple and interacting risk factors to produce damaging outcomes seems to come up with precisely that finding.

When research psychologist Arnold Sameroff decided to put his clinical observation—that risk factors seemed to pile up in the families whose children were in the most trouble—to some statistical tests, he and his colleagues selected eleven variables which they thought likely to interfere with the development of competence at the age of four. Confirming his hunch, Dr. Sameroff found a direct relationship: in 215 families in Rochester, New York, the higher the number of risk factors, the lower the competence of the four-year olds.

In a quite different cultural and social setting, British psychiatrist Michael Rutter came to an identical—if arithmetically more elegant—conclusion. He found that children who encountered only one risk factor were no more likely to suffer serious consequences than children experiencing no risk factors at all. By contrast, when two or more stresses occurred together, the chance of a damaging outcome went up at least fourfold, and when four factors were present, the risk increased tenfold. Concluded Dr. Rutter: "Stresses potentiate each other so that the combination of chronic stresses provides very much more than a summation of the separate stresses singly."

The extraordinary synchrony of findings from such a variety of sources—a group of delinquents, an entire island population, two groups of vulnerable newborns, city families on two continents, and even a colony of monkeys—provide powerful evidence that it takes more than a single risk factor to produce damaging outcomes. Lasting damage occurs when a child's constitutional vulnerabilities interact with an unsupportive environment. Lasting damage occurs when the elements of a child's environment—at home, at school, in the neighborhood—multiply each other's destructive effects.

The implication is clear: The prevention of rotten outcomes is not a matter of all or nothing. It will make a difference if we can reduce the incidence of low birthweight or of vision defects, if the isolated mother is helped to respond to her difficult infant, if more children come to school better prepared, succeed in mastering fundamental academic skills, and have reason to look forward to a better future.

It will be of value if we can eliminate one risk factor or two, even if others remain.

This insight lets us sort what is known about the antecedents of rotten outcomes to provide a basis for action. By distinguishing between those factors we can do something about and those we can't, the problem becomes less intractable. Some risk factors are not amenable to modification through deliberate social action; others are too difficult to change with our state of knowledge. For example, we can do little about the finding that delinquency rates rise as the proportion of adolescents in the population rises. But we do know how to reduce the incidence of low birthweight and how to provide social support. So the finding that a child born at low birthweight or to a mother without social support stands an increased chance of being abused or of failing in elementary school is a finding we must seize on. Not only do we seek to prevent child abuse and early school problems for their own sake, we also know that these are important risk factors for delinquency, for school-age childbearing, and for dropping out of school. That is a powerful chain of knowledge, for it provides a basis for action.

REDUCING THE RISK FACTORS THAT LEAD TO ROTTEN OUTCOMES

Many of the antecedents of adolescent crime, school failure, and early childbearing have been identified. The research findings of the last twenty years linking risk factors to outcomes converge dramatically. Risk factors implicated in one adverse outcome appear again with another. The common strands are the more startling because the findings come from such diverse research.

Three clear themes emerge: First, *risk factors leading to later damage occur more frequently among children in families that are poor* and still more frequently among families that are persistently poor and live in areas of concentrated poverty. Second, *the plight of the children bearing these risks is not just individual and personal;* it requires a societal response. Third, *the knowledge to help is available;* there is a reasonably good match between known risk factors and the interventions to reduce them.

The close association between poverty and risk holds for every component of risk—from premature birth to poor health and nutrition, from failure to develop warm, secure, trusting relationships early in life to child abuse, from family stress and chaos to failure to master school skills. Persistent and concentrated poverty virtually guarantee the presence of a vast collection of risk factors and their continuing destructive impact over time. (The converse is also true. Middle-class status is an effective buffer against a wide variety of risk factors.)

The child in a poor family who is malnourished and living in an unheated apartment is more susceptible to ear infection; once the ear infection takes hold, inaccessible or inattentive health care may mean it will not be properly treated; hearing loss in the midst of economic stress may go undetected at home, in day care, and by the health system; undetected hearing loss will do long-term damage to a child who needs all the help he can get to cope with a world more complicated than the world of most middle-class children. When this child enters school, his chances of being in an overcrowded classroom with an overwhelmed teacher further compromise his chances of successful learning. Thus risk factors join to shorten the odds of favorable long-term outcomes.

Both the informal supports from family and friends and the institutions and services that could buffer these risks are also less likely to be there for the poorest children. Given the way helping systems operate, these are the children who will not get the kind of attention that could provide them with protection against adversity.

The absence of good services and schooling have, for a high proportion of vulnerable children, actually become additional risk factors. The institutions and services now in place have not interrupted the downward spiral for the children of the shadows because the services these children need are inaccessible or do not exist. The services they can obtain are often the wrong ones, too cumbersome to reach, too fragmented, or too narrow in scope. With a few noteworthy exceptions, these children, who, along with their families, should be getting the attention of the most skilled and wise professionals, the best-organized and best-funded institutions and agencies, and the most comprehensive services, have to make do with doctors, clinics, social agencies, child care, and schools that offer the worst and the least.

Putting together what is known about childhood risk factors shows clearly that *the plight of the children bearing these risks is not just individual and personal,* and therefore requires a societal response.

- These are the children growing up with parents who are not only poor but isolated, impaired, undermined by their surroundings, and stressed beyond their ability to endure. The adversity that assaults these children persists over time, continually reinforcing its destructive impact.
- These are the children who have been accumulating burdens from before birth, when their mothers' health was not well cared for, nor was their own health as infants and small children. They are more vulnerable than others to stress, yet additional stresses are heaped on them as they grow, and they are far less likely to be protected against the effects of these stresses.
- These are the children growing up in families whose lives are out of control, with parents too drained to provide the consistent nurturance, structure, and stimulation that prepares other children for school and for life. They experience failure as soon as they enter the world outside the family (and often before) and rapidly become convinced that they are born to fail.
- These are the children whose experience of failure is compounded and reinforced by not learning the skills that schools are meant to teach, who soon become aware that the future holds little promise for them. Their prospects for a satisfying and well-paying job and for a stable family life seem bleak. Because they perceive a future that holds few attractions, they enter adolescence with no reason to believe that anything worthwhile will be lost by dropping out of school, committing crimes, or having babies as unmarried teenagers.
- These are the children who lack the hope, dreams, and stake in the future that is the basis for coping successfully with adversity and for sacrificing immediate rewards for long-term gains.

The third theme that emerges from a review of risk factors is that *the knowledge to help is available*. The match between the crucial risk factors and the known effective interventions* is good enough to produce a rich agenda for action:

- The *risk factors* of unwanted children, children born too close together, and children born to teenagers can be reduced through the *interventions* of better access to more effective and appropriate

---

* I use the term "intervention" to mean "any systematic attempt to alter the course of development from either its established or predicted path."

family planning services, and by measures that help youngsters to develop a greater stake in their own futures.

- The *risk factors* of babies born at low birthweight, prematurely, or with congenital handicaps can be reduced through the *interventions* of better access to enriched and more effective forms of prenatal care.
- The *risk factors* of children suffering from poor health, malnutrition, and correctable physical defects can be reduced through the *interventions* of broader and more effective child health services.
- The *risk factors* of children who are neglected, abused, unnecessarily removed from their homes, or otherwise growing up without the nurturance, protection, and guidance they need from their families can be reduced through the *interventions* of more widely available effective and intensive social and family support services.
- The *risk factors* of children who encounter early problems at school and ultimately fail to acquire the skills needed to become independent and productive can be reduced through the *interventions* of family support services, high-quality child care and preschool education, and elementary schools that are more responsive to the needs of high-risk children and families.

As we have seen, no one circumstance, no single event, is the cause of a rotten outcome. School failure, delinquency, teenage pregnancy—none is dependent on a single devastating risk factor. But each risk factor vanquished does enhance the odds of averting later serious damage. A healthy birth, a family helped to function even though one parent is depressed and the other seldom there, effective preparation for school entry—all powerfully tip the scales toward favorable outcomes.

So even when a family unassisted and alone cannot provide the necessary material and psychological resources, it is now clear that it is within our power to harness social institutions for a clearly focused attack on a complex but well-defined set of problems.

As will become plain in the following chapters, there is a foundation to build on—programs that have succeeded in significantly reducing the probabilities of adverse outcomes for children growing up at risk and thereby helping to break the cycle of disadvantage.

Fewer Early
and Unplanned Pregnancies

"It's just amazing, it's like nobody discovered parenthood before," said *Doonesbury* creator Garry Trudeau, finishing Halloween preparations while explaining to a young Washington *Post* reporter how it feels to be the father of three-year-old twins and a newborn baby. "It's something you and your wife will decide together and, God willing, everything will go well and you'll have this baby. And it will be the most important thing in your life."

Any child so cherished by its parents will have a powerful psychic shield against future harm. Any child—not just the children of Garry Trudeau and Jane Pauley—born wanted, to parents with the emotional and economic resources to make child rearing a joy, starts with a big leg up on the future.

THE CONSEQUENCES OF UNWANTED
OR TOO-EARLY CHILDBEARING

Research findings confirm what every kitchen philosopher knows. "A child whose birth is eagerly awaited," reported the Select Panel for the Promotion of Child Health, "has the best chance of getting a healthy start in life. A wanted child is far more likely than an unwanted one to enter a loving, nurturing home environment that encourages healthy growth and development." A woman who welcomes her pregnancy is more likely to guard her health, watch her diet, and get early and continuing prenatal care, thereby improving the odds that she will have a healthy child.

The child of a reluctant mother, by contrast, faces significant risks of being born prematurely, at low birthweight, and with congenital defects, as well as longer-term perils. American and Czechoslovakian researchers together examined the histories of 220 children born in Prague between 1961 and 1963 to women who had been refused abortions—children they judged could reasonably be classified as unwanted. Compared to 220 otherwise similar children at age nine, the "unwanted" children were more apt to have suffered acute illness, to have been hospitalized, and to be overly aggressive. Their behavior in grade school led the investigators to predict difficulties at puberty and during adolescence. At later follow-up, again in comparison with the control children, fewer of the unwanted children were found to have attended high school, and more had had intercourse before the age of fifteen.

Equally dramatic findings came from a Swedish study, which followed to the age of twenty-one a group of 120 children of women who had been refused abortions. The "unwanted" children, each of whom was compared to the next child of the same sex born in the same hospital, had significantly less education and were significantly more likely to be dependent on public assistance, and more than twice as many had become delinquent.

Another category of risk—too many children born in too-rapid succession—may be underestimated in a nation where large, wealthy families like the Kennedys have contributed so much. But the evidence shows that, especially when the family is poor, the larger the number of children and the more closely together they are born, the greater the chances of adverse outcomes.

A birth that occurs within a year of a previous birth is associated with a higher frequency of health complications, including a three- to fourfold increase in the chances of low birthweight.

Children from families of four or more were at significantly greater risk of becoming delinquent or developing conduct disorders, according to psychiatrist Michael Rutter's studies of poor children in London and on the Isle of Wight in the English Channel. Dr. Rutter believes the association probably arises from a combination of socioeconomic disadvantage, less intensive interaction between parents and children in large families, and the difficulty of maintaining discipline and supervision when there are a lot of children to look after. Also in England, in a study of boys from London working-class families, David Farrington and Donald West calculated that the chances of delinquency increase by 57 percent when a child has more than three siblings before the age of ten.

Half a world away, in what was almost a mirror image of the British studies, psychologists Emmy Werner and Ruth Smith found that the resilient children of Kauai who performed well above the norm despite a history of family poverty and instability, typically were born more than two years apart from their siblings.

Risks to healthy development also occur when the mother is close to the end of her reproductive years, but these are often compensated for by her more propitious economic circumstances. The converse is true for mothers who bear children at too early an age. As we saw in Chapter i, childbearing by school-age mothers carries high risks for the future of both mother and child.

THE ORIGINS OF FEDERAL SUPPORT OF FAMILY PLANNING

Society has an interest in well-spaced and wanted children. But there is a strong consensus in this country that these are matters to be decided privately by individuals in a family setting.

The stormy evolution of governmental policy toward family planning got under way in the mid-sixties, when the growing realization of society's stake in the outcome of these private decisions converged with the understanding that only government had sufficient resources to help families realize their private wishes. Given the current concern about teenage pregnancy and unmarried childbearing, it is easy to lose sight of the contribution that public support of family planning services has made to enabling most American families to have the number of children they want, and to have them when they want them. One sixth as many women had a fifth child in 1983 as in 1965, when systematic government support of family planning services began.

Except for teenagers, to whom we will shortly return, the greatest reduction in birthrates occurred in populations whose children would be at highest risk of damaging outcomes. Between 1965 and 1981 federally supported family planning programs played an important role in significantly narrowing the gap in contraceptive use between blacks and whites and between more and less educated women.

Government support for family planning services has become so familiar a part of the national landscape that we forget how recently the federal government began to play its vital role.

When I joined President Johnson's War on Poverty early in 1965 to direct the health activities of the Community Action Program, I was surprised to discover that my responsibilities included family planning matters. In fact, the first appointment scheduled for me on my first day on the job was lunch with two senior officials of the Planned Parenthood Federation of America, Dr. Alan Guttmacher, the famed obstetrician, and his persuasive associate, Fred Jaffe. They made a forceful presentation: If our objective was really to reduce poverty and dependency, it was incumbent on the Office of Economic Opportunity (OEO) to spearhead a clear new federal policy to make family planning services affordable and available nationwide.

Until then the national government had avoided what was regarded as a political hot potato. But, as with a CIA covert action program, it allowed some money to trickle into family planning activities under other headings. Funding was buried in appropriations for general health services for government employees, both civilian and military, and in flexible grants to the states for maternal and child health. It was assumed that states and localities were using some of the grant money to support family planning activities, but officially Congress and the Department of Health, Education and Welfare (HEW) preferred not to know about it.

It was, said Dr. Guttmacher, as though HEW, fearing to be caught supporting family planning, would deposit the money on a tree stump in the dark of the night and scurry away.

Under the lash of President Johnson's demand for demonstrable cost-effectiveness, OEO's Division of Research, Planning and Program Evaluation assessed the comparative contribution that each of its proposed programs could make toward the elimination of poverty.

Dr. Joseph A. Kershaw, head of that division, reported to OEO Director Sargent Shriver and the agency staff that federal support of locally sponsored family planning programs promised, far and away, to provide the biggest bang for a buck of the contemplated assaults on poverty. The magic cost-effectiveness ratio assigned to it was eighteen to one.

Dr. Kershaw explained that OEO-supported family planning programs would simply give the poor the same option open to the rest of the population—to choose whether and when they wanted children. Supplying advice and contraceptive devices to about 5 million poor women of childbearing age at the then prevailing cost of $20 a person would total $100 million if they all availed themselves of the option. Not all of them would, of course, but nothing could beat this as a way of reducing family poverty and dependency, and at the same time giving poor families a greater degree of control over their own lives.

The argument gained still greater force on June 7, 1965, when the U.S. Supreme Court struck down the laws of twenty-nine states that, in various ways, put restrictions on the use of contraceptives.

One hurdle remained to be cleared before support of family planning could become an official federal policy. On a Saturday morning, Dr. Kershaw was invited to Timberlawn, Sargent Shriver's home in suburban Rockville, Maryland. Led out to the verandah overlooking acres of rolling green serenity, the former Williams College economics professor was surprised to find not only the director, but his wife, Eunice Kennedy Shriver, sister of the late President, flanked by two Roman Catholic priests in clerical garb.

Shriver listened mainly in silence while this unofficial review panel questioned Dr. Kershaw about the wisdom of federal support for family planning. Mrs. Shriver stated bluntly that, to her mind, it was not fair to keep children from being born, and that government support for family planning was not good public policy. The priests supported her argument. In the end, Shriver thanked the bewildered research director for coming and said he would be seeing him on Monday at the office.

Significant numbers of local communities were, by this time, preparing requests to OEO for funds to support family planning programs. The paperwork was rolling through the bureaucratic mills. Monday arrived and nothing was said. The days went by, and confusion reigned in the new OEO headquarters on 19th Street in downtown Washington. Community action leaders called Dr. Kershaw to say they hesitated to submit new applications for family planning funds in the light of rumors that the director opposed the idea. Finally, Dr. Kershaw, himself now fully committed, buttonholed Shriver and told him, "They're saying all over the place that you don't want this program."

Painting his own profile in courage, Shriver replied that despite his wife's personal views, he would issue a policy statement dispelling the rumors and affirming that antipoverty agencies, at local option, could request family planning funds. There would be restrictions. Eligibility for services would be limited to married women over twenty-one years of age and women who had already had children.

It was a hesitant start, but considering that the majority of health departments, and even hospitals with maternity services, were not making birth control available to poor women, OEO, the maverick new federal agency, had made an important breakthrough in national policy. Its full significance was not recognized at the time, perhaps because of how slowly and falteringly the program got under way. In the first year only five communities started OEO-financed family planning projects. In 1967 Congress raised family planning to the status of a "special emphasis" program in the war on poverty. In addition, it earmarked 6 percent of all of HEW's maternal and child health funds for that purpose. By 1968 there were 159 OEO-financed family planning projects scattered around the country among trailblazing antipoverty community action agencies. They operated within narrow confines—birth control services were still generally denied to unmarried women. The whole program cost about $13.5 million, a drop in the budgetary bucket.

But from the experience of these adventurous communities, supported by a temporary agency willing to rub up against political taboos, some important lessons were learned. Contrary to prevailing myth, low-income women, like better-off women, availed themselves of birth control when the services were offered in accessible settings that respected their needs, wishes, and privacy.

The beachhead established by the antipoverty warriors was expanded under President Nixon. In a 1969 message to Congress on population problems, he called for stepping up spending for family planning by the OEO and the more tradition-bound HEW. In 1970 President Nixon signed into law the Family Planning Services and Population Research Act, incorporated into the Public Health Service Act as Title X. In five years, family planning had blossomed from a timid experiment to a full-fledged national policy, reflecting a broad consensus.

The federal government had recognized and acted on the nation's interest in helping to enable all Americans to determine the number and spacing of their children. The federal interest was based on the documented effectiveness of family planning in improving the health of mothers and children in general, and its predictable effect on reducing poverty and helping to break the cycle of dependency.

For relatively modest tax expenditures, the government enabled American families to exercise more control over the number of children they would have and when they would have them and reduced the likelihood that income, education, and race would determine who would have access to effective contraception.

Between 1965 and 1982 unwanted births among black married women fell by 71 percent; among married women with less than a twelfth-grade education, by 60 percent. In 1965 black married women were half as likely as white married women to use contraception; by 1982 that gap had narrowed to 6 percent. Unplanned births to married women plummeted from 65 to 29 percent in the same period. Contributing to this decline was the introduction of the birth control pill and the legalization of abortion, but the magnitude of the reduction would not have occurred without the increased availability of subsidized family planning services.

The greater availability of family planning services was also a major factor in the reduction of infant mortality over the last twenty years. Among low-income black women, only the availability of legal abortion seems to have been of comparable significance.

Despite their favorable impact on infant health and on giving families more control over how many children they will have and when, publicly supported family planning services were cut back and became mired in controversy throughout the years of the Reagan Administration. Federal funds for family planning services under Title X of the Public Health Service Act were cut from $150 million in 1980 to $100 million in 1982; under Title XX, the Social

Services block grant of the Social Security Act, they were cut by more than half between 1980 and 1983. The suspicions of Right to Life organizations that federally supported family planning agencies were encouraging abortions, and the opposition of some administration officials to all government-subsidized family planning services, created turbulence in the ranks of family planning providers. Much of their energy was diverted into fighting to maintain their programs and services, at the expense of program development.

Even before the Reagan Administration began its attack it had become clear that the prevention of unplanned births was not progressing equally smoothly on all fronts. In the early 1980s, unplanned pregnancy among adults continued to recede; a substantial number of teenagers also avoided unintended pregnancies through the use of contraception, but unplanned and too-early pregnancy among teenagers emerged as an increasingly troublesome social problem. Although the rate of teenage births declined during the 1970s, the rate of births among *unmarried* teenagers climbed. It also became clear that the problem was too profound to be solved only through making family planning services and information more widely available.

FAMILY PLANNING AND BEYOND

The prevention of unwanted childbearing among teenagers raises different issues than it does among adults. First, there is much less agreement about a reasonable public policy on the dissemination of contraceptive services and education to teenagers. Second, and even more important, to reduce too-early childbearing it is not enough to make contraceptive information and services more available; at least as critical are the environments that encourage early childbearing, especially outside of marriage.

At the outset it is important to recognize that for teenagers, the line between "wanted" and "unwanted" pregnancy and childbearing is much hazier than it is for adults.

Take fifteen-year-old Mary, a Chicago ninth-grader. She first had intercourse the week she was suspended from school as punishment for her chronic truancy. She had not been sure she wanted to "go all the way" with her sixteen-year-old boyfriend, but he insisted. She had heard you couldn't get pregnant the very first time, but about six weeks later she started to worry. She went to a family planning clinic for contraceptive advice and learned that, yes, she was pregnant. Her story of ignorance and confusion, of intercourse too early and a clinic visit too late, has been repeated, in its essentials, hundreds of thousands of times.

High rates of school-age pregnancy and childbearing represent a particularly American tragedy. As we saw in Chapter 1, American girls younger than eighteen have twice as many babies, proportionately, as British and Canadian girls, more than three times as many as the French, and more than four times as many as the Swedish and Dutch.

Asked why Dutch rates were so low, Dutch sociologist Evert Ketting replied, "We in Holland don't think of our rates as low. We would like to see them drop even further. What amazes me is how high rates are in the United States. How can the richest country in the world allow a situation to continue that would not be tolerated in other countries?"

What our "Dutch uncle" was saying, in effect, was that the United States was neglecting to act in response to factors known to be responsible for abnormally high rates of school-age pregnancy.

The most fundamental reason for high rates of school-age pregnancy in the United States is that far too many youngsters reach adolescence without hopes or plans for a future that seem compelling enough to deter them from early parenthood. This paucity of options is frequently intertwined with ignorance about reproduction and lack of access to the kind of counseling and contraceptive services that would enable teenagers to avoid pregnancy. For some, the problem is that they are so young they could not possibly be expected to use contraceptives effectively, much less to be responsible parents.

The young people who must be encouraged to postpone sex, those who need better access to accurate information and appropriate services, and those who need more realistic alternatives to early parenthood are not clearly distinguishable groups.

We know that the majority of teenage pregnancies are neither planned nor wanted, but attempts to be more precise run into the ambiguities of complex human behavior.

Sherita Dreher, testifying before the Washington, D.C., Blue Ribbon Panel on Teenage Pregnancy, seemed to exemplify the need for better sex information and contraceptive services, and to confirm what panel members had been hearing throughout their deliberations. Sherita told of succumbing, at the age of fifteen, to the advances of her sixteen-year-old boyfriend and not using contraception because she believed you couldn't get pregnant right away. She was still fifteen when her son was born.

But Sherita had not told her true story. Several months later, Washington *Post* reporter Leon Dash interviewed Sherita, having spent weeks winning her confidence. She told Dash that actually she and her boyfriend had begun having sex when she was eleven and he was twelve. At fifteen, she became afraid of losing him, and decided to get pregnant in the hope of "holding on to him."

There are many reasons for teenage motherhood. Ignorance is one. Lack of access to the means for avoiding it is another. Not wanting—or not wanting enough—to avoid it is still another.

How much weight to assign to each of these intertwined reasons is far from clear.

As Sherita's two versions of painful reality illustrate, reliable data about attitudes and motivations are hard to come by. Especially for teenagers, a "wanted" and an "unwanted" baby are not opposites but more like two ends of a blurred spectrum. Some have babies by design, some by lack of design, some because they want to, others because they don't sufficiently *not* want to. It is much harder to learn *how* to prevent conception when you don't know *why* to prevent it.

The information we do have, however, provides clear guides to action. There is no reason to choose between efforts to improve family planning services and efforts to change the social and economic conditions that lead to early sex and childbearing. Rather, our policies must reflect the reality that disadvantaged teenagers need access to more effective family planning services *and* fundamental changes in the environment in which early childbearing occurs.

We turn first to the question of family planning programs that work for teenagers.

FAMILY PLANNING PROGRAMS THAT WORK FOR TEENAGERS

To understand how family planning services can be made to work better for teenagers, one must begin by discarding the image of a world divided into two kinds of teenagers—those who want to avoid childbearing, and therefore will, and those who don't want to, and therefore won't. Seeking a simple answer, many a policymaker and editorial writer has been tempted to conclude that since family planning services do, after all, exist, a youngster who does not avoid pregnancy must be actively choosing to have a child. But the real world is infinitely more complex.

Of course there are youngsters who, although economically and emotionally unequipped for parenthood, plan, hope, and even scheme to have children. And, of course, there are also youngsters who avoid pregnancy and childbearing because they are able to surmount obstacles and to make effective use of whatever contraceptive services are available. Between these extremes fall the vast majority of young people at risk of becoming parents too soon. Some want to avoid parenthood just enough to do so if the impediments were reduced. Some, who neither look nor plan far ahead, passively accept whatever fate may bring—including babies.

For all of these youngsters, early sexual activity and the prospect of parenthood at an early age are enmeshed in complicated and contradictory feelings. And critical for all of these youngsters, is the question of where, how, by whom, and under what circumstances family planning services are provided.

After all, what to most adult users and providers is considered "available" and "accessible" may not seem so to an ambivalent teenager. Teenagers may avoid or hesitate to use programs that do not offer assurance of confidentiality, time-intensive counseling, and clear, individualized guidance.

Even a youngster who has many reasons not to can be helped to use contraceptives effectively—but rarely by a fifteen-minute visit to a professional she has never seen before.

Twenty years of research and experience have clearly identified the barriers standing between teenagers and the effective use of contraception, and the kind of programs that have succeeded in significantly reducing teenage childbearing among the groups at highest risk.

First, the barriers:

1. Teenagers are often uninformed, unrealistic, or confused about contraception. Many believe they cannot get pregnant the first time they have sex; they have very little comprehension of the risks of pregnancy. This helps to explain why most teenagers are sexually

active for about a year before ever seeking birth control help from a professional.

The price of ignorance and unrealistic attitudes about risks is high: One out of every five girls gets pregnant during the first six months of sexual activity. Half of all initial premarital teenage pregnancies occur in the six months following first intercourse and more than one fifth in the first month.

2. Teenagers delay seeking family planning services not only because they do not believe they will become pregnant, but because they fear their parents will find out about the visit. Poor communication between partners, typical of many early sexual relationships, adds another impediment to successful contraceptive use.

3. Many youngsters hesitate to obtain contraceptives because they think it "unromantic" to anticipate a sexual encounter by making preparations for it. As one young teenager explained, "The first time, it was like totally out of the blue. You don't . . . say 'Well, I'm going to his house, and he's probably going to try to get to bed with me, so I better make sure I'm prepared.' I mean, you don't know it's coming, so how are you to be prepared?"

4. No method of contraception yet available is well suited for use by teenagers. One study found that even among adolescents who do obtain a contraceptive at a family planning clinic, fewer than half used it every time they had intercourse over the next fifteen months. Currently available techniques for preventing pregnancy do not yet include a safe postcoital method, a once-a-month method, or other means with fewer disadvantages from the teenager's perspective. There is considerable confusion about the risks and benefits of methods currently available. The pill, a highly effective method of preventing pregnancy, sometimes has unpleasant side effects; it is not ideal for a young person for whom sexual encounters are occasional or episodic and for whom it is difficult to plan ahead. A young Chicago woman says, "I wouldn't go on the pill only if I was going to meet somebody, maybe to have sex casually, like once a month. I feel it's more for somebody who has a steady boyfriend."

More important, birth control pills are regarded by many women, and especially teenagers, as dangerous. "Birth control pills give you cancer," a young mother of three told CBS's Bill Moyers. Despite irrefutable data that the health benefits of the pill outweigh the risks, a Gallup survey found Americans consistently overestimating the risks and underestimating the effectiveness of oral contraceptives.

The intrauterine device (IUD), long regarded as medically inappropriate for teenagers who have not had children, has been virtually eliminated from the American market. Diaphragms are unpopular with youngsters not yet comfortable with their own bodies. One young woman explains her reluctance to use a diaphragm, "It's like a coily spring around the thing, and you've got to hold it and when it's going in you, it, like, starts to expand and it hurts. I mean, because it's like all this pressure. It's worse than going to bed with the guy."

As for condoms, the precise effect that the fear of acquired immune deficiency syndrome (AIDS) and the campaigns for "safe sex" have had on their use is still unclear. We do know that although once hidden in the back of the drugstore, they are now openly displayed on self-service racks, that their sales have increased dramatically, and that at least a third of all condoms are now bought by women. ("Don't go out without your rubbers," proclaimed a New York City Health Department subway ad.)

Pending the availability of effective new contraceptives better adapted to the reluctance of the young to plan ahead, present technology and knowledge can serve to reduce rates of school-age childbearing—even among those most at risk, those least equipped for planning ahead, and those most inept at negotiating complex bureaucratic or professional systems.

The circumstances in which contraceptive services are provided play a critical role in actual contraceptive use. Recent research clearly identifies the major factors in the design of family planning services for teenagers: clinic accessibility, confidentiality, appropriate choice of method, and special attention to follow-up and staff-client rapport.

The choice of contraceptive method emerged as the key issue in a recent study among adolescents in Pennsylvania. No other factor—not social relationships, not race or other demographic characteristics, not even personal attitudes and motivation—was as clearly associated with successful use of contraception as the adolescent's satisfaction with her contraceptive method.

A closely related factor—professional influence on the choice of method—was identified as an important ingredient in another study of teenagers making their first contraceptive visit to seventy-eight county health department family planning clinics. The study tried to understand the influence of client-provider relationships on teenage women's subsequent use of contraception. The critical ingredient seemed to be the willingness and ability of professional staff to provide clear direction and authoritative guidance to teenage clients. Clinics most successful in encouraging consistent contraceptive use and in preventing unwanted pregnancies were those where staff exhibited a strong sense of authority, and where clients showed a high sense of trust in the practitioner.

Professors Laurie S. Zabin and Samuel D. Clark at Johns Hopkins University were curious about what teenagers themselves identified as important elements in obtaining contraceptive services and advice. Teenagers using various sources of family planning services gave three main reasons for choosing a specific clinic: confidentiality, proximity, and a staff perceived as caring about and relating well to teenagers.

Choices of clinics clearly reflect different needs. Drs. Zabin and Clark concluded that the full spectrum of needs is best met by a service network that includes different types of facilities with a mix of programs, operated by a variety of agencies.

Here, as in other areas, there is no single magic formula, and a diversity of approaches seems to be part of the recipe for success.

The importance of a variety of sources of contraceptive services and advice is supported by another study, which looked not at users' attitudes and opinions, but at differences in the extent of contraceptive use among thirty-seven U.S. counties, in relation to the services available. Counties in which a high proportion of the need was met showed a great diversity in types of agencies, auspices, and sources of funding, and twice as many clinics relative to teens at risk. The clinics in the well-served counties also had a number of attributes in common: they provided more hours of service each week, and they were more likely to have special outreach, recruitment, and follow-up programs involving teenagers, to encourage but not require parental consent or notification, and to provide prenatal care, abortions, and other health services along with contraceptive services; their services are also more likely to be free. Where clinics specifically for adolescents have been established, they were found to be in the counties with a high proportion of need met.

As for sex education, a major survey completed in 1984 found that the form most prevalent in schools—traditional didactic methods to convey a body of information—generally increased knowledge but had little impact on behavior. The recognition of AIDS as a national problem has added a new dimension to the issue of sex education, but little systematic information is yet available about the nature of the schools' responses.

The methods and objectives of sex education had already been undergoing considerable change. There was increasing understanding that teenagers need to learn not only about anatomy but also about sexuality and parenthood in a social context, and that they need to be able to explore their own situations and feelings. "It's not enough to tell kids to say 'No,' " Harvard child psychiatrist William Beardslee explained to me. "They're much more likely to listen, to hear you, if you do so in the context of acknowledging their sexuality." Recognition of the weakness of exclusively didactic approaches has led many school districts to develop a process rather than a curriculum, usually involving parents actively in all aspects of planning. These programs have increasingly departed from the "value-free" approach of earlier years. They explicitly affirm that sexuality is a precious part of life to be used wisely, that it is better for very young teenagers not to have intercourse, and that abstinence is the best method of birth control.

"The biggest recent shift," says Douglas Kirby of the Center for Population Options, "is in the emphasis placed on getting teens to delay sex."

In addition, the recognition is growing that youngsters need certain basic attitudes and specific skills not only to abstain from premature sex and to use contraception effectively when they do have sex, but also to make wise decisions about smoking, drinking, and drugs. They need self-esteem, a clear sense of values, and the ability to assert themselves in the face of social and peer pressures. Whether these values and skills are best inculcated under the aegis of sex education is not clear, nor is the extent to which these can be effectively taught in a school setting. One large-scale experiment is testing whether youngsters can be taught techniques that would help them to postpone sexual activity. Under the auspices of the Emory University School of Medicine in Atlanta, Dr. Marian Howard, director of the Emory/Grady Teen Services Program, developed a curriculum to give youngsters the practical skills to help them to avoid having sex at an early age.

It is too early for a systematic assessment of the effects of these variants of traditional sex education.

It is also too early to know with any precision how the fear of AIDS has changed sexual behavior, use of contraceptives, and attitudes toward sex education. Clearly, however, we are experiencing the most rapid upheaval in public perceptions and beliefs about sexual activity that has occurred in our lifetime. It remains to be seen whether the changed climate will mean greater receptivity to a more aggressive public role in sex education and the provision of contraceptives.

Clear guidance for action is, however, provided by the experience of programs which have combined sex education with the provision of contraceptive and other health services and which have been operating long enough to permit careful assessment.

The Pioneering School-Based Program in St. Paul

The first of the currently burgeoning school-based programs, and perhaps the most influential, began in St. Paul's Mechanics Arts High School. An inner city school, Mechanics Arts had a 40 percent minority enrollment—ten times the city average. Its dropout rate was 30 percent—double the city average. It held a city-wide record for absenteeism and, alas, for fertility among students fifteen to seventeen years of age.

One day in 1971, the principal of Mechanics Arts High called the St. Paul–Ramsey County Medical Center, a public hospital only two blocks away, asking whether the hospital could furnish day care services to the school and set up a place on the school grounds where not only teachers but students could leave their children.

Dr. Homer Venters, chief of pediatrics, consulted with Dr. Erick Hakanson, chief of obstetrics. Dr. Hakanson, a laconic Scandinavian, recalls telling Dr. Venters that there were three things that made him angry: running a teenage family planning clinic to which nobody came, fifteen-year-olds coming in for prenatal care nine months pregnant, and the same kids coming back a year later, pregnant again. He asked Dr. Laura Edwards, whom he had appointed two years earlier to head the hospital's federally funded maternal and infant care project, to join the conversation. Dr. Edwards, as it happened, had served as an obstetrician for many years in a remote area of India. On her return to her native St. Paul, she had been shocked at the high rate of pregnancy among school-age girls.

What the school needed, the three quickly agreed, was a lot more than a day care center. "Wouldn't it be neat if we had a clinic right in the high school?" asked one. (Forgetfulness or modesty shrouds the source of the galvanizing remark.)

When they called the principal back, it was to say, yes, they'd get him his day care program, but they wanted something from him in return—his help in developing a center at Mechanics Arts that would combine day care with health care for pregnant school girls, and birth control information and services as well.

St. Paul became the scene of a great debate. For the next two years, teachers, parents, school board members, and religious groups questioned and argued. Would prenatal care for pregnant students and the provision of contraceptive information and services give the school a bad reputation? Would the clinic divert resources from classroom education? Students worried that parents would be notified about birth control counseling, and parents worried that they would not be.

In February 1973 the school board voted to give the clinic a one-year tryout, with the condition that contraceptives would not be dispensed in the school. (They would be available at the hospital, two blocks away.) Dr. Hakanson recalls getting dozens of phone calls from anxious parents and telling them, "Look, I'm on your side. I don't want fifteen-year-olds having sexual relations either. But, face the facts—those fifteen-year-olds are having sex whether we like it or not. And some of them are getting pregnant and ruining their lives."

In the end, Dr. Hakanson recalls, "it was the students who carried the day. They stood up at these meetings and said they wanted the clinic."

The clinic opened in a renovated storage room, later moving to an attractive classroom. Services were expanded to include physicals for athletes, immunizations, and a weight control program, providing a measure of protective anonymity for the sexually active. Mechanics Arts was torn down in 1976, but the kind of clinic it pioneered now thrives in four of St. Paul's six high schools. Utilization of the clinics has steadily increased; at last word, more than two thirds of the students at the four schools were receiving services. Thirty-five percent of the female students were coming for family planning services.

What did the clinics do for St. Paul? First and foremost, child-bearing in the four high schools decreased by more than half. Furthermore, fewer than 2 percent of students had second pregnancies before graduation. (Nationwide, one third of women under the age of eighteen who have been pregnant become pregnant again within twenty-four months.)

Equally impressive, nine of ten students who do have babies now finish high school. While completing their education, they receive prenatal care as well as counseling and support from the health clinic, and learn parenting skills and work with children in the day care center. Day care, says Dr. Hakanson, also serves as a pregnancy preventer. "We've taken the glamor out of being a student parent."

A SCHOOL-UNIVERSITY COLLABORATION IN BALTIMORE

A researcher and two clinicians at Johns Hopkins University provided the impetus, in 1981, for establishing a school-based program in Baltimore, Maryland. Begun under circumstances very different from those in St. Paul, the Johns Hopkins program had similarly dramatic results.

The Johns Hopkins program had its roots in a serendipitous combination of research findings and clinical experience.

Laurie S. Zabin, active in the family planning field for more than two decades, had gone back to school to acquire a Ph.D. and formal research skills. She wanted to explore more systematically what could be done about the high proportion of unexpected pregnancies that occur so soon after youngsters first become sexually active. The research team she joined established that the risk of pregnancy is highest during the first months of intercourse, and the younger the girl, the higher the risk. Building on these findings, Dr. Zabin went to thirty-two family planning clinics in eight cities to find out why young teenagers waited so long to use contraception and why so many stayed away until they feared they were already pregnant.

Dr. Zabin concluded that while some teenagers lacked the motivation to avoid pregnancy, many more lacked accurate information and appropriate services. Her research convinced her that child-bearing among school-age girls could be reduced if they had access to information and services that were "close, cost-free, confidential and caring."

Some years earlier, in another part of the medical school, pediatrician Janet Hardy had been overseeing Johns Hopkins' participation in a large-scale, multicity, federally sponsored perinatal study. She recalls being appalled at the number of very young mothers bearing babies that were too small or otherwise damaged.

"Just about all the babies at the bottom of the heap," in Dr. Hardy's words, were born to school-age mothers.

Patrician in bearing, determined in manner, Dr. Hardy is accustomed to acting on her observations. Moving quickly to set up a clinic to provide more accessible and more appropriate prenatal care to adolescents, she found that it was indeed possible significantly to improve the outcomes for their babies at birth, but that the future still looked dismal for both mothers and babies. With her health educator colleague, Rosalie Streett, Dr. Hardy established a second program, which would provide health care for the babies and parenting education and family planning services for the young mothers.

Although both programs produced satisfying results, Ms. Streett recalls that she and Dr. Hardy would often talk about how much better off even the most successful young mothers would be had they postponed childbearing. Physician and educator discussed how antithetical were the characteristics of normal adolescents and the characteristics of a good parent. So the indefatigable Dr. Hardy decided the time had come to establish a program aimed at preventing pregnancy among school-age girls.

Having engaged the interest of a local foundation, she approached Dr. Zabin. The clinical experiences of the pediatrician and the educator blended perfectly with the studies of the researcher. The three energetic, committed women took their proposal to the Baltimore Health Department and School Board. A social worker and nurse practitioner would provide information about sex-related issues to individuals and groups in the junior high school and senior high school closest to Johns Hopkins Hospital. The same professionals would be available every afternoon, with physician backup as necessary, to provide reproduction-related medical services and education at a storefront clinic across the street from one of the schools and three blocks from the other. Staff selection and training and the organization of services would emphasize confidentiality, continuity, and a warm supportive environment. Lastly, there would be rigorous evaluation, data to be gathered before services began and periodically thereafter, both in the participating schools and in two neighboring schools to be used for comparison.

With full support from the health department, school principals, and school superintendent, the clinics opened in January 1982. The two participating schools have all-black student bodies. A large proportion of the junior high school students live in the high-rise public housing projects around the school; more than 85 percent qualify for the free lunch program. The senior high school is in part a magnet school drawing students from the whole city, and therefore with a slightly smaller proportion of students poor enough to qualify for free lunches. A nurse practitioner and a social worker were placed in one school, and a nurse midwife and a social worker in the other. The nurse–social worker team gave classroom presentations, counseled small groups or individuals in the school health suite, and made appointments for further education, consultation, and treatment at the clinic. Youngsters who went to the clinic received education, counseling, and medical services during a single visit, on the assumption that young adolescents were unlikely to return for education alone once their immediate medical needs were met. Medical services, including physical exams and contraceptives, were provided without cost. The program was organized to make sure that the students would be able to see the same professional over time, in the belief that consistency of relationship builds trust, helps youngsters to synthesize what they have learned, and makes it possible for them to share very private concerns. The clinic also became the scene of many value-oriented discussions of sexual attitudes and behavior.

Perhaps most important, Dr. Hardy and Ms. Streett made sure that the clinic atmosphere reflected what Dr. Zabin considers her key research finding. "Teenagers must perceive that the place cares about them. Over and over, in the surveys we did, in the interviews we did, caring was always at the top of the list." The clinic has clearly succeeded in conveying a caring atmosphere—by always seeing whoever came in, by responding promptly to the expressed needs of their student clients, by adapting professional schedules and habits to teenage needs.

"Remember," Ms. Streett asked Dr. Hardy, "the girl who came in at four o'clock on a Friday and said she *had* to see the doctor that afternoon, before going off to the senior prom that evening?" Dr. Hardy recalled that, and the ensuing counseling session that lasted until it was time for the girl to dress for the dance.

The demonstration program continued until June 1984, with impressive results. Rates of pregnancy and childbirth were reduced in a period when rates went up in the comparison schools. In less than three years of the program's operation, the proportion of sexually active ninth- to twelfth-grade girls who had borne babies went down 25 percent.

Fears that the availability of contraceptive information and services might encourage greater sexual activity proved to be unfounded. In the schools served by the program, girls became sexually active *later* than before the program was instituted. The final evaluation found that the proportion of girls who became sexually active by the age of fourteen went down by 40 percent, and the median age at which girls began sexual activity rose by seven months, from age fifteen and a half before the program started to a little over sixteen at the program's end. With their excellent services and careful research, Dr. Hardy, Dr. Zabin, and Ms. Streett have been able to refute, with hard data, the fears that the provision of contraceptives in schools causes promiscuity.

THE FUTURE OF SCHOOL-BASED CLINICS

Communities all around the country, recognizing problems like St. Paul's and Baltimore's, have developed similar programs. Some arrived at their programs independently, some were stimulated by word of the successes elsewhere. Most of those that began with an emphasis on family planning found that adding a broader array of health services—including athletic physicals, immunizations, general health assessments, and weight reduction programs—made all elements of the program more acceptable and more widely utilized. Some began with a more traditional school health orientation, later adding family planning services.

By 1987 comprehensive health services, including family planning, were being offered in eighty-five school-based clinics in twenty-five states, with additional programs in the planning stage. Most offer easy geographical and psychological access, special efforts to reach out and follow up, and an emphasis on confidentiality. Early reports suggested that the clinics were not only decreasing school-age pregnancy but also improving school attendance and possibly decreasing dropout rates.

A Support Center for School-Based Clinics has been established at the Center for Population Options in Washington, D.C., to provide technical assistance and other encouragement to communities contemplating setting up such clinics. A two-year study by the National Academy of Sciences concluded by recommending better access to contraceptives for school-age youngsters through school-based clinics, and the Robert Wood Johnson Foundation announced it is awarding grants totaling $12 million to twenty cities under its School-Based Adolescent Health Care program, begun in 1987.

In many areas, state and local governments provided the impetus, and sometimes some of the funds, to establish school-based clinics. The dramatic increase in public attention to the issue of teenage pregnancy and the growing evidence of program success have made it easier to get initial financial support. Joy Dryfoos, chair of the board of the Center for Population Options, predicted in 1985 that an "artful combination of private and public funding" would be forthcoming to start new programs. And it has turned out that way. Less clear is whether sufficient funds will be available to sustain the continued operation of these clinics. Dr. Douglas Kirby, the center's research director, worries whether the funds will be forthcoming to continue these programs over the long haul, once their effectiveness has been established and they are no longer considered "demonstrations." Even as new programs were beginning, some of the older ones feared a funding crisis in the near future.

Another major impediment to the spread of school-based clinics is community opposition. Although only 15 to 20 percent of clinic visits are made for family planning services, and although careful studies show that school-based clinics do not lead to increased sexual activity, many people continue to believe that the clinics, by making contraception more readily available, are an invitation to adolescents to engage in sex.

Chicago's DuSable High School health clinic is one of several to face vigorous and well-publicized opposition from the Catholic Church, the Moral Majority, and Right to Life groups. The Chicago school board nevertheless voted in 1985 to allow the DuSable health clinic to continue operating and to continue dispensing contraceptives. DuSable is located in one of the nation's poorest neighborhoods. Many of its students are among the 27,000 residents crammed into the Robert Taylor Homes, the world's largest housing project.

Supporters of the clinic pointed out that in 1984, before the clinic was established, 40 percent of babies born to teenagers in the census tracts surrounding the school were second, third, or fourth children. Chicago's Cardinal Bernadin maintains that teaching about contraception leads teens to think "they can have sex without consequences." But the parents, who have to sign consent forms before their children can use the clinic, are generally supportive. Patricia Davis Scott, the nurse who runs the clinic, says, "DuSable parents seem to appreciate our being here." DuSable principal Judith Steinhagen recalled fears among parents when the clinic opened in 1985, but these abated as parents came to realize that 250 to 300, or about a third of the girls in the school, gave birth every year, "and we didn't have a clinic in the school—well, they figured, how much worse can we do?"

Betty Bonow, a school board member who voted in favor of closing the clinic, asked, "How can we, on one hand, tell high school students to refrain from sex and, on the other, provide them with materials to make sex?" She said she worried that the community was not addressing the more fundamental causes of early childbearing. She is not alone. Even those supporting more effective and more accessible family planning services are increasingly convinced that family planning services are not enough, and that school-age youngsters need not only the means but the will to avoid having children.

The achievement of that objective requires the creation of an environment in which sex is not portrayed consistently and exclusively as trivial, an environment that can offset the profound effects of early deprivation, an environment that offers more attractive future options than early parenthood.

Environments That Influence Early Childbearing

The family planning community was a relatively late, and sometimes reluctant, convert to the conviction emerging in the early 1980s that family planning alone was not enough to reduce unacceptably high rates of childbearing among unmarried school-age youngsters.

In the governing council of the Alan Guttmacher Institute, on which I served at the time, we assumed that if we didn't have all the solutions to reducing teenage pregnancy, we at least knew the problem—unwanted children. That had been a major focus of our deliberations beginning in the mid-1970s and was the subject of the Institute's landmark publications, *Eleven Million Teenagers,* issued in 1976, and its 1981 sequel, *Teenage Pregnancy: The Problem That Hasn't Gone Away.*

I remember the meeting of the AGI council at which I came to realize that the terms of the debate had fundamentally changed. It was early in 1983, and a newly elected member, Judge Clinton De-Veaux of Atlanta, rose to say that the council's discussion of "unwanted children" being born to teenagers didn't square with the reality he was witnessing. A great many of the fourteen-, fifteen-, and sixteen-year-olds who came before him were having babies because that was what they seemed to want to do or because it was something that seemed just to happen, entirely out of their control.

So, the judge observed, you could offer more informative sex education and you could provide readier access to contraceptive services, but that wasn't going to do much for those who didn't see school-age motherhood as a problem, or who saw it as a problem that they couldn't do anything about.

In a stunningly rapid change of perceptions, the fulcrum has shifted and a new consensus has emerged. Across a wide ideological spectrum, there is a new commitment to finding ways to combat early childbearing that go beyond making contraception more available. The rhetoric and action implied by this new commitment, once the exclusive preserve of conservatives and religious fundamentalists, have been given new life and new meaning by civil rights activists, child advocates, social reformers, and professionals who work directly with teenagers.

A ten-year campaign to prevent teenage pregnancy moved to the top of the agenda of the Children's Defense Fund (CDF) in 1983. The vigorous advocacy organization declared that teenagers need both the capacity to delay childbearing and the motivation which comes from hope and positive life options.

"The best contraceptive," says CDF President Marian Wright Edelman, "is a real future."

This perspective gained adherents with growing awareness that pregnancy rates dipped only slightly in the late seventies and early eighties despite increased availability of family planning services. As the age of initiating sexual intercourse dropped, the pool of sexually active youngsters increased, canceling out much of the effect of expanded family planning services for teenagers. It will not reliably be known for some time what impact the fear of AIDS will have on the trend toward a constantly earlier age of first intercourse. In 1979, the latest year for which national data exist, the average age was 16.4 for whites and 15.3 for blacks.

Local surveys indicate that in some inner city areas the average age of first intercourse is much lower than the national average. Judith Jones, director of Columbia University's National Resource Center for Children in Poverty, reports that in the deprived Washington Heights area of Manhattan, "It is not unusual for 11-year-old boys and slightly older girls to 'make out'; with mother at work, there are plenty of opportunities right at home. . . . Junior high school personnel have described 'catching' students 'doing it' in hallways, bathrooms and locker rooms." Tauscha Vaughn confided to Washington *Post* reporter Leon Dash that she was taunted at a pajama party as "Miss Goody Two Shoes," because she was still a virgin at twelve.

As the age of first intercourse goes down, the problem of school-age childbearing becomes more acute. Statistically, the younger the girl, the less likely she is to use contraception. The earlier she bears her first child, the more children she will ultimately have.

School-age childbearing is also, as we saw in Chapter 1, a greater problem today because the consequences—in terms of interrupted education, skills acquisition, and maturation for the mother, and long-term risks for the child—have become more serious.

Thus the spotlight has fallen on the environment that lures young people to bed at earlier and earlier ages and deters them from avoiding pregnancy.

Teenagers see sex on television, hear about it in popular music, and are exposed to sex in its most trivialized form in advertisements of everything from blue jeans to deodorants. It remains to be seen to what extent tantalizing sexual messages will be offset by alarm signals about AIDS, with their emphasis on restraint and "safe sex," and whether media attention to the risk of contracting AIDS will change the way teenagers think about sex, leading them to postpone sexual activity and to make greater use of condoms.

"When I was growing up, sex was a dirty word," Newark Police Detective Shahid Jackson told Bill Moyers. "Now sex is what's happening. You know, they see sex on TV, sex in the movies, sex everywhere . . ."

On ABC's *Love Boat* the overarching goal of almost every character is to "score" before the ship docks. On CBS's *Hometown,* Peter longs for "someone I can talk to—naked." In an average year, reported *TV Guide,* American television viewers are "exposed to some 9,230 scenes of suggested sexual intercourse or innuendo," and "fully 94 percent of the sex on soap operas involves people not married to each other." In the exciting and glamorized sex of movieland, videoland, and rock-musicland, no one uses contraceptives, and hardly anyone gets pregnant—except when a soap opera plot requires an agonizing decision about abortion. Sex is rarely explored as a serious and meaningful aspect of the lives of television characters. Enduring human relationships built on warmth, affection, reliability, and mutual understanding have been glimpsed briefly on the *Bill Cosby Show* but are seldom seen elsewhere on television or heard in the lyrics of today's most popular songs.

Adults, eager to appear liberated and tolerant, fearing to make moral judgments that might appear hackneyed or hypocritical, often stand mute amid the tide of sexual incitement.

The problem is compounded by adolescents' unrealistic expectations of parenthood. Teenagers seldom perceive the impact of having a baby on their own educations and future incomes. They do not foresee the demands a baby makes or the burdens of child rearing, especially for a single parent.

Duane Michaels took hundreds of pictures of teen mothers—white and black, urban and rural, middle-class and poor—for a *Time* cover story, "Children Having Children." The photographer observed, "They came across as girls, not women. They seemed to be playing house. A lot of them did not understand the enormousness of having a child."

Many of this generation's young women see child rearing as easier than marriage and babies as more malleable than husbands. Garry Trudeau's *Doonesbury* depicted a teenage woman, young man at her side, reassuring her mother about their decision not to rush into marriage and to postpone their wedding until they figure out what to do with their lives. Interrupting the mother's relieved congratulations on their mature decision, the daughter says, "We're still going to go ahead with the kid, though," the young man chiming in, "Right! While we're still young enough to enjoy him."

But the same media that titillate can also serve as a vehicle for accurate information about contraception and the importance of avoiding too early sex and pregnancy. But that rarely happens except in the context of a public service campaign, with considerably less impact than the more subtle but persuasive messages of television entertainment.

"The media say it's cool to have sex and say nothing about the consequences," comments Marian Wright Edelman. "We've got to say it's uncool to have a baby too young."

To make sure that the message is heard, the Children's Defense Fund has launched a sophisticated five-year multimedia advertising campaign. One ad shows an attractive young schoolgirl, baby in arms, with the caption, "It's like being grounded for eighteen years."

Both the Urban League and the Children's Defense Fund have also been conducting media campaigns aimed specifically at encouraging young men to avoid fathering children they cannot care for. Radio spots and billboards carry such messages as "Be a real man . . . don't make a baby if you can't be a father," and "Don't let a hot date turn into a due date."

Church, civic, and fraternal organizations, especially in the black community, are working hard to create a climate that conveys to children and youth the undesirability of early sexual activity, pregnancy, and parenthood.

While prevailing societal attitudes toward sex, sexuality, and parenthood have made it harder for all American youngsters to postpone sex and childbearing, poverty and other forms of disadvantage operate more selectively to encourage early sex and childbearing.

Economic factors and race. Economic and emotional deprivation intertwine as crucial factors in explaining many aspects of adolescent pregnancy. On behalf of the Rockefeller Foundation, researcher Joy Dryfoos combed the literature and interviewed academics, clinicians, and young mothers. She found "a depressing composite portrait . . . of children from disadvantaged families living in chaotic conditions; of parents unable to support their children either economically or emotionally; of families besieged with the daily struggle for food, housing and jobs, with no time or energy left over for their children; of children uncared for, abused and lonely." Most of them had been in trouble long before they became pregnant. A new baby only deepened their plight.

Other investigations, including cross-national studies, yield similar conclusions. A study of teenage childbearing in the United States, France, the Netherlands, Sweden, England, and Canada found that in each of the six countries, the young women most likely to bear children were "adolescents who have been deprived, emotionally as well as economically, and . . . unrealistically seek gratification and fulfillment in a child of their own."

For blacks, the high incidence of poverty combines with dismal future economic prospects to account for high rates of teenage childbearing. Although birth rates among black U.S. teenagers have been going down steadily since 1970, they are still twice as high as among white teens. This is in part because of higher rates of poverty among blacks. In determining whether a teenager is sexually active or uses contraceptives effectively, poverty is more decisive than race. A black teenager living in a poor area of Chicago is twice as likely to have sexual intercourse as a black teenager living in a more affluent part of the same city. In Washington, D.C., the rate of teenage births correlates more closely with ratios of poor households than with ratios of black households in each ward.

Black teen birthrates are also high because blacks become sexually active at an earlier age, when all girls are less reliable contraceptive users than at later ages, and because fewer black than white teenagers have abortions. (Precise figures are disputed, but a substantially higher proportion of white than black teenagers have abortions. Rates also differ markedly by social class. One study in Rhode Island found that 56 percent of pregnancies occurring in teenagers from high-income areas ended in abortion, compared with 22 percent among teenagers from poverty areas.)

But the biggest reason for the difference between black and white rates of early, unmarried childbearing is the undermining of the economic basis for marriage for a high proportion of black young people. Not only are an unprecedented proportion of black teen males unemployed, but many of those who find jobs do not earn enough to support a family.

What we are seeing, as University of Chicago sociologist William J. Wilson has documented, is a long-term decline in the proportion of black men, and particularly young black men, in a position to support a family. Joblessness and low earnings, resulting primarily from changes in the economy, combine with high mortality and incarceration rates to result in a shrinking pool of marriageable black males relative to the number of young black women. Professor Wilson's "male marriage pool index" shows twenty years of sharply declining ratios of black men aged sixteen to twenty-four compared to black women of similar age. (This trend, which began in the 1960s, is the more startling, as Wilson points out, when compared to the rising ratios for white men.) For every hundred black women between the ages of twenty and twenty-four, there are only forty-five employed black men! Women in poor black communities grow up not only without seeing men marry, but without seeing eligible black men.

This one stark fact—that so many black women have such slim prospects of marriage to a man who can contribute substantial support to them and their children—goes a long way towards explaining high rates of teenage childbearing and the enormous increase in poor black female-headed families. Marriage to a reliable provider has always been and remains the most frequent way that women escape poverty and avoid welfare dependency. If marriage is so unlikely, then one more incentive to postponing early childbearing is removed. The salience of psychological and cultural explanations fades by comparison.

The role of school failure. School failure is such a powerful factor in early childbearing that efforts to promote school success must be central to any efforts to reduce teenage pregnancy. The seeds of school failure are sown early: Girls who become pregnant as teenagers usually have long histories of school difficulties, beginning in elementary school, and are below average in academic performance for a substantial period before they become pregnant.

For youngsters growing up in poverty, especially if they have little adult guidance and encouragement, trouble with school virtually guarantees bleak prospects for the future, for psychological as well as practical reasons. Disadvantaged young people who have never had the experience of acquiring skills and of mastering a socially valued body of knowledge, lack a personal sense of mastery and self-esteem. If they see only minimal prospects of a decent job and economic independence for themselves or their partners, they have little reason to postpone sex and parenthood because they have nothing to lose.

As Howard University sociologist Joyce Ladner explains, a girl without opportunities to "achieve a sense of self-worth through education, through employment, through positive interaction at home

. . . feels she has very little else to offer except her body, so she gives her body in exchange for [a young man's] treating her nice and making her feel that she's somebody."

By contrast, the higher a young woman's educational expectations, the more likely she is to avoid pregnancy. High aspirations rank with high socioeconomic status as the two biggest factors associated with postponing sex and with more effective use of contraception.

Young men with little educational and vocational achievement or ambition are also the most likely to have early sexual experience and least likely to use contraception. Eighteen- and nineteen-year-old males with poor basic skills are three times as likely to be fathers as those with average basic skills.

The prowess demonstrated by fathering a baby can serve as a powerful consolation for lack of skills, education, and job prospects. As illuminating as any academic finding is the testimony that Bill Moyers' CBS camera captured in a hospital delivery room during the birth of the latest of six children fathered by Timothy McSeed. As the baby emerged from its mother's womb, McSeed, in mask and gown, jumped up and down, shouting, "I'm the king!" Viewing this, and aware that McSeed supported none of his children, I thought of the opportunities missed for helping Timothy McSeed achieve other than biological triumphs.

GIVING YOUNGSTERS A GREATER STAKE IN THEIR OWN FUTURE

The implications of these findings are clear. Many powerful antecedents of premature sex and premature pregnancy have done their damage long before a youngster reaches adolescence. Many of the strongest determinants of high rates of teenage childbearing originate far from where the vulnerable teenagers hang out, far from where they may drift into sexual relations, far from where they may decide to use contraceptives.

We now know that the availability of income support through AFDC can be ruled out as a determinant of unmarried and teenage childbearing. Of course, other questions remain unanswered. Experts will continue to debate the relative contribution of economic and psychological factors, of blighted early experience, of a discouraging present or of dismal future prospects. But these questions need not deter us from action. We already know more than enough to act.

We must ensure that disadvantaged young people can acquire needed skills and work habits, become connected with the world of work and achievement, and have the opportunities to use their skills to earn a decent income. This would go far toward providing the missing economic basis for marriage and the formation of stable families.

We must ensure that young people believe in these opportunities and become convinced they have a real stake in their own future. Only then are they likely to believe in the value of postponing sex and childbearing.

It is time to move beyond arguments about family planning services as the only answer, beyond appeals to morality as the only answer, and beyond the withdrawal of welfare benefits as any kind of answer at all.

The state of our knowledge beckons us to broaden our vision.

A realistic commitment to improving the life prospects of disadvantaged youngsters means starting early. It means expanded job opportunities and training for their parents, along with income support where necessary. It also means:

- Improved prenatal and child health care.
- Services to strengthen family functioning.
- Much greater emphasis on the development of competence and the prevention of academic failure through high-quality child care and preschool programs, and changes in schools to heighten the chances that high-risk children will succeed in school.

These interventions, which are explored in detail in subsequent chapters, must be included in the wider framework of teenage pregnancy prevention. All must become part of our arsenal to increase the odds that children growing up in the shadows will become adults before they become parents.

Brighter Beginnings Through Improved Prenatal Care

"The room [was] full of tiny, naked, wrinkled infants, each enclosed in a glass cage. Festooned with tubes and needles, they looked less like babies than like ancient, shrunken little men and women, prisoners gathered for some bizarre reason to die together under the sizzling lights . . .

"Jamila's arms and legs were thinner than my thinnest finger. Her threadlike veins were always breaking down from the pressure of I.V.'s. Each time she received an injection or had her veins probed for an I.V., Jamila would holler as if she'd received the final insult, as if after all the willpower she'd expended enduring the pain and discomfort of birth, no one had anything better to do than jab her one more time. What made her cries even harder to bear was their tininess. In my mind her cries rocked the foundations of the universe."

Anyone who has ever entered a neonatal intensive care unit will resonate to novelist John Wideman's description of his first visit to his prematurely born daughter.

Twenty years ago, babies like Jamila Wideman might not have survived. Today, along with thousands of others born too small or too soon, she is growing up healthy and robust, saved by the miracle of neonatal intensive care.

The "miracle" can, in fact, be quite rationally explained. It resulted from the development of dazzling new technologies, from the training of exquisitely skilled professionals, and from the determination of a powerful combination of professional and philanthropic forces to make these technologies and skills available to all who need them. This nation's present capacity to care for infants at high medical risk represents a triumph not only of science and technology but also of professional and administrative willingness to regionalize services—thereby changing time-honored practices and organizational arrangements.

No similarly determined effort has ever been made, in the United States, to attack the conditions which produce so many high-risk infants. There is a great shortage of the less dramatic services that would obviate some of the need for the heroic high-tech rescues. No comparable effort has gone into ensuring universal access to the kind of prenatal care that would maximize the chances for healthy pregnancy and childbirth. Socioeconomic risk is not addressed with anything like the zeal applied to medical risk. It is like ignoring safety measures at the launch site and mobilizing resources only for the crash landing.

Although the prospects of further progress with still greater investments in highly specialized care are uncertain, prenatal care, a form of intervention which offers less drama but more long-term payoff, exerts little pull on scarce public resources. Playing the odds, we bet that most pregnant women will have healthy babies even if they don't get the health care they may need. The abstract baby-to-be cannot tug at our heartstrings and purse strings like the identifiable frail infant for whom something has already gone wrong. It is easier to respond to an emergency than to a probability.

Legislatures more readily appropriate money to repair a disaster than to prevent one.

Dr. Ann Wilson writes from the School of Medicine at the University of South Dakota that in 1983, eight infants who received no prenatal care were admitted to the state's most specialized neonatal intensive care unit at a cost of over half a million dollars. Two of these babies, one of whom had a second hospitalization costing over a hundred thousand dollars, died before they were two. Another will require a lifetime of state-supported services. Dr. Wilson calculates that half the dollars expended on this group of eight babies would have paid, that year, for prenatal care for all of the women in the state who did not receive it.

Resources flow readily to neonatal intensive care not only because we value treatment over prevention, but also because it involves the medical technology in which this nation leads the world. When it comes to the design and application of social interventions aimed at populations at risk that would reduce the incidence of poor birth outcomes and low birthweight, we are far behind other Western nations, and even some developing countries.

It is no wonder, then, that low birthweight has become the single greatest threat to the health and well-being of infants in the United States today. While America is number one in saving tiny and premature babies, it is number fifteen in the proportion of babies born at low birthweight.

Consequences of Low Birthweight and Prematurity

Babies born too small or too early face severely reduced life chances. A low birthweight baby is almost forty times as likely to die in its first month as a normal birthweight infant.

Low-birthweight babies who survive run a substantially higher risk of:

- Having a congenital anomaly or a neurodevelopmental handicap such as a seizure disorder.
- Needing intensive, high-technology hospital care immediately after birth, and often for as long as two to three months.
- Suffering throughout infancy from a variety of illnesses and infections, especially respiratory problems. Almost 40 percent of very-low-birthweight infants (under two pounds) and 20 percent of

low-birthweight infants are rehospitalized more than once during the first year of life.

Every one of these factors has long-term consequences. The British psychiatrist-researcher, Michael Rutter, who has done much of the landmark longitudinal research on the relationship between early experience and later outcomes, found that both congenital anomalies and neurodevelopmental handicaps are forerunners of increased rates of later psychosocial problems.

Life in the neonatal intensive care unit (ICU), hooked up to tubes and wires and devoid of parental hugs, rocking, and holding, impedes the process of forging the bonds which would normally smooth the way for the normal give-and-take between parents and their baby. The pain can be acute for new parents who suddenly find they "have no child, for the child belongs not to them, but to the neonatal ICU." Family functioning may be severely disrupted. Some studies suggest that child abuse is more frequent in families with low-birthweight babies. A low-birthweight baby, which is typically very hard to care for and raises a host of uncertainties, is likely to be traumatic even to a well-functioning middle-class family. Many poor families, with fewer buffers against the resulting economic and emotional stress, never recover fully.

Hospitalization in later infancy and childhood, which occurs much more frequently among children born at low birthweight, is also connected to subsequent adverse outcomes. Dr. Rutter found that children who are hospitalized twice or more in early childhood have markedly increased rates of later psychiatric disorders.

A fourth consequence of low birthweight with an even more direct bearing on later outcomes is that many low-birthweight babies grow up with learning disorders and behavior problems. Centers that follow low-birthweight infants report rates of learning disability running as high as 40 to 45 percent, as well as high rates of poor language development and reading problems, difficulty with abstract concepts, poor impulse control, and attention deficit disorder.

The likelihood of adverse consequences among low-birthweight babies increases substantially if the baby is born into a family that has other strikes against it, such as poverty, unemployment, social isolation, or an impaired parent—or if the mother is a teenager.

THE IMPORTANCE OF PRENATAL CARE

The chances of having a full-term, normal-weight baby without handicaps are substantially increased when a woman receives prompt, appropriate, high-quality care during pregnancy and childbirth. Women who get no prenatal care are about three times as likely to have a low-birthweight infant as those who receive routine care. As the National Academy of Sciences concluded, "The overwhelming weight of the evidence indicates that prenatal care reduces low birthweight, and that the effect is greatest among high-risk women." When prenatal care is comprehensive and begun promptly, the results are reflected in improved infant health and fewer difficulties in early parent-child relationships, including child abuse. Teenage mothers who get excellent and comprehensive prenatal care have babies at least as healthy as those of women in their twenties. If every pregnant woman in the United States were to get the prenatal care she needed, birth outcomes and life prospects would be dramatically improved for many now born at risk.

The central role of prenatal care in infant health and later outcomes is not reflected in public policy. The United States is virtually alone among nations—and absolutely alone among the Western industrial democracies—in its grudging approach to the provision of maternity care.

Government in the United States has long taken some role in helping to make prenatal care available to some segments of the population, but has never assumed responsibility for assuring that every pregnant woman gets the health care she needs to maximize the chances of a healthy birth.

Federal and state funds have helped many pregnant women to obtain maternity care, have helped to get services to places where they were lacking, and—in the hands of particularly talented individuals—have even been harnessed to support superior and comprehensive prenatal care. But by and large, an accumulation of fragmentary and disconnected laws, regulations, and appropriations has produced a jumble of incoherent services.

More than eight hundred thousand pregnant women annually do not get prompt prenatal care (i.e., in the first trimester) and probably twice as many don't get the kind of care they need. This is often attributed to their own negligence. One Reagan Administration official came up with something called the "apathy factor" to explain a decrease in the use of prenatal care in the early 1980s. *Losing Ground* author Charles Murray asserts that when mothers don't get proper care during pregnancy, "it is not because there is no doctor available, it is because the mother . . . [is] not functioning in the ways that parents have to function."

However comforting the idea that women who do not utilize prenatal services have somehow failed us, closer to the truth is that we have failed *them*. The data indicate a clear relationship between ease in obtaining services and the percentage of expectant mothers using these services. The nature and content of the services—how closely they respond to the individual's needs—is also a factor in whether high-risk women use prenatal care. The message is that it is the system that is in need of reform, not the pregnant women.

We know this in part because the proportion of pregnant women who received timely prenatal care over the last thirty years tracks closely with the gradual lowering of barriers to care and the subsequent reimposition of barriers. The percentage of women utilizing prenatal care early in pregnancy rose steadily from the mid-1960s until 1979, paralleling the expansion of Medicaid and private insurance coverage and increases in public support of maternity services rendered by health departments and community health centers. Reaching a peak in 1980, the proportion of women receiving prompt prenatal care began dropping among black mothers and teenagers of all races. After a decade of steady decline the percentage of women receiving late or no prenatal care increased for three consecutive years, 1981, 1982, and 1983, and leveled off once more beginning in 1984.

Decreases in prenatal care among high-risk groups are closely related to cutbacks in government support for these services, reaching low points at times and in places where the cutbacks coincided with economic recession. Clearly, when finances are tight, families will skimp on items such as preventive health care, which may seem less urgent. When public support for such services is simultaneously curtailed, the result can be devastating. In 1983, as prenatal care continued to decline among high-risk groups, the proportion of low-birthweight births went up in twenty-one states; for black babies, the rates went up in twenty-eight states. Overall, low-birthweight rates also rose slightly nationwide. For white infants, this was the first increase in eighteen years.

In a shocking indicator of the combined effects of economic recession and service cutbacks, in 1983 the gap between black and white infant mortality reached a forty-year peak.

Consistently, over the years, black and Hispanic women, poor women, poorly educated women, and very young women—the very women who would benefit most from prenatal care—have been the least likely to obtain prenatal care promptly or at all. In a pattern that defies any logic in the allocation of resources, the poor and minorities, for whom high-quality services could make the biggest difference, are least likely to get the services they need. They are also most likely to end up as mothers of the frail infants eligible for neonatal care miracles, and of babies who face the most serious long-term consequences of prenatal neglect.

PRENATAL CARE FOR HIGH-RISK PREGNANT WOMEN

Lack of money and insurance coverage are the most fundamental reasons that more women do not receive timely prenatal care. We will return to the problems of financial barriers and access to care in Chapter 6. Here we consider the less obvious, but often equally important, nonfinancial barriers—the bad fit between patterns of care and patterns of need.

A simple example of the mismatch between prevailing care and the services high-risk women need is that, despite overwhelming evidence that smoking during pregnancy is a major reversible cause of low birthweight, very few obstetricians place high priority on helping pregnant patients to stop smoking. Similarly, alcoholics who continue drinking heavily and addicts who continue using drugs during pregnancy are at high risk of bearing children with central nervous system damage and a variety of severe malformations. Yet the obstetrical community has made little progress in helping women to reduce their use of drugs and alcohol during pregnancy, although techniques for bringing about significant reductions in substance abuse by pregnant women have been successfully demonstrated.

Efforts to change smoking, drinking, drug, and eating habits and to respond to problems with social or psychological components are notoriously time-consuming and poorly compensated. With some notable exceptions, physicians are reluctant to commit the time it takes even to try to alter behavior—especially among poorly educated patients. Nurses and nurse practitioners, as well as physicians who work in settings where they can collaborate with other health professionals, are often in a better position to attend to these issues.

Jenie James, a nurse midwife in South Carolina, explains that, in working with pregnant teenagers, "We take a great deal of time with each girl. We feel it is important not to generalize about anything, but to find out about *her* . . . to ask about social and emotional issues and to take time for behavioral problems and questions." Sarah Piechnick, another nurse midwife working in South Carolina, agrees. "It can take an hour to establish rapport. If you're rushed, there's no communication. It takes time to enlist people—especially adolescents and very poor women—in their own care, and allow the discovery process to unfold."

Teenagers are often frightened about what pregnancy is doing to their bodies and their sense of themselves. Many continue to wear excessively tight jeans, try to keep their weight down, and, in general, retain a nonpregnant appearance—practices that can contribute significantly to stunted fetal growth. Obstetrician Henry Heins of the Medical University of South Carolina observes that many teenagers gain only very little weight because they believe that will mean a smaller baby, easier to deliver. "It takes time, a lot of time, to get all that straightened out," he says.

A number of clinicians report that histories of physical and sexual abuse are distressingly common among the pregnant teens they see. In the absence of skilled and sustained help, these girls simply stay away from medical care, as the idea of a pelvic exam is too frightening. For girls with unusual needs for reassurance and support, extensive counseling may be necessary, and a nurse midwife or other sympathetic clinician who sticks with the expectant mother throughout her pregnancy and during labor and delivery may make the difference between consistent prenatal care and a smooth delivery and no prenatal care and a traumatic birth.

Anthropologist Margaret Boone studied poor black women in Washington, D.C., whose low-birthweight babies died early in infancy. She found they had in common a fatalistic outlook on life, tending not to plan and leaving tomorrow to take care of itself. Dr. Boone also found that these women were profoundly afraid of doctors. Most of them did not know exactly what constitutes "poor health." Although at high risk of premature labor, they had not been taught enough about the signs of premature labor to know when they might need medical help. Dr. Boone concluded that while more advantaged people were likely to seek out preventive health services on their own, these women would need a great deal of talented help to make good use of prenatal care.

The lack of a comprehensive national policy to eliminate financial barriers and expand the content of conventional prenatal care means that extraordinary efforts and ingenuity are required to maintain effective state or local prenatal care programs. Nevertheless, progress, although uneven and small in scale, can be and has been made. The three successful programs described here show what can be done, even in an adverse climate. They show that the "apathy factor" quickly recedes when services are readily accessible and when the mix of services and the circumstances in which they are provided respond to the needs of the women they aim to serve. The diverse populations served by these programs include low-income women in thirteen of California's poorest counties, high school students in a depressed Baltimore neighborhood, and adolescents in a poor rural area of South Carolina.

Each of these programs goes well beyond routine obstetrical services. For programs like these, the Robert Wood Johnson Foundation has coined the word "transmedical." They reduce barriers to access and availability and provide an enriched form of prenatal care. They recognize that social isolation, poor nutrition, and drug and alcohol abuse can present as much of a risk to healthy pregnancy as a low hematocrit or elevated blood pressure. They see prenatal care as an opportunity to help parents focus on the needs of their unborn infants in ways that prepare them not only for childbirth but also for the responsibilities of parenthood.

Most of these programs have chalked up substantial monetary savings. Each has been able to document that the services it provided during the prenatal period improved pregnancy outcomes. In short, they have everything going for them—except adequate recognition and secure financial support. Every one of these programs has been sufficiently successful on a small scale to warrant serious attention and wider implementation.

CALIFORNIA'S TRAILBLAZING EXPERIMENT

In 1977 the California legislature became aware that infant mortality in many neighborhoods was frighteningly and unacceptably high. In poor districts of Oakland, babies were dying at twice the rates of the rest of the county and state. Similar disparities were found in other areas with high concentrations of poor families. With the help of the state health department, the legislature identified improved access to good prenatal care for the poor as the most hopeful route to better infant health.

Physicians said they could not provide adequate care at the rates fixed by Medi-Cal, the California Medicaid program. Poor women complained that they were having trouble finding physicians. Twenty of the State's fifty-eight counties had no resident obstetrician-gynecologist who would accept Medi-Cal patients. Statewide, the proportion of practicing obstetricians willing to treat poor patients had declined from 65 to 46 percent in three years.

Alarm bells rang in Sacramento. The legislature passed an emergency bill to revise reimbursement for physicians and stimulate their participation in maternity care. That didn't help. Two years later, in a 1979 resolution, the legislature declared that its emergency efforts had been ineffective. Prodded by an intense advocacy campaign led by several women's health groups and the March of Dimes, the legislature began to work with the state health department to come up with more fundamental solutions. It soon authorized the department to develop an innovative pilot program. Seven years later, that experiment blossomed into a statewide system, pointing the way for other states and perhaps for the nation.

The pilot program was called the "OB Access Project," short for Access to Obstetrical Care. It was designed to operate in thirteen of California's neediest counties, testing the theory that the number of low-birthweight babies could be reduced, with financial as well as human benefits, by increasing access to prenatal care for several thousand women over a three-year period. "It is believed," the project prospectus said, "that by improvement in prenatal care, a percentage of those who would have been low birthweight infants can be converted to normal birthweight."

That was more easily said than done.

Before the planning had gone very far, it became clear that the problem of "access" was more than a matter of opening the prenatal care door. It also involved expanding the content of prenatal care.

The state found it would have to be able to assure that the right kind of prenatal care was made available to high-risk women, and that it actually reached them. After extensive study, the state health department concluded that this meant several major departures from previous practice.

Instead of paying the bills for whatever services the provider chose to offer, the department went into the thirteen target counties, found providers that were willing and able to offer a comprehensive array of services, and contracted with them to furnish eligible pregnant women with a set of agreed-upon services. The participating contractors were an interesting mix, ethnically and professionally. In the county of Trinidad, in northern California, it was United Indian Health Services, an Indian community nonprofit clinic that signed on. In Oakland, it was the East Oakland Health Alliance, serving a predominantly black population, and La Clínica de la Raza, serving a mainly Hispanic population. In San Diego, which accounted for almost half of the client population, it was a consortium of county, university, and community resources.

In working out what services would be covered, the OB Access staff became increasingly aware of the gaps between what high-risk women needed and what Medi-Cal would pay for.

"We had to redefine reimbursement," recalls Dr. Lyn Headley, the state's chief of program development in maternal and child health. "Medi-Cal had never paid for health education, nutrition, or psychosocial services. Boy, was that a struggle! Before we were through we even got vitamin and mineral supplements reimbursed under OB Access."

The package of prenatal care offered to OB Access participants was truly "transmedical." In addition to medical services starting early in pregnancy and a complete screening for medical and associated risks, it included a thorough nutritional assessment, vitamin supplements, a psychosocial evaluation and follow-up services, health education, coordination with the Special Supplemental Food Program for Women, Infants and Children (WIC) and family planning services, and parenting classes.

The commitment to comprehensiveness and to individualizing services was impressive. Services could be provided in homes as well as clinics. A patient unable to attend classes because of medical, transportation, language, cultural, or job problems could receive individual instruction. Special supplementary services could be provided to patients who had emotional or learning handicaps, had trouble complying with medical advice, or used cigarettes, drugs, or alcohol. Nutritional and psychosocial assessments sought out the everyday problems that can interfere with a healthy pregnancy and healthy parenting. Where needed, the contractors had bilingual staffs. Providers were explicitly asked to consider patient and family anxieties about pregnancy and delivery, psychiatric problems, unmet needs for child care, employment, or education, and the absence of social support.

Contractors agreed to inform women of the program through systematic outreach efforts, including public service announcements on local television, in newspapers, church meetings, brochures, and by word of mouth through welfare workers. Eventually almost seven thousand women were registered in the thirteen counties. A quarter were teenagers; half were Mexican-Americans, a quarter were white, and 10 percent were black. Half of the total were Medi-Cal beneficiaries, and the rest were poor but not eligible for Medi-Cal.

The usual state financing arrangements were modified and Medicaid regulations waived to permit more flexible methods of paying providers, so that once a woman was in the program she could be guaranteed continued care until after the birth of her baby regardless of changes in her eligibility status.

It was clear from the outset that more comprehensive services would mean increased public expenditures, which would be justifiable only if they resulted in improved health outcomes and savings in postnatal care. Thus, a rigorous evaluation of the program was agreed upon and supported with federal funds.

Evaluation was designed to focus on two kinds of outcomes: the impact on health costs and the proportion of babies born at low birthweight. To head the evaluation team, the state chose Joe Klun, a statistician from the California Highway Patrol. "There we were," says Dr. Headley, "sitting down to develop the evaluation plan, and I was trying to explain very basic terms—the difference between perinatal and prenatal—to someone who had spent the last several years studying whether more pedestrians get hit inside or outside crosswalks." But it didn't take long for the new researcher to catch on and for Dr. Headley to realize what a gem had become part of her maternal and child health team.

Between 1979 and 1982, more than five thousand babies were born to the women participating in the pilot program. It took another two years to complete the evaluation, and the results were spectacular.

The percentage of babies who were of low birthweight was one third lower among the OB Access participants than in a matched comparison group of Medi-Cal women: 4.7 percent versus 7 percent. The percentage of very low birthweight was less than half of the comparison group: 0.5 percent versus 1.3 percent.

The cost impact was even more striking. Enhanced care under OB Access cost 5 percent more than the average cost of Medi-Cal prenatal care, but every additional dollar spent on OB Access saved an estimated $1.70 to $2.60 just in neonatal intensive care for low-birthweight babies.

The final report to Governor George Deukmejian in December 1984 said, "Although it is the end of the project, it is also the beginning of a new era in prenatal care."

Its recommendation, "The adoption of the OB Access pilot program scope of benefits statewide for the Medi-Cal program," was soon passed by the legislature. Despite the added cost, a tight budget, and the Gramm-Rudman budget-cutting climate, Republican Governor Deukmejian signed the bill into law.

Under the new program, in operation since January 1987, the state of California takes responsibility for assuring that an enriched form of prenatal care will be available to all Medicaid-eligible residents.

"There are still people in the state government squirming about having to put in some of the up-front dollars," Dr. Headley says. "They know that you don't realize the cost savings right away. But they know that ultimately they will be there. That is why that program is in effect today."

Statistician Joe Klun, still working in maternal and child health, is proud of his part in documenting that significantly improved prenatal care, offered to widely diverse populations extending from the northernmost to the southernmost borders of the state, can have a measurable beneficial effect.

Dr. Headley, who now heads the successor program to OB Access, counts herself lucky to have seen a research theory and a dream turn into a statewide program in less than a decade. She is working diligently to make sure that the lessons of the pilot program are applied, as a vastly expanded array of prenatal care is made available and accessible to poor pregnant women throughout America's most populous state, where one of every eight U.S. babies is born.

A Storefront Program in Baltimore

The medical value of providing more than the medical parts of prenatal care was also demonstrated with adolescent mothers in Baltimore. Prestigious Johns Hopkins University Hospital provided "prenatal-plus" services in a bright, poster-festooned storefront clinic located in a slightly seedy shopping center. Participants were all seventeen or younger, most of them black, single, and poor.

The founder of the program, Dr. Janet Hardy (whom we met in the last chapter, working to prevent school-age pregnancies), explains, "Pregnant adolescents need more than good medical care. They need more services, a case management system to assure that no problem is overlooked, and—perhaps most important of all— they need an environment which makes them feel comfortable and cared about."

The program established by Dr. Hardy, and conducted with her health educator colleague, Rosalie Streett, was based on these convictions. Serious continuing attention was given to health education, nutrition, preparation for parenthood, and many kinds of supports to help the youngsters maintain the self-esteem essential to caring properly for oneself during pregnancy and for one's baby later.

The many pressing medical, social, and personal needs typical of pregnant adolescents were addressed by a team consisting of an obstetrician, two obstetrical nurses, a social worker, and a health educator. The medical director and nurses frequently reviewed the medical record of each patient to make sure that pressing individual needs had been identified and were being responded to, whether they were related to the young woman's health and nutrition, her schoolwork, job prospects, fears of childbirth or motherhood, her relations with family or friends, or worries about where she would live and how she would take care of her baby. Missed appointments were meticulously followed up and contact maintained between scheduled visits.

An invaluable member of the team was the community outreach worker, who got to know each expectant mother in the clinic and stayed with her during delivery. She became the young woman's advocate, friend, and role model. She visited the homes of the youngest and highest-risk girls. With the social worker she also worked with schools, churches, and other community groups, developing a rich support network. The staff helped the teenagers surmount numerous logistical and administrative obstacles to obtain a wide variety of social services, including WIC nutrition benefits. ("Most of our girls got on WIC," says Rosalie Streett, "and that has not always been easy here in Baltimore.")

Obstetrical nurses and other staff were always available to provide support, not only during crises. The nurses developed a close personal relationship with each of the adolescents through group and individual education activities. They saw the youngster on each clinic visit, and made sure that no girl left the clinic without fully understanding what had happened during her time with the doctor.

Each visit with a physician or other clinician was preceded by a session of health education and discussion, usually in a group setting. "Kids listen to each other—often they learn more from each other than they do from us," observes Rosalie Streett.

Prime subjects tended to be caring for one's own health, proper nutrition during pregnancy, and preparation for childbirth and parenting. Much time was devoted to discussions of infant feeding, cleanliness, safety and health, and how to respond to the subtle cues of the newborn infant. To emphasize the importance the staff attaches to helping these young mothers-to-be to acquire the skills and motivation to interact sensitively with their babies, Ms. Streett brought out a Raggedy Ann doll with a face made of a mirror, which she uses to encourage pregnant youngsters to think about the importance of getting their babies to look into their mother's eyes, and of looking back at them. "Waiting until after delivery to talk about the job of being a parent is too late," notes Dr. Hardy.

The Johns Hopkins program for pregnant adolescents was carefully evaluated between 1979 and 1981. Participants were compared to a matched group of pregnant teenagers receiving care from several other programs, also affiliated with Johns Hopkins University Hospital. The basic medical care, prenatally and during childbirth, was fundamentally the same for both groups. But the control group did not receive the added educational, social, and support services, and the atmosphere in which the care was provided was very different.

And the outcomes were markedly different.

Fewer mothers in the experimental program had anemia and fewer had preeclampsia (a dangerous toxic condition that can develop in late pregnancy). More gained an appropriate amount of weight. Even more dramatic was the difference between the two groups of babies: in the control group, the rate of low birthweight was 60 percent greater; very low birthweight was twice as great among the controls as in the experimental group. The babies in the experimental group had higher Apgar scores (a measure of general health in newborns) and shorter hospital stays. Of the demonstration group babies, one third fewer died during their first month of life.

In discussing the prospects of reproducing their model elsewhere, Dr. Hardy and Ms. Streett emphasize that they consider the small size and intimacy of their program essential to its success. "Huge doesn't work in human services," observed Ms. Streett. Dr. Hardy agrees, adding that the favorable outcomes they achieved were, in her view, "in some fundamental sense, the result of warm and wonderful relationships." She is convinced that these factors of size and relationships must be taken into account in the organization and funding of prenatal care if it is to be effective with high-risk populations such as the teenagers she has been working with.

SOUTH CAROLINA'S RESOURCE MOTHERS

Several hundred miles south of Baltimore, in Florence, South Carolina, an extended family—five women, an infant, four other children, plus several dogs—makes a noisy scene, crowded as they are into a small, sparsely furnished home in a public housing development. So it causes no great disturbance when Libby Wiersema arrives to counsel seventeen-year-old Nancy, who comes in looking breathless, pretty, and pregnant.

Nancy does not know what to expect in labor or delivery, how to get Medicaid to pay for the doctor and hospital, how or where to find a pediatrician, or how to feed an infant. When Ms. Wiersema mentions breast-feeding, Nancy winces. "It's too embarrassing!" As to her own diet, she had orange juice for breakfast, but can't remember what she had for lunch at school. She is vague about using contraceptives after the baby is born. Before Ms. Wiersema leaves, Nancy will know a lot more about such things and will have pamphlets to study in the week before the next visit.

Not far away, in a mobile home on a winding rural road, another seventeen-year-old, Audrey, shows her healthy six-week-old baby to Julie Tilford, eager to tell of his habits and progress. Audrey has had a long-standing relationship with Ms. Tilford, dating back to early pregnancy. On this day Audrey talks of her forthcoming marriage to the child's father and her trouble fitting into a borrowed wedding dress. That is Ms. Tilford's cue to discuss diet, postpartum exercises, and the physical changes caused by childbirth. They also discuss Audrey's contraceptive practices, the importance of talking and responding to the baby, and how to store infant formula safely. As the older woman leaves, Audrey calls, "Now remember to come to my wedding! I told Jamie I won't get married unless you're there."

Libby Wiersema and Julie Tilford are "Resource Mothers," part of a program designed to help fill gaps in prenatal care for teenagers. Resource Mothers, as Governor Richard W. Riley reported on a 1985 visit to Washington, are a key element in a high-intensity campaign to improve maternity care in a state that until recently had the highest infant mortality rate in the nation.

Governor Riley spoke with quiet passion of his efforts in South Carolina, and through the National Governors' Association, to combat poverty and promote child health. As deeply conversant as any staff expert with the details of the policies he espouses, the governor cited studies showing that prenatal care costing $1,000 a person frequently prevents premature births of infants who may require hospital care costing more than $100,000. He voiced dismay that Reagan Administration officials seemed unable to see beyond immediate costs.

"I tell them, yes, it would cost the government more—for about six months! But these programs pay for themselves many times over in dollars as well as in the reduction of human suffering."

To direct South Carolina's maternal and child health activities, Governor Riley chose Marie Meglen, a nurse midwife who had spent five years in the 1960s as a visiting nurse in rural Mississippi and already had a considerable reputation as a dedicated and experienced clinician, educator, and public health administrator.

For many years, Ms. Meglen recalls, South Carolina—like most other states—dealt with the problem of low birthweight after the fact. It upgraded its neonatal intensive care system, reducing both mortality and morbidity. But South Carolina remained stuck near the bottom in state rankings of infant mortality, low birthweight, and receipt of prenatal care. Public health authorities began to wonder whether further progress might not require increased investment in prevention.

Armed with funding from the Robert Wood Johnson Foundation's Rural Infant Care Program, Ms. Meglen enlisted Dr. Henry Heins, professor of obstetrics at the Medical University of South Carolina. Together they would put together a program to get prenatal care to high-risk pregnant women who were not being reached. Tiring of nearly a lifetime of "taking care of a lot of healthy women" as he put it, Dr. Heins had quit private practice to earn a master's degree in public health and become a prime mover in efforts to improve maternal and child health among high-risk families in his state.

Determined to change outcomes in the face of daunting odds, Ms. Meglen and Dr. Heins chose as their target population pregnant girls under eighteen living in a poor, rural, three-county region with very primitive health facilities at the northern edge of the state. The Pee-Dee area, as it is known, is notable for having the state's highest teenage pregnancy rate and the nation's highest rate of postneonatal mortality.

The program they launched in 1981, initially funded by the Robert Wood Johnson Foundation, operates today with state and federal support in all fifteen health districts in the state. It was designed to provide young pregnant women with the elements missing from available prenatal care. A group of community women would be trained to work closely with the pregnant teenagers. These are the women who have become known throughout the community—and now more widely—as Resource Mothers.

The first six, selected from a hundred applicants, had all raised children, and most of them had themselves been teenage mothers. They were selected for their empathy and warmth, their coping skills, and their ability to communicate with teenagers.

Their training was intensive and covered family planning, labor and delivery, infant safety, sanitation and feeding, stages of child development, parent-infant interaction, and key points of the physical, emotional, and social aspects of pregnancy, including prenatal nutrition. They were taught counseling, recordkeeping, and how to mobilize community resources. They receive continuing consultation and supervision from a public health nurse and a senior social worker at the health department.

Resource Mothers work with about thirty teenagers at a time, visiting each girl at home or in some other agreed-upon place at least monthly, but more frequently when special problems arise. They systematically provide information about a wide variety of maternal and child health topics.

Nutrition is almost always on the agenda when the Resource Mother meets with her client. "I'm always asking them what's in their refrigerator that they can eat right now that would be good for the baby," says Resource Mother Brenda Hicks. To warn the young expectant mothers about the dangers of smoking and drugs, they try to help them visualize the developing fetus. Several Resource Mothers have found—macabre as it may seem—that showing the pregnant girls pictures of damaged newborns can be an effective tool.

High priority is assigned to helping the teenagers make and get to prenatal care appointments and to interpreting the doctor's instructions. One middle-aged Resource Mother, who herself had had a baby at sixteen, told of Glenda, one of her charges, rapidly gaining too much weight on a diet of cake and candy, having understood her doctor to have told her to "eat sweets all the time" because her blood sugar was low. A call to the doctor's office enabled the Resource Mother quickly to correct the misunderstanding.

Resource Mothers spend considerable time helping their teenage clients to establish eligibility for Medicaid, WIC, and other supports and to make realistic plans for their future employment and education. In addition, most Resource Mothers become friends, confidantes, advocates, and role models during pregnancy and afterwards. They are as likely to be consulted about problems of housing and schooling as about bathing a newborn.

Resource Mothers are enthusiastically received by teenagers and their families. A measure of their sophisticated skills is that few have become embroiled in competition with family members about whose advice should be heeded. In fact, several of the teenagers' mothers said they wished they could have had the help of such counselors. "When they were pregnant, no one helped them out at all," observes Brenda Hicks.

Beyond pleasing the beneficiaries, what have the Resource Mothers accomplished?

To assess the impact of the program, between 1981 and 1983 one quarter of the eligible pregnant teenagers were randomly assigned to a control group and not visited by a Resource Mother. They were telephoned every three months to monitor their progress and provided with encouragement and referrals as needed.

There were striking differences in birth outcomes. The control group had 55 percent more low-birthweight babies and four and a half times as many very-low-birthweight babies.

Positive effects continued after birth. Among the experimental group, during the infant's first year of life, researchers were able to document superior parenting skills as well as better infant health.

Studying these results, along with the results of attempts by others to get high-risk pregnant women into care, Marie Meglen concluded that successful programs are distinguished by the extent to which they contribute to the pregnant woman's sense of comfort, acceptance, dignity, belonging, and feeling of support. "For a disadvantaged woman," she says, "understanding, support, and respect can be every bit as important in determining outcomes as the physiological aspects of health care." She believes that early pregnancy is a time of great susceptibility, a time when "minimal intervention can have great long-range impact in either a healthy or unhealthy direction." To take advantage of this most "teachable moment" in the life cycle, Ms. Meglen believes it is essential that prenatal care programs for disadvantaged women be designed to meet their needs in ways rarely attempted in the past. This means eliciting and addressing the immediate needs of the pregnant woman, taking into account that her life is likely to be crisis-ridden and filled with stress due to poverty, poor housing, unemployment, and daily struggles to obtain food.

The most far-reaching conclusion that emerges from Ms. Meglen's review of the work of others, from the innovative program she founded, as well as from the California OB Access program and the Johns Hopkins program for adolescent mothers, is that traditional standards for acceptable prenatal care must be fundamentally revised to assure that high-risk women receive a far broader spectrum of services than those traditionally considered to be adequate prenatal care. In Chapter 6 we will examine the health policies that could support expanded forms of prenatal care for high-risk pregnant women.

Child Health Services
That Make a Difference

Archie Douglas spent three years in the first grade, often missed school, and, when he attended, paid little attention and was disruptive. At eight, when he finally got a complete evaluation, he excelled on nonverbal tests, but his language skills were those of a five-year-old, and he was found to have a significant hearing loss—probably as a result of frequent and inadequately treated middle ear infections which began when he was one and a half. Now Archie has a hearing aid, and remedial education is helping him catch up with his schoolwork. But neither can make up for Archie's deep sense of having failed in a world beyond his comprehension.

Childhood hearing loss is most commonly the result of untreated or inadequately treated recurrent middle ear infection (otitis media), the most frequent childhood illness requiring medical attention. About 45 percent of children have seven or more episodes during the first three years of life. The risk is higher for the disadvantaged: All types of otitis media are more prevalent among poor children, and so is the residual hearing impairment that often results.

Repeated periods of hearing loss from recurrent middle ear infections, especially when not adequately treated, interfere with the ability to process sounds and understand speech, delaying the development of language and threatening the whole educational process. Behavior problems may also result, when the inability to hear is misunderstood as unwillingness to pay attention or as disrespect.

> In a classroom in Canton, Mississippi, Kenny had trouble seeing the blackboard. His teachers showed impatience as he fell behind in his schoolwork. One teacher slapped him when he did not move out of her way. Another told his mother that she "didn't have the time to teach him." When Kenny was nine, his third-grade teacher called him "a fool," and his mother took him out of school. Not until he was fourteen was his eyesight tested. He was found to have a serious but correctable vision problem. His mother tried to re-enroll him in school, but Kenny, ashamed of failure and unwilling to start again with younger children, remains at home, unhappy and unschooled.

Seeing well is not only fundamental to learning to read and write, but to grasping concepts of space and form, the foundations of perception and perhaps much of what we call intelligence.

About 20 percent of the nation's children suffer from vision defects. Only a fraction of these are identified and properly treated. Poor children are the ones most likely to have serious uncorrected vision problems.

Educator Theodore Sizer's observation reflects the statistics. In the course of visiting dozens of schools for his five-year study of U.S. high schools, he noted one of the most striking class differences: "There are fewer spectacles on poor kids—and it is not because their eyes are better."

The effects of uncorrected seeing and hearing difficulties go well beyond scholastic achievement. Judge Julian Houston of the Roxbury, Massachusetts, juvenile court was struck by the number of young people in serious legal trouble who had long-undetected vision and hearing problems. Along with many of his colleagues, he believes that these may be among the most preventable precursors of delinquency.

The judge's conclusion is supported by a number of studies. The annals of juvenile delinquency and school failure abound in case histories pointing to early physical problems as a significant factor contributing to later antisocial activities.

Learning disabilities, a more complex form of perceptual disorder than vision or hearing problems, can also significantly impair normal development and academic achievement. The learning-disabled child may be seen by adults as a slow learner and a disciplinary problem, by other children as awkward, clumsy, and an undesirable playmate, and by himself as a loser. He is likely to find school an agony from the start and to take refuge in truancy and misbehavior. He may be held back or put in special classes, which may fortify a sense of failure. His problems may be complicated by general impulsiveness and a limited ability to learn from experience or accurately perceive social cues. By the time he reaches adolescence, a learning-disabled youngster, like a hyperactive youngster, is likely to have low self-esteem, difficulty in making close friends, and poor social skills. He may have failed one or more grades, and has a higher than average chance of having been in court for theft or truancy.

Poor health and biological handicaps, although rarely *causes* of damaging outcomes, represent significant risk factors. With proper health care, a substantial number of these conditions can be prevented or detected and treated, averting many of their damaging consequences.

Whether present at birth (like low birthweight or congenital defects), or acquired later (like lead poisoning, anemia, and brain damage resulting from illness or injury), health problems become risk factors by interfering with the development of healthy relationships within the family—especially when family tensions run high—and by impeding learning and early success at school.

Central nervous system disorders may also, especially in combination with an adverse environment, produce serious damage, even some forms of violent behavior. Take the case of Gail:

Gail was thirteen, pretty, shy, and soft-spoken. While being teased by schoolmates on the playground, she fatally stabbed an eleven-year-old boy. She wandered away from school, and, several hours later, confused as to her whereabouts, telephoned her grandmother to pick her up. Later, she had no memory of the stabbing, and only vaguely recalled that the boy had pointed a knife at her. Witnesses said the boy had been pointing a pencil at Gail when she stabbed him. Neurologists subsequently concluded that Gail probably suffered from a psychomotor disturbance, and that the killing may have resulted from a seizure—which might have been averted with proper medical attention. Gail, growing up in a poor and chaotic family, had not received such attention.

Her case is not unique. Psychiatrist Dorothy Otnow Lewis, who uncovered and investigated Gail's story while working in the psychiatric clinic of the New Haven juvenile court, was astounded at the large proportion of children coming before the court with previously undiagnosed central nervous system problems.

Some health conditions will lead to later damaging outcomes if they are not recognized and treated promptly. Some are completely preventable, such as the neurological complications which can occur as a result of pertussis (whooping cough) and measles, both of which can be prevented through immunizations.

Some conditions, such as iron-deficiency anemia, are both treatable and preventable. Anemia, the most common consequence of inadequate nutrition in infants and young children, can be prevented with proper diet and dietary supplements. Anemia is associated with slow development in infants, inattentiveness among school-age children, and conduct disorders in adolescents. It is three times as prevalent among youngsters in poor families as in the general child population, and it occurs much more frequently among black than among white children.

Lead poisoning, another severe blood abnormality most likely to afflict poor children and also preventable, can produce verbal, perceptual, motor, and behavioral problems, including irritability, inattentiveness, and inability to follow instructions, often reflected in lowered test scores.

Hyperactivity is another health problem that often has long-term consequences. Hyperactive infants sleep poorly and irregularly, often have feeding problems, and may object to being held. The trouble is compounded when parents find themselves unable to comfort their baby. As toddlers, hyperactive children keep their caretakers chronically off balance by their constant demands, by getting into dangerous situations, by not heeding, by not being content to play either alone or with other children. When a hyperactive child reaches school, with its requirements for group discipline, sitting still, and concentrating, he is likely to be in deep trouble.

A substantial proportion of hyperactive youngsters "lose" their symptoms as they grow up, but a significant number of these continue to be at high risk, especially for antisocial behavior and substance abuse. Good health care can make a difference in how the family fares and how the youngster fares, sometimes by treating the child and often by providing parents with support and guidance in dealing with their hyperactive youngster.

The strength of the link between biological factors and later adverse outcomes, as we saw in Chapter 2, is heavily dependent on the intervening environment. Where there is family stress and poverty, early biological insults become much more powerful; more favorable circumstances protect against long-term negative effects. The other major variable in accounting for long-term outcomes is the adequacy of child health services.

BARRIERS TO GOOD HEALTH CARE FOR HIGH-RISK CHILDREN

Millions of American youngsters lack the services needed to meet their health needs, especially children growing up with other odds already stacked against them.

Archie, the hearing-impaired boy who failed in school, might have had a different life story if he had received the health services he needed. When Archie had an earache and fever at the age of eighteen months, there were many things that deterred Mrs. Douglas from taking him to the clinic—the expense, the distance, the inconvenient hours, the long wait, and the prospect of being treated brusquely and impatiently. So, relying on her own mother's advice, Mrs. Douglas gave Archie half an aspirin and a commercial eardrop preparation every few hours and rocked him to soothe his pain. When fluid began to drain from Archie's ear, he seemed less distressed, and after a few days, he was better. Three months later, the fever and earache recurred; this time home remedies brought no relief. His mother took Archie to the city clinic. The doctor diagnosed bilateral otitis media, and prescribed a ten-day course of antibiotics. To pay for the prescription, Mrs. Douglas deferred paying the rent. Archie seemed to recover in a few days; his mother saw no reason to continue the medication. Within a month, the earache returned. This time the rocking and ear drops were supplemented by the left-over antibiotic pills, and Archie once more seemed to recover.

The significant hearing loss that went undiagnosed until Archie was eight could have been prevented by prompt medical attention along with a careful explanation of the importance of continuing the antibiotics for the full ten days and a follow-up by the clinic to make sure that full recovery had in fact occurred. Thus, Archie's later difficulties in school might have been averted with good health care during early childhood.

Gail's story is similarly instructive. After the fatal stabbing on the playground, an official of the juvenile court reviewed Gail's medical records at the local hospital. They showed that Gail had been seen there more than thirty times for problems ranging from recurrent headaches to sore throats. The juvenile court reviewer discovered, in the midst of the thick file, an inconspicuous note by a resident physician saying that Gail had twice lost consciousness for no apparent reason while being examined. The resident had recommended an electroencephalogram to determine whether Gail was suffering from seizures. None was performed until after Gail had killed her schoolmate.

What went wrong? First, this example illustrates the fact that most health care works best for families with the means and knowledge to monitor their own care, identify their needs, and see to it that they are met. Gail's family had little education, was overwhelmed by other problems, and had no idea what Gail's examination had shown or that follow-up neurological tests had been recommended.

Second, no single professional had a continuing responsibility for making sense of the many complicated factors in Gail's background. Not until after the killing did anyone take the careful history that revealed that Gail had been the product of a long labor and traumatic delivery, that her mother had had syphilis during her pregnancy, that Gail's behavior since kindergarten had oscillated between withdrawal and fighting, that Gail often flew into a rage for no apparent reason. Following such outbursts, Gail would feel tired and have to sleep—a history which might have suggested some sort of psychomotor symptomatology.

But Gail's family was dependent on episodic care in a local hospital clinic, where patients typically see physicians they have never seen before and do not expect to see again. In such circumstances accurate diagnosis is difficult, and the prospects for proper treatment and management of complex conditions are low. In a different environment with different health care, Gail's delusional stabbing of a schoolmate might have been averted, and Gail's own life might have had a better outcome.

More Effective Health Care for High-Risk Children

Good health care can help to prevent adverse outcomes not only by improving health status but by identifying and responding to problems that are not exclusively biological. Alert health professionals can often spot subtle problems in a child's behavior, in relationships within the family, which when ignored become established and compounded and later contribute to adverse outcomes.

Because, especially in early childhood, physical and emotional health are so closely related, health professionals are frequently in the best position to detect early signs of a variety of troubles, sometimes going beyond those the family is explicitly asking help for. Health professionals are often more acceptable and less stigmatized than other sources of support and guidance, especially when physical symptoms signal a broader and more complex set of problems, whether these originate from a sick or difficult child, an impaired parent, or an overwhelming accumulation of stresses.

Yet the gulf is wide between the kind of health care that could respond to such needs and the health care available to most high-risk families. It is created by a combination of financial barriers (to be discussed in Chapter 6), hurdles of distance, inappropriate hours, fragmented and impersonal services, the absence of outreach and follow-up, and in many instances enormous cultural differences. In addition, prevailing health services are poorly matched to the special needs of families handicapped by poverty, lack of education, mental illness, alcoholism or drug addiction, or who live in particularly harsh environments.

Physicians whose orientation is narrowly biological—as a result of their training and the medical ethos and settings within which they practice—often miss opportunities to help. A study of the early medical histories of one group of young delinquents found an extraordinary number who had been seen in hospital outpatient departments for problems that might signal extreme family disorganization (including a high incidence of head trauma and possible child abuse). But the study found that, particularly among the blacks in the study population, "any needs beyond care of the immediate presenting problem are likely to be overlooked."

A similar picture of the physician-in-biomedical-straitjacket emerged from a meeting on medical ethics in which I was a participant. The issue before us was whether a physician was ethically required to file a child abuse report on a baby who had been brought to a big-city emergency room for treatment of diarrhea and dehydration for the fourth time within two months. Perceiving that the pediatrician describing the case was drawing on his own experience, I asked whether during the second and third visits there had been indications that the baby was not being fed or properly cared for. He recalled that there had been many signs of neglect, and I expressed astonishment that the baby's diarrhea and dehydration had merely been treated and the family sent home. He, in turn, seemed astonished at my suggestion that he might have done more. Talking to the family to discover what was going wrong and why, or sending a social worker, public health nurse, or homemaker to the home to help—none of these fell within his definition of an appropriate medical response. His way of mobilizing others to help was limited to filing—at the time of the family's fourth appearance in the emergency room—a child abuse report.

Of course, there are physicians everywhere who are aware of and responsive to the children they see in the context of their family and other surroundings, but the broader perspective brings little in the way of financial reward or recognition from valued colleagues.

Many of the children in greatest need of help from the health system would benefit from a much broader approach than is the norm. A study in the Boston schools found that prolonged or frequent absences reflect not so much simple biological problems as a more general "state of disequilibrium or social dysfunction." Truancy often signaled masked depression, learning disabilities, family problems, inappropriate responses to minor illness, or poor management of chronic illness. Health care for these youngsters going beyond the biomedical could be expected to reduce school absenteeism, itself a major precursor of school failure.

So what can be done? Every impediment to good health care for high-risk children has been recognized, understood, and successfully dealt with somewhere in this country, at some level, during the past twenty years.

In a multitude of settings, dedicated individuals have deflected, ignored, and defied prevailing pressures to meet the health needs of high-risk children. Let me describe three programs which epitomize the imagination, skill, and hard work with which this has been done, in locations as diverse as Mississippi, Maryland, and California.

THE HEALTH CENTER IN MISSISSIPPI WHERE "COMPREHENSIVE" INCLUDES CLEAN WATER

What is now the Jackson-Hinds Comprehensive Health Center started in 1970 in the Sunday school classrooms of a church in Jackson, and in a renovated bus that served the outlying area of rural Hinds County. The center's founder was Dr. Aaron Shirley, Mississippi's first black pediatrician, who has the voice and charisma of a Paul Robeson and the sure touch of a sophisticated political operator.

From his 1960s experience in the Mississippi Delta, Dr. Shirley had learned that health, especially for the poor, involved a lot more than treating disease. As part of the pioneering Mound Bayou neighborhood health center, funded by the federal Office of Economic Opportunity (OEO) and sponsored by the Tufts University School of Medicine, Dr. Shirley helped to provide a full range of preventive and curative health services to the residents of the oldest all-black community in the nation. That center, which also organized a farm cooperative as part of its broad approach to health, was an almost instant success, cutting infant mortality by more than half within four years.

In 1970, together with several other practicing physicians and concerned citizens, Dr. Shirley secured support from OEO and other federal programs to bring the comprehensive health center concept to Jackson, the state capital, and to a nearby rural area of Hinds County. Mississippi then led the nation in maternal and infant death rates and other indicators of preventable mortality and morbidity. Dr. Shirley and the other founders believed that "health problems cannot be separated from the poverty, isolation, ignorance, and threatening environments which cause them." They proceeded to build a truly comprehensive health care system, aimed at preventing sickness as much as treating it.

Within five years Jackson-Hinds had enrolled about twelve thousand members, 40 percent of them children. Members, who paid what they could—and nothing if they couldn't—learned about getting regular health care from professionals who got to know them and their families. In 1976 the Jackson center moved into a cluster of new single-story buildings on a 10,000-square-foot tract located at a main intersection.

I visited there in 1979, as chairman of the congressionally established Select Panel for the Promotion of Child Health. Dr. Shirley, a member of the panel, had invited us to Mississippi to see both problems and solutions at first hand.

We found family physicians, internists, pediatricians, obstetricians, surgeons, and nurses at work in modern, well-equipped facilities alongside nutritionists, social workers, community organizers, and outreach workers. Nurses and nurse practitioners provide much of the preventive care and conduct a county-wide home health program for the chronically ill. Dental care is available, an early survey having shown three-quarters of the county's children suffering from tooth and gum problems. Mental health professionals are on hand to help with the many emotional problems compounded by poverty and stress. Patients who are malnourished are helped to obtain food, and those who can't prepare or store food (mainly the elderly) are provided with meals.

For those who have trouble getting to the clinic, the health center has fourteen minibuses which provide door-to-door service for more than one hundred fifty people a day. Dr. Shirley believes that the center's transportation system is at least in part responsible for the fact that so many children from families who had never seen a doctor before are now thoroughly examined every six months.

Since our visit, the center has continued to grow. Fifteen years after its founding, its clientele numbered thirty-two thousand, and the center was bursting its seams and expanding into additional facilities. Thirty percent of its budget comes from Medicaid payments, but it is still largely dependent on grant funds. The center's core budget was frozen as a result of Reagan Administration fiscal restraints, even as its ratio of nonpaying patients rose because of cuts in other programs. Yet it continues to launch new projects. Recently it established a colony of single-unit dwellings for the aging adjacent to the health center as an alternative to nursing home care.

The center also operates adolescent health clinics in two Jackson high schools and a junior high school. Nurse practitioners, health educators, and counselors, along with physicians, provide comprehensive health services to the students. Initial returns show that pregnancies among school-age youngsters have been markedly reduced, and school completion has risen dramatically since the inception of the program.

On our 1979 trip we visited one of the high school clinics, among the first school-based comprehensive health clinics in the country. After we talked with both staff and students, Dr. Shirley loaded us into his van to take us to rural Hinds County and the outpost clinic which had replaced the secondhand bus. Twenty miles beyond the Jackson city limits, the scenery became increasingly desolate. We covered many miles of dusty road, stopping once briefly for Dr. Shirley to remind an elderly lady, pulling up weeds at the roadside, that her great-grandson was overdue for his shots.

Finally we pulled up in front of an isolated shack and got out of the van. Dr. Shirley said he wanted us to see what the phrase "growing up at risk" means in rural Mississippi. "But just one of you come in with me," he said, "I don't want to overwhelm these folks with a delegation." As we stood looking at the dilapidated shack with the broken-down porch and the newspapers stuffing the cracks in the walls, my colleagues pushed me forward, and I found myself following Dr. Shirley up what passed for steps.

Perhaps because of the contrast with the sunlight outside or perhaps because I was so unprepared, it took me a while before I began to take in what I saw. The flies and cockroaches are etched in my memory. The bugs were everywhere—on every flat surface, on the baby bottles, on the baby's cheeks, on the grandmother's legs. The infant, on the floor, sucked sporadically on a bottle. A toddler—not quite asleep, not quite awake—was also on the floor. Their mother had gone to Chicago to look for work, and the children had stayed on here with their grandparents. Grandfather Boren dozed on the only visible chair in the room. The grandmother was clearly prepared to respond to my questions.

There was obviously no indoor bathroom and no running water in the kitchen. No point asking about that. I finally asked where everyone slept at night. Mrs. Boren directed my attention to two mattresses in a corner darker than the rest of the room. When I said it must be hard trying to care for two little children without any plumbing at all, Mrs. Boren smiled for the first time and said it would not be long now before "Dr. Shirley's truck" would be there to bring a barrel of clean water. We left on that small note of cheer.

There was no time to reflect on what I had just seen. Before I could finish a brief report to my colleagues back in the van, we had arrived in Utica, at the rural outpost of the Jackson-Hinds Clinic. We pulled up next to the WIC food distribution center, which operates out of the health center's parking lot. Dr. Shirley asked two WIC workers to interrupt their lunch break to attend to a woman waiting with an infant in her arms and two toddlers clinging to her legs. "At least we do better than the food stamp office," Dr. Shirley observed. "Yesterday they had nine people in line from 5 A.M., started giving out numbers at 9 A.M., and turned away fifty people when they closed at 4 P.M." He shook his head.

Inside the center, the preschoolers in the day care program were about to join the senior citizens' group for lunch. Dr. Shirley explained how central the feeding programs were to the operation of the center. "When I see a child for the first time, if he's not part of an organized program like Head Start, I know there's at least a one in four chance that child will be seriously malnourished."

We were invited to come to the table, too. The volunteer cooks had prepared enough chicken and sweet potatoes to feed their Northern visitors along with their regular charges. Shown around the center after lunch, we observed physicians and nurses in their offices and examining rooms, and talked briefly with a health educator and an outreach worker about their plans to reach all eligible children with the screening and follow-up services made possible through the Medicaid Early and Periodic Screening, Diagnosis and Treatment (EPSDT) program.

Then we were off again, this time our van following the truck that goes out once a week from the health center, delivering barrels of clean water and lumber to build privies for homes that lack plumbing, such as the one we had seen that morning. A 1974 survey had shown that half the homes in the area were using contaminated water from catch basins or shallow wells, and two thirds had no piped water or plumbing, indoors or out. The health center began by digging wells for those without running water, operating its own drilling rig. The well-digging program, too expensive to maintain, has now ended, but water is supplied weekly by a 5,000-gallon tank truck. Homes with small children get first priority, since children are most susceptible to diseases that come from exposure to untreated wastewater as well as from drinking contaminated water.

En route, we asked Dr. Shirley how things were changing in Mississippi and for how long he expected his federally funded health center to continue to perform functions that elsewhere were the responsibility of state and local health departments. He told us of the important role of federal funds and federal standards. Even a substantial expansion of Medicaid would not be enough in Mississippi, he said, especially when it comes to serving poor blacks and others who can't negotiate their way around a complex system and don't live in an area served by a community health center. "Heaven help you if you can't find your own way, for there is just no one reaching out."

To illustrate his point, Dr. Shirley told of a little girl who had died at the age of five, of secondary pneumonia brought about by an infection caused by Ascaris worms in her intestines. The family had no privy and no access to clean drinking water—which might have accounted for the worm infestation. But they also had no regular source of health care. "That little girl's symptoms of worms may have looked like a cold and runny nose, and didn't signal the need for an emergency trip to the hospital. That's why we need outreach and easy access to a familiar source of care. Our outreach workers are not frills, our attempts to eliminate barriers and to maintain a friendly atmosphere are not trivial, the broad range of services we offer is not a luxury. For many of the families we see, all these are an absolute necessity."

The comprehensive approach to health care taken by the Jackson-Hinds Center has resulted in both cost savings and improved health. Like other comprehensive health centers, Jackson-Hinds finds it can provide complete care, including preventive and supportive services, to a population that is medically as well as economically underprivileged, at less cost than other sources of care. Among Medicaid patients, for whom comparisons are easier to make, hospital costs of Jackson-Hinds participants run $600 less per person each year.

The center has been able to document its success in reaching children, including infants and preschoolers, with immunizations and screening for anemia at much higher rates than other populations in similar circumstances. It has also reached a high proportion of sexually active adolescents with family planning counseling and services. Adolescents who do get pregnant get special services, with the result that 90 percent receive nutrition supplements, only 5 percent of the school-age mothers became pregnant again within a year, and only 9 percent dropped out of school (compared to 50 percent before the program began.)

"No one gets sick in a vacuum," says Dr. Shirley. The program's dual emphasis on changing high-risk environments and providing high-quality services in a way that makes them easy to use is paying off, not just for the families being served by the center today but also, Dr. Shirley is convinced, for the next generation.

"A CHAIN OF CONCERNED PEOPLE"—IN BALTIMORE

"From the minute that baby was born, from the first second, they showed concern for him," said Bertha Cross, a handsome, fiftyish retired schoolteacher, speaking of her grandson Jeffrey, born two and a half years earlier to her schizophrenic daughter at Baltimore's Sinai Hospital.

I met Mrs. Cross and Jeffrey on a visit to the Greenspring Pediatric Associates primary care center, which provides superb and respectful care to a population with a high proportion of poor and disorganized families. Greenspring is a private medical group on the grounds of Sinai Hospital, organized by Sinai's chief of pediatrics, Dr. Evan Charney, and several of his colleagues. It has demonstrated that good medicine can save lives in many ways. And it has been able to show residents in training that prestige can attach to attentive caring for families traditionally given short shrift.

From Mrs. Cross I learned much of what makes Greenspring a model program. Arranging for me to talk with her seemed a way for the self-effacing Dr. Charney to let me find out what he and the staff actually do that makes it so special. Mrs. Cross told her story in the doctors' conference room while Jeffrey went off to play nearby.

Her daughter, Lena, Jeffrey's mother, had been diagnosed as schizophrenic several years earlier. Lena had met Jeffrey's father during one of her periodic hospitalizations—he was also mentally ill. Jeffrey's birth put the grandmother in a position of responsibility and trepidation. She recalled her sense of relief at the way the staff mobilized in support.

"Everyone, starting with Dr. Straus [Dr. John Straus, Jeffrey's pediatrician and the medical director of the group] knew what the situation was from the beginning. My daughter couldn't have had a pediatrician who paid her any more attention or cared more about that baby.

"And after Lena came home from the hospital with Jeffrey, it continued. It's really been like a chain of concerned people. Because then Mrs. Bruce [the outreach worker] came to visit the baby and follow up. And she talked with my daughter, and played with Jeffrey and examined him, and tried to see that his functioning was what it should be. And she did that periodically.

"Whenever I saw a problem, I got on the telephone and called her, and she came right out. I felt confident, knowing she would do that. And I'm sure she relayed what was going on to the doctor because everybody at all times knew what was going on. We didn't have to always start over again and repeat everything, like at other hospitals.

"When Jeffrey was just a few months old, Lena got worse and was hospitalized again. So I kept him and took care of him and brought him here for his shots and whatever else he needed. When Lena came home from the hospital she wouldn't let Jeffrey have the medicine he was supposed to be taking—I think it was for an ear infection. I felt free to talk to Dr. Straus about that, and also about whether the father, who was coming to visit, should be alone with the baby for even a few minutes—personal things like that. It strengthened me to know that I could get professional advice from someone I could trust and who was aware of the situation.

"After a while, I came to see that much as I'd like to think Lena could care for her own baby, it was wishful thinking. When Lena was home from the hospital she didn't really care for the baby properly. It was not easy to acknowledge, but it was the truth. I got to the point where I couldn't be on the scene and see Jeffrey being neglected—not willfully, but it was neglect. She wouldn't bathe him, wouldn't let water touch him. And the only thing she'd feed him was pizzas and noodles and grits. And she wouldn't let me care for him.

"I talked to Mrs. Bruce, and she came in and talked to Lena about feeding him properly, about his health, his cleanliness. But Lena refused. The only other thing to do was to let the Department of Social Services know. We called them in, thinking that maybe they'd send somebody out who could persuade her. But they sent somebody who told me that if Lena remained at home they would have to take the baby and put him in a foster home."

Step by step, Mrs. Cross reviewed how the outreach worker and Greenspring's social worker, Mrs. Rebecca Polen, helped her to get her daughter back into hospital care and to get temporary guardianship of her grandson, a painful process that she could never have managed, she said, without the help of the pediatric group.

"All these people know that this is a child that really needed special attention. Dr. Straus, you know, he really *knows* Jeffrey! He not only checks him physically, he takes time out to see what his interests are. As for Mrs. Polen, from the day I met her until this time, she's been, like, right there with me. And Mrs. Bruce, she really became like a member of the family. There wasn't a time when we came in for the appointments that she didn't look Jeffrey over, to see how he had grown. She was like Jeffrey's—I would say appointed mother from the hospital. She always came. One day we opened the door and the snow was knee high and icy, but there she was. She never, never failed to keep an appointment."

Jeffrey reappeared from the playroom and collected a hug from his grandmother. As we said goodbye, Mrs. Cross talked about the need for more people like Dr. Straus, Mrs. Bruce, and Mrs. Polen— people "with genuine concern," as she put it.

When I talked with Dr. Charney later about Mrs. Cross's perceptions, he acknowledged the essential role of skilled and dedicated individuals but stressed the importance of institutional principles and practices.

"We reinforce and legitimize certain attitudes—like treating all families with respect," he said. "We make sure that star quality attaches not just to high-tech and high-chrome medicine but also to spending time with the family of a dying child. We teach how you deal with why a child isn't sleeping at night as carefully as we teach about meningitis. And our residents feel comfortable dealing with diabetics or kids with asthma because they've learned how the social problems interact with the physical diseases."

Dr. Straus added that when their residents complete their training, they are confident that they have the skills to provide care to diverse population groups. Members of the medical group all believe that a central reason that their program works so well is the mix of backgrounds among their patients. Both financially and psychologically, they note, it is much harder to serve an exclusively low-income population. They have overcome the "burnout" phenomenon (four of the six senior professionals have been there more than eight years), partly by combining clinical work with research and teaching but even more by being able to see middle-class patients with relatively simple problems along with low-income families with multiple and complex problems.

The pediatric group also believes that it could not have succeeded in obtaining high-quality specialist care for its low-income patients without the leverage gained by being able to refer middle-class patients as well. As Dr. Straus explained, an orthopedist in the famous tertiary care facility across town gets six times the fee for setting an arm from Blue Cross as from Medicaid. Consequently he treats Blue Cross patients himself and sends Medicaid patients to the residents in the clinic. There a child may have to wait many hours and may get less careful attention, and the family is left on its own to negotiate its way around a medical system that is very hard to manage.

"So we make sure our medical assistance (Medicaid) patients see the same specialist as the suburban family and are treated the same way," explains Dr. Straus's colleague, Dr. Steven Caplan. "If they don't take everybody we refer and don't treat everybody equally, then they won't get any of our referrals. And we follow up to make sure the family made the appointment, to make sure the child with the heart murmur was seen by the cardiologist. And we try to make up for the anonymity they encounter there—we find out what happened and make sure the family understands what happened, and we help the family to follow through with what needs to be done."

Continuity of care, which the Greenspring group holds to be so central to good practice, starts at birth. No baby born in Sinai Hospital—the busiest obstetrical service in Baltimore—is discharged before a pediatrician accepts responsibility for that baby. Most babies from poor or otherwise high-risk families become patients of Greenspring Pediatric Associates. The group takes continuing responsibility for these children, aided by a computer-based reminder system, outreach workers, transportation when needed, and a carefully designed after-hours telephone system.

The Greenspring group, through its computerized record keeping, has been able to document three quantifiable indicators of success. First, the rate of children who continue in care is unusually high; 90 percent of the children enrolled as newborns (about five hundred a year) are up to date on immunizations and screening procedures at the age of two. Second, the group's patients are much less likely than a comparable population to overuse the emergency room—a matter of importance, for reasons of both cost and quality of care. And third, in contrast with most of the rest of the health system, at Greenspring black and white children, poor and nonpoor children, use health services in virtually identical ways, showing that the barriers to needed health care have been successfully removed for everyone.

Such results, of course, do not come about automatically. I spoke to a young woman who was in the eighth grade when her daughter Livvy was born. At six months, the baby was found to have sickle-cell anemia. The mother told me how hard that was:

"I used to watch my baby when she was sick and in pain, and I just felt like I would give anything just to get that pain off of her."

She told me how the baby's constant crying scared her, and what a relief it was when "they had nurses come to my house and teach me a lot of things I needed to know, like being able to tell when she was really—you know, *really*—sick.

"When it's only a baby, they can't tell you what's wrong," the young mother said. "The nurses showed me how to tell when she was hurting; at first I never knew how to look at something and tell it was swollen, and they taught me all that." Livvy is now five years old, and her mother told me that even when Livvy has a crisis, "I don't rush in to the emergency room. Mrs. Polen helped me to get a phone, and I call and somebody in primary care who knows her will see her, no matter what hour it is."

The experiences of Livvy's mother and of Jeffrey's grandmother tell the same story as the studies and statistics: The determined ways in which the Greenspring group has set about eliminating organizational and psychological barriers to an enriched form of health care for low-income children have paid off in healthier and stronger families.

Sinai Hospital's Department of Pediatrics serves the children of Baltimore through a second model program. This one is in a community setting, providing an imaginative response to previously unmet needs in health, child development, nutrition, and family support.

Dr. Barbara Howard, the pediatrician who conceived the program, took me to the site, about a half mile from the hospital in a new community development. Perched on a hilltop in a cheery modern building is the Cold Spring Head Start Center, containing four classrooms filled with exuberant, busy, well-supervised preschoolers. When we arrived in the last of the four classrooms, Dr. Howard remarked that it looked like the others now but had looked much different three months earlier, at the start of the term. Then the children in this group were screaming, hitting each other, and in total chaos, for this was a group of children with lead poisoning.

Dr. Howard had been thinking for a long time about how powerfully the odds were arrayed against children with lead poisoning. Not only do they come from poor and often disorganized families and live in dilapidated housing and rundown neighborhoods, but they are likely to have experienced both malnutrition and inadequate parenting. They also tend to come from families that have difficulty in utilizing traditional programs aimed at improving children's health and learning.

Dr. Howard set about designing a program that could reach these high-risk children and make some lasting improvements in both their physical and social environment. Using funds available through Head Start and various nutrition and lead control programs, she sought to develop a model that would be economical and replicable and would demonstrate that organized intervention for multiply disadvantaged families could make a difference.

The program represents an ingenious combination of interventions. The children, between three and five years of age, come from all over Baltimore on referral by the city's health department. They were having a nutritious breakfast in their classroom when I arrived. Meals are planned to make up for the deficiencies in calcium, iron, and protein and the excess of fat that characterize the diets of most lead-poisoned children.

The fourteen children in the room were supervised by a teacher, a trained teacher's aide, and a parent volunteer. Activities were thoughtfully organized to provide ample opportunity for verbal exchange, and some of the structure and stimulation that is often missing in these children's lives.

In an adjoining room, the mothers were about to start one of their regular sessions with a nutrition aide from the Expanded Food and Nutrition Education Program of the University of Maryland

Cooperative Extension Service. They would be planning and preparing lunch for the children and learning how to improve their children's diets at home. The women were an amazingly diverse group. One young woman looked more like a member of a motorcycle gang than a mother's group and several were openly skeptical about what was going on. But most seemed eager to participate.

While much of the parent education focuses on nutrition, the educator responsible for the group also tries to engage the mothers in discussions of child development, the hows and whys of emotional nurturing, and how to organize their homes to reduce lead contamination. The mothers also work as aides in the classroom, where they see examples of sensitive adult-child interactions and ways of providing both structure and stimulation to their children.

In its second year of working with these mothers and their children, the program already displayed encouraging preliminary results. The children's behavior has improved noticeably—they went from nonverbal, overly active, disorganized, and uncooperative to cooperative group participants with less hyperactivity and improved verbal and fine motor skills. Of the six children initially in the retarded or borderline range, three improved to the normal IQ range. The children put fewer harmful objects in their mouths, and their blood lead levels decreased.

Participation by both children and mothers has been regular and enthusiastic. Dr. Howard believes that the mothers have not only acquired increased skills in caring for their children but, as a result of participation in the program, are less socially isolated and have gained some of the social supports that were previously lacking. She expects to see these changes reflected in more responsive and responsible mothering, better ongoing nutrition, continually decreasing blood lead levels among the children, and ultimately a reversal of the declines in developmental function which usually characterize children who have suffered from lead poisoning.

Impressed though I was with the model primary care and community center activities I had seen, I asked Dr. Charney at the end of the day to what extent he thought they reflected an unusual, and perhaps unreplicable, combination of talented leadership and propitious circumstances. The pioneering pediatrician nodded, recognizing my concern. Then he told me about a summer camp he had gone to as a boy.

"They had all kinds of kids there, many different races and religions. The counselors were selected to be particularly caring and sensitive. Some people complained that it was all too artificial. It was crazy, they said, to expose kids to this—there isn't any place in the real world like this, where people of such different backgrounds work together and get along so well. They'll never see this again in their lives. And the head of the camp said, 'But this is the way it should be. You've got to show people how it should be.' And I never forgot that. Now, what we've done here is hardly ideal, but—especially when you're teaching—there isn't anything wrong with trying to create an ideal."

FROM THE NEONATAL UNIT INTO THE WATTS COMMUNITY

Walking briskly, talking intensely to two residents as he comes out the door of the Martin Luther King General Hospital in the Watts area of Los Angeles, the trim-bearded Dr. Ronald Bloom seems to fit his title—Director of the Division of Neonatology.

But at the moment his animated discussion is not about saving newborn infants in crisis. He is talking about tracking the progress of infants after discharge from the hospital and about helping their families to cope with the problems of frail and damaged babies. And he is striding in a direction unusual for a neonatologist—to the far end of the hospital grounds, where stands the high school he helped to create in 1982 in partnership with the Los Angeles Unified School District. The school is part of an experiment in enriching the lives of young people who will be tomorrow's parents, in the hope thereby of reducing the number of damaged infants.

The Magnet High School for the Health Professions has 180 students, mostly black, mostly from disadvantaged families, who come from all over the Los Angeles area. Eighty percent are poor enough to qualify for free lunches. Most had abysmally low aptitude scores when they entered the school in tenth grade. Now they are learning to become health professionals and experiencing the excitement of new goals and achievements.

"We don't think that, in the few years they're here, they will overcome all their deficiencies," says Dr. Bloom. "But a lot of them are going to be ready to make something of their lives."

The students, in addition to classroom instruction, work as apprentices in the King/Drew Medical Center laboratories and in patient care, and some of them talk with a professional air.

Demetrius, a tall, serious, and vocal senior ("He came to the school straight out of the streets," says Dr. Bloom), has been assigned to show us around the school and the hospital, where he is a familiar figure, greeting doctors and nurses along the way in collegial fashion.

Obviously turned on by his surroundings, he talks knowledgeably about the metabolism of bacteria, about making a homogenate out of a rat's brain and feeding the data into the computer for analysis. Other eleventh and twelfth graders, equally excited, tell us how they remove clots from blood before it goes into the analyzing machine, how they incubate brain cells, and how they assist with oral surgery.

At graduation, Demetrius and his fellow students will be prepared, psychologically as well as academically, for further training on their way to becoming anything from nurse's aides to physicians.

Dr. Bloom is not a lone visionary. His work is central to the King/Drew Medical Center belief that reducing the number of low-birthweight babies crowding the intensive care unit requires improving the life prospects of future parents in the Watts community. The idea of health professionals joining with community organizations, foundations and the school district to create the magnet high school may at first glance seem a long leap out of medical boundaries. But such extramural activities spring directly from the philosophy of the King/Drew Department of Pediatrics—that the health of Watts children can only be addressed in the context of their surroundings. Dr. Bloom's idea for a high school under the aegis of the hospital followed logically from earlier decisions of the department to establish a model child care center, a family day care network, a Head Start program, a training program for child care workers, and a consortium of community early childhood centers.

The King/Drew Medical Center itself was an offspring of the Watts riots of 1965, one of the first of the urban outbreaks that swept the nation in the mid-sixties. The burning and looting in Watts left thirty-four persons dead and more than a thousand injured and destroyed $40 million in property. A presidential investigating commission, headed by John McCone, identified the lack of decent, accessible health services in Watts as a major aggravating factor. It recommended the establishment of a comprehensive, well-equipped hospital in the middle of Watts.

It was not long after the opening of the King/Drew Medical

Center in 1972 that its new pediatrics department realized it would be necessary to go beyond traditional teaching hospital approaches to medicine and public health if any real improvement were to be made in the dismal health conditions of this community.

The young pediatric staff perceived both a need and an opportunity for a new strategy. Though most of them had been taught in the course of their training that they could have no higher calling than as healers of biomedical problems, many came to the new teaching hospital feeling uneasy with a form of practice that subordinated the social preconditions of illness as secondary matters, to be relegated to social workers. In Watts it didn't seem to make sense to view health and illness simply as biological entities residing in individuals in isolation from their surroundings.

One of the original members of the department of pediatrics and now its chairman, crew-cut Robert Schlegel, recalls, "We had to be willing to apply biological interventions where they are most relevant and social interventions where they are most relevant, knowing that the social antecedents of disease and death among children dwarf in magnitude the biological causes, particularly among youngsters growing up in the inner city."

The new strategy proved itself by its results.

Between 1977 and 1984, the neonatal mortality rate at the new hospital dropped from 17.5 to 6.5 per thousand births. In 1977, it had been 177 percent of the national rate; in seven years it dipped below the national average. In the entire area served by the hospital, despite the continuing abject poverty, infant mortality is now the same as the overall U.S. rate. Immunization levels have also improved significantly and at school entry are above 90 percent for polio, measles, and mumps.

At King/Drew, faculty, residents, and students seem equally at home discussing changes in body fluid composition that are due to midbrain lesion, the management of bronchial asthma, the assessment of cervical lymphadenopathy, and the high numbers of children left at home without supervision. They respond to even minor problems at night, knowing that for overstressed families, one way to prevent child abuse is being available at times of high anxiety. They provide support to foster families caring for PCP-addicted newborns while trying to reduce drug abuse among adolescents.

Dr. Alice Faye Singleton, the slim young black pediatrician who is director of ambulatory care, moves swiftly and easily between examining room and the Tillmon Day Care Center, a training and demonstration unit that has stimulated the formation of fifty new child care centers throughout the region.

In their daily lives, Dr. Bloom, Dr. Schlegel, Dr. Singleton, and Dr. Ernest Smith (director of community programming), as well as the newest medical student on rotation, blend the routine of their practice with their guiding philosophy. While teaching, they are always learning, never forgetting to take into account the tangled world from which their patients come and to which they will return.

One resident recalls prescribing a course of home-based physical therapy for a handicapped child. The community worker, who had visited the child at home, pointed out to him that this child's family consisted of ten people in a two-bedroom home, and that the parents couldn't possibly carry out his elaborate program. The community worker insisted that the resident come out to the house with her. "It wasn't until that visit," the resident explained, "that I began to understand who these people really were, where they lived, where they went to church, where their children went to school, what they really thought, what they were saying about the hospital and the physicians and the nurses. It was only then that I fully realized that we had to take a different approach to meeting this child's needs."

Dr. Schlegel explains that once pediatricians get used to thinking about children in a larger context, once they can visualize the children's lives beyond the examining table and the stethoscope, they are propelled into acquiring and training others in new skills, into setting up and running community programs, and into collaborating with professionals and agencies from outside the health care arena.

Thus the Department of Pediatrics went into partnership with the local high school's program for adolescent mothers and their babies. The school had set up a day care program to encourage youngsters with children to finish high school. The young mothers were enrolled in a special class on child development and were being helped to acquire parenting skills, but the teachers were concerned that the girls needed much more help than the school could provide. The King/Drew child development staff organized a weekly group meeting to talk with these girls about issues other than parenting, a group in which they could be adolescents first and mothers second. They found that this made a significant difference.

Pediatrician Kerry English tells the story of Alice and her son, Bo.

"Alice came into our group very quiet, found it very difficult to communicate. She had grown up as one of three children with her biological mother and stepfather. Slowly, over the weeks, we found out that she had been sexually abused by the stepfather. Her relationship with her mother was very poor. Mother and daughter were unable to talk, in large part because the mother had been aware of the abuse, had not protected her, and had blamed the daughter for seducing her stepfather. It seemed as though two things converged to enable Alice to face up to her disastrous home situation and to talk about it for the first time. She had become more and more comfortable in the group. Simultaneously she had become aware that her stepfather was starting to abuse her younger sister. She made a decision, with the support of the leaders of the group as well as the other girls, to move out of the home with her baby and to move her little sister out as well.

"She set up housekeeping with her boyfriend, and maintained that relationship until she graduated from high school—as an honor student. When we originally encountered this girl, both she and her son were heading for serious problems. But in our group she found an environment where it was safe to be vulnerable, and her considerable strengths started coming out. Now, four years later, she is living alone with her son, who is thriving, and she is about to graduate from UCLA."

Over a six-year period more than four hundred girls have gone through this program, under the joint auspices of the schools and the Department of Pediatrics. Dr. Kathy Sanders-Phillips of the Division of Child Development told us proudly that "although we know that the pattern among adolescent mothers is a high rate of child abuse, repeat pregnancies, and dropping out of school, we have had only a single case of child abuse, and, among these four hundred girls, only five have become pregnant again during the six years we have followed them!"

At the end of our visit to King/Drew, we returned to the neonatal intensive care unit with Dr. Bloom. As he described what was going on with each of these tiny handfuls of life in his charge, he seemed to be speaking as much to himself as to his visitor.

"The amount of money and effort that goes into keeping these kids alive . . . and then they grow up in a community like this, their options taken away from them, their lives functionally finished before they begin. Society isn't willing to approach that question . . ."

Suddenly his voice rose.

"As a neonatologist who is present at the beginning—at the beginning of any process there's always hope—but over a period of years I began to ask what then happened to these kids? I was simply keeping a succession of biological organisms alive . . . unless we started to attack the other issues. I have no intention of discontinuing my efforts to save these lives. But if you say to me that this child, just because it exists, should be kept alive, then you incur the obligation of making sure that it be given the opportunity to reach its potential.

"You come to a place like this. You see the amount of money and effort that go into it. I would not think of discontinuing care, though I know that many kids will come out damaged. A lot of other kids will come out well, but then their options will be taken away after they have left here, and their lives will be finished.

"Is the job done when I have saved them here? Is the child simply a biological organism? We think otherwise. We think of health as not just providing health services. We think that over the years we have to care about what happens to these kids. That's why we are in the business of day care and prenatal care and home visits and magnet high schools."

Dr. Bloom's convictions, like those of his colleagues in Watts, in Baltimore, and in Mississippi, are almost impossible to act on in the context of present health policies. Programs like those described here cannot be made to work on a large scale without fundamental changes in health policy. The next chapter explores these changes.

• 6 •

Reforming National
Health Policies

Prenatal and child health programs which succeed in improving the odds for children at risk should be the rule, but they are the exception. They survive in an inhospitable health system as a result of many fortuitous circumstances, including inspired leadership, adroit budgeting, and luck. But a little band of professionals willing and able to buck a health system based on perverse incentives is hardly a solid base from which to meet the health needs of millions of American mothers and children.

Current national health policies threaten the survival and deter the expansion of demonstrably effective health care programs for high-risk families. Prevailing policies are in direct conflict with the very elements that make these programs successful.

If today's model prenatal and child health programs are to become tomorrow's norm—especially for high-risk populations—and if ordinary local communities are to be able to build on past successes and establish more effective health programs, reforms are required not just at the bottom, but also at the top.

Health programs that improve the odds of favorable outcomes for children at risk work because they deal with the social as well as biological components of health and disease and because they offer a range of services broad enough to match the needs of the population they serve. Rural or urban, based in a hospital, community health center, or health department, successful programs take into account the special needs of high-risk families for ready and continuing access to services, for caring and respectful relationships. All of them somehow manage to put the needs of patients and communities above the pressures exerted by market forces, and by accountants oriented to short-run costs.

Fundamental changes in health policy are required if exemplary prenatal and child health programs are to serve the patients who most need them.

THE POWERFUL IMPACT OF NATIONAL POLICIES

Only a generation ago, universal access to the benefits of modern medicine seemed a feasible goal. The financial implications were modest. In 1965 personal health expenditures averaged about $200 per person. In the payment system that had evolved, it seemed proper for private insurers and public third-party payers to tell doctors and hospitals, in effect, "Do what you think best for the patient and take what you consider to be 'reasonable' and 'customary' compensation." That arrangement seemed to work, at least for insured persons needing treatment for acute illnesses. It was assumed to be only a matter of time until insurance would become universal.

Coverage was extended to the aged with the passage of Medicare in 1965. That legislation was the end product of a long, hard-fought battle. None of us involved in designing and campaigning for Medicare (I participated as a representative of the AFL-CIO) anticipated the magnitude of the scientific revolution that would transform medical care in our lifetime and increase its costs tenfold. John W. Gardner, Secretary of Health, Education and Welfare at the time, said twenty years later that he had anticipated some inflation in medical costs, "but it happened faster and worse than any of us had expected."

None of us who worked so fervently in the early 1960s to extend the benefits of health insurance foresaw the meteoric rise in health costs and expenditures, ignited by the explosion in expensive new technology and fueled by new funds which came with few budgetary or regulatory constraints. Least of all did we foresee how the expansion of public and private insurance would accelerate the pace and even determine the direction of technological change. By making expensive new medical procedures more affordable to patients as well as more profitable to providers, insurance had the effect of stimulating both the development and utilization of high-tech medicine.

As the price for passage of the Medicare legislation, doctors, hospitals, and the insurance industry exacted a promise that government-sponsored insurance for the aged would not be used as an entering wedge for governmental reform of reimbursement arrangements. Even those Medicare advocates who were most avid for health systems reform reluctantly agreed that the enactment of Medicare was worth the price. The concession was enshrined on the first page of the law: "Nothing in this title shall be construed to authorize any federal officer . . . to exercise any supervision or control over the compensation of any institution . . . or person providing health services." This provision, like many that are added to assure passage of a piece of legislation, ultimately caused great difficulties in the administration of the program. Most of the supporters of the legislation were fully aware that we were sacrificing the possibility of health system reform to achieve more immediate —and obviously vital—goals: protecting the aged against destitution from high medical costs and lowering financial barriers to the health care they needed.

The surprise eleventh-hour addition of Medicaid for the poor to the legislation originally designed only to cover hospital and doctor insurance for the aged received little attention at the time. It emerged in the spring of 1965 from intense negotiations between the late Wilbur J. Cohen, then under secretary of HEW, and Congressman Wilbur Mills, chairman of the House Ways and Means Committee. I remember the midafternoon call, asking a small group of us, hardcore advocates of Medicare legislation over the years, to come immediately to the under secretary's office. The under secretary dashed in, having just left Congressman Mills, and described the package they had come up with, which at last would command the majority of Ways and Means Committee votes. The compromise would combine hospital insurance and doctors' insurance for the aged (the two elements which together would become Medicare) with a new program of means-tested health insurance for the poor, soon to become known as Medicaid. It was now, the ebullient Cohen announced triumphantly, "a three-layered cake."

As Cohen had predicted, this artfully crafted combination swiftly won Congressional approval. The legislation became law on July 30, 1965, in Independence, Missouri, signed by President Johnson with a beaming eighty-one-year-old Harry Truman looking on. It left a momentous legacy of improved health and alleviation of suffering for millions of the aged and poor, as well as significant protection against economic devastation from medical bills for the aged and their families.

It also brought an unprecedented escalation in health care spending, which rose from 6 percent of the gross national product in 1965 to 11 percent in 1985—from $42 billion to an incredible $425 billion. At the same time, by making Medicaid benefits contingent on eligibility for income assistance, the legislation cemented the link—at least for more than two decades, and perhaps for much longer—between health insurance for the poor and welfare. Sociologist and medical historian Paul Starr has branded that decision—to attach health insurance for the aged to Social Security while attaching health insurance for the poor to the welfare system—as "the original sin of American health policy."

In the twenty years following the passage of Medicare and Medicaid, dismay over cost inflation has obscured both their contributions to health and the obstacles they placed in the way of health systems reform.

WHEN COST CONTAINMENT DOMINATES

In the early 1980s, cost escalation combined with sharpened concern about budget deficits to create new public pressures to contain costs. Savings were to be achieved by cutting back direct public financing and by changing economic incentives, with heavy reliance on market mechanisms and price competition. In an antiregulatory atmosphere, the chosen way to curb inflation was to reduce demand. Costs would be contained through pressures on patients, as well as on doctors and hospitals, to reduce utilization of health services.

Advocates of bringing more of a market orientation into the health system hold that free market forces should determine not only the decisions of individual patients and health professionals but also the distribution of health facilities. The location of new hospitals and the closing of uncompetitive facilities should be determined by the play of market pressures rather than by government regulation, with all its clumsy procedures and politics. But the free market's invisible hand, notes health economist Rashi Fein, operates without a mailing address, telephone number, or appeals board. Thus it forces crisp, if draconian, decisions. Survival of the "fittest" hospitals may have some appeal over decisions based on which administrator went to college with the local supervisor or congressman, or which group is most successful in mobilizing public outrage against a hospital closing. But market mechanisms, seeking to maximize profits, inevitably lead some providers to skim off the healthier populations, simpler ailments, and better-reimbursed procedures, obliging others to follow suit to survive the competitive battle. Institutions committed to teaching and research or to treating large numbers of people who are unable to pay or have multiple and complex needs—such institutions simply cannot compete successfully. When health services are reduced to a balance sheet, nice guys finish last—and often out of business.

In the five years ending in 1985, at least seventy public hospitals closed. Large urban hospitals serving high proportions of uninsured and Medicaid patients operate under severe financial strain. Health providers of all kinds gravitate toward patients who are easy to reach, easy to treat, and easy to collect from.

While hospitals and clinics serving the poor curtail their services and attempt to make do with disintegrating facilities, services for the rich expand. Diet clinics thrive, and psychiatric hospitals invite affluent parents to send their troubled adolescents. One new pediatric clinic specializing in behaviorally related health problems restricts its clientele to healthy children of parents with health insurance or private means. Its literature announces it does not intend to serve children with "serious pathology, including . . . those with family histories of alcohol, depression or severe marital discord."

Thus the new "health market" screens out the children who need health services most.

Simultaneously and devastatingly, changes in reimbursement methods and rate controls have virtually ended "cost shifting," which used to allow hospitals to use the income from insured patients to subsidize treatment of at least the seriously ill among the uninsured poor.

American voters may not have embraced universal health insurance, but they are also not prepared to see people die because they cannot afford treatment. Americans have long accepted, tacitly, a system slack enough to buffer the impact of our failure to assure universal access to health services. Cost shifting made it possible to care at least for those of the poor who showed up at the hospital door. Cost shifting, in fact, served—in the words of health economist Uwe Reinhardt—as "the fig-leaf that covered up what would have otherwise revealed itself to the world as a national disgrace." That fig leaf has now been removed.

Women in labor who come to the hospital in Beaumont, Texas, without money or insurance are given bus tickets to Galveston— seventy miles away, across the bay. The baby of one such woman was born and died in the Beaumont Hospital parking lot.

A pediatrician in Rock Hill, South Carolina, called three hospitals before he could find one—a hundred miles away—that would admit a comatose three-year-old whose family had no health insurance.

Dr. Arnold Relman, editor of *The New England Journal of Medicine,* wrote in February 1985, "In practice, many very sick patients are denied adequate care. . . . Medical judgment, compassion and common sense are nowadays too often overruled by the economic concerns of hospital managers."

Although the denial of care to the critically ill is what makes the occasional headlines and evokes sporadic public outrage, subtler indicators of trouble suggest alarming long-term trends. Recent reports of decreased and delayed use of prenatal care, especially among black and Hispanic mothers, the higher incidence of measles, the increasing numbers of tracheotomies for croup and of ruptured appendixes, and the increased use of emergency rooms for asthma and upper respiratory infections all suggest postponement of needed care until the problem reaches emergency proportions. Black babies continue to die at twice the rate of white babies. Between 1983 and 1984, infant mortality increased in six of America's twenty-two largest cities; black infant mortality went up in four additional cities. The U.S. infant mortality ranking among twenty industrialized nations declined from sixth in 1950–55 to last place in 1980.

In this era of fierce competition, hospital managers are forced to behave like any entrepreneur trying to survive. The director of the division of ambulatory care of the American Hospital Association suggested in 1982 that member hospitals consider "selective demarketing" to keep away "relatively unprofitable" customers and those "undesirable in terms of their impact on other valued segments of the market." Among the recommended "demarketing" tactics:

- Providing an unlisted phone number for the emergency department and deliberately allowing lengthy waiting times to develop for emergency care.
- Segregating the waiting areas for paying and nonpaying patients and providing few seats, poor lighting, few signs, and no food or drinks in the nonpaying patient area.
- Eliminating alcohol, and drug abuse programs and primary care programs that serve the poor.

Prestigious journals feature learned papers debating the merits of a two-class system versus three or more "tiers" of health care. William G. Anlyan, M.D., Duke University's vice president for health affairs, argued in 1982, "We've accepted a two-tiered airline system, with first class and coach seats, so it should not be so foreign to us."

Unlike airlines, which deliver passengers of all classes to their destinations, hospitals do not limit class distinctions to amenities. The question is not whether the poor should eat gelatinous meals with plastic cutlery while the rich get china, silver, and midafternoon wine and cheese. "No frills" in hospitals frequently means the elimination of services especially important to high-risk children and families. Teenage mothers, drug-abusing adolescents, child-abusing parents, families that can't cope are the ones left by the wayside as funds which were once bootlegged under the looser reimbursement schemes of the past disappear.

Even before the recent attempts to restrain it, the U.S. health system had produced an array of services not well matched to the needs of many population groups, including the poor, the hard-to-reach, the chronically ill, and multiproblem families. Current pressures compound the problems of access as well as the magnitude of the mismatch.

The health policy of the 1980s is clear. The purpose is cost containment. Improving health and reaching the unreached are incidental at best. Population groups that were already inadequately served by the health system are, of course, the hardest hit. Richard Berman, executive vice president of the New York University Medical Center, described it in a report for the Robert Wood Johnson Foundation: "Resources are allocated on the ability to pay, while maximizing profits—otherwise known as competition. No one is really talking about equity. . . . mainstreaming is out; now, you get what you pay for."

That orientation bodes ill for most Americans. For high-risk children and pregnant women, it spells disaster.

THE BIZARRE WORLD OF HEALTH CARE FINANCING

How health services are paid for determines, more than anything else, how the health system operates—what services are available, who provides them, and who receives them.

One way of understanding the peculiar impact of financing arrangements on our health system is to visualize what schools would look like if they were financed the same way—that is, through fees for individual services, paid for directly by families and through insurance.

Most families would pay for most of their children's basic schooling out of their pockets. Children whose families lacked private means or insurance, but were poor enough to meet their state's criteria as to income, assets, and family composition, would qualify for school payment assistance from public funds. Only about half of all poor children would qualify for such help, and only certain kinds of schooling would be paid for. The specific services covered would be defined differently by each state. Some children would never go to school, because their parents couldn't pay and didn't qualify for public assistance. Some children would go to school sporadically, because they would be eligible for public support for part of the year, or for one year and not the next.

Teachers and schools would naturally be drawn to areas with high concentrations of families able to pay. Inner city areas and many rural counties would simply have no schools or teachers. Since market forces would also shape the curriculum, the ability to teach young children who enter school ill prepared, as many low-income children do, would receive scant attention in teacher training institutions or in practice. English composition would cease to be taught entirely, as teachers found that correcting written work was unprofitably time-consuming.

With college-bound children dominating the private market and public reimbursement set at lower rates, courses other than college preparatory would be uneconomic. Foundations might fund some demonstration programs in vocational education, but there would be few teachers with skills to teach them. Soon even private support would dry up when it became evident that schools could not make these courses self-supporting in the long run.

What may seem like an absurdity when applied to education is a reality in our increasingly market-oriented health system. The real-life effects of bizarre financial incentives are apparent everywhere. For example:

· Mrs. Bruce, the outreach worker at the Sinai program who probably saved Jeffrey from being cast adrift in foster care, was let go in the summer of 1985 because a reduced grant to the pediatric group eliminated money for outreach, and because outreach services are not reimbursable through third-party payments.

· The Denver Department of Health and Hospitals, sponsor of one of the first OEO Neighborhood Health Centers, later expanded into a highly successful citywide program, reported in 1982 that it was obliged to reduce ambulatory services because they are "less well reimbursed." It also eliminated outreach services because they were not reimbursed at all and because outreach services "most often increase utilization of treatment services."

· Poor children with serious behavioral problems typically cannot get the mental health services that are most likely to be effective, because Medicaid regulations confine reimbursement to a narrow range of traditional psychiatric interventions. This has a "chilling effect" on the development of broader and more effective services, ultimately necessitating "more restrictive and more costly interventions."

From the perspective of at-risk families, the most obvious problem with prevailing health financing arrangements is simply that not enough money goes to support their most basic health service needs. This results from three fundamental flaws that pervade health care financing today. (1) Millions of people are not covered by insurance, public or private, and are unable to pay for the health services they need. (2) Many crucial health services are not covered by insurance. (3) Financing arrangements are loaded with incentives and deterrents that are in fundamental conflict with the needs of vulnerable families.

Gaps in who is covered. The cost of health care has soared so high that the average American family can no longer defray it from its own income. Employer-paid insurance is linked to current employment, leaving uncovered the jobless, many in the service sector, and the marginally employed and their dependents. Medicaid coverage reaches only half of the poor and is subject to the varying income and welfare eligibility rules of fifty different states. Many pregnant women and families with children simply fall through the cracks and cannot obtain the health care they need. And many programs and institutions serving poor families, increasingly burdened by uncompensated care (the "free" or "charity" care provided to poor and uninsured persons by physicians and hospitals), are being forced to close their doors.

High rates of unemployment and poverty have operated to price many families out of the health insurance market altogether. The number of Americans unprotected by health insurance, after a long, steady decline, rose by 9.9 million between 1979 and 1982. In 1984, 35 million Americans had no health insurance—a 22.3 percent increase since 1979 in the number of uninsured. Not only did unemployment and poverty increase between 1979 and 1983, but even as workers were reemployed, many returned to lower-paying jobs with less adequate fringe benefits for themselves and their dependents; many employers curtailed their fringe benefits even for current employees.

The problems created by diminished protection by private health insurance have been compounded by cutbacks in eligibility for AFDC and Medicaid, which deprived more than a million persons of Medicaid benefits. Between 1976 and 1984 the percentage of the poor and near-poor covered by Medicaid dropped from 65 to 46 percent. Although the number of poor children in the country increased, fewer children were covered by Medicaid, and the proportion of Medicaid funds spent on children and their families went down from 38 percent in 1973 to 28 percent in 1983. Fewer than half of poor children qualified for Medicaid in 1985. State eligibility policies and spending levels vary widely, and many states continue to impose severe restrictions on who is covered. In most states, a single pregnant woman living alone must have an income far below the federal poverty level to qualify. (In Alabama, for example, a single woman earning more than $59 a month, or a woman with a baby earning more than $88 a month, is not eligible for Medicaid.) However, if the 1986 amendments to Medicaid are vigorously implemented in 1987 and 1988, coverage of poor children under the age of five and pregnant women will be significantly expanded.

Families living on the borderline of poverty find it almost impossible to maintain continuity of care. A family which belonged to a Health Maintenance Organization (HMO) through the father's employment would lose that coverage if the father lost his job. They might turn to a local health department or community health center for health care for the children. Several months later, their savings exhausted, the family might qualify for Medicaid if they lived in one of the twenty-six states that extend Medicaid to unemployed families. If the family lives in a state in which the Medicaid agency attempts to enroll eligible families with office-based physicians, this might mean a change to yet a third provider.

In some states a woman may be eligible for Medicaid at the start of her pregnancy but not at the end. Obstetricians complain of having to refuse further care just before delivery or providing it at their own expense. In other states women cannot become eligible until close to the end of their pregnancy.

Hospitals and doctors typically require that pregnant patients have private insurance or Medicaid coverage before accepting them as patients, because of the high cost of many hospital deliveries. Some private hospitals in south Texas demand preadmission deposits as high as $3,500 before admitting high-risk women in labor. Financial barriers and lengthy eligibility determinations often cause risky delays in obtaining care. In Los Angeles the waiting time for a first prenatal care appointment at the health department in early 1987 was nineteen weeks.

Gaps and distortions in what is covered. The prevailing reimbursement system puts a premium on diagnostic and therapeutic procedures, discourages time-consuming counseling and teaching in ambulatory settings, and underrates basic clinical knowledge and skills. New methods of paying hospitals (prospectively, by diagnosis-related groups) reinforce the long-standing bias in favor of technological, invasive, hospital-oriented therapeutic approaches.

Financial incentives operate to narrow the range of services available from the health system and circumscribe the physician's role. Their impact is exacerbated by public expectations of instant diagnoses and miracle cures, by the wider, technology-worshipping culture within which medical care is rendered and physicians selected and trained, and by the effect of reimbursement incentives on the content of medical training. While these forces have combined to bring about extraordinary technological and pharmacological advances, they have also resulted in the neglect of many of the health needs of high-risk populations. Reimbursement policies create and reflect an ethos where saving a baby in the neonatal intensive care unit is valued over a nursing visit to the home of the fragile infant a week after hospital discharge; where fiber-optic gastroscopies take precedence over time-consuming talking and listening as a way of understanding a child's stomachache.

Thanks to its system of health care financing, the United States is a world leader in discovering the body's secrets through miniaturized probes and computerized scans, but lags far behind in dealing with problems where nonbiological factors are important in etiology, prevention, diagnosis, and management. When these problems arise in families that are poor or simultaneously trying to deal with a lot of other troubles, the health system is rarely a source of effective help.

Pressures intended to contain costs not only deny care to many who can't afford to pay and are uninsured, they have also resulted in the mushrooming of intensive care, of high technology and specialists' care, and of surgical procedures and diagnostic tests. "Anytime a doctor sticks something into someone he receives a bonus," says *Newsweek*. It might have added that every time a doctor stops to think, synthesize, listen, or explain, he loses money. Or, in the more elegant phrasing of *The New England Journal of Medicine*'s Dr. Relman, speaking for the Institute of Medicine, "The method by which most physicians are paid now seems, on a number of grounds, to be rather a poor reflection of society's objectives for health care . . . It provides large rewards for the provision of high-technology procedures and little or none for preventive and cognitive activities."

The economic incentives that drive physician practice also drive physician training. Because it is easier to get reimbursed for technological interventions, it is easier to spend time teaching about them, rather than about getting an uneducated, non-English-speaking family to adhere to a prescribed regimen.

Reimbursement policies reflect and reinforce an approach to medicine where a problem is seen as medical, and therefore within the physician's proper purview, only if it can be approached by the theory and techniques of biomedical science.

This narrow view of medicine seriously limits physician effectiveness. It goes far toward explaining why children and families at risk often derive little benefit from their encounters with the health system, even when they have them.

Physicians often neglect the health problems that go beyond those contained within the child before them on the examining table. This is in part because of time pressures, in part because they see problems not exclusively biological as not amenable to "scientific" intervention, and sometimes because they are inadequately trained to deal effectively with nonbiological issues. But perhaps the most frequent reason it is so difficult for physicians to respond adequately to the needs of disadvantaged families is that the environment in which they practice makes an adequate response almost impossible.

A pediatric group in Jackson, Mississippi, told the Select Panel for the Promotion of Child Health of having given up on trying to affect how the low-income mothers in their practice fed and cared for their babies. They explained, in tones of resigned despair and frustration, that "the reservoir of Medicaid patients is just unlimited, and they just won't listen. Education is the key, but we just don't know how to reach them."

Four physicians high up in the hierarchy of pediatric politics once explained to me why three of the four of them excluded Medicaid patients from their practice. They said that for them the problem was neither too little reimbursement nor too much red tape. The problem was simply that "you couldn't practice good medicine with those families. They don't do what you tell them, they don't come in when they should, and they can't communicate properly so you can find out what's going on."

Pediatrician Jack L. Mayer wrote movingly in the New York *Times Magazine* of his pain at not being able to realize his vision of bringing the quality medical care he learned at Stanford Medical School to the families in one of the poorest towns in Vermont. "Despair and human stubbornness have undermined the compassion and dedication of which I was once so proud." Mystified by his failure to make inroads against the malnutrition, child abuse, chronic illness, and teenage pregnancy that became progressively worse with "budget cuts, Medicaid cuts, and worker cuts at the hockey stick factory," he was leaving for a gentler clime. Reading his tragic story of self-doubt made me wonder why they hadn't taught him at Stanford that he couldn't do it alone. Why they hadn't taught him that good medicine in that town couldn't be practiced without outreach workers and nurses and social workers who could take the time to visit homes and chat with the grandmothers who were undermining his advice about when to start the baby on solid foods. Why he didn't know that a health system that doesn't come up with the money to support those additional services cannot—no matter how dedicated and well-trained the pediatrician at the hub—meet the health needs of the children in that poor town any more than it can meet the health needs of the children in Harlem or Watts.

Corroborating the experiences of these individual physicians, careful studies of the health care of low-income and minority children suggest that the elimination of financial barriers is an important beginning, but that private practitioners operating in a fee-for-service setting are severely handicapped in trying to meet the needs of disadvantaged families.

FEDERAL PROGRAMS THAT HAVE HELPED

Four federal programs stand out as successes in improving maternal and child health over the last two decades, in part by reducing financial barriers to needed care, in part by developing new ways to bring appropriate health services to high-risk mothers and children: Medicaid, Medicaid's Early and Periodic Screening, Diagnosis and Treatment (EPSDT) program, the Special Supplemental Food Program for Women, Infants, and Children (WIC), and federal support of neighborhood health centers and maternal and child health clinics.

Medicaid is the single biggest source of public money spent on maternal and child health. Even though only about 30 percent of total Medicaid expenditures are made on behalf of children and pregnant women, the size and scope of the program give it a profound influence over the circumstances in which poor children and pregnant women receive health care. Medicaid uses a combination of federal and state funds and is administered by the states to pay doctor and hospital bills for eligible poor people.

Most analyses of Medicaid's impact agree that although only about half of all poor children are covered and state programs vary widely, the program can be credited with a substantial increase in access to health services among the poor. Before Medicaid was inaugurated in 1966, poor families went without needed care or depended on charity. As public health official Dr. Alonzo Yerby put it to the White House Conference on Health in 1965, the poor were "forced to barter their dignity for their health." Poor people visited doctors much less frequently than the average American. By 1978 Medicaid recipients were using physicians' services with about the same frequency as other Americans, although access cannot be said to be equal in view of the greater need for health services among the poor.

The steady drop in infant mortality rates between 1965 and 1980 is the most notable example of Medicaid's contribution to improved child health. Other favorable effects have also been well documented. In Rochester, for example, Medicaid coverage was associated with higher immunization rates. Children covered by Medicaid are more likely to receive preventive health care than uninsured low-income children. David Rogers, M.D., then president of the Robert Wood Johnson Foundation, and several colleagues concluded in 1982 that although a direct causal link had not been established, "Medicaid has been far more valuable than is commonly realized." They point out that Medicaid and other public programs started in the mid-1960s coincide with a dramatic drop in infant death rates among blacks, and decreases in death rates from diseases in which medical care can clearly be lifesaving—deaths during childbirth were down by 72 percent, from influenza and pneumonia down by 53 percent, from tuberculosis down by 52 percent, and from diabetes down by 31 percent.

Between 1981 and 1984, many states cut children from Medicaid coverage, reduced services to those who remained eligible, and decreased the amounts they paid providers. In 1984 and 1986, the Children's Defense Fund, virtually single-handedly, was able to persuade the Congress that these reductions were counterproductive, even in stark economic terms. Congress enacted several amendments to Medicaid which extended coverage to more poor children under the age of five and to poor pregnant women. Efforts to extend Medicaid coverage to all children and pregnant women in poverty regardless of their AFDC eligibility, to expand covered services, and to speed up enrollment for pregnant women were also receiving favorable consideration. If fully implemented by the states, these changes would reduce the number of uninsured poor children and pregnant women by one third and would provide more solid financial support for the kind of organized programs effectively serving high-risk mothers and children described in Chapters 4 and 5.

Early and Periodic Screening, Diagnosis and Treatment (EPSDT) was added to Medicaid in 1967, only two years after the enactment of the original law. It sought to adapt Medicaid to the major unmet health needs of children by providing separate reimbursement for certain cost-effective preventive services.

Public concern had been aroused in 1966 by a Selective Service System study that found more than 15 percent of eighteen-year-olds examined for military service were rejected because of health-related conditions, including dental, eye, and ear problems and emotional and developmental disorders. A Department of Health, Education and Welfare task force on maternal and child health estimated that 62 percent of these conditions could have been prevented or corrected by comprehensive and continuous health care, and that 33 percent could have been prevented or corrected through periodic screening and treatment.

In a don't-rock-the-boat frame of mind, the department recommended the less expensive screening option for enactment and chose Medicaid as the funding vehicle. The latter choice carried with it the advantages as well as the disadvantages of latching on to prevailing arrangements for financing ambulatory care. Medicaid, then as now, spent about ten times as much on child health and prenatal care as does the Maternal and Child Health program, established in 1935 as Title V of the Social Security Act, which might have provided an alternative administrative home. Grafting EPSDT to Medicaid meant access to more ample funds, but also narrow and cumbersome eligibility requirements tied to welfare status and little leverage on how services could be provided.

Over the years, mainly as a result of the unremitting efforts of child advocates, which included vigorously pursued lawsuits, EPSDT developed into a source of substantially increased funding for preventive services for poor children. It has also provided child advocates with tools to cajole and coerce state agencies and some private practitioners into providing additional services to more poor children some of the time.

In the main, however, EPSDT did not fulfill the hopes of its founders. In my own view, not universally shared by others concerned with improving child health services, this is because its premises were fundamentally flawed. With eligibility for EPSDT services tied to fluctuating Medicaid eligibility, with administration housed in a setting emphasizing funding rather than the provision of services, and with the initial decision to support only selected services, EPSDT was hobbled from the start.

EPSDT was erected on the assumption that the nation could save money and that poor children could best be aided through government funding of specified, targeted services which had a particularly high payoff. Illnesses and handicaps would be found and treated before they did long-term damage and became harder and more costly to treat. But the attempt to bypass the need for continuing, comprehensive care has proved both uneconomical and ineffective. Health professionals cannot discover, in a single screening session, the myriad conditions that reveal themselves over time. They cannot effectively treat children whom they do not know and with whose family they have established no relationship. Many EPSDT providers cannot mobilize the necessary supportive services. And many families are reluctant to take on the hardship and hassle to bring their children to providers who will only screen for specified problems, provide preventive services of whose value they are not convinced, and are not set up to respond to the health needs the family considers most important.

Despite its weaknesses, the EPSDT program has been remarkably successful in making additional money available for preventive services for poor children. By doing so, it has succeeded in improving the health of many. Careful studies have shown that EPSDT has contributed to significant improvements in the health of low-income children by funding of immunizations, eye examinations, hearing tests, and dental care and by its identification and treatment of many previously undiagnosed conditions. Studies in Michigan and Pennsylvania documented that children who had received EPSDT screening services had fewer abnormalities requiring medical attention than similar children who had not.

The Special Supplemental Food Program for Women, Infants and Children (WIC) was enacted by Congress in 1972 in response to documentation linking nutritional inadequacy to mental and physical defects and poor health. It provides carefully designed packages of highly nutritious food and nutrition education to low-income, nutritionally at-risk women who are pregnant or breast-feeding, and infants and children up to the age of five. Recognizing the close relationship between good nutrition and good health services, the law requires local agencies distributing food under the WIC program also to offer health services to beneficiaries, directly or by referral.

The program got off to a sputtering start with President Nixon's impoundment of funds and the occasionally lackadaisical administration by the Department of Agriculture, but it grew steadily during the 1970s. At an annual cost of $1.56 billion, WIC in 1986 was serving about 3.3 million participants. More than twice that number meet the health and income requirements to participate but cannot be served with the funds appropriated, even though the program enjoys considerable Congressional support. More than a hundred U.S. counties have no WIC program at all; many counties turn away eligible mothers and children simply for lack of money.

Cumbersome eligibility determinations also hold down the number of beneficiaries. Visiting one migrant workers' health clinic outside San Antonio, I found the building jammed with mothers and children. Many of the women told of having come long distances. They were now waiting for the children to be assessed for WIC eligibility. If the child was found to be anemic, eligibility for WIC assistance would be established, but the family would have to return on another day—when a different group of professionals would treat the child's anemia or provide the more comprehensive screening to which the child might be entitled under EPSDT.

Despite such problems, every one of the successful prenatal care programs described earlier identified WIC as a critical ingredient in improving the health of the mothers and babies in their care. These local program reports corroborate earlier studies which found the WIC program to be effective in improving health and cost-effective as well, particularly because the food supplements were instrumental in reducing the incidence of low birthweight and therefore the need for expensive neonatal intensive care.

One major researcher in the field, however, continued to be skeptical. Dr. David Rush, pediatrician and epidemiologist, had published extensive critiques of several of the major studies of the effects of the WIC program, finding them methodologically flawed and calling for more and better research. It seemed not surprising, therefore, that the Department of Agriculture, having called early in the Reagan Administration for a 30 percent cut in WIC funds, engaged Dr. Rush to conduct a massive evaluation of WIC's program performance and health benefits. The $5 million contract called for four concurrent studies over a five-year period. This most comprehensive evaluation of WIC ever undertaken was completed in 1985, but then, to the amazement of Dr. Rush and his colleagues, the Department of Agriculture refused to release it. A year of pressure, threats, and entreaties finally pried loose the five volume report, but without the Executive Summary and the Chapter Summaries, which the department ordered deleted. The reason soon became apparent—the report found unequivocally that WIC had made impressive contributions to women's and children's health. The New York *Times* stated editorially that the Agriculture Department "is willing to work more diligently to keep findings—that so simple an undertaking [as WIC] can produce such spectacular results—from the public than it is to get food and medical attention to mothers who need it."

Among the study's findings:

- WIC participation reduces premature births among high-risk mothers by 15 to 25 percent.
- WIC participation helps bring more women into prenatal care earlier in their pregnancy and increases the likelihood that they will have the desirable number of prenatal visits.
- WIC participation raises the chances that children will have a regular source of medical care and be better immunized.
- WIC participation has the largest impact among minorities and the least well educated. Among children, the greatest benefits are reaped by those who are poor, small of stature, black, and in single-parent families.

The study also found promising, although not conclusive, evidence of improved cognitive development among infants of participating

WIC mothers and among preschoolers who became WIC participants as infants. Further, probably reflecting the program's nutrition education efforts, WIC families were found to purchase and consume more nutritious foods than comparable non-WIC families. There was also a significant relationship between the quality of the local WIC program, as judged by state WIC directors, and increased birthweight.

The Neighborhood Health Center program, launched in 1965 by the Office of Economic Opportunity, is notable not only because it improved the health services available to the poor but because it represented a serious federal effort at fundamental reform of the financing and delivery of health care. Like the Maternal and Infant Care Centers and the Children and Youth Centers begun in the early 1960s with support from the Department of Health, Education and Welfare, the OEO program not only paid for health services but supported efforts to organize services in new ways that proved to be more effective than those available on the open health care market.

I vividly remember the birth of the Neighborhood Health Center program. Early in 1965, about to join the staff of the Office of Economic Opportunity but still in my office at the AFL-CIO, I received a telephone call from Dr. William Kissick, assistant to the Surgeon General of the U.S. Public Health Service.

"Hey, Lee," he said, "there's a wild man in my office, and he's got some ideas we can't do much with over here, but I think you people in the War on Poverty would find him pretty interesting. I'm sending him right over."

The "wild man" materialized in my office in the person of H. Jack Geiger, M.D., internist, Harvard professor, science writer, man-about-medicine, and frequent critic of the status quo. Within two months he and a fellow physician at Tufts University, Dr. Count Gibson, produced the first proposal asking OEO support to establish a new kind of institution, which became known as a "neighborhood health center."

The Geiger-Gibson proposal was not unusual in its diagnosis of defects in the health system: too many financial and other barriers, too few doctors and other resources where the poor could reach them, and too many services important to high-risk families not available. Unorthodox was the way in which they proposed to address the problem.

"The need," wrote Dr. Geiger, "is not merely for the provision of more preventive and curative health services, but also for the development of new organizational patterns to make the distribution of such services uniquely effective for severely deprived populations."

As Bill Kissick had surmised, Jack Geiger's analysis struck a responsive chord in an agency looking for new ways to address old problems. In its first few months, OEO had received many requests from local communities to help pay for treatment for poor people whose health problems kept them from utilizing newly opened education, training, and employment opportunities. But leaders of OEO's Community Action Program, reluctant to use new funds simply to plug old loopholes, sought innovative ways to address fundamental problems of delivering health services to the poor. We were thus highly receptive to proposals like Dr. Geiger's to try out new approaches that might prove more effective and more economical than the traditional inaccessible, sporadic, and hurried care that was working so badly for the disadvantaged.

Within a year, OEO had made grants to hospitals, health departments, and community action organizations to establish eight demonstration neighborhood health centers. We specified no preferences between public or private sponsorship, stipulating only that these centers were to offer "the residents of neighborhoods with a high concentration of poverty virtually all ambulatory services, in a one-door facility, readily accessible in terms of time and place." Services were to be "personalized, of high quality, rendered by professional staff of the highest caliber, and closely coordinated with other community resources."

Trying to concentrate OEO funds on start-up costs and on services and functions not otherwise covered, we insisted that the centers make use of all existing sources of funds in combination with our grants. They would have to reach agreements with state Medicaid agencies, maternal and child health programs and other sources of categorical grant funds.

Our grantees expressed varying combinations of dismay and outrage at being obliged to engage in burdensome negotiations with agencies which already resented the presence of OEO grantees—the brash new kid on the block—whose activities they viewed dimly even before being asked to subsidize them. Project directors found it hard to believe we would really insist on their meeting this requirement. I remember the reaction of Dr. Roger Egeberg, dean of the University of Southern California Medical School, (later HEW assistant secretary of health). As the person responsible for planning the neighborhood health center in Watts, he announced to OEO Director Sargent Shriver that he would no longer deal with me because of my stubborn insistence that the center make use of other sources of funds. Shriver later told me that it had taken all his diplomatic skills to calm down Dr. Egeberg and convince him that he was dealing not with my personal eccentricity but a considered policy that went to the heart of our demonstration program concept.

Our hope was that as soon as Medicaid agencies and other third-party payers, maternal and child agencies, and other categorical grant programs became aware of how effectively their dollars were being used in the new centers, the integration of funds would become a smooth and simple process. Administrative and regulatory adjustments would come first; ultimately, state and federal legislation would be modified to channel health money into communities in more rational ways.

As the first centers got under way, initial reports were promising. Long-neglected illness and disabilities were being discovered and treated at much earlier stages. The use of hospitals and emergency rooms decreased as primary care became easier to obtain, with substantial savings in public expenditures.

In 1967 Congress amended the Economic Opportunity Act to earmark $50 million for the Neighborhood Health Center program; thirty-three new centers were rapidly established. Additional centers were funded in succeeding years by OEO and later by the Public Health Service, as responsibility for the centers was shifted in the early 1970s from OEO to HEW. Today there are nearly 800 centers —now known as community health centers—providing comprehensive primary health care to nearly six million poor and previously underserved Americans in fifty states.

A multitude of studies have shown that, in their impact on the poor families they were intended to serve, the neighborhood health centers succeeded beyond our fondest early hopes. They have reduced infant mortality, low birthweight, rheumatic fever, and untreated middle ear infections. They have brought about greater use of prenatal care and an increase in the number of immunized children. They have reduced health care costs because their populations require fewer hospital admissions and shorter hospital stays and make less inappropriate use of emergency rooms.

But the demonstration of successful new ways of organizing services for high-risk families did not rub off on the larger world of health financing, as we had hoped.

Despite strong evidence of their effectiveness, community health centers find money harder to come by than ever before. It is almost impossible today to obtain grant money for the nonmedical services needed by hard-to-reach families, such as health education, counseling, outreach, and support. Except for programs serving pregnant adolescents, grant funds from all sources have been slashed. The subsidies that had previously come from training funds, from the assignment of National Health Service Corps personnel, or through ample third-party reimbursement formulas have dried up. The number of individuals and families whose services are paid for through private insurance or Medicaid has been cut. The centers find it almost impossible to get support to provide services to people not certified as eligible for Medicaid or some other third-party payment program. And the range of services reimbursable by third parties, already too narrow to meet the needs of the families at highest risk, is being further curtailed.

Reviewing two decades of health policy aimed at the poor, sociologist Paul Starr observed in 1986, "The community health centers have enjoyed a decidedly positive record . . . better health at lower cost. And yet the health centers have never received the acclaim or policy support given to health maintenance organizations (HMOs), the other great success in health care innovation." In part this results from the fact that community health centers serve primarily poor populations, while HMOs serve the middle class. Not only do the HMOs have a more popular constituency, but successful HMOs become self-supporting, while successful community health centers require continuing public support—a considerable flaw in a market-oriented climate.

An additional explanation, suggested by Professor Starr, lies in ideology. "If health centers exemplify the ideological distinctiveness of the War on Poverty, the failure to capitalize on their achievements illustrates the ideological repudiation of the War on Poverty."

Yet lessons have been learned that may survive ideological conflicts. The Neighborhood Health Center program demonstrated that new institutions can be created to provide a broad range of services under conditions that meet the needs of high-risk families —while saving money.

Antiregulatory, antigovernment, and cost containment pressures have been the order of the day so far in this decade. It may be hard to maintain confidence in the potential for an expanded governmental role in assuring high-quality health care at a time of emphasis on limits and restraints rather than on ideas for expanding the health system's reach. But the record is clear that well-organized, comprehensive health services for poor children have proved to be a cost-effective public expenditure. The foundation for progress has already been laid by federal action—and is ready to be built upon.

PROTECTING POOR CHILDREN IN A CHANGING HEALTH SYSTEM

The way health care is organized and paid for in the United States has produced many phenomenal medical achievements but has never fully responded to the special needs of poor children and pregnant women, the chronically ill, and others whose needs are not for dramatic cures and heroic measures but for basic primary health care.

The medical successes of this century are reflected in falling death rates and increased life expectancy in every age group and continually rising rates of survival from heart disease, cancer, and premature birth.

But within the overall success story lie hidden failures. These failures may bring about the fundamental reforms which pressures for equity alone have not.

- Medical costs continue to escalate.
- Thirty-five million uninsured citizens have only uncertain and fragmentary access to health care of any kind.
- Incremental improvements in access to health care add new layers of complexity to a health system flawed at its base. Each new category of recipient—whether defined by employment status, income, residence, welfare eligibility, or handicap—imposes new bureaucratic and financial burdens on providers as well as recipients. Each incremental change also stands in the way of later reform; it is harder and harder to fit the simple reforms that are

politically most feasible into today's incoherent health system structure.

- The complexities of current health financing arrangements result in a rising proportion of funds, energy, and ingenuity going into costly administrative activities that save no lives and alleviate no suffering. A recent study calculates that 22 percent of the $355 billion spent in the American health sector in 1983 went for administrative expenses, nearly half of it "wasted on the excess administrative apparatus needed to maintain our present health care system and to enforce differential access to care."

As market forces increasingly dominate resource allocation, matters are bound to get worse for poor mothers and children. The most costly consequences of inadequate health care of children and pregnant women do not (except for neonatal intensive care) show up in the health system. The costs of unattended malnutrition, anemia, child abuse, or lead poisoning do not become incentives to greater prevention or outreach efforts, because these costs do not ultimately fall on the health plan, or even the health system. Rather they show up on the ledgers of the social services, education or corrections systems. Greater reliance on market pressures will take resources away from poor children and pregnant women, because the market cannot take account of the fact that good health care has effects that are deferred, and that go well beyond health status.

Significant improvement in the health care of high risk children and pregnant women may come in the form of new programs for children and pregnant women. Or it may be part of a fundamental reform of the health system.

The chaos and cost of the present unwieldy structure may force basic changes. It is slowly becoming clear that a sane and fiscally sound health system cannot be erected atop a jerry-built accretion of compromises and accommodations. Good health services and effective health programs are almost impossible to sustain amid rules that change erratically in response to the dictates of employers and insurers, federal and state governments, speaking in dissonant voices about who should receive health services and what services they should receive.

Among Western industrialized nations, only the greatest and richest one leaves the allocation of health resources—and therefore the health of its citizens—at the mercy of market forces. Other countries constrain the economic and medical decisions of health care providers, so as to maintain access for all citizens to a broad range of effective health services. They accomplish this at a substantially lower per capita cost than ours—8 percent of national income for France and Canada and 6 percent for England, for example, compared to 11 percent for the United States.

Fundamental health system reform, remote as it seems today, may be less so tomorrow. "The cost of our present market-driven system may prove to be so high, and its inequities so onerous," wrote Dr. Relman in *The New England Journal* in 1986, "that universal tax-supported health insurance may become a far more attractive political option than many now suspect."

More than 50 million adult Americans believe, according to a 1982 survey by the Robert Wood Johnson Foundation, that the American health care system "has so much wrong with it that we need to rebuild it completely." In August 1987, a nationwide poll commissioned by the Los Angeles *Times* found that nearly two of three Americans support a federally run national health insurance program.

Chrysler chairman Lee A. Iacocca has asserted, "The country needs an orderly system, and if that means some kind of national health insurance, then I'm for it."

Paul Starr, author of the definitive social history of American medicine, sees a rational system, including decent health care for the poor, as neither a fiscal nor political impossibility—"unless we become utterly resigned to a kind of national incompetence in public policy."

Others have incisively described the means by which this nation could assure access to health care or to health insurance for all its citizens and put in place a more rational system of allocating health resources.

I am more concerned with how we can be sure that a reformed health care system—or even a strengthened maternal and child health system—will respond to the distinctive health care needs of disadvantaged children and pregnant women.

The assurance of universal access to basic health services would of course be the greatest single step forward. Because access to care is so central an issue, and because it is more easily defined in political terms than are issues of the quality, content, and circumstances of care, the expansion of access has been the main focus of those concerned with achieving greater equity in health care. But expanded access can be a hollow victory if what is behind the newly opened door is not well matched to the needs of those who can now enter. It is essential to attend, therefore, to the question of how health resources shall be allocated.

If the income of health professionals were less closely linked to their performance of specific procedures, and if enough health care funds were to flow through one national or a few regional health authorities, a rational and deliberate allocation of health resources would become possible.

How would the body politic respond to the prospect of replacing our current implicit rationing of health resources with more explicit rationing? We tend not to think of our present system, where ability to pay is often decisive in determining who gets what services, as being based on rationing. But actually, highly specialized care is the only kind of care that is furnished without regard to income.

Social historian David Rothman, who periodically joins the physicians making rounds at New York's Columbia-Presbyterian Hospital, tells of a destitute street person admitted near death to the intensive care unit. He was given state-of-the-art care, and his life was saved. A few days later, after expenditures that probably amounted to $30,000 to $40,000, the attending physician pronounced him ready for discharge, which meant a return to the street without so much as a blanket, there being no money in the hospital budget for blankets or food or preventive health care for street people.

When twenty-five-year-old Ollie Hill of Detroit gave birth to a four-pound baby on June 9, 1987, she had had no prenatal care. While her baby was on a heart monitor in the thousand-dollar-a-day intensive care unit of Hutzel Hospital, Ms. Hill told of being unmarried and unemployed and unable to pay for a doctor's visit during her pregnancy. Also, she said, based on the experience of her prenatal care during her first pregnancy, the trip wouldn't have been worth the effort.

"You wait four hours to see the doctor for five minutes," she said. "He just pokes at your stomach and tells you everything's okay."

Would we do it differently if we had the mechanisms to decide? Would we come to a shared understanding that it was worth investing in the kind of prenatal care that would have brought Ollie Hill back in the first trimester of her second pregnancy? Would we pay

Strengthening Families
from Outside

Father James Harvey is a New York City priest who has worked with hundreds of young men in trouble. They come to him from their world of robbery, burglary, stabbings and shootings, and he has helped many to change direction. But he is angry about the one thing he cannot change: their past.

"These youngsters come in, they don't have food, they don't have clothes, many of them don't have a place to sleep," he told a television interviewer. "And people say, 'What is the one biggest thing they don't have?' And I believe it's memory. These young people have no good memories of the past."

The streetwise priest without a parish has reached the same conclusion as has the world-renowned child psychiatrist, Yale University's Albert J. Solnit.

To become a productive and responsible adult, says Dr. Solnit, a youngster needs "a useful and self-respecting past, one that gives him or her a sound sense of self-worth and of a future worth anticipating."

Children whose memories are storehouses of deprivation, neglect, or violence are robbed of the ability to cope with the present or to envision a future bright enough to justify postponing immediate rewards. Children whose families were never able to convey to them a sense of being valued and a feeling of coherence are in a poor position to cope with the world of school or work. They are likely to be in deep trouble by the time they become adolescents.

It is no coincidence that adolescents who are delinquent, lack the skills and motivation to work, or are otherwise destined for serious difficulty are described by those who come to know them in terms that evoke images of a blighted past.

George Cadwalader, who runs a school for delinquent teenagers on an island off the coast of Massachusetts, says, "Their only guide to behavior is simply to satisfy the impulse of the moment. A childhood that never gave them the chance to make consistent connections between cause and effect leaves them feeling powerless to influence the course of their lives."

Ronald White, a successful black professional, describes the triumphs and defeats of tutoring K., a seventeen-year-old black high school student. After many months K. began to respond to White's devotion, only to disappear suddenly after White felt they had finally made a real connection. "I wondered about his absentee father, about the mother who never set foot in K.'s school," wrote White. "I pictured teachers giving him passing marks for work never done. I pictured a younger K. who knew no one was backing him up. When he found people who would, it was too late for him to believe. Too many people had failed him."

Leon Dash, the Washington *Post* reporter who spent a year learning about life in one of Washington's poorest neighborhoods, tells about three young people he came to know, two brothers and their sister. None was married, each of the men had a child and their sister had two. All had dropped out of high school. They worked sporadically at low pay in fast food restaurants, even though they had participated in training programs to equip them for skilled work. The two young men held journeymen's certificates, one in bricklaying, the other in house painting, and the young woman had been enrolled in a nurse training program.

Dash describes how these young people were frustrated in their efforts to become part of the regular work force. Unable to find jobs near home, to arrange for transportation from their isolated ghetto to where the good jobs are, to return to a job after a disagreement with a supervisor—none of the three could surmount the difficulties they encountered. Dash believes they were defeated so easily because they never got the emotional nurturing they needed to cope with life. Their mother told Dash that since the children were small, she had been preoccupied with trying to figure out how to feed them and was able to give them little else. She remembers that she would often tell them, "You'll never be nothing." Now, Dash says, the three are passing on to their children the same sense of defeat that is keeping them "without hope and without goals—at the very bottom of our society." He says he would not be surprised to hear them saying to one of their children, "You'll never be nothing."

These three young people grew up with few supports from inside or outside the family and went to schools that provided only a marginal education. Their background makes it easier to understand why all three so quickly gave up on what they had started out to be when they encountered the first barrier, their fragile egos and scant skills unable to withstand the slightest setback. Their story reminded me of these lines of Carson McCullers:

> The hearts of small children are delicate organs. A cruel beginning in the world can twist them into curious shapes. The heart of a hurt child . . . may fester and swell until it is a misery to carry within the body, easily chafed and hurt by the most ordinary things.

The story of these three young people, "hurt by the most ordinary things," sheds light on the crucial spot where childhood experiences, economic prospects, and the lessons young parents convey to their own children all intersect.

FAMILY ENVIRONMENTS THAT JEOPARDIZE DEVELOPMENT

The connections between dismal childhoods and damage in adolescence form clear patterns, if not always straight lines.

The rich knowledge gathered over the past twenty years clarifies some of the most basic connections between early family environments and damaging outcomes in adolescence and later life.

The family environments under discussion here are not, I want to emphasize, a matter of minor variations within the panoply of reasonably favorable circumstances for child development. This is not a matter of flash cards versus lullabies, or picking up the baby at the first cry or second. This is not about choosing among nuances of child-rearing styles. As the renowned Harvard psychologist, Jerome Kagan, puts it, while there is probably a broad range of early environments that have similar effects, it is also true that there is a threshold function, and that "once that threshold is crossed, the consequences are more serious." Research has documented what common sense has taught: Economic stress, lack of social support and other protective factors, a fragile, impaired, or immature parent, and sometimes a difficult infant can combine, in the absence of outside help, to create an environment so bad that it prejudices the normal development of the child.

Six-year-old blond, blue-eyed Martha is a child growing up in circumstances that jeopardize healthy development. She came to the attention of Dr. Ellen Bassuk, a Harvard psychiatrist studying children in Massachusetts shelters for the homeless.

> Martha was born nine months after her mother, Diane H., then fifteen years old, had been raped by a boy at school. Earlier, the mother had been sexually abused by her godfather and beaten by her alcoholic mother. As a teenager she was addicted to drugs; she was depressed and attempted suicide. She lived successively with two different men who severely abused her and eventually, with Martha, took refuge in a Boston shelter for homeless families. Soon thereafter, a doctor discovered that Martha, having been raped by her mother's last boyfriend, had gonorrhea.
>
> They had lived in the shelter for two months when a psychiatric evaluation, done in connection with Dr. Bassuk's study of homeless families, found six-year-old Martha weepy, clinging, demanding, and preoccupied with her body. The psychiatric team recommended immediate intervention through Boston's Beth Israel Hospital. The recommendation was never acted on, because simultaneously a Department of Social Services worker became aware that Martha was being left rather casually by her mother with other shelter residents—and was being picked up after school by the rapist/boyfriend. In Diane's absence, the worker packed up Martha's belongings and took her away, to be placed in foster care by court order. Martha, considered vulnerable and trau-

matized even before the separation, is unlikely to be reunited with her mother, who is without prospects of a job, permanent housing, or the chance to learn and to show that she could adequately care for her daughter.

For another example, consider six-year-old Lenore and her baby sister Dalia, who live in the Anacostia section of Washington, D.C.

At 8:30 one evening, Lenore arrived at a neighbor's door, her face contorted, cheeks and cream-colored party dress stained with tears. Through the sobs that wracked her body, the child finally managed to explain: Her mother, who had gone out early that morning, leaving her in charge of her seven-month-old sister, had just called to say she was spending the night away, and the girl should fix a bottle of formula for the baby. The six-year-old was confused about how to prepare the formula and frightened about spending the night alone with the baby. This was not the first time little Lenore had shown up in panic, but the young mother did not seem to recognize that this arrangement could be harmful to both little Lenore and her baby sister.

The early childhoods of Martha, Lenore, and Dalia are filled with the kind of deprivation that teaches the lesson that there is no one to trust or count on, that even as a small child one is altogether alone. Their experiences are the stuff of which memories of youngsters in trouble are made.

When it comes to serious, long-term consequences, the results of longitudinal and epidemiological studies of the last two decades converge dramatically with those of firsthand observers. It is now possible to identify a few elements of early family experience that put children in serious jeopardy of significant damage in adolescence. A young child who fails to form strong and loving bonds with one or two caring adults and fails to experience a reasonable amount of coherence in his surroundings during the first few years of life is probably headed for trouble.

A loving and predictable relationship between infant and mother (or between infant and one or two other caring and committed adults), leading over time to the development of a child's sense of trust, is probably the condition most fundamental to normal human development. This relationship has for some years been referred to in the child development and psychiatric literature as "attachment" and is considered by many scientists actually to be a basic biological survival mechanism in human and other species whose young are born immature and dependent.

In the human infant, a sense of trust is most likely to develop when the baby is cared for by someone who, with reasonable consistency, brings comfort and pleasure and resolves distress and uncertainty—especially when the baby is hungry, anxious, fearful, or tired. The relationship becomes secure over time as the adult is sensitive and responsive to the baby's cues and derives pleasure from the interaction.

When the process goes smoothly, it is sheer poetry. Writer Judith Viorst describes it eloquently: "In the beginning mother and baby do something akin to a dance, a dance in which neither partner is wholly the leader, a dance in which the rhythms of rest and activity, distance and contact, clatter and calm, are regulated by both the dancing partners. Together this one specific mother and one specific child fit into each other's back-and-forth cues and responses, and the synchrony—this 'goodness of fit'—facilitates both the infant's inner harmony and his first relationships with the outside world."

Psychologists, psychoanalysts, novelists, and other observers of the human condition have long regarded a reasonably secure connection with a caring adult early in life as the precursor of later capacities for love, trust, conscience, self-confidence, and the ability to form healthy social relationships.

To psychoanalyst Selma Fraiberg the process that lays the early foundations for adult love relationships was an object of continuing study and awe. She wrote, "During the first six months, the baby learns the essential vocabulary of love before he can speak of love. . . . There is the language of the embrace, the language of the eyes, the language of the smile . . . Eighteen years later, when this baby is fully grown and 'falls in love' for the first time, he will woo his partner through the language of the eyes, the language of the smile, and the joy of the embrace. And naturally, in his exalted state, he will believe that he invented this love song."

Clinicians' observations about the enduring consequences of stable early relationships are borne out by large-scale empirical studies. Professor Emmy Werner found, in her work in Kauai, that among the children who were raised in poverty, with high rates of prematurity and perinatal stress and with poorly educated mothers, those who became competent and autonomous young adults—working, playing, and loving well—were most likely to have in common the experience of a strong bond forged with a primary caretaker during the first year of life.

Secure early relationships promote healthy development because they allow the toddler to explore the wider world with some sense of comfort and make a youngster more amenable to societal demands, be they for good manners during Grandpa's visit or for listening during story time—the child does not want to jeopardize a valued relationship. At elementary school age, the child who generally accepts adult restrictions elicits praise and acceptance and comes to feel valued and even virtuous.

An early positive outlook toward parental authority remains important to later development, by buffering the child against stress. "When children are following the instructions of others whom they trust, they experience little anxiety about the outcome, and are at least partially protected from guilt or a sense of failure over negative outcomes."

Children who are less receptive to the standards promoted by family, church, or school, who consistently refuse to accept adult restrictions, may gain a sense of freedom but may also develop a feeling of unworthiness. Such children may adopt what Professor Kagan calls a "deviant behavioral profile," causing them to be rejected by the mainstream culture, making them ever more vulnerable to uncertainty and to the blandishments of surroundings that sanction their antisocial attitudes and actions.

The failure to develop strong early connections with someone who, in Professor Urie Bronfenbrenner's phrase, "is crazy about the kid" has been found to lead, with haunting frequency, to an adult personality "characterized by lack of guilt, an inability to keep rules, and an inability to form lasting relationships."

If the early connections are not forged, normal development is jeopardized. If the infant is deprived of affection and predictability, especially when in distress, if a familiar caregiver is consistently unavailable when the baby is in need, repeated disappointments will lead the baby to conclude that it is futile to anticipate adult care or help. Such a child will withdraw to find more solitary sources of comfort and will learn to distrust the surrounding world.

Healthy growth is also threatened when the baby is in the care of someone who is incapable of responding because of alcoholism, drug addiction, or mental illness, because her own life experience has left her defeated or otherwise impaired. The chances of harm increase when the impaired parent is responsible for a baby who is —for any of a number of reasons—particularly difficult to care for.

In Kauai, public health nurses, observing one-year-olds in their homes, identified families where the mother-child interaction was permeated by "nonrewarding patterns." At two years of age, children and mothers seemed "locked in a vicious cycle of increasing frustration for both parent and child." When the same children were ten, professionals unaware of the earlier observations noted "a pronounced lack of emotional support" in these homes. The children in these families were found the likeliest to have serious mental health problems as adolescents and to have been involved in repeated, serious delinquencies.

A fundamental mismatch between the child's temperament or developmental needs and the parent's temperament, expectations, and capacities has been found to be a critical issue in accounting for early behavior disorders.

The process of development can also be subverted when young children lead a pillar-to-post existence and have to cope with a large and changing cast of caretakers. This can happen when a child is in substandard day care or in a rapid succession of different day care arrangements, is shifted from one foster home to another, or—less common today—is reared in a large, impersonal institution.

Warm and loving relationships can develop after infancy, but their early absence appears to have a lasting effect. British studies found high rates of problems among elementary school children who spent their first few years in institutions. Problems occurred with the same frequency, whether or not the children were adopted after the age of four. British psychiatrist Michael Rutter concluded that "the lack of opportunity to form early emotional bonds to particular individuals" is most likely to be the damaging factor.

As important to normal development as close and dependable early relationships is a child's experience of a reasonably stable, protective, and responsive environment which provides protection from hunger and harm while teaching a reasonable connection between actions and their consequences.

Pervasive family chaos and discord—two of the major factors that interfere with a child's acquiring a sense of coherence—are found in longitudinal research to play very important roles. Although the death of a parent during childhood has long been regarded as a prime reason for trouble in adolescence and adulthood, recent research has shown that a background of family discord and chaos is more strongly associated with antisocial disorders, including delinquency, than is a parent's death.

A sense of coherence and an absence of chaos and discord distinguished the resilient children and youth of Kauai from their less fortunate fellows. The children with favorable outcomes grew up in households with structure and rules; all seemed to have "a feeling of confidence that one's internal and external environment is predictable and that things will probably work out as well as can be reasonably expected." As the Kauai researchers concluded, "The central component of effective coping . . . appears to be a sense of coherence. . . . The real issue may well be whether the families and societies in which children grow up and live their daily lives facilitate or impede the development and maintenance of such a sense."

The coherence that seems to be so important does not require a standard family of two parents and 2.3 children eating dinner together at the same time each evening. It does mean stimulating and supportive interaction between adults and children, changing in specifics as children grow. It does mean that both authority and love come with some consistency from the adults perceived by the child as responsible for his welfare, that family conflicts are resolved without resort to violence, that chaos, discord, and unmanageable stress are not the constant backdrops to family life.

Children need coherent experiences in order to mature. They need the help of concerned, competent adults in order to meet new demands, to cope with new stresses, and to achieve new levels of organization.

Of course, the qualities adults need in order to convey a sense of coherence to their children change as children grow. An impaired or limited parent may be able to meet a child's needs at some stages of development but not at others. A mother who rejoices in accommodating to her infant may be unable, when infant turns toddler, to set firm rules or to tolerate his new sense of independence.

Disequilibrium is a normal part of development which accompanies the newly found ability to stand or walk, the birth of a sibling, the onset of puberty, a death in the family. But demands and stresses that produce disequilibrium must be within the range of the child's ability to master them. They are more likely to lead to growth, rather than defeat, if the child is surrounded by familiar routines and a predictable, understandable physical and social environment.

Infancy researcher Kathryn Barnard emphasizes the importance of this kind of structure. For example, while every family with a new baby is under great stress, she notes that families with ample resources protect children from the effects of such stress by their organization and structure. Working in Seattle with young mothers who live at society's margins, Dr. Barnard finds that families without adequate incomes, with no support, and in chaotic surroundings face a superhuman task in making things predictable for their infants. (Dr. Barnard's current "home visit" clientele includes one woman who lives in a car and another who lives in four different places every week. She says, "These families are so devoid of structure, of organization, they can disorganize *you!* When you leave after a visit, *you* have a headache!")

The specific ways in which extreme family distress can lead to failed relationships and incoherence in very early childhood, and in turn to long-term damage, are well documented. Few of these connections fall into the category of the "counterintuitive":

When the fussy infant, instead of being rocked and soothed, is shaken and told that he is bad . . .

When the one-year-old, triumphantly standing up in her crib, is not applauded but ignored . . .

When her frustrated screams at not being able to let herself down again are met not with assistance, but with blows . . .

When the two-year-old, trying to get a drink from the faucet, is not shown how to make the water flow into the cup, but is cursed and slapped . . .

When the five-year-old, venturing out the front door, finds not a brother who might read to him but huddled bodies of junkies sleeping in the doorway . . .

When the eight-year-old, bringing home a truancy complaint, discovers that no one cares whether he goes to school or not . . .

These are the experiences of early family life that create adolescents who are helpless, hostile, and alienated, who lack self-esteem, a sense of being valued, and the conviction that their actions matter. Adolescents who are helpless, hostile, and alienated are quick to yield to impulse, to seek immediate gratification of desires, to find minor obstacles at school, work, or training insurmountable, to see little reason to finish school or postpone early childbearing, to show no regard for others' feelings, and to become easy recruits to the ranks of crime. Unsupported at a crucial stage of their lives, they are unlikely to become self-supporting and will have few of the resources required for successful parenting.

HELPING FAMILIES WITH OUTSIDE SUPPORT

No one doubts that good memories and a proud past are—at the most fundamental level—created by concerned and competent families. But can the interior functioning of the family be significantly affected by exterior social action?

Many Americans find it hard to believe that intervention from outside could be effective in helping families raise children who have self-esteem, feel valued, and are convinced their actions matter. The processes of developing these qualities are so subtle, so fragile, so private, so internal to the life of the family that they seem at first blush beyond the reach of social policy.

But are they really?

Harvard Professor of Government James Q. Wilson addressed this question in his 1975 book, *Thinking About Crime,* when he asked, "What agency do we create, what budget do we allocate, that will supply the missing 'parental affection' and restore to the child consistent discipline by a stable and loving family?"

The question suggests that we are expected to reply: Nothing that society can do will make any difference, we are indeed helpless.

But we are not helpless.

The affectionate, stable, and loving families invoked by Professor Wilson are not random blessings, the result of some cosmic roll of the dice, nor are they genetically ordained.

The circumstances in which they develop are in large measure the product of social forces and are therefore amenable to social action.

First, many social policies—ranging from those that stimulate the economy to those that support family planning, prenatal care, child health services, child care, preschool education, and improved schools—have a substantial role in strengthening families.

But in addition, as we shall see later in this chapter, high-risk families are able to make use of interventions and support focused directly on family functioning to mend the interiors of their lives— in ways that have significantly changed outcomes for vulnerable children. These interventions have helped families to give their chil-

dren the essential nutrients for normal growth and to cope successfully with life transitions (like the birth of a baby) as well as with
the frequent crises of daily life that, in high-risk environments, are
almost impossible to surmount without outside help. Especially
when there is a particularly difficult baby or child or when someone
else in the family is sick or impaired, these interventions have
helped. Even families as disintegrated as those of Martha, Lenore,
and Dalia, even families so overwhelmed as to be unable to provide
their children with the most basic conditions for normal growth can
be helped.

Both common sense and research tell us that as family stress,
regardless of its source, increases, the capacity for nurturing decreases, and the likelihood of abuse and neglect increases. Whether
the stress stems from insufficient income, a difficult child, an impaired adult, family violence and discord, inadequate housing,
chronic hunger and poor health, or surroundings of brutality, hopelessness, and despair—these are the circumstances in which affection withers into hostility, discipline turns into abuse, stability dis-
solves into chaos, and love becomes neglect.

Even the fragile and intimate process that culminates in a loving
and trusting relationship between young child and adult can be
helped along by outside intervention. The mother or other caretaker
who is isolated, feels defeated, and lacks confidence in her own
ability to make a difference for her child, can be helped by a skilled
home visitor to muster the physical and emotional energy to meet
her child's most fundamental demands.

A child's need for coherence, structure, and predictability—almost impossible to meet when the adults around him are caught up
in a chaotic struggle for survival—is similarly amenable to intervention. The mother who cannot respond appropriately to a child's
evolving needs while simultaneously coping with unemployment, an
abusive husband or boyfriend, an apartment without hot water, insufficient money for food, and her own memories of past neglect—
even a mother who is stressed to the breaking point can be helped
by a neighborhood agency that provides day care, counseling, and
the support that convinces her that she is not helpless and alone.

All families rearing children need support, be it from friends,
relatives, neighbors, or more organized sources. The job is simply
too hard to handle alone. But for parents who are isolated and beset
by a multitude of other stresses, the stakes are higher and support

can prevent severe damage. A vast body of research now illuminates the importance of support:

- Unusually high rates of child abuse and neglect and of juvenile delinquency have been consistently found in families that have few social relationships and believe that help would not be forthcoming if they needed it.
- Adolescent mothers who have not completed high school and are unemployed and have low levels of support tend to be hostile, indifferent, and rejecting of their children. By contrast, the teenage mothers with high levels of support are "more affectionate . . . comforting, cuddling, playing with and praising their children."
- The absence of social supports during pregnancy, combined with a high degree of stress, was found to be "highly predictive" of medical complications during pregnancy and at birth.
- A consistent association has been demonstrated between the adequacy of maternal social support and the security of the infant-mother relationship at twelve months. Irritable infants showed the strongest favorable effects, when social support was available to the family.
- Being brought up by a mother living alone and in social isolation is associated with early school failure, truancy, fighting in school, dropping out of school, and childbearing in early adolescence.
- Even animals put under stress while in isolation show more long-term pathology than do those stressed in the company of littermates, mothers, and siblings.

The support that seems to make such a difference in family life can come from a spouse, a grandmother, a friend, a family support group, a day care center, a pediatrician, or a mental health professional. It can occur naturally (informal supports), or through intentional social planning (formal supports). It can confirm to a young mother the value of her role as a parent, give her a respite from the cries of her colicky infant, provide her with the experiences that give her some sense of control over what happens to her child, or provide her with money for a washing machine. (Barbara Blum, President of the Foundation for Child Development, says that as Commissioner of Special Services for Children in New York City, the funds she could use to provide concrete help, such as assistance to the family to buy a washing machine, were among the most helpful tools she had.) Ultimately, the supports that improve life for young children are those which convey the message that one is not alone in carrying out one's child-rearing responsibilities.

No one knows exactly how support operates to produce such significant effects. Its presence seems somehow to enable people to mobilize coping strategies and adaptive behaviors which, in turn, seem to reduce stress.

Today, as in years past, support for most families comes primarily from an informal network of friends and relatives. The rockbottom buffer against the raw assaults of multiple stresses, if all goes well, are those who share one's home. When there is only one adult, the buffer is much harder to come by. Once again, research confirms intuition: A parent, especially a very young one, who is raising a child alone is in a particularly vulnerable position.

Among children of teenage mothers studied in Baltimore and Chicago, those raised by the mother alone did least well (at high school age in Baltimore, and in first grade in Chicago). The critical factor turned out to be whether the mother was the lone adult in the household and not whether the additional adult, when there was one, was the father or grandmother.

Of course, support can also come from family members who are not part of the household. One study found that an informal multigenerational network of kin available to help with child rearing was one of the variables that differentiated between the vulnerable children who grew into competent adults and those who did not.

The plight of American families today stems partly from the fact that even as the number of adults in households with children decreases, support from outside the immediate family becomes harder to mobilize. There are simply fewer people around to provide it. "In earlier stages of human history, mothers moved in a world crowded with supportive kin who supplemented their care of infants, a situation in sharp contrast to the experience of most American women today." In increasing proportions, grandmothers, aunts, and sisters are employed outside the home. Job requirements and urbanization have divided extended families, leaving fewer adults to help with child care responsibilities.

Neighborly assistance has become almost as scarce as family help. Fewer people with long-standing relationships live nearby. Those who might help often can't, because they themselves are depleted.

Social isolation cuts across class lines but is worst in poor neighborhoods, where everyone is stressed and few have energy to spare. James Garbarino and D. Sherman, experts in the social context of child abuse, believe that the increasing incidence of child abuse is directly related to the spread of "socially impoverished environments, denuded of enduring supportive relationships" and the scarcity of people "free from drain" who can afford to be supportive to neighbors because their own needs do not exceed their resources.

This drying up of informal supports has occurred even as the need for such support has multiplied.

- More women, including many more mothers of young children are working, the vast majority in response to economic pressures.
- More children are growing up in poverty and many more in concentrated poverty, subject to the strains that low incomes and depleted neighborhoods impose on family life.
- Greater population mobility not only means fewer relatives and friends nearby to lend an extra pair of hands, but also that parent(s) and children themselves move much more frequently than did earlier generations, adding yet another element of strain.
- Greater mobility also means the erosion of the sense of community which develops over generations of living in proximity (whether or not reinforced by kinship ties) that provided structure and a framework for the process of childrearing. For many Americans, community has been replaced by a climate of anonymity, often accompanied by alienation, hostility, and violence.
- Child rearing itself has become more difficult. Gone are the clear, shared values and precepts to be passed on to the children. From outside the family have come the lure of drugs and powerful pressures to define oneself by acquiring material goods. The pace of change is so rapid, values are so much in conflict, that everyone, including parents of young children, has to make up instant new rules to live by—a task that older societies never imposed.

The gap left by the decreasing availability of informal supports has been deepened by America's failure to provide families with the economic and social benefits that are standard in other Western democracies. The extent to which these shields against increased pressures on the family are so unavailable is particularly shocking in view of the clear evidence of their effectiveness.

Organized programs of family support have similar effects as the informal supports they supplement or replace. Formal social supports protect people from an amazing variety of pathological states, including destructive family functioning, low birthweight, depression, arthritis, tuberculosis, and even premature death.

Over the last few years, programs to provide families with outside supports from a wide variety of sources have mushroomed. These programs are generally able to provide a combination of services, material goods, information, and emotional support. Most try to convey to participants that they are "cared for . . . esteemed and valued, and part of a network of communication and mutual obligation." They seek to cushion individuals against the harmful effects of stress and thereby help them to function better as parents, friends, and productive citizens. They "assist families to become involved in shaping their environment."

Support programs may be oriented to helping during important transitions such as the birth of a new baby. (Periods of transition—pregnancy and childbirth especially—are not only times of great vulnerability, but tend also to be times when individuals and families are particularly receptive to new learning.) Other support programs assist families in dealing with crises—the threat of out-of-home placement of a child in danger of abuse or neglect, a father's death, a mother's or child's hospitalization. Some programs primarily serve those families in greatest need of support. Others make continuing support services available to a broad range of families, on the ground that supportive interventions should be continuous during the child-rearing years, just as the care and attention of parents in secure families are not limited to periods of crisis.

In families at greatest risk, where stress has become unmanageable and lives are out of control, informal support is least likely to be available. In addition, for these families, informal support may not be sufficiently powerful to be an effective buffer. For example, among teenage mothers and their infants, informal social supports were found to have positive effects only among the mothers who had relatively little stress in their lives. Furthermore, among poor single mothers, efforts to maintain informal supports actually can themselves become a significant source of stress.

Families with few supports but great needs are often inept at using available supports, formal or informal. They often need help in using help. They are unlikely to be able to make good use of services offered in circumstances that may meet professional and bureaucratic requirements but do not sufficiently take into account the obstacles faced by very depleted families. As Norman Polansky, University of Georgia Regents' Professor of Social Work, concluded after a lengthy study of abusive and neglectful families, these families are "poor prospects" for traditional services. "Their deficits in ordinary social skills require us to meet them well over halfway."

Programs that meet families more than halfway with support services have demonstrated some stunning victories.

Strewn across the bleak landscape of America's struggles to prevent damage to children through understaffed and underfunded child protection and child welfare services are some gleaming success stories. These programs have broken new bureaucratic and professional ground and have been able, by supporting families, to salvage young lives.

Intensive Care at Home in Tacoma and the Bronx

In Tacoma, Washington, one day in 1974, the staff of the Catholic Children's Services were bemoaning the sorry state of organized help to families in crisis. There seemed to be only two alternatives, both unacceptable. One was to remove the child from its family; chances were that this would destroy continuity of caretaking for years. Or one could try once more to prop up the family with available services known to be inadequate; this would ultimately fail and could endanger a child's life in the process.

The services the agency could offer seemed out of synch with the needs of troubled families.

"When a family is in turmoil, they don't want you once a week on Wednesdays," says Jill Kinney, then director of the agency's family crisis program. "They want you when they are feeling the pain."

It seemed grotesque that disintegrating families, facing removal of children, should be subjected to further burdens, required to show up at inconvenient times in faraway places to meet with people, each of whom would deal, at best, with one small piece of their problem.

Staff members of the Catholic agency met with a visiting grant officer from the National Institute of Mental Health and ardently made their case. Available services, remote and disjointed, were futile and failed to reflect the importance of preventing unnecessary removal of children from their families.

Everyone present recognized that children removed from their families and placed in foster care, group care, or residential institutions face bleak futures; that half of children in foster care are placed in more than one foster home, and that over one quarter live in three or more consecutive placements; that thousands of children are effectively stranded, shuttled back and forth, even sent to institutions far from their own homes, where they are not visited, rescued, or even recorded.

From that 1974 meeting emerged a plan that swiftly turned one agency's services upside down. It created a social service version of the medical intensive care unit.

The new program, called Homebuilders, assembled a team of professionals with masters' degrees in social work, psychology, or counseling. The services of one or more of the staff were offered to any family which, in the judgment of a child welfare, juvenile justice, or mental health agency, stood in imminent peril of the removal of a child.

Homebuilders staff met with the family on its own turf, heard family members define the nature of their crisis, and remained on hand as long as necessary, for many hours or even days, for periods of up to six weeks.

"We help clients take control of their own lives," is how Homebuilders therapist Charlotte Booth describes the process that has now been in operation for over a decade. No team member is responsible for more than three families at once. This allows time to resolve the immediate crisis and to help the family to learn new ways of coping, so the family will not fall back into crisis after the intensive intervention ends.

The staff works closely with schools, the juvenile court, and other youth-serving agencies, using a variety of individual and group therapy methods and teaching more effective parent-child interactions. Counselors also find themselves offering practical help—a spare part to fix the family car, a ride to the market, help in getting rid of the rats.

Homebuilders always responds within twenty-four hours after referral. Prompt response, says Jill Kinney, is one key to defusing potentially violent family conflicts. Therapists then usually separate the participants and spend enough time "listening carefully, until each family member feels that his or her point of view has been heard and understood." Usually, she says, when family members are reassured that enough help will be available, much of the immediate pressure seems to dissipate.

One family that Homebuilders visited during its first year had a long history of child neglect—four children previously placed in foster care. The house was extremely dirty, the mother and children unkempt. The children, truant from school, explained they were ashamed of their appearance and ridiculed by classmates. The family had been involved with many social service agencies, and the mother said that what she did not need was "somebody else telling us what to do." All she wanted was some help in "getting the house together" so that the children wouldn't be taken away again.

The Homebuilders therapist got a refrigerator, mattresses, sheets, blankets, and other basic necessities for the family and pitched in to help the mother scrub the walls and floors. Impressed by the therapist's responsiveness to her immediate needs, the mother gradually began to trust the other woman and to express her feelings of despair.

Soon she was able to work with the therapist to organize household tasks and to set realistic goals for herself and her children. She learned how to obtain food stamps, and enrolled in vocational school classes in budgeting and food buying and preparation. She posted charts to encourage the children to take their turn with the chores. She began seeing a therapist from the mental health center as a continuing source of help after the Homebuilders ended their intensive home visits.

The Homebuilders worker also spent several hours with each of the children, gradually winning their confidence. School personnel provided support to encourage regular attendance. The two older children got jobs picking berries and mowing lawns.

A year later, the mother proudly showed her newly painted, neat living room. The children were doing well in school and were helpful at home, and the eldest child, previously intent on leaving school at sixteen, had decided to continue.

In the first six years of Homebuilders in Tacoma, placement became unnecessary for 92 percent of the client families, which included 849 children originally headed for foster care or other out-of-home placement. In the most recent evaluation, which followed the families for a longer period, 90 percent of the children helped by Homebuilders were still with their families.

Homebuilders credits its success to several factors:

First, the families are highly motivated. Cases are accepted only when referring agencies sign statements saying that out-of-family placement is imminent. Referral is often triggered by a climactic event such as an arrest, a suicide attempt, a child running away, or an incident of child abuse. At such times, points out Dr. Kinney, families seem more willing to experiment with new ways of behaving than "when their pain seems more bearable."

Second, meeting at home rather than in distant offices facilitates treatment. On their own ground, more family members are willing to participate in counseling. The caseworker or therapist coming to the family's home is perceived as less threatening, more concerned and respectful. Also, says therapist Karen Elmore, "you get a different perspective being in the home." The worker can observe the family's lifestyle, demonstrate different ways of interacting, and join the family in monitoring the process of change and modifying plans on the basis of the family's new experiences.

Third, Homebuilders allows staff members to devote ample time —more than a hundred hours with some families. Sometimes they work in pairs, especially at the outset, to ensure that every member of the family gets prompt attention, and they remain until everyone feels better. Therapists are freed from the pressure of trying to meet many types of needs within a tightly scheduled one-hour-a-week structure.

Fourth, staff can draw on a wide variety of resources. They call upon and coordinate other community services, as needed. (One young girl had previously dealt with fifteen different case managers using often conflicting treatment plans.) Dr. Kinney says that Homebuilders must often be "aggressive advocates to secure services from other providers that have given up on a family."

Fifth, Homebuilders staff have in their repertory a wide variety of ways to help. These range from individual and family therapy and lessons in relaxation, assertiveness, and behavior management, to providing very practical help, rarely available from agencies that offer professional expertise.

In the early days of Homebuilders, skeptics expressed three major concerns—that the demands on the staff would be unreasonable, that unlimited access to therapists would reinforce dependency, and that costs would be too high. Experience has been reassuring on all three counts.

The home visits are more demanding on the staff than seeing clients at conveniently scheduled times from behind one's desk in the comfort of one's own office. Staff who go into clients' homes must be able to function well in unstructured, unpredictable, and sometimes dangerous situations. On call twenty-four hours a day, seven days a week, workers must be able to juggle personal schedules to meet the sometimes overwhelming needs of their clients. But staff members agree that a caseload small enough to enable them to do justice to their clients' needs and the sense they are succeeding more than compensate for the personal convenience they sacrifice.

"Seeing a family pull things together is a tremendous energizer for therapists," says Dr. Kinney.

"It's the results," says social worker Don Bender. Because Homebuilders can provide intervention so much more intensive than traditional forms of social work, Bender says, "We're in a position to see changes. I feel a lot more productive and successful."

As for dependency, it often occurs at the outset but can usually be resolved before the intensive phase has ended. Jill Kinney says that most Homebuilders staff have been moved by the strength of the families' desire to pull their own weight.

"They don't call unless there really is a crisis, and once they have learned options for handling situations on their own, they much prefer to do so," she observes. After the first few sessions, therapist and client generally develop a relationship of team members working together toward a common goal.

To estimate cost-effectiveness, Homebuilders compares the cost of its intervention (which averaged about $2,600 per family in 1985) with the projected long-term cost of the foster care, group care, or psychiatric hospitalization that was prevented, and finds a five- to six-fold return on every dollar invested.

The Tacoma success story has attracted enormous attention from local and state human service agencies, foundations, and the child welfare profession. There is growing recognition that the removal of abused or neglected children from their homes offers few of them good futures. Under present circumstances, it is only rarely in their best interest.

"For too many children, foster care becomes a bottomless pit," says Columbia Professor David Fanshel, the country's leading foster care expert. In New York City, not unique in this respect, the average length of time a child spends in foster care is 4.8 years. The scarcity and inadequacy of services to prevent placement is a nationwide problem. Removing a child from home is the response of first resort to troubled families—a system norm, even though, as Peter Forsythe of the Edna McConnell Clark Foundation points out, the consequences of putting a child in out-of-home care are very costly to the children, their families, and the taxpayer. Recent rises in the number of children removed from home reflect in part the fact that financing arrangements continue to provide incentives for out-of-home care and in part the persistent pessimism about whether families, particularly disadvantaged families, can be helped to change for the better.

This is the context in which the Tacoma Homebuilders experience has been widely regarded as a ray of hope and a model to be replicated. The Edna McConnell Clark Foundation has put the expansion of intensive family support programs at the top of its agenda. Training and technical assistance to spur the growth of similar programs are also being provided by the Child Welfare League of America, the National Child Welfare Leadership Center, and the National Research Center on Family Based Services, recently established at the University of Iowa.

By mid-1987 at least eight states were experimenting with large-scale implementation of the intensive family services idea under public auspices. Oregon, Florida, Iowa, Colorado, and Maine have made significant progress in applying the principles pioneered in Tacoma and seem to be achieving similarly impressive results, preventing both unnecessary placements and unnecessary public expenditures. In addition, an unknown number of local agencies are employing the principles developed in Tacoma, often with assistance from the rapidly growing Homebuilders organization itself.

In what may be its most daring venture in replication, the Homebuilders group has responded to an invitation to help several New York City agencies to adapt the program for use in the Bronx.

This experiment in social diffusion had its origin in early 1986, when a consortium of five public and private agencies, including the New York City Department of Juvenile Justice and Office of Special Services for Children, began exploring ways to improve the city's existing services for keeping families together. Organizations and individuals long at war with each other began to work together for the first time. "It was as though they were suddenly in a demilitarized zone," says David Tobis, who directed the consortium's planning activities. Tobis believes that the cooperative atmosphere was a product of the participants' shared conviction that "families need far more, and could be helped in far better ways, than they now are being helped."

Early in the process, says Tobis, "we had our socks knocked off by a presentation from the originators of Homebuilders." A grant from the Clark Foundation allowed the group to proceed very slowly, "to touch every base, and get everyone involved and informed." (All participants emphasize that the generous planning time was crucial to enabling them to work together so successfully.) In early 1987, after more than a year of searching discussion and planning, the consortium invited Jill Kinney and David Haapala, cofounders and directors of Homebuilders in Tacoma and Seattle, to come to New York City for a year. Together they would find out whether an intervention that clearly works in the predominantly white, comparatively uncomplicated state of Washington can be made to work in a part of the Bronx that is devastatingly poor, predominantly black and Hispanic, and dependent on the services of the most bureaucratically complicated city in America.

Dr. Kinney and Dr. Haapala came to New York to hire the therapists, who returned with them to the West Coast for ten weeks of training, followed by more training in New York, focused on the range of public and private services that both therapists and families would be involved with locally. On May 4, 1987, the first Seattle-trained Homebuilder called on a family in the Bronx. Initial impressions after the first few months were consistent with the expectations of the consortium. The staff found poverty in New York to be much more intrusive and determining of people's lives than it is in Washington State, and the task of obtaining additional services for their clients infinitely more difficult in the Bronx than in Seattle. The staff was not prepared, however, for the larger and more destructive role that drugs, especially crack, play in the lives of distressed families in the Bronx. One of the Homebuilders staff told of shopping for a family which had no food in the house. As she put the grocery bag on the kitchen counter, the mother unloaded the cans and proceeded to open them one by one. When the puzzled Homebuilders worker asked why, the mother explained that unopened cans were simply too great a temptation to the relatives and others who came through the house, stealing what they could to get money for another purchase of crack.

Nevertheless, Dr. Kinney and Dr. Haapala, the Clark Foundation, and the consortium were optimistic about the prospects for helping families in jeopardy in the Bronx to stay together, to prevent harm to children, and to equip all members with greater skills to deal with future crises. They were also impressed with accumulating evidence that the very process of importing the Homebuilders model to New York is shifting the focus of the city's public and private agencies toward a much greater emphasis on preserving families, preventing out-of-home placement, and rendering intensive, round-the-clock services.

"A PARTNERSHIP IN BEHALF OF THE CHILD" IN NEW HAVEN

Crisis intervention as provided by Homebuilders is effective and essential, but so is earlier intervention. About two thirds of the children whose imminent removal from home triggers the Homebuilders services are between eleven and fifteen years old. Trouble in these families has usually been incubating for years. Programs to strengthen such families when the children are much younger can often prevent a spiral into crisis.

One such program was created by Dr. Sally Provence under the auspices of the Yale University Child Study Center. She and her professional colleagues worked closely with parents to forge what she called "a partnership in behalf of the child." It was a trailblazing concept.

With a mildness that masks her incisive intelligence and persistence and with an energy that belies her emeritus status as professor of pediatrics and child development at the Yale Child Study Center, Dr. Provence looks back on the history of that experiment.

Trained in pediatrics at the Children's Medical Center in Dallas, Texas, and in psychoanalysis at the New York Psychoanalytic Institute, Dr. Provence became persuaded that both pediatrics and psychiatry focused too comfortably on individuals with identified diagnoses and neglected children growing up in surroundings that threatened healthy development.

In the mid-sixties, Dr. Provence recalls, "we were all interested in working with disadvantaged families, to address the waste of human potential associated with poverty and with inadequate care of children in the early years." With her colleague, clinical professor of social work Audrey Naylor, she designed a program to provide medical, educational, social, and psychological services to disadvantaged young parents and their children in New Haven. Their objective was to modify the poverty-related high-risk environments of both parents and children and alleviate stresses that diminish parents' capacity to nurture their children.

The participants, recruited in 1968 from women attending the obstetric clinic of the Yale–New Haven Medical Center, were seventeen young women living in the depressed inner city of New Haven, with incomes at or below the poverty line. The mothers ranged in age from eighteen to twenty-four. Nine were unmarried, and two were separated from their husbands. The mothers were enrolled before the birth of their babies and served by the program until the children were two and a half years old. (A second child of one family was later included.) Of the eighteen participating children, twelve were black, two white, two Puerto Rican, and two of mixed racial background.

The project was housed in a remodeled old inner city residence renamed Children's House. There pediatricians, nurses, developmental specialists, early childhood educators, and social workers met with parents and children to provide health care and periodic developmental appraisals for the children and guidance, counseling, and other supports for the parents. Families could also bring their children for day care and toddler school. An informal atmosphere helped the mothers—and the few fathers who came in—to feel at home. They could exchange thoughts and observations with day care staff over a cup of coffee. "There was always the intention," says Dr. Provence, "to convey to parents our interest in hearing their wishes, opinions, and concerns about their children, and to create an atmosphere in which easy communication would be possible."

Supplementing the Children's House services were home visits during the baby's first week by the pediatrician and thereafter by a social worker, psychologist, or staff nurse about twice monthly.

The blend of comprehensive health care with family support, education, and day care was an unusual aspect of the Yale program. Dr. Provence considers health services an important component, both because good continuous health care is often not available to disadvantaged families and because it was highly valued by participants. The pediatrician got to know the mother in the hospital at the time of delivery and telephoned her at least once a week during the first month in response to "the almost universal need of young parents for support in caring for their child during their early months as parents." The doctor saw the baby at Children's House monthly during the first year and every three months thereafter, as well as at home as necessary, especially when children were ill.

When one of the children in the project, six-week-old Steven, became seriously ill, the pediatrician came to the home, found him much sicker than when she had examined him the day before, and took him and his mother to the hospital. Steven was admitted to the intensive care unit with a severe respiratory infection, which ultimately required a tracheostomy. During eight weeks in the hospital, the pediatrician was in daily contact with the hospital staff and with Steven. Along with the family social worker, the pediatrician also saw Steven's mother regularly, to answer her questions and to provide support.

Dr. Provence believes that parents' awareness of the doctor's availability was one big reason for their attachment to the project. The pediatrician also helped parents feel increasingly able to decide when they needed the doctor's help and to participate actively in the health care of their children. Doctors always allowed ample time for listening to and discussing parents' opinions, questions, and concerns. When pediatricians gave advice, Dr. Provence emphasizes, it was not in recipe form but in specific relation to individual children and parents.

Developmental evaluations were done at eight points during the program's thirty months, always in the presence of one or both parents.

The program offered participating families day care whenever they wanted to use it, beginning when the baby was six weeks old, and a "toddler school," beginning at thirteen months. The purpose of the day care component was to provide children with experiences that promote learning, coping, and adaptation and to provide parents with the possibility of going to school or work and some easing of day-to-day stress. For parents whose personal problems resulted in a chaotic, neglectful, or abusive home environment, day care provided not only support for the parent but the daily care and special individualized services urgently required by the children.

The Yale project's view of parents as the single greatest influence on their children's early lives is reflected in the way all members of the staff worked with families. The social worker was particularly "the parents' person," charged with learning about and responding to the problems each parent faced. This meant providing help with obtaining education, training, jobs, housing, birth control, and food stamps, as well as supporting mothers who had not been adequately nurtured in their own growing-up years in ways that would free them to better nurture their own children.

Dr. Provence believes that for a group of parents deprived of many social supports available to the more advantaged, the project's supports were of particular significance, for practical as well as psychological reasons. She believes that for most of the parents, participation in the study became "a corrective emotional experience, making up for some of the deficits in their early life experiences, supplying the caring 'parents' that some still needed."

Before Steven, the child with the tracheostomy, was discharged from the hospital, the pediatrician and social worker helped his mother get the special equipment needed for his care. The social worker sometimes drove mother and son to the hospital for weekly aftercare visits, occasionally combining these trips with stops for grocery shopping and other errands that were difficult during Steven's convalescence.

Social workers attempted to build a relationship in which the parent felt safe sharing the information and feelings that can help in problem solving. Their objective was to increase the parents' capacity to function effectively on their own behalf, to heighten their self-esteem, and to enable them to take greater charge of their own lives.

From the inception of the program, Dr. Provence and her colleagues wanted to make sure that their work, if successful, would be useful to others, and they attached a major research and assessment component to the service program.

The program was in operation from 1968 to 1972. Two years after the program participants were initially recruited, the researchers returned to Yale–New Haven Hospital to select another group of eighteen children, using similar criteria, in order to provide a comparison group.

The mothers and children in the program and in the control group were studied five years after the end of the program and once more five years later—by separate groups of researchers. The results of program participation turned out to be striking.

Ten years after the end of the program, there were enormous changes in the participating mothers. Almost all of the intervention families were off welfare and self-supporting, while only about half the control families were. (The effects of the program on the mothers were not immediate. But at five-year follow-up they were found to have "changed dramatically as a result of their involvement in the program," having smaller families and being more frequently employed. The big changes in welfare status were not found until the ten-year follow-up.)

Compared to the control mothers, the participating mothers had also completed more years of education (though they had had similar amounts at the time their children were born), waited longer to have a second child, and had fewer children (an average of 1.7 compared to 2.2).

As for the children, using a combined measurement of test performance, absenteeism, and special services, only 28 percent (five out of eighteen) of the intervention children suffered from serious school adjustment problems, compared to 69 percent (eleven out of sixteen) control children.

The outside evaluators agreed with the professionals who designed and ran this program about the keys to its success:

- High-quality services, rendered by a stable group of well-trained professionals and paraprofessionals who were able to maintain strong and continuous relationships with participating families.
- Services that covered a wide spectrum and responded to the diverse and changing needs of participants; a commitment by program staff to resist the predictable pressures to routinize services.
- Recognition that both children and parents were equally important targets of the intervention.
- The conviction that professionals who respect, care about, and empathize with those they serve provide more effective services. (Dr. Provence says it was a first experience for many parents to have professional people spend as much time with them as their questions required, and to have their comments responded to as worthy of serious consideration.)
- The incorporation of mental health principles and professionals into every aspect of the program. Dr. Provence believes that while many kinds of support can be provided by a relatively untrained "friendly home visitor," work with a disadvantaged popu-

lation requires training and experience best obtained in the context of psychiatry, clinical social work, or psychology. Mental health skills help the professional to distinguish "between outreach and intrusiveness, between guiding parents and lecturing them, between providing them with the tangible supports they appear to need and enabling them to get these for themselves, between imposing . . . one's own goals for them and helping them to define their goals for themselves."

As to the actual processes responsible for the improved outcomes, the evaluators believe that the changes that occurred in the mother-child relationships, and in the mothers themselves, provide the most reasonable explanation:

- The extensive emotional support given the mothers helped strengthen their children's attachment to them. The mothers' child-rearing competence increased as a result of steady contact with the staff and frequent observation of the staff's child care practices.
- The services and support the mothers received in the program made them feel valued, increased their self-esteem, and "made a great difference in how they saw themselves as parents and as individuals." This in turn helped them achieve greater control over their lives and probably led to the children's improved school performance.
- An increased sense of self-worth may also have allowed the participating mothers to exercise greater control over their childbearing, resulting in their smaller family size. The decision of some of the women, during their firstborn's preschool years, to obtain more education instead of having another child may have been a major factor in the steady rise of so many of these families toward becoming self-supporting.

Yale's Dr. Solnit has described a high-risk environment as one that "tends to complicate rather than facilitate a healthy development, one that uncovers and magnifies the infant's and parents' vulnerabilities rather than providing the built-in support that will enable them to overcome weaknesses or deficits." Dr. Provence's program, he says, demonstrates "how to transform high-risk environments into environments in which the average expectable outcome is progressive development for the baby and the achievement of competence and self-fulfillment for the parents."

THE NURSE COMES TO VISIT IN ELMIRA

Like the New Haven program, the Prenatal/Early Infancy Project (PEIP) in Elmira, New York, provided support to mothers and infants and succeeded in changing their long-term outcomes. The intervention in Elmira consisted of a program of intensive nurse home visiting.

It was a beautiful spring day when I visited Elmira, accompanied by psychologist David Olds, professor of pediatrics at the University of Rochester and organizer of PEIP. Elmira looked a lot less grim, bathed in sunshine, than I had expected on the basis of what I had read. The New York *Times,* in a front-page article on economic disasters around the country, described it as a community "of lost jobs, broken families and fading hope." The *Times* wrote that no other small city in the Northeast provides a more vivid example of how American manufacturing has declined.

The semirural area at the northern end of Appalachia, in which Elmira is located, with a population that is 95 percent white, was rated in the 1980 census as economically the worst-off section of the country. Its rates of confirmed cases of child abuse and neglect were the highest recorded in New York State—exceeding those of some of the nation's worst urban slums.

In this inauspicious setting, a program of home visiting to pregnant women, new mothers, and infants was launched in 1978. Remarkably, over the next four years the nurse visitors succeeded in reducing the incidence of child abuse, neglect, and accidents. They were able to help mothers to obtain various kinds of support during and after pregnancy and to improve the health of participating mothers and babies. The program also resulted in an increase in the number of teenage mothers returning to school and employment, a decrease in the number who became pregnant again, and a reduction in welfare dependency among the participants. The program also took pains to document its achievements by rigorous research.

I had read the research findings and descriptions of the program before my visit. The dry words and numbers came alive as I accompanied nurse Jan Diello on a home visit, met with the original nurse home visitors and with the current staff, and talked at length with David Olds.

The earliest impetus for the program was an outgrowth of Dr. Olds's reservations about a new child health screening program he had been brought to Elmira to evaluate. He considered the proposed program, which consisted of a battery of tests to identify children with defects such as anemia or vision, hearing, dental, or developmental problems, as too limited an intervention. Dr. Olds was fresh from graduate training under Cornell's Urie Bronfenbrenner, intellectual pioneer of the ecological approach to child development, which sees parents as the most important influence on how their children develop and the parent-child relationship, in turn, as the product of a wider environment. Dr. Olds was convinced that health screening by itself could make only a limited contribution to the lives of socially disadvantaged children. He urged that the proposed program, funded by the Appalachian Regional Commission, be substantially expanded.

Following a year of planning with the local health and human services community and the University of Rochester's Department of Pediatrics and Obstetrics/Gynecology, a consensus evolved around the idea that a home visiting service would be the most promising means to protect families with young children from a wide range of risk factors.

The planners decided to recruit and train registered nurses to work with families in their own homes, to help them learn about pregnancy, infant health, and child rearing, to help them obtain support from families, friends, and the health and human services systems in the community, and to provide them with the direct support they otherwise lacked.

Four hundred families participated in the experimental phase. Dr. Olds and his colleagues, wishing to avoid the impression of a program restricted to people who were poor or had serious problems, welcomed into the program any woman in Chemung County pregnant with her first child. But they made special efforts to enroll teenagers and women who were unmarried, unemployed, or on welfare, believing that a comprehensive home visiting program provided a unique opportunity to reach those women at greatest risk of pregnancy complications, yet most reluctant to use traditional health and human services. Eighty percent of participants fell into at least one of these socioeconomic risk categories, and many fell into all of them.

The registered nurses who would make the home visits had received two and a half months of special training, were themselves parents, and were selected in part because they were considered compassionate, sensitive, and mature enough to provide emotional support along with education and nursing care.

During the prenatal period, there were usually about nine home visits, each more than an hour long, during which the nurse

- Tried to help mothers understand how their behavior affects their health and that of their unborn child.
- Helped to prepare them for labor, delivery, and the early care of their newborn.
- Discussed the mother's, or parents', plans for employment, schooling, contraceptive use, and spacing of future children.

After the baby was born, the same nurse, now having a solid relationship, continued helping the mother or parents to understand —and act on their understanding of—the unique characteristics and abilities of their infant, and the infant's nutrition and health needs. Nurse and mother would discuss the importance of responding to the baby's cues and encouraging the baby to enjoy progressively more complex motor, social, and intellectual experiences—all the way from cooing and smiling to sitting, standing, walking, and talking.

The nurses knew they had to be especially alert to the parents' preoccupation with survival problems—what Dr. Olds calls the "unending chain of stressful events" experienced by so many socially disadvantaged women during pregnancy and the first two years of their baby's life. Unemployment, marital conflicts, and difficulties with finances and housing can be strong barriers to converting knowledge about good health practices and child care into action. The nurses worked explicitly on strengthening the women's supports, helping them to establish links with other family members and friends and with community services.

One nurse told of visiting a young couple three months before the baby was due and finding they had not eaten in two days. Quickly revising her plan to discuss the nutritional demands of pregnancy on this visit, the nurse arranged for emergency food relief through a local church and began working with the couple to find a stable source of food and income.

The time devoted to specific subjects varied tremendously from family to family. The nurses emphasized the strengths of the women and their families and tailored the content of visits to individual circumstances. They were able to provide emotional support by listening carefully to parents and helping them to clarify their feelings. Together with parents they identified areas they were handling well. They tried always to be available in times of stress, while encouraging the young mothers and fathers to develop their own problem-solving skills.

The nurses often acted as a bridge between the women and their obstetricians and pediatricians or clinics. They sent the physicians written reports about nutritional inadequacies, health hazards, and emotional and social disturbances, thus helping to assure more informed and sensitive care in the office. They also interpreted and reinforced physicians' recommendations and advice. Dr. Olds says this was a particularly important contribution because office-bound practitioners are often unaware of how the stresses associated with poverty can interfere with good health habits during pregnancy and interact to undermine the family's care of the child.

Program evaluation became a prominent part of the Elmira PEIP. Dr. Olds is convinced that further progress in the prevention of damage among socially disadvantaged families requires rigorous measurement of promising interventions and careful documentation of their effects on low birthweight, child abuse and neglect, and—among school-age mothers—repeat pregnancies, school dropout, and welfare dependency.

Dr. Olds's strong commitment to program evaluation attracted the interest of the Bureau of Community Health Services of the federal Department of Health and Human Services, the Robert Wood Johnson Foundation, and the W. T. Grant Foundation. About the time the PEIP program was getting started, all of them had become interested in whether home visiting programs could improve health and related outcomes among women who were pregnant or mothers of young children. They welcomed the opportunity to support the serious research and evaluation effort that Dr. Olds and his colleagues were proposing. As a result, thirteen university-based researchers were ultimately involved in evaluating the Elmira program.

The Elmira PEIP based its evaluation on the random assignment of participants into control and treatment groups, overcoming the many difficulties of using this method in a human service program. One group received no services through the project except screening. Another received screening as well as transportation to prenatal and well-child care at local clinics and physicians' offices. A third received screening, transportation, and nurse home visits during pregnancy only. The fourth group received the full intervention, with home visits beginning during pregnancy and continuing until the child was two years old.

The results were dramatic.

- Among mothers under the age of seventeen and mothers who smoked, the nurse-visited women had heavier babies and fewer premature babies than their unvisited counterparts.
- Among the women at highest risk, the "visited" had one fifth the verified cases of child abuse and neglect of the "unvisited" during the first two years of their children's lives.
- Among the poor unmarried women, the "visited" returned to school more rapidly after delivery, were employed a greater part of the time, obtained more help with child care, and had fewer pregnancies over the next four years.

In addition, the nurse-visited women were aware of and made better use of community services, talked more frequently with service providers, friends, and relatives about their pregnancy and family life, and reported that the father showed a greater interest in their pregnancy. During pregnancy they had fewer kidney infections, improved their diets and had a more favorable pattern of weight gain, smoked fewer cigarettes, and were less likely to be alone when they came to the hospital to deliver.

The nurse-visited women restricted and punished their infants less frequently and provided more appropriate play materials. Their babies were seen less frequently in the hospital emergency room and had fewer accidents and fewer incidents of swallowing foreign substances. This apparently reflected better supervision and better control of the children's immediate environments.

Despite favorable findings from each new analysis of the data, Dr. Olds cautiously shuns any claim that every aspect of the program's design represents the optimum approach. He is confident, however, that the Elmira experience warrants these conclusions:

First, organized home visiting of very young, poor, or unmarried women before and after the birth of their first child will have high payoffs, measurable in improved functioning of both mother and child and in significant monetary savings.

Second, because pregnancy and infancy are highly labile phases in the life cycle of families, with a strong potential for good as well as harm to both family and child, help during this period is best begun during pregnancy, even if directed towards what happens after birth (such as the prevention of child abuse). Mothers find it easier to accept help when they are going through the profound and sensitive biological, psychological, and social changes produced by pregnancy. Furthermore, Dr. Olds notes, if assistance is offered before the arrival of the first child, at a time when all families have questions and special needs, it is less likely to be interpreted as criticism, as a message that parents have cared for their child poorly.

Convinced of the wisdom of investing in this type of intervention, Dr. Olds is eager to further improve his model. He especially wants to experiment with ways of adapting it to other kinds of populations.

Dr. Olds has already learned what can happen to a successful model program supported by foundations, the federal government, and academic luminaries, when it comes out of its sheltered incubator into the cold world of budget-pinched local services. Home visiting in Elmira today is run by the local health department and funded by Medicaid. The health department—besieged by funding cuts and demands that seemed more urgent—doubled the nurses' caseloads on the day it took over the program.

The original nurses resented the pressure to shorten their visits and to drop families from the program when the babies were only four months old. They suddenly found themselves in an environment in which their work seemed less valued and felt that they couldn't give their clients the kind of support they required. Within months of the program's conversion from demonstration project to mainstream operation, all the original nurses had resigned. Their replacements are competent and committed nurses but are aware that they are no longer able to provide the same intensive care their predecessors did.

Jan Diello, the nurse who took me with her for a home visit, says there just isn't time. On this visit, she showed her seventeen-year-old client, Debbie, who except for the worried frown on her face looked more like a high school cheerleader than a mother, how to use a rectal thermometer. Having demonstrated the use of the thermometer and given Debbie a chance to try it, Ms. Diello told her under what circumstances to phone the doctor. She carefully explained how high a temperature required the doctor's attention and what other symptoms to look for and report. Finally, she emphasized that it was much better to phone the doctor than to take the baby to the emergency room.

After we had left, I asked Ms. Diello if there was a telephone in Debbie's apartment. It turned out that there was none, nor any in the building. Ms. Diello was quick to acknowledge that the practical problem of how to phone the doctor should have been addressed. "But we can't take the time to go into that sort of thing," she said. "We just don't have that luxury anymore."

She responded similarly when I expressed surprise that on this visit she had learned for the first time that Debbie's father, who lives in Florida, had been found, three months earlier, to have cancer, and that Debbie was vaguely considering going to see him instead of starting back to school as she had planned. Conversations about how Debbie felt about her father's illness and her responsibilities to him, and how that might affect her plans for completing high school, were also casualties, it seemed, of the doubled caseload and brisker climate in which the nurses now worked.

There is no way to know for sure (there being no money in the current budget for evaluation) whether the exchanges that no longer happen are indeed luxuries that can be dispensed with without affecting outcomes, or whether they are the subtle but essential stuff of which support of vulnerable families is made. The nurses who worked in the original program believe that their experience and much research supports the view that the watered-down program is far less effective. They explain that that's why they are no longer with PEIP.

High-Risk Families Need High-Intensity Services

The most striking fact about the programs that have accomplished the seeming miracle of helping high-risk families to change the conditions in which their children grow up is how much these successful programs have in common.

All of them offer services that are comprehensive and intensive. All have highly professional staffs (some of whom work closely with paraprofessionals). All use insights and skills from psychiatry and child development in working with families to establish an atmosphere of trust and confidence.

The lessons from Tacoma, New Haven, and Elmira are virtually identical to those that come from programs that support families in entirely different circumstances and under different auspices in Maine, Maryland, Seattle, Brooklyn, and Chicago:

- A Maine Department of Human Services official observes, "The families we're working with are so alienated, so put off by their experiences of trying to obtain help from agencies and institutions that could only deal with a piece of their troubles, that it wasn't until we were able to provide intensive family-centered services that we were able to help some of those families learn a new skill, like better ways to discipline their children."

- Psychiatrist Stanley Greenspan, who works with families whose infants are in jeopardy of abuse, neglect, or stunted development, finds that the mothers tend to be under great stress, isolated, and depressed, with few personal, economic, and social resources; many are suspicious of offers of help and idiosyncratic in their styles of receiving information. That is why the therapists in his program persist, even if it takes several visits before a leery mother opens the door, and why the "treatment" itself may take place on the way to the supermarket or at the laundromat.

- Nurse researcher Kathryn Barnard, who works in Seattle with pregnant women and young mothers with virtually no other source of social support, describes her clients as "psychologically unavailable" for help offered on traditional terms. She believes that much of the success of her program can be attributed to the enormous amounts of time and effort that the trained nursing staff are able to invest in developing a relationship with their clients.

- Sister Mary Paul, who works day and night to serve the most seriously troubled families in the decaying Sunset Park section of Brooklyn, says that only individual needs—not professional preferences or bureaucratic dictates—can be allowed to determine the nature of an agency's services to a family. She says that in her program no staff member is ever put in the position of denying help to a family on bureaucratic grounds or of having to justify to a cost accountant the time they take to develop a relationship, because help to hurting families is not likely to be effective in the absence of a relationship of trust—which takes time and skill to build.

· In Chicago, the Ounce of Prevention, a partnership between the State of Illinois and visionary Chicago businessman-philanthropist Irving R. Harris, decided to "take the best of what we've learned" from running forty family support programs over a period of five years "and put it all in a very concentrated program." Named the Beethoven Project for the Beethoven elementary school which the children it serves will be attending, the program has been called "a Marshall Plan for preschoolers." With funding help from the U.S. Department of Health and Human Services, and under the sponsorship of the Chicago Urban League, the project is putting together virtually every kind of service needed by pregnant women, young mothers, and children between birth and school entry, and making them available right on the premises of the housing project where these families live. The services include full prenatal care, home visiting, help with nutrition, counseling, and support to raise the chances of a healthy birth, to enable the young mothers to complete school and get job training, and at the same time to equip them to help their babies develop socially, cognitively, and psychologically, so they will be fully prepared for school entry. Gina McLaughlin, the project director, says the program will work because "it is so comprehensive and so intense" and because it will operate on so many levels at once—just as poverty does.

The convergence is amazing. People with experience in providing effective help to seriously disadvantaged families all agree: Services for families at greatest risk work if they are comprehensive and intensive enough to respond to the full range of their needs, and if they are prepared to provide help as concrete as a ride to the hospital or a box of diapers and as subtle as trust and understanding.

These conclusions, powerfully supported by a wealth of evidence, are constantly "discovered" anew. They are not acted upon on a large scale for several reasons.

First, interventions with multiple components, applied selectively in response to individual needs, are costly. Proof of cost-effectiveness becomes essential, but effectiveness is hard to measure and document in complex programs aiming at long-term gains.

Second, the process of applying a wide array of services on a flexible and individualized basis runs counter to the traditions of many of the helping professions and the requirements of most bureaucracies. Helping a seriously disrupted family requires professional expertise to distinguish between providing support and creating dependency, while also utilizing skills not reserved exclusively to professionals—from displaying personal warmth to helping a mother clean house. This mix of highly professional skills and a willingness to provide very practical help requires a redefinition of what is considered "professional," which is not easy for the professionals themselves nor for policy analysts, administrators, and policymakers.

In Chapter 10 I shall describe ways of surmounting these and other impediments to widespread replication of efforts like the Yale, Tacoma, and Elmira programs. Here it is enough to note that the evidence is now overwhelming: Programs that succeed in helping the children and families who live in the shadows are intensive, comprehensive, flexible, and staffed by professionals with the time and skills to establish solid relationships with their clients. Intensive medical care for fragile newborn or aged patients who are barely clinging to life, costly though it may be, encounters no general resistance. Intensive care for fragile families requires similar support.

The Care and Education
of Young Children:
Inseparable Combination

The nation's provisions for the care and education of children under five cannot long survive in their present neglected and chaotic state. New arrangements will emerge, sooner or later, from the turbulence generated by the massive social changes that have occurred so rapidly as to have outstripped the capacity of the country's institutions to respond.

The most important of these changes:

· The majority of women with children under five work—some in quest of a fuller life, many more to maintain their foothold in the middle class. More frequent family breakup is also a factor, by leaving many more divorced and abandoned women as the sole source of support of their children.

- The number of unmarried teenagers with babies who need to complete their education and become prepared to enter the job market continues to rise.
- The consensus around the view that welfare recipients with young children should be employed or in training is rapidly growing stronger.

The absence of reliable and affordable child care imposes a heavy —and unnecessary—burden on all these families and interferes with the realization of both personal and public purposes.

In danger of being overlooked in the search for better answers to these pressing needs are the lessons of two decades of dazzling successes in providing care and education for disadvantaged preschool children. In danger of going unmet are the special needs of disadvantaged children.

Simultaneously with the explosion in the need for child care, the public policy world was learning of the enormous importance for long-term outcomes of giving disadvantaged children the best possible start in school. It was learning, too, that this objective could be achieved—by providing children with preschool experiences that would improve their health and their competence and by offering support to their families. These lessons are currently in danger of being forgotten amid the preoccupation with improving child care and preschool arrangements for other purposes and other populations. This *despite the fact that there is no inherent conflict but rather a basic congruence of interest among all the groups seeking a more rational child care policy for the nation.*

We will return, at the end of this chapter, to consider the implications of the current state of knowledge for future policy development. But let us first examine the special preschool care and education needs of disadvantaged children, the success of Head Start, the confusion about where day care ends and preschool education begins, and the turf conflicts among schools, childhood development programs, family day care providers, and commercial child care interests. I urge the reader to bear in mind throughout two organizing themes:

1. In the period between womb and school, one cannot care for children without educating them, and one cannot educate them without caring for them.

2. Whatever provisions are made by the nation, the states, or localities to increase access to a more orderly and higher-quality

system of child care and preschool education, it is children of disadvantaged families who have both the most to lose and the most to gain.

THE LINKS BETWEEN BEING WELL PREPARED FOR SCHOOL AND LATER OUTCOMES

The experiences that prepare most children in well-functioning families intellectually and socially for school begin in early infancy. Long before a child can reason, his daily experiences ("When I cry, she will come . . . when I hear the water running, I will be bathed") are teaching him that the world is safe and predictable, that human beings can be relied upon. The same experiences are simultaneously helping him to master the fundamentals of time and space, now and later, cause and effect.

Children surrounded by chaos, defeat, unpredictability, and despair are less likely to learn the rules of an orderly universe, to develop logical reasoning skills, or to believe in their own efficacy. In homes where economic and social stresses are high and parental education low, children are less likely to have conversations with adults of a kind and frequency that stimulate the development of language and logical reasoning.

Already by the age of two or three, children in families of low socioeconomic status often lag measurably behind their middle-class counterparts in the ability to reason and use language.

The ways in which these theories play out in the daily lives of small children, are illustrated by the stories of Aja in Washington, D.C., and of the Rossis in Boston.

On a sweltering summer afternoon, two-year-old Aja was perched on the edge of the lap of her great-grandmother, Edna Adams, in the shade of the front porch. A visitor had come to interview Mrs. Adams and her husband about the childhood of their grandson, recently convicted of a brutal murder.

Aja was playing with a large metal cup, quietly at first. When she discovered she could use the cup to produce interesting noises, she repeatedly banged it against the chair. Mrs. Adams snapped at her several times to "shet up." Aja's mother arrived, bringing a Popsicle, which she handed to Mrs. Adams to give to the child. Mrs. Adams unwrapped the Popsicle, and then seemed to forget about it. Aja, tantalized by the treat just out of her reach, began to cry. Annoyed, Mrs.

Adams handed the child to her husband. As the child's cries became increasingly vigorous, Mrs. Adams recalled the thawing Popsicle, and handed it to Aja. The tears vanished instantly as Aja began to lick the Popsicle—and to drip it on her nightgown and bare legs. Mrs. Adams' attention was attracted once more when the last chunk of Popsicle fell to the ground. In a rising voice she told the child that she was "a mess," that she was "disgusting," and that it was stupid to have given her a Popsicle in the first place. The diatribe ended with the words, "God love you," delivered in a tone that struck the visitor as more threatening than reassuring.

The Rossis lived in a North Boston slum. Mrs. Rossi, at twenty-five, was the mother of seven children. Mr. Rossi was in and out of work, in and out of prison, and in and out of fatherhood. He had abandoned his family during each pregnancy, but had always eventually returned. Mrs. Rossi, despite her own background of neglect and deprivation, managed somehow to meet many of the needs of her children, including those of her congenitally handicapped fourth child.

Mrs. Rossi's relationship with her children was primarily nonverbal. When they were infants she carried them about a great deal, and communicated her love through feeding, smiling, and occasional patting. With the first baby, she had been frightened, but loving and tender. When the second arrived, her interest shifted to the newcomer. This pattern repeated itself with the third and fourth, as though each baby, when small, were a part of herself, a part she could love. But with each additional child her reservoir of energy ebbed. When the fifth was born, Mrs. Rossi's interest in her children seemed to reach a cutoff point, and the last three children were virtually isolated from the family.

We know enough to predict that in the absence of intervention neither the Adams nor the Rossi children are likely to go far, during their preschool years, in developing the language skills, social competence, self-confidence, and ways of thinking that would help them discover how the world works. They would have a hard time developing the confidence that they could affect what happens to them. Yet these are among the attributes that help in the mastery of school tasks. "A culture of literacy is a precondition for learning how to read and write . . . for starting school not as aliens to the mores, materials, expectations and themes of academic life, but as natives to that culture," says Dr. James Garbarino of Chicago's Erikson Institute. Without outside help, seriously disadvantaged children usually miss the kind of experiences in the preschool period that promote a bright school future.

No one knows how many children share the crippling early experiences of Aja and the Rossi children. What is known is that when lower-class children enter school, they are much less likely than middle-class children to believe in their own power, command rich language, and be confident of success and motivated to gain the teacher's approval.

Much of the evidence linking long-term damage to early school difficulties has emerged since the mid-1970s, but in the early 1960s there was already a considerable awareness of sharp socioeconomic disparities in preschoolers' ability to benefit from schooling and a suspicion that many poor children carried handicaps already at the time of school entry that could substantially diminish their life chances.

In that period many notable experiments, demonstrations, and studies were launched, which sought to modify preschool environments of poor and minority children and to reduce the disparities between these children and their more advantaged counterparts. Some projects focused primarily on raising IQ scores, some on inculcating specific learning skills, some on improving social competence and home environment, and some on all of the above.

These pioneering experiments were the forerunners of the preschool programs now widely recognized as the most successful large-scale attempts in the last quarter century to improve the prospects for high-risk children.

As we will see, preschool programs have succeeded directly in reducing the incidence of many serious adverse outcomes and in preventing or ameliorating the effects of risk factors such as early school difficulties, failure to acquire basic skills (reading, writing, arithmetic), low self-esteem, alienation, a weak sense of efficacy, and chronic truancy. Good preschool programs affect parents' experience and expectations, as well as children's school performance and self-perception. Good preschool programs, in fostering a child's disposition to learn—to question, listen, and persevere—can end up actually starting an upward spiral of motivation.

HEAD START: EARLY DREAMS, LONG-TERM TRIUMPHS

Within a few short months in early 1965, preschool education for disadvantaged children exploded from a handful of experiments into a nationwide crusade. Project Head Start provided preschool children and their families with education, health, and social services on a scale unprecedented in American history. Its creators, though thrilled by its potential, were soberly aware it would be no panacea. This did not keep some of its supporters, including the President of the United States, from seeing Head Start as mighty enough in itself to protect children against the cumulative effects of serious deprivation.

Thus President Lyndon B. Johnson proclaimed on May 18, 1965, that the educational, health, and social services to be provided that summer to half a million poor children through Head Start could "make certain that poverty's children would not be forevermore poverty's captives." Expansively he predicted that "this program, this year means that 30 million man-years—the combined lifespan of [the participating] youngsters—will be spent productively and rewardingly, rather than wasted in tax-supported institutions or in welfare-supported lethargy."

Such grandiose expectations seemed unrealistic even then to many of the program's planners, as they stood in the White House Rose Garden listening to the onetime schoolteacher giving voice to his dreams in rhetoric that seemed more a reflection of wishful thinking than of political scheming.

However unrealistic the President's vision, Head Start soared on the wings of his enthusiasm and that of the First Lady. Lady Bird Johnson, who became honorary chairman of Head Start, was not new to child care issues. A year earlier, over tea with Cornell Professor Urie Bronfenbrenner, Mrs. Johnson had listened with fascination to accounts of highly valued child care programs abroad. She had also visited the pioneering preschool program established in 1961 in four Harlem public schools under the auspices of New York University—one of the forerunners of Head Start.

By midsummer of 1965, Head Start was helping half a million poor children and their families—in some measure—to overcome physical, intellectual, and social impediments to a successful start at school. More than twenty-five hundred communities had been cajoled and encouraged to enlist, almost overnight, and to provide these children with an unprecedented package of services.

In retrospect one can see how Head Start became such an important component of the War on Poverty. The personal experiences of a few key individuals had fortuitously converged with evolving theories of child development and new empirical research findings in a new climate of confidence in the possibilities of social change.

Head Start, now hailed as one of the most successful legacies of the War on Poverty, was not, in fact, a part of its original design. The original antipoverty proposal, mainly the product of a group of socially conscious economists, emphasized economic development, job creation, and training, especially for teenagers and young adults. That was the plan awaiting presidential approval in November 1963, when Lyndon Johnson succeeded the slain John Kennedy. Only two days in office, President Johnson met with Dr. Walter Heller, chairman of the Council of Economic Advisers and told him to move full speed ahead on the pending antipoverty program—it was his kind of program, he said.

In February 1964 President Johnson asked R. Sargent Shriver, the late President's brother-in-law and flamboyantly successful founding director of the Peace Corps, to take charge of planning the War on Poverty. Shriver recalls that it took several months for him to realize that more than half of the poor were children and to start thinking about this fact in programmatic terms. He recalled that the Kennedy Foundation (in which he had long been active and of which his wife, Eunice Kennedy Shriver, was executive vice president), had funded studies showing that early intervention with high-risk children and their families could raise IQ scores and that good nutrition early in life could affect mental development. As president of the Chicago Board of Education he had become aware that "the cards are stacked against kids in the slums in a huge number of ways," but that their life chances could be radically improved by preschool exposure to "books, teachers, desks, pencils, chalk and school buildings," along with proper food, immunizations, and medical exams to uncover hearing and vision problems and other impediments to learning.

Shriver discussed with friends and colleagues the idea of a massive new effort to help preschool children. Always anxious to anticipate potential opposition from Washington cynics, he tried the idea out on journalist-curmudgeon Joseph Alsop. "To my surprise,"

Shriver recalls, "Joe thought it was a great idea." He concluded, quite correctly as it turned out, that certain kinds of help for poor children appeal even to conservative skeptics.

Shriver proceeded to consult several eminent child development experts, most of whom responded enthusiastically. They cited a growing body of evidence that intellectual ability was more malleable than previously thought, that development was heavily influenced by a child's environment, that infants and young children reared in adverse circumstances frequently suffered serious developmental attrition, that early childhood was a critical period for intervention, and that interventions to stimulate the development of poor children seemed to have significant effects.

In the light of this evidence, the heavy emphasis in the proposed antipoverty legislation on helping sixteen-to-twenty-two-year-olds to become economically productive struck many child development experts as shortsighted. Dr. Urie Bronfenbrenner argued in congressional hearings in 1964 that for the same money a program directed at preschoolers would accomplish more. He urged broadening the antipoverty bill to earmark money to strike "at poverty where it hits first and most damagingly—in early childhood."

Although money for early childhood programs was not earmarked by Congress until five years later, within a few months a program would be under way far larger than Dr. Bronfenbrenner had dreamed of.

In October 1964 Shriver—now operating from an abandoned hotel on Fifteenth Street in downtown Washington, surrounded by a bright, energetic staff, which included volunteers from private life and government workers borrowed from more traditional agencies —called for a memorandum on what a preschool program might look like. The first proposal, prepared by Polly Greenberg, an early childhood education specialist on loan from the Office of Education, was considered at an OEO staff meeting in November. (I was invited to the meeting by the Deputy Director of the OEO Community Action Program Staff, who was about to hire me to take charge of health activities of the community action program but hoped to entice me to first spend six months helping develop the new early childhood project.)

The question up for discussion was whether it would be possible, in the seven months remaining before school ended for the summer, to enroll ten to twenty-five thousand poor children in a program still on the drawing boards. A few said it was unrealistic to undertake such a massive social program without more extensive planning and experimentation, and that a summer's worth of intervention was hardly worth the effort and the risk of failure. But the majority, eager to seize the opportunity for a major federal effort to better prepare poor children for school, were cheerfully ready to help "Sarge" mount a national program, come summertime, for several thousand—or several hundred thousand—children.

Shriver was not blind to the limited results that could be expected in one summer nor to the risks of starting with a very large number of children. Harvard professor of psychology Jerome Bruner had cautioned him not to aim for more than twenty-five hundred children during the first year. Shriver recalls being discouraged by his conversation with Dr. Bruner but deciding to go "charging ahead" anyway. He was convinced of the importance of signaling that the War on Poverty would not be fought with just a handful of model programs. He also felt that his best chance to launch the program on a massive scale would be during the summer, when school buildings were empty and teachers on vacation. He resolved "to write Head Start across the face of this nation so that no Congress and no President can ever destroy it."

Early in January 1965, Shriver asked Dr. Robert E. Cooke, the Shriver family's pediatrician and chief of pediatrics at Johns Hopkins University Hospital, to assemble an interdisciplinary group of recognized professionals who would, within six weeks, formulate the outlines of a preschool program. To its everlasting credit, the committee recognized its unique opportunity, acted boldly and came up with a program of unprecedented breadth.

Several committee members maintained from the outset that to have the desired impact, the program had to be comprehensive. Others saw a comprehensive program as essential to encompass the diverse purposes and outlooks among the planners. Some on the committee started with the idea that disadvantaged children simply needed to be taught certain cognitive academic skills to put them on an equal footing with more fortunate first-graders. Several developmental psychologists, led by Dr. Edward Zigler of Yale, called this approach too narrow. They pressed for a program that would motivate children and help them to acquire social competence and the know-how to succeed in the classroom, a program that would let the children experience success in mastering new tasks and would teach them not only letters and numbers, but concepts and relation-ships.

Some held that more fundamental to school success than any of these were health, nutrition, and social services to ameliorate the educational handicaps that arise from urban poverty. Still others put emphasis on getting parents involved to improve the home and community environment of children and to help them upgrade their own economic prospects.

Wrapped together in the proposal the committee submitted to Shriver were all these elements. The committee also recommended unusual flexibility in implementation for reasons both practical and philosophical. To work, the program had to reflect the enormous diversity of American communities. Its projected size and rapid expansion militated against detailed uniform rules and require-ments. Dr. Zigler later recalled that the committee realized it lacked "the time, the knowledge or the human resources with which to create the ideal program," and therefore agreed on a few firm fed-eral requirements, leaving the rest to local initiative. National head-quarters would sound a federal theme, to be enriched by an infinite variety of local variations.

To direct this ambitious enterprise, Shriver sought out the noted pediatrician (who subsequently became Surgeon General of the United States) Julius B. Richmond. When he got Shriver's call in January 1965, Dr. Richmond was chief of pediatrics at the State University of New York at Syracuse and about to become dean of its medical school. Supersalesman Shriver was not deterred. On a snowy Sunday at Shriver's suburban Maryland home, Dr. Rich-mond recalls, Shriver told him that his long experience in develop-ing programs for disadvantaged children and in advocating their large-scale implementation made him uniquely suited to direct Head Start. Even more compelling was Shriver's argument "that this was my chance to make some of my dreams come true." Less than four weeks later, Dr. Richmond was at work in Washington.

Looking back, Dr. Richmond considers that the most important decision he made in the initial days was to set the teacher/child ratio. I remember how much weight he attached to that decision at the time. Learning with alarm that a ratio of one adult to thirty children was under consideration, he insisted on at least one quali-fied teacher and two aides for every fifteen children. He later said, "I didn't know whether with one teacher and two aides per fifteen children the program would succeed, but I did know that with one teacher to thirty children it would surely fail."

Project Head Start was formally announced with great fanfare by President Johnson at the White House in May, but word had gone out to the nation's poor communities well in advance. Shriver had ordered that every public health commissioner, school superintendent, and welfare director in the country be personally notified of the availability of funds to provide poor preschool children with early education as well as immunizations, medical checkups, hot meals, and social services. It was left to the ingenuity of the hastily assembled staff, still quartered in the ramshackle hotel, many in bathrooms with boarded-over tubs for desks, to issue the notification nationwide using the single available typewriter and the one telephone they all shared.

Head Start's Associate Director, Jule Sugarman, former vice chairman of the Civil Service Commission and an imaginative administrator, was worried that without specific outreach efforts, most of the Head Start money would flow to the more affluent communities which would be better equipped to develop grant proposals. Determined that the nation's neediest children not be left out, he acted to target Head Start resources on the three hundred poorest counties in the nation. He enlisted a group of prominent women—many of them wives of Congressmen and other officials—to spend days, and sometimes nights, on the telephone, locating the leaders of interested community organizations, church groups, and adventurous school boards in these counties.

Leading the volunteers, all of whom had impressive previous records of accomplishment, were Lindy Boggs, the wife of House Democratic Whip Hale Boggs (later to succeed him in representing Louisiana's Second Congressional District); Sherri Henry, the wife of Federal Communications Commissioner William Henry; and Miriam Bazelon, the wife of Federal Appeals Court Judge David L. Bazelon.

To supplement the work of the volunteers in Washington, 125 federal interns pledged to devote four long weekends that spring, going out into the field. The interns were trained to assist local community leaders in developing programs that would meet federal Head Start guidelines. (These included racial integration, specified adult-child ratios, standards of professional, parental, and community involvement, and mobilization of health, nutrition, and social services.) In March and April the interns would arrive at OEO headquarters on Thursday afternoon and receive a manila folder containing a plane ticket, blank Head Start applications, and all the information and leads the "Wives" and the staff had been able to compile from Washington about a handful of geographically clustered impoverished communities. On Sunday nights, after three strenuous days and often sleepless nights, they returned to Washington, manila folders now grubby but filled with completed applications.

"The selling of Head Start," recalls Sugarman, "exceeded all expectations and created a major crisis." Three thousand applications had to be processed within a few weeks. Funds, training materials, and technical assistance had to be delivered to more than twenty-five hundred communities. Demands on the staff grew so rapidly that, as one story had it, a young messenger delivering a package was asked if he could type and was immediately put to work. The overwhelming response from communities around the country could have resulted in disaster had Richmond, Sugarman, and their colleagues not been able to elicit an equally massive response from the nation's pediatricians, child development specialists, clergy, teachers, social workers, and other professionals. Sugarman remembers with wonderment how that spring and summer "more than 500 professionals totally disrupted their professional lives to do what had to be done, traveling to every type of community, working unbelievable hours, tearing apart their own summer class schedules and giving up vacations—all because they believed in what was happening."

As the brief summer programs were getting under way in the heady mid-1965 atmosphere, proposals for full-year Head Start programs were already coming in for review and funding. In 1966 nearly two hundred thousand children were participating in year-round programs and nearly six hundred thousand in summer programs. By 1970 the majority of Head Start children were in full-year programs. Federal Head Start appropriations continued to grow over the next decade and have hovered around one billion dollars annually since 1984.

Shriver's wish had been rapidly realized—Head Start was so deeply embedded in the American landscape that no administration could uproot it or even significantly cut it back. Head Start parents and citizens' groups formed effective lobbies to keep Head Start going and growing. It is true that by the mid-1980s Head Start was still serving less than one fifth of potentially eligible children, and that while enrollment increased by 97 percent between 1970 and 1985, federal funding (in constant dollars) increased by only 19 percent. Nevertheless, its popularity shielded it at least partially from the Reagan Administration's assault on domestic programs. This is particularly noteworthy because it contradicts the conventional wisdom that programs targeted on the disadvantaged lack a constituency broad enough to survive political adversity.

In retrospect, Head Start's success stems in large part from its founders' courageous insistence on setting multiple goals—which ultimately brought both programmatic and political payoffs.

The diverse constituency for Head Start included those who believed it would raise poor children's IQs along with those who were skeptical on that score but anxious to see more poor children fully immunized before starting school. It appealed to those who thought slum children needed more structure in their lives as well as those who sought ways of involving, training, and employing low-income parents who had never had a say about how community institutions dealt with them and their children. Some scholars and citizens liked Head Start because it promised to compensate for poor children's initial disadvantage in school; others liked it because it promised to build on the strengths of children and families long treated as though they were devoid of strength.

This melange of purposes and rationales did not undermine Head Start's effectiveness, nor its continuing popularity. It did, however, interfere with its getting high marks on its initial outside national evaluation in 1969. Focusing primarily on changes in IQ as the outcome most easily measured, researchers from the Westinghouse Learning Corporation reported that after a few years in elementary school, the cognitive gains made by Head Start children were often lost.

Subsequent evaluations took a broader look and told a different story.

The long-term effects of Head Start and other preschool programs on participating children and families are today better documented than any of the other interventions considered in this book. Preschool programs have attracted the attention of many more researchers than most other forms of intervention, perhaps because child development academics were so heavily involved in initiating

Head Start, because the Head Start leadership stimulated the interest of outstanding researchers, or because the early optimism surrounding the effects of preschool interventions encouraged investment by public and private agencies in evaluation and research.

We now know that the education, health, nutrition, and social services and parent support provided by these programs have prevented or ameliorated many of the educational handicaps associated with growing up in poverty. We now know that children who have attended quality early childhood programs develop social and academic competencies later manifested in increased school success. They "enter school healthier, better fed and with parents who are better equipped to support their educational development."

The basic Head Start model has proved to be sound. When three to five-year-old children are systematically helped to think, reason, and speak clearly; when they are provided hot meals, social services, health evaluations, and health care; when families become partners in their children's learning experiences, are helped toward self-sufficiency, and gain greater confidence in themselves as parents and as contributing members of the community, the results are measurable and dramatic.

EFFECTS OF EARLY PRESCHOOL PROGRAMS

The early models for Project Head Start are the same programs that now provide the most definitive information about the powerful real-world impact of preschool intervention. The three programs described here all began in the early 1960s, under widely different conditions, but sharing many elements of philosophy and program design. Remarkably, all were able to collect information about participating and comparison children until they were eighteen to twenty-one years old. They tell a dramatic and strikingly consistent story of long-term impact.

The Early Training Project. This Tennessee program, created by Dr. Susan Gray, is the one Sargent Shriver remembered because it began with Kennedy Foundation support in 1962. Local school officials in Murfreesboro, a town of 20,000 in central Tennessee, had become concerned over the "progressive retardation" observed in the still-segregated elementary school serving low-income black children, and had approached Peabody Teachers College in nearby Nashville for help.

Dr. Gray, a psychologist and highly regarded childhood educator, and several colleagues at Peabody set out to design an intervention that would address what they judged, after years of study, to be the most important causes of school failure among disadvantaged children.

The project had the use of a new, well-designed school building with spacious playgrounds for ten weeks during three summers. Here groups of twenty children, aged three to five, were taught, hugged, supervised, and encouraged by two experienced teachers and eight assistant teachers. The staff was chosen with an eye to giving the children role models they could identify with, and the program was geared to stimulating acquisition of language, concepts, motivation to achieve, persistence, and interest in school activities.

During the fall, winter, and spring, home visitors— "mature black women with experience in early education and in group work"—visited the families of these children weekly. They brought materials and ideas for activities involving both mother and child. In early spring, for example, the mother, child, and home visitor together found daffodils and measured their growing leaves. The visits were carefully planned to enlist "the mother's concerns to become herself the teacher of her child."

The Perry Preschool Program. This program, begun in 1962 in Ypsilanti, Michigan, is possibly the most famous early preschool experiment because of its extensive, well-publicized follow-up studies and reports. David P. Weikart, who has presided over the dissemination and follow-up efforts for more than twenty years, was also the originator of the program. Working in the Ypsilanti schools as a psychologist, he was impressed with the concern of the black community in Ypsilanti to reduce the high number of school dropouts and frustrated in his efforts to persuade the schools to respond to the special needs of disadvantaged children. He concluded that the best way to improve their chances of success in the school system was through better preparation for school.

With support from the Carnegie Corporation of New York, he recruited three- and four-year-old children from low-income black families living on the south side of Ypsilanti, "one of the worst-congested slum areas in the State of Michigan." Participating children were randomly assigned either to the experimental or the control group; all had family incomes below the poverty line, none had organic handicaps, and their IQs were between 60 and 90. Almost half the children lived in single-parent homes, and fewer than 20 percent of the parents had completed high school.

The daily two-and-a-half-hour organized educational program extended over two school years, with a ratio of one adult for every five or six children. Teachers also made home visits to every mother and child for one and a half hours each week. The program was designed to help children acquire the intellectual and social strengths they would need in school, with a focus on learning directly from concrete experience and its expression in language. The children were encouraged to plan some of their own activities each day; teachers helped them to think through and talk about their plans.

The IDS Harlem Project. In Central and East Harlem, a tougher neighborhood than Ypsilanti, Martin and Cynthia Deutsch of the Institute for Developmental Studies (IDS) of New York University established in 1963, also with Carnegie support, an enrichment program for preschoolers.

The 750 participants came from poor families living in crowded and unsafe housing, in areas with a high incidence of drug addiction, low employment, inadequate income, and poor health facilities. The sponsors found widespread community awareness of children's unmet educational needs and a desire for increased community participation in schools. They reported finding support for the effort to establish "a mutually reinforcing cycle of school, community and family structures . . . to provide children the opportunity to acquire essential concepts and skills in a consistently supportive environment."

Special classes were set up for four-year-olds in neighborhood schools in Central and East Harlem. Each class of seventeen preschoolers had one certified teacher and a specially trained teacher's aide. Their techniques, highly innovative at the time included tape recorders, "talking typewriters," and telephones—all designed "to help children master basic academic skills and become independent learners." Special games to build language and cognitive skills were devised that could be used by individual children working at their own pace to help them experience a sense of mastery and success.

Staff members, finding that the youngsters often arrived at school lethargic and listless because they were hungry, initiated what may have been the first school-based breakfast program of the 1960s. The project also encouraged parents to read frequently with their children. Parents were actively involved through a center that worked with them on their own needs and on their relationship to the community and the schools.

Unlike other early programs that ended when the children started school, the IDS Harlem Project maintained enriched classes for participating children and continued to work with them and their families until the children had completed the third grade.

Evidence of consistent impact into adulthood. As word spread of the long-term effects of these and similar programs, the results seemed so extraordinary that they were initially greeted with some doubt. Eventually, the uniformity of the conclusions convinced even hardened skeptics that they could not be explained away by peculiarities of research design, small samples, or good luck.

Follow-up of participants in the Early Training Project to age twenty-one found that the rate of high school dropouts was one third higher in the control group and that children in the control group were placed in special education classes at six times the rate of program children.

In the Perry Preschool Program, at the age of nineteen, twice as many program participants as control children were employed, attending college, or receiving further training. Their high school graduation rate was one third higher, their arrest rates 40 percent lower, and their teen pregnancy rates 42 percent lower.

Equally astounding results came out of the IDS Harlem project. When participants reached the age of twenty-one, compared to a randomly assigned control group, twice as many were employed, one third more had obtained high school or equivalency diplomas, and 30 percent more had gone on to college or vocational training.

Any doubts about the significance of what these individual projects were finding were soon dispelled. Several university groups joined to analyze the combined results of all the large-scale research studies of preschool education for the disadvantaged conducted in the 1960s. In the most extensive investigation ever undertaken of the long-term effects of preschool education, the Consortium for Longitudinal Studies invited participation from programs that used a specific curriculum, were completed before 1969, and included an original sample of more than one hundred children.

The consortium found, as many earlier assessments had, that preschool education for disadvantaged children raised IQ and achievement test scores in both math and reading in the early school years but that most of these gains later disappeared, usually by third or fourth grade. But with data on later ages, the consortium found enduring positive effects on real-world performance.

The most striking and consistent findings were the effects on school competence. Significantly fewer children from preschool programs were kept back in grade, and only 30 percent failed to meet school requirements, compared to 45 percent of the nonprogram children. The effect on grade retention and special education placement, which increased throughout the elementary and junior high school years, has important consequences. Youngsters who never have to repeat a grade and are not in special placement are more likely to stay in school and to go on to be employed and are less likely to go to prison or become dependent on public assistance. Alumni of preschool programs also expressed greater pride than the comparison group in accomplishments related to school or work—another measure related to a greater likelihood of being employed and completing school.

These findings clearly show, said IDS founder Dr. Martin Deutsch, that "if you offer a child enough opportunity, something can happen." That goes even for youngsters who "come from areas with (extremely) high dropout and failure rates."

Perry Preschool founder David Weikart observed that what used to be dismissed as rhetoric is now documented fact: "Early childhood education has a lasting impact on adult life," and the benefits to society in reduced costs of remedial education, increased earnings, decreased welfare payments, and less crime are demonstrable in hard economic analysis.

Striking the same note, the 1985 report of the prestigious corporate Committee for Economic Development, reviewing the findings on preschool education, called it "an extraordinary economic buy," adding, "It would be hard to imagine that society could find a higher yield for a dollar of investment than that found in preschool programs for its at-risk children."

That conclusion was echoed in a 1986 conference on early childhood intervention sponsored by the National Governors' Association. Governor Martha Layne Collins of Kentucky summed up: "Early childhood programs cost money—sometimes a lot of it. But crime costs more."

Evidence of the enduring effects of preschool interventions began seeping into public consciousness in the early 1980s. In a different political climate, such knowledge might have spurred a massive effort to provide Head Start–type services for all the nation's disadvantaged youngsters. The bad news was that this didn't happen, that appropriations did not keep up with the increases in the number of children served, and that there were indications of deteriorating quality. But the good news was that the spreading awareness of the value of preschool programs had been instrumental in protecting Head Start from the devastating cutbacks imposed by the Reagan Administration on most other federally supported programs serving the poor.

In fact, the number of children enrolled continued to increase, and in 1985 Head Start was serving four hundred fifty thousand children. Its program goals are strikingly similar to those established in that first tumultuous summer of 1965.

HEAD START TODAY

To see an example of how the program whose birth pangs I had witnessed was faring now, I went to nearby Fairfax County, Virginia, which I had heard had a thriving Head Start program, with some centers operated by the school system and others in churches and other community settings.

The County's Head Start coordinator, Sharon Glynne, had agreed to be my guide. I found her at the County Department of Community Action in Fairfax.

Ms. Glynne had once been an elementary school teacher, but had stayed home for several years with her own small children. During that time she had become increasingly interested in preschool education. She started a preschool program in her church, obtained some training in child development, and soon became attracted to a school-based Head Start program—in part because of its splendid facilities, and in part because of the higher salaries the schools were able to pay. She rapidly moved up the ladder, obtained further training, and now serves as both Head Start teacher and county coordinator.

On our way to Timber Lane Head Start, a nearby school-based center, Ms. Glynne talked about the importance of Head Start's noneducational components. It was almost eerie, to hear phrases echoing from hot debates of twenty years earlier, now part of a county civil servant's everyday vocabulary.

"You have to understand," she said, "Head Start is much more than just preschool education. Our new child-initiated learning curriculum is exciting, and it works, but it wouldn't work without the health and nutrition and social services we also provide. Fifty percent of our staff's time is spent working with families. Our teachers understand that a child whose family got evicted that day can't pay a lot of attention to classroom routines. We also know that if we want the child to learn, we have to help the family."

I asked whether there was pressure to eliminate services that are not strictly educational, either because of budget constraints or because the schools where most of the programs operate are geared to accomplishing narrower educational purposes. She was aware of no such pressure. "Everyone recognizes the importance of the health and nutrition aspects of what we do. And everyone knows how important it is to work with families to help them to provide a home environment that encourages their children's learning, and to help them to become self-sufficient." It sounded more anachronistic than nostalgic to hear her add, "Besides, if we didn't include those parts of the program we'd be out of compliance with federal regulations!"

Ms. Glynne told me of her enthusiasm for the new active learning curriculum, developed by the High Scope Educational Research Foundation. It was now the basis of her own training of preschool teachers, and of an increasing number of preschool programs in Fairfax County and around the country.

We arrived at the modern elementary school just in time to see one group of three- and four-year-olds accompanied by a teacher, an aide, and several parents leaving for the local public library. Another group was piling into a school bus to go to the county health department to see the dentist.

The school's preschool wing housed five Head Start classes in rooms made surplus by declining elementary school enrollments. The classrooms were bright, cheerful, and carefully organized to encourage children to find and explore, and to work and play with a great variety of materials. As I looked around the room, it was clear that I was about to witness the "active learning" curriculum in action.

I joined a teacher engaged with five children at a low table, planning the morning's activities. The teacher, Ms. Brownlee, talked with each child in turn about his or her choice of activities and work area—arts, blocks, housekeeping, music, sand, or quiet games. I was impressed with how the teacher responded to each child's choice, sometimes helping the child to elaborate his plan, sometimes helping two children to make a plan together. Then the children went off, taking with them their individual signs (bearing name and Polaroid picture) to be hung in the chosen activity area. Soon the children were busy painting, doing puzzles, building with blocks, putting dolls to bed, or sending sand through sieves and funnels.

While keeping an eye out for anyone who needed help, Ms. Brownlee explained, "We believe children learn best when they can make choices and act on them. I am persuaded by both my training and my experience that disadvantaged children in particular need to have the opportunity to set their own goals and follow through on them."

A child with dark, lively eyes approached and invited me, with a rich set of gestures and facial expressions, to join him in the quiet games area, matching various odd shapes with their pictures on a board. Completing that task with great satisfaction, he engaged me in his next endeavor, sorting out beads of various colors and sizes, also accomplished with zest but without a spoken word. Ms. Brownlee explained later that Anh Loh, now three and a half years old, had come to the United States from Vietnam two years before and had never spoken—not in any language. A meeting with his family was scheduled for the following day to discuss getting extra help from either a speech therapist or a psychologist.

Now it was cleanup time, and the children scurried about, returning materials to clearly marked containers on well-organized shelves, with both teacher and aide encouraging the children to name and classify what they were putting away. Then the children helped themselves to milk and grapes—set out for each child on his or her own sign. There were also signs to show where each child's toothbrush hung. After the snack, to my amazement, they all—unreminded—used their toothbrushes, returned them to the designated place, and proceeded to gather again around the tables, now for "recall time." At one table the teacher spoke into a toy telephone, the children answering in turn, on a second telephone, the teacher's questions about what they had done during work time. At the other table the aide was helping a second group of children to incorporate what each had done into a song.

As the boys and girls went out to the playground in a jovial but orderly line, I remarked to Ms. Glynne how carefully thought through the morning's activities had seemed. She said this was part of the strength of the High Scope curriculum. "Consistently giving children who come from disadvantaged families a structured way to express themselves, make choices, and learn they can act on their own decisions has to be a very promising road to social as well as academic competence."

THE EXPLODING NEED FOR NEW CHILD CARE ARRANGEMENTS

The original rationale for Head Start—that disadvantaged children need some extra boosts if they are to have successful school careers—applies with even greater force today. Over the last twenty years the long-term benefits of preschool care have been solidly documented; changes in economics and technology have made success at school ever more important, and the number of poor children has increased. Furthermore, for a growing subset of poor children, good preschool care can mean not just a lift, but a lifeline. For the children of the shadows—children with parents who are isolated or impaired (by drugs, alcohol, or mental illness), children at special risk of abuse, children growing up in persistent and concentrated poverty, children being raised by a single parent, and children of school-age mothers—for these children and their parents, good preschool programs are a necessity.

A political strategy to respond to this necessity must take into account a social context totally transformed since the days in which Head Start was launched. The increase in the number of working mothers, the heightened concern that unmarried teenage mothers obtain the necessary education, skills, and supports to enter the job market, and the growing consensus that more welfare recipients should be working has shifted the ground under public policy-making on the care and education of disadvantaged young children.

At the national, state, and local level, new approaches to the care of children under school age all reflect the overriding fact that the needs of disadvantaged children represent only one of the many imperatives to which new policies must respond. Middle-class families who seek and can't find affordable, high-quality child care are one driving force, predominant in numbers and political clout. Add the pressures of those demanding that welfare-dependent mothers be free for employment, and the economic stake of child care providers (who include large corporations, small entrepreneurs, struggling nonprofit agencies, schools, and other public institutions), and one can readily see how the interests of children, and especially disadvantaged children, can sink out of sight.

None of these factors, however, is as powerful in shaping the new context for child care policymaking as the fact that the need for out-of-family arrangements is no longer confined primarily to three- and four-year-olds but now includes equally large numbers of infants and toddlers.

The care of children under the age of three has become the fastest-growing type of child care. The long-term effects of early out-of-home care are the subject of passionate debates. Many important questions remain unanswered, particularly because of the wide range of circumstances in which infant day care is provided, most of them difficult to monitor and study.

Several propositions, however, are widely agreed upon: First, good out-of-home care, even for very young children, is possible when staff are adequately trained and well paid, staff turnover is low, and recommended standards for group size and child-staff ratios are not exceeded. Second, infant day care of poor quality can be damaging. For children from disadvantaged families, inferior and discontinuous out-of-home care can be devastating. It adds to the risk factors these children already face and may, in fact, multiply their effect.

It is not hard to understand why poor infant day care poses such dangers to infants from stressed and disorganized homes. Children under the age of two have an especially great need for a predictable environment with no more than two or possibly three caregivers, all of whom have a continuous and emotionally satisfying relationship with the young child. Research findings on quality of day care are consistent with those on family influences in child development. Caregivers in day care settings, just like parents, need to be a source of comfort and succor to the young child, involved with and sensitive to the child's developmental needs, and able to encourage verbal communication and to control behavior without being overly restrictive.

Too many high-risk children don't get what they need at home, and they don't get it away from home. Child care that builds on

and children. It furnishes prenatal care, help in preparing for child-birth and parenthood, and family counseling. It sponsors a men's counseling group and intergenerational community workshops aimed at building a supportive environment for the teen parent. The center coordinates home visits by public health nurses and mental health counselors from state and local agencies.

Jean Ekins, who is responsible for keeping it all going, talks about how difficult it is for a youngster to learn to cope with the demands of parenthood and to stay in school at the same time. "At least we can put the services they need together for them, and we can help them overcome the isolation and rejection so often experienced by teen parents."

FLC has been able to document some remarkable results:

- In 1985, 97 percent of its pregnant and parenting eighth- to eleventh-graders were staying in school, and 91 percent of the seniors graduated.
- Despite the high-risk status of the young women served by the center, their babies had a lower-than-average rate of perinatal problems: among the sixty babies born between 1982 and 1985, only four were born at low birthweight, one was premature, and one had a birth defect.
- Between 1982 and 1985, there were only two repeat pregnancies to single mothers.
- Teen parents were able to increase their grade point averages and showed improved attitudes and behavior, greater confidence in their abilities, and higher self-esteem.

The program sponsors believe it has also succeeded in improving the children's socialization and motor and verbal skills and significantly lowering the incidence of child abuse and neglect among the families served.

In recognition of its achievements, the Ford Foundation conferred one of its ten 1986 awards for outstanding innovations in public service on the Family Learning Center of the Leslie Public Schools.

For many teenagers, a day care opportunity that is connected to school and provides a cornucopia of supportive services can make an enormous difference. By facilitating the return to school, such programs allow teen parents an alternative to being at home alone with their babies, not studying or working, tempted to fill their lives with an additional child. The kind of comprehensive child care program provided in Leslie also furnishes the information, role models, and experiences which the teens might otherwise lack and which help them to function as responsible parents.

CHILD CARE CHOICES—NOT ENOUGH THAT ARE GOOD ENOUGH

For a teenage girl who hasn't finished school and needs intensive help in the process of learning to be a mother in the face of her youth and inexperience, infant day care may be an enormous blessing. For a high proportion of mothers in their twenties and thirties, on the other hand, putting their babies in out-of-home care before they are six months old is more likely to be a matter of dreaded necessity than desirable choice. Mothers return to work as early as they do most frequently because they need the income and the benefits that come with the job. In Europe, where maternity leaves are the norm, one sees very few infants in out-of-home care, even in countries where a higher proportion of women are in the work force than in the United States. To protect families from having to choose between losing jobs and leaving their newborn before either mother or baby is ready, a star-studded panel of experts recommended national action to guarantee infant care leaves of at least six months. This imposing group of scholars and professionals in social policy, child development, and related fields met over a two-year period and gathered on November 26, 1985, to announce agreement that, at a minimum, 75 percent of salaries should be reimbursed for three months after childbirth and benefits and jobs protected for six months. The enactment of legislation embodying the committee's recommendations would send a message that child rearing is more than a private concern, would help to give many parents and children a healthier start, and would end the unique position of the United States among industrialized countries as the only one that has no national legislation guaranteeing a woman her job after childbirth.

Almost every civilized country in the world has developed systems in which maternity leaves, job guarantees after childbirth, and out-of-home child care combine to make it possible for women to be part of the labor force without risking their children's well-being.

But most Americans with young children face problems getting child care when they can't provide it themselves.

In Denver, Susan J. Montgomery's four-year-old was in a publicly funded day care program while she trained at a community college to become a licensed practical nurse. When day care ended because of funding cutbacks, she had to drop out of school and once again became entirely dependent on welfare and food stamps. "I work so hard to get off welfare," she said, "and this puts me right back to it."

A recent Washington State survey found that more than two thirds of single mothers receiving AFDC benefits said difficulties in locating adequate child care interfered with their seeking and keeping a job. Of the women who had given up looking for work, 76 percent cited child care difficulties as the reason. The availability of good child care has now been reliably shown to be a crucial factor in whether young mothers will become financially self-sufficient.

One young mother in Atlanta, bent on finishing high school, went through her neighborhood knocking on doors, asking "Can you keep my baby?" According to Dr. Marian Howard, Director of Teen Services at Atlanta's Grady Hospital, she finally found a neighbor willing to take care of the child during school hours. The arrangement broke down after six weeks, and the student was back on the streets again canvassing for care of her baby. Many babies, says Dr. Howard, just get "passed around from caregiver to caregiver instead of getting what they desperately need, which is consistency in their environment to grow and thrive."

For poor mothers, the decision to work towards financial independence often means putting their children into child care arrangements that will virtually guarantee adverse outcomes, says Bernice Weissbourd, president of the Chicago-based family support organization Family Focus.

Even a professor of child development can be stymied in the child care quest. A parent recounted this story in a Washington, D.C., magazine:

> Both the professor and her husband worked full-time. Their baby daughter was enrolled in one of the few high-quality infant day centers in the area. When she was eight months old, she came down with an illness that required her to be withdrawn from the center. For three weeks, the family scrambled—the mother, father, and twelve-year-old

daughter each took turns staying home. Finally, after a frantic search, they found a woman willing to care for the baby at her apartment.

Because the building management did not allow tenants to operate businesses in their apartments, the baby could not be brought in through the lobby each morning. The parents were told they would have to drive up through the alley behind the woman's ground floor apartment and hand the baby through the window.

"Of course," wrote the man telling the story, "the child care specialist reacted to such a bizarre arrangement just as I or any other local parent would—she agreed. We're desperate, you see."

The couple subsequently learned that the woman was taking in a large number of other children, and leaving them all in the care of her twelve-year-old daughter while she went out to clean homes. The arrangement ended when one of the infants ended up in the hospital after swallowing thirty aspirin tablets.

While delivering a child through the window and aspirin poisonings are not the norm, few families—unless they have the means and the luck to have found their own version of Mary Poppins—have been able to work out satisfactory solutions to their child care problems, especially if they need full day care or if their children are younger than three.

The state of Florida, which keeps track of such things, had twenty-two thousand children on its waiting list for subsidized child care in 1986. Two of the children on that waiting list, left alone at home on a day when makeshift arrangements fell through, were playing in a clothes dryer when the door closed—and they tumbled and burned to death.

Day care that is affordable is hard to find everywhere. Even harder to find is care that meets basic standards of quality, care that parents can be reasonably sure will be good for their children.

Surveying seventy-seven communities throughout the United States, the National Council of Jewish Women found in the early 1970s that half of the day care provided in homes by nonrelatives was only "custodial," and another 11 percent was rated "poor." Among proprietary centers, an alarming 85 percent were providing care rated as custodial or poor. Visitors found wailing babies strapped to infant seats, double-decker cardboard cribs stacked in rooms with open gas heaters, centers where one untrained person was responsible for the care of as many as forty infants and children. In one day care home where five infants and six other small children were under the charge of one sullen, untrained woman, "the children were screaming and running, almost naked, in the four-room house. The strong urine smell, the stale odor of uneaten food everywhere and the bugs crawling around made one nauseous . . ."

In 1984 Deborah Fallows, professor of linguistics and mother of two young boys, undertook a less systematic but highly informative —and disturbing—multicommunity survey of child care. She decided to take time off from her academic career to become a full-time mother and to write about the options available to women like herself. Her mornings observing in dozens of day care centers and family day care homes in Massachusetts, Maryland, the District of Columbia, and Texas are recorded in her book, *A Mother's Work*, containing heartwarming as well as heartbreaking stories. She tells of children cared about, respected, and thriving, and of children abandoned. Time and again she found children wandering "aimlessly, with no attention from an adult, little ones confined in cribs or playpens, forbidden to roam or play, the only source of distraction the game show or soap opera on the eternally babbling television."

The majority of child care for children under the age of four is provided in other people's homes by nonrelatives. These are usually referred to as "family day care homes," because they are expected to provide a family setting for child care outside the child's own home. Quality varies widely, and there is little solid data from which to draw systematic conclusions about just what happens in these settings. As Professor Edward Zigler of Yale University explained to the House Select Committee on Children, "It is very likely that both the best and worst of day care situations take place in family day care homes."

It is extremely difficult to create structures that assure minimum quality standards in these settings or even to provide training and support, because they are small, scattered, and often difficult to locate. Family day care providers tend to be "women who have not been part of organizations in the past; they are not paper pushers or people who have responded to influences outside the home," observes June Solnit Sale, who has worked extensively with family day care providers. Ms. Sale, a social worker by training, was able to demonstrate, in cooperation with the Pacific Oaks College in Pasadena, California, that it is possible to join family day care homes into networks to provide mutual support and training, and to help assure quality of care. She is convinced that, since family day care is so popular with families and has the potential for providing excellent developmentally oriented care in a setting that can be warm, intimate and responsive, efforts to work with family day care providers deserve vastly more attention from policymakers and professionals than they have received in the past.

Whether out-of-family child care is provided in homes or centers, concern about the quality of child care is growing. Funds for services have been cut back, as have funds for monitoring, and there is a reluctance to promulgate—much less enforce—any kind of uniform minimum standards.

Most states do not limit the number of infants and toddlers in day care centers or homes. Even where regulations exist, one adult is often responsible for eight infants and toddlers. That makes responsive child care almost impossible. Furthermore, the child care worker, not obligated to her charges by the emotional commitment that binds most family members, needs two things that parents caring for their own infants or toddlers do not: training and a salary. Yet only eight states require that caregivers in day care centers and group care homes be trained. Eighty-seven percent of family day care providers and 50 percent of all child care workers earn less than poverty-level wages.

The results are predictable. For example:

> Jerel, age two years and four months, stands up on a chair. The woman in charge tells him to get down. He loudly asserts himself by saying, "No!" The caregiver approaches him and he takes off running. She catches him and yells at him. He hits at her. She sits on him, yelling, "You don't need to think you're better than anyone else. You're going to learn to listen." He begins to cry. She lets him up.

Most day care workers are well intentioned but often overstressed and overwhelmed by the large numbers of children to be taken care of. Their own poor pay and lack of training make it almost impossible for them to feel they have an important and socially valued job. Turnover among child care workers is higher than in any other occupation.

In some day care centers 50 percent of the children are there because they have been abused or neglected and the court has ordered them placed in day care. But most of these centers receive no special funds for training caregivers or providing social support services.

> Eighteen-month-old Jayne goes from teacher to teacher crying, hands held high in a clear plea to be picked up. The staff ignore her or say, "No!" She cries in despair, and finally goes to a young high school boy who is temporarily assisting in the classroom. He looks to the head teacher for permission to pick Jayne up and comfort her. The teacher says, "No, if we pick her up, she'll always want to be picked up." Jayne continues crying. Finally she drops to the floor and begins pounding her head on the floor. A teacher picks her up and places her on a chair. Jayne cries, screams, and kicks so hard that the chair falls backward, and Jayne hits her head. An assistant picks her up, puts her face down on her lap and pats her back, as Jayne sobs herself to sleep.

On a visit to an exemplary infant day care program in an affluent Maryland suburb of Washington, D.C., I asked a pregnant staff member her plans after her baby came. "I intend to continue working, and I'd give anything to be able to bring the baby here," she said, "but it's out of the question. This place costs just about what I earn every week." Her answer, though shocking, was not surprising once one had made the calculations. The program, under the auspices of the nonprofit Montgomery County Child Care Association, was staffed by four capable, cheerful, well-trained young women. Each day they provide nine, ten, or eleven infants with sensitive, loving care—costing each parent $145 a week (1986 figures). And, not surprising in an unsubsidized program, every baby came from a two-parent family, both full-time professionals.

The most alarming part of the present situation, in which out-of-home child care is not reliably and predictably available to the majority of Americans, is that the families whose children are already at greatest risk are least likely to be able to find the care they need. This is especially true for the youngest children, for whom good care is the most costly. Good out-of-home infant day care requires at least one trained staff person for every three infants. Very few public programs have been able to muster the resources needed to provide or pay for high-quality infant day care.

Having allowed American child care to be shaped by market forces and the ability to pay, we now have a grab bag of arrangements in which the children at highest risk are least likely to get the kind of child care that could reduce the chances of adverse outcomes.

Head Start is an exception, but an insufficient one, because it serves less than a fifth of all disadvantaged three- and four-year-olds, and because only a fraction of its centers take children for more than four hours a day, although a high proportion of the children need full day care. (Children in a half-day program who have a mother who is completing school or single and working, or two parents who work, have to learn to accommodate to three separate sets of surroundings, caretakers, and expectations every day—the Head Start or other preschool program, day care, and their own families. For very young children, this can be a damaging burden.)

Although the preschool experience is much less crucial to the development of middle-class children than lower-class children, the greater the income and education of parents, the more likely it is that their children will be in an organized child care program with an educational component. Of families with incomes higher than $25,000, 75 percent of children attend a preschool program by the age of four, compared to 33 percent of children from families with incomes of under $15,000. The higher a mother's education, the more likely her children are to be in a preschool program. Further compounding the dissonance between who needs care most and who is most likely to get it, minority children tend to be in the more custodial programs, while white children are more often enrolled in programs with substantial educational components.

As the Carnegie Foundation for the Advancement of Teaching summed up, children of low- and moderate-income families have simply been priced out of the market for high-quality preschool care.

THE NEW POLITICS OF CHILD CARE

The most up-to-date research confirms what every parent and grandparent knows—young children need, at home and elsewhere, competent, warm, responsive adults who are not so overwhelmed that they can't be joyfully involved with them. But in the United States we have not yet succeeded in translating this understanding into workable child care policies.

The child care policy paralysis may, however, be nearing an end.

The explosion in women's employment has fundamentally changed the politics of child care.

Big business, concerned about work force stability, morale, and productivity, has joined women's organizations, child advocates, and worried parents in recognizing that out-of-home child care is too important to the national well-being and too complex to be left to families to grapple with on their own.

The growing ranks supporting improved national child care policies now also include many who recognize that good child care is essential to the education, training, and employment of many young mothers, for whom child care may be the alternative to welfare. Even politicians whose main interest is in putting welfare mothers to work have recognized that they cannot achieve their objectives without vastly expanded and improved arrangements for child care.

Undeniably, today's lobby for more available, more affordable child care derives less force from children's needs for care than from adults' needs to have children looked after. It may be wise to mute this distinction in the interest of building broad coalitions in support of a common program. But the distinction should be borne in mind to assure that, in the inevitable accommodation between child care demands and the realities of scarce resources, the needs of children will not be relegated to last place behind the claims of child care providers, of employers, and of parents as wage earners. Unless policies to expand preschool programs and child care arrangements are designed specifically to meet the distinct needs of children growing up at risk, they will not help to eliminate—and may indeed perpetuate—adverse outcomes into the next generation.

The reasons for child care may be different for the employed, the would-be employed, and the unemployed, but neither philosophically nor programmatically are these constituencies likely to be adequately served at each other's expense. The mother on Wall Street may require child care with different characteristics than the mother on welfare, but in planning for one we had best not neglect the other.

All those committed by profession, public mandate, public interest, or personal conscience to the future of American children must join together, under public and private auspices, to work out the detailed specifications for launching a vastly expanded network of child care.

The basic principles are simple:

First, *the needs of families with the fewest economic and political resources must receive the highest priority* in current efforts to make out-of-home child care more widely available. This means recognizing that child care for high-risk families, whose children have the most at stake, must meet a broad range of children's needs. It is neither enough to get them out of the way during the workday, nor to provide for their educational needs for half a day, leaving parents to scramble once more to put together pieces of care that don't fit.

Second, *Head Start and other developmentally oriented preschool programs must be expanded and supplemented.* They must be given financial and technical assistance to *serve more children,* and to *expand their hours* of care, freeing parents to complete education and training and seek employment. Programs now successfully serving poor children younger than three must be helped to expand, to include *more very young children and their families.* Programs now providing full-day care for infants, toddlers, or preschool children at risk, but without special provision to meet the children's developmental needs, must be assisted to *expand the content of their services.*

Third, *new sources and methods of funding* must be found. Existing sources do not provide enough money to assure that publicly supported care will be of high quality. Funds come from many different sources with sometimes conflicting requirements which are confusing to parents and providers alike. Funds must be made available in ways that allow for sensible local planning. Eligibility for subsidies must be designed to avoid disincentives to paid employment and to take into account the importance for young children of continuity of care. Most important, public funds must be provided in sufficient amounts to make possible adequate salaries and training for caregivers, and reasonable staff-child ratios.

Fourth, *parents must be made partners* with early childhood educators and child development professionals at the local level in new efforts to prepare their children to achieve academic success and social competence. This is especially important for parents who are not well educated and not sophisticated in dealing with large or unfamiliar institutions, and who see themselves as powerless and overwhelmed.

Fifth, *schools must become a major (although not exclusive) source of preschool care,* since they have a readily available structure for institutionalizing a vastly expanded preschool program, especially for three- and four-year-olds. Special provision for separate administration and staffing of these programs is probably essential. Such separation, together with training of staff in the development of children under the age of five, should assure that these programs will not narrowly and exclusively focus on cognitive and academic achievement and will emphasize the characteristics of preschool programs that are different from traditional elementary school education. They must make special efforts to recognize the value of caring, curiosity, and play and the importance of social and emotional development; to respond to the individual needs of children and their families and work closely with parents; and to forge strong ties to community institutions that can provide a variety of supports to high-risk and disadvantaged families.

Sixth, *the quality of child care* can be maintained at high levels only through the active involvement of parents, private agencies, academic institutions, and local and state governments. Each has a role in providing information and training to all sources of care, including family day care providers. Each has a role in developing, promulgating, and monitoring standards of reasonable care.

Every one of these principles has been adopted and successfully implemented somewhere in this country. They will be adopted on a much broader scale as more Americans come to realize how much we have that we can build on, how vital is the task of caring for young children—one's own and others'—and what an enormous collective stake we have in the arrangements that prepare young children for school and for life.

Schools, Balance Wheel
of the Social Machinery

"Education, then, beyond all other devices of human origin, is a great equalizer of the conditions of men—the balance wheel of the social machinery. . . . It does better than to disarm the poor of their hostility toward the rich; it prevents being poor. That political economy, therefore, which busies itself about capital and labor, supply and demand, interests and rents, favorable and unfavorable balances of trade, but leaves out of account the elements of a widespread mental development, is naught but stupendous folly."

HORACE MANN, *Report to the Massachusetts State Board of Education,* 1848 need a serious education. By getting out of the way, as they did in large numbers before World War II, these children helped to make the process of universal public education appear to be working smoothly.

But the mythology of what schools *could* do was very much alive, and it became the reason that the National Association for the Advancement of Colored People, soon after the end of World War II, picked the schools as the arena in which to open its fight to desegregate America. In 1954, in *Brown v. Topeka Board of Education,* a unanimous Supreme Court said that segregated education is inherently unequal. Although that finding hardly created a utopia, it did stimulate dramatic improvements in the education available to many blacks, and the court's decision was and remains an important symbol of American intolerance for the most blatant differences in access to opportunity.

The Soviet launching in 1957 of two earth-orbiting Sputnik satellites sent a tremor of fear through America that it was losing out in the space race to Soviet concentration on mathematics and science. In haste Congress passed the National Defense Education Act (NDEA), authorizing federal funds to help close a perceived technical education gap.

The NDEA was useful in that it established a beachhead for the expanded federal aid to education that was to come, provided new support for the teaching of science, math, and foreign languages, and led to a reexamination of curriculum content and quality. But it also diverted attention from the schools' weaknesses in educating their least advantaged students.

In the sixties, national attention was drawn to persistent differences in academic achievement, not only between black and white but also between rich and poor. Congress was impressed by studies showing that low-income areas produced disproportionate numbers of delinquents and school dropouts. President Johnson, newly returned to office in a landslide election and deeply committed to education, announced that bringing better education to millions of disadvantaged youths was one of the four major tasks facing the nation. The presidential message transmitting the Elementary and Secondary Education Act of 1965 was titled "Toward Full Educational Opportunity" and provided the rationale for forging a successful coalition with Southerners, Catholics, and others traditionally nervous about federal aid to education. With its enactment a new era in education seemed to be in the making. Title I of the act provided federal funds to the nation's local school districts for "imaginative new approaches for meeting the educational needs of poor children." The President called it "the most important bill I will ever sign."

In education, as in other domestic policy arenas, the buoyant hopes of the sixties were punctured by the nay-saying of the seventies. Suddenly everybody seemed to know that nothing worked. Harvard Yard was abuzz, reported Godfrey Hodgson in *The Atlantic* in 1973, with successive revelations that "schools make no difference." Social science confirmed the cynics' worst suspicions: Schools could not be fashioned into springboards to opportunity. They simply reinforced the advantages and disadvantages, genetic and environmental, that children bring to school; even large federal expenditures could not change the preordained outcomes.

A public now turned skeptical about social interventions was receptive to research showing that a child's skills, length of schooling, and success in adult work were determined primarily by family background. And educators, already despondent about the difficulty of the task assigned to them, were grateful for this "weighty rationalization for pessimism." If social class was what really mattered, schools couldn't be held responsible for their shortcomings in educating poor and minority children.

Then, in the eighties, other researchers found better news about the effectiveness of compensatory education, and it looked more reasonable to ask schools to take greater responsibility for the basic skills and other educational achievements of their charges. At the same time, attention focussed anew on the schools as a result of a fundamental shift in the economy. Toyota cars and Sony televisions were challenging Fords and RCAs. American industry, striving for competitiveness and needing good workers, expressed outrage at the number of youngsters getting out of school without being able to read, spell, add, or get to work on time. The demographics were also alarming. Industry would no longer be able to skim off the best and forget the rest, because there would not be enough of "the best" to fill the growing number of jobs requiring sophisticated skills. (See Chapter 1.) Commissions were appointed and studies funded to determine what was wrong with American schooling.

SHORTCOMINGS OF CURRENT EDUCATIONAL REFORMS

The commissions, highly critical of the state of U.S. education, called for massive educational reform, aimed primarily at raising standards. Everybody—educators, pupils, parents, school boards—was challenged to shape up. The states responded mainly by mandating stiffer graduation requirements, boosting salaries, reassessing teacher competence, and enriching school curricula. In 1987, four years after the commission reports, many questioned how deep their impact had been. "The 1983 reforms did not change the system at all —just tightened the screws," said David R. Mandel of the Carnegie Forum on Education and the Economy.

It also soon became clear that neither the reports nor the responses to the reports adequately recognized that the American economy had reached a point where every citizen—not just those who take easily to education—must be well educated. *All* young people, concluded a National Academy of Sciences report, whether or not they go on to college, need a similar set of core competencies in order to succeed in today's labor market. The Carnegie Forum on Education and the Economy declared, "America must now provide to the many the same quality of education presently reserved for the fortunate few."

But the spotlight of reform had simply not been aimed at the young people on whom the schools had basically given up. A year after the completion of the 1983 report of the National Commission on Excellence in Education, *A Nation at Risk,* a member of that commission, Harvard physics professor Gerald Holton, acknowledged that the report had not come to grips with what he called "the most ominous question of all"—how schools can meet the needs of the "large and growing fraction of our society that appears to languish in the darkness, below the security provided by any safety net."

Terrel H. Bell, who as Secretary of Education had commissioned *A Nation At Risk,* said four years later, "The school reform movement has had no significant impact on the 30 percent of our students who are the low-income minority students. We are still not effectively educating them."

Ernest L. Boyer, president of the Carnegie Foundation for the Advancement of Teaching, said urban schools with students largely from minority groups were getting worse even as "advantaged schools are getting better." The first wave of educational reform, declared the Committee for Economic Development in its 1987 report, "has either ignored or underplayed the plight of the disadvantaged."

Most of the proposed reforms have "relatively little to offer educationally disadvantaged students," agrees Henry M. Levin, Stanford University educational economist. Levin found that in 1985, about 30 percent of the public school population was educationally disadvantaged, and believes the proportion is rapidly rising. These students, typically from minority and immigrant families, with parents who have low incomes and little education, see scant evidence connecting education, hard work, and success. Levin fears that, in the absence of explicit efforts to improve education for these youngsters, some of the current reforms, such as stiffer graduation requirements, may actually increase dropout rates, contributing in turn to increased unemployment, welfare dependency, crime, and the emergence of a large and permanent underclass.

There is agreement, at least at the level of rhetoric, that the failure of our education system to provide all American youngsters with basic skills exacts a high price, whether measured in personal, moral, or economic terms. There is also increasing recognition that early school experiences, especially for disadvantaged youngsters, impact powerfully not only on educational outcomes, but, because of the centrality of schooling in children's lives, also on rates of delinquency and early childbearing.

LONG-TERM EFFECTS OF ELEMENTARY SCHOOL EXPERIENCE

For an astonishingly high proportion of youngsters in serious trouble as adolescents, the trouble didn't begin when they dropped out or became unruly or withdrawn or stopped learning in high school. Most had had many years of unrewarding and unhappy school experiences before they ever got to high school. Their school difficulties had begun in the elementary grades. School failure and poor reading performance *as early as third grade,* truancy, poor achievement, and misbehavior in elementary school, and the failure to master school skills throughout schooling are among the most reliable predictors of early childbearing, delinquency, and dropping out of school.

Painstaking investigations over time have also identified "a distinctly encouraging school environment that enhances a child's values and competencies" as an important factor in ameliorating a child's risk status.

But why should difficulties in elementary school have such far-reaching consequences? What happens during those early school years that could have such a powerful impact? The mechanisms by which many disadvantaged youngsters are sucked into a downward slide that is often destiny-determining are now fairly well understood.

First come the predisposing factors: The disadvantaged child may arrive in first grade not well prepared for school. Schools and teachers may not be geared to the special needs of disadvantaged children. Teachers may be poorly trained, burned out, or insensitive. In some children, aggressive and hyperactive temperaments or learning disabilities may play a role. Others may be precociously angry in response to racial or class prejudice or an early perception of limited future prospects.

As the result of these or similar factors, a child may fail to meet the initial demands of school. Teachers often reach—and display—lasting judgments as early as the first few days of school. The first-grader who is called upon to count, recognize letters, shapes, or colors, or simply to sit still or not grab, and who is unable or unwilling to respond as expected—that child is in trouble. This is especially true when the schoolroom atmosphere is unsupportive. The converse, of course, is also true: In a group of Head Start children followed to the age of nine, the ones who made the greatest gains were those with teachers who were enthusiastic, warm, positively motivating, cognitively stimulating, and able to teach in a one-to-one or small-group setting. Children whose home environments provide comparatively less structure and support may have a special need for a nurturing atmosphere at school, but, by third or fourth grade, teacher styles tend to become less nurturing.

Beginning around third or fourth grade, new socioeconomic factors seem to intrude to reduce the chances of school success for the disadvantaged child. Test scores show a greater divergence by class, race, and income, and even the children with a successful compensatory preschool experience through Head Start seem to fall behind again. It seems that at this point the awareness of discrepant values between home and school increases, and the gulf widens between the skills acquired at home and the skills needed for school success. In the first three years of school, children are learning to read; around fourth grade they are reading to learn. Keeping up with reading now requires a far broader vocabulary and the kind of familiarity with current events, history, and culture that is more likely to characterize the out-of-school environment of a middle-class child than a child from the ghetto. It is after third grade that the below-average readers fall further and further behind. After third grade, math skills seem to be more affected by extra instruction at school than are reading skills—probably because reading, especially from fourth grade on, relies more on general knowledge acquired outside the classroom than does math, which is more formal and more uniquely learned in school.

Elementary school children are quite aware that learning to read, spell, write, and do arithmetic is the number one mission assigned them by society. Those that come to see themselves as inferior to their classmates or as unable to meet the challenge of schooling, are likely to become alienated. Failure to master what is taught (whether or not that involves repeating a grade or placement in a special education class) erodes whatever self-esteem they may have started with.

Such a child, having once concluded he won't make it, may stop trying to learn the things valued by those in charge and behave in ways that will turn low expectations into a self-fulfilling prophecy. It now becomes difficult to persuade him to obey the rules of the school—and of society.

In the absence of intervention, hostility, truancy, and misbehavior are likely to become chronic and serious. Soon the child is suspended, loses whatever adult approval and support he had, and concludes that the future holds so little promise that there is no sense investing further effort in acquiring academic skills.

Any remaining commitment to learning is likely to be scuttled by the evidence accumulating from outside. As he looks around him, the youngster growing up surrounded by deprivation may find very little to sustain the belief that school learning will be useful.

WHAT SCHOOLS CAN DO—CHANGING THE PARTS

Knowing something of what can happen to place a child on a downward drift and having seen the difference that a good preschoool experience can make, we arrive at the question of how much a child's life prospects can be affected by changes that can be made in and by the schools.

From research on compensatory education supported under Title I of the Elementary and Secondary Education Act from 1965 to 1981 and its successor, Chapter 1, since 1981, we have learned that even piecemeal change can make a difference.

Targeted to low-achieving children in poverty-area school districts, Title I funds were used for individualized instruction in reading and math as well as extracurricular trips and activities, hiring and training of special teachers and aides, and the purchase of new equipment. Local expenditure decisions were not closely monitored at first, raising questions about how much of the effort really addressed the most serious educational needs of the most disadvantaged children. Federal control was tightened in 1978 but loosened again in 1981 in the name of local autonomy, spurred by Reagan Administration pressure for decentralization of authority. Today most of the Chapter 1 money—which has become steadily less adequate to the need—goes for basic instructional services in reading and math, often by specially trained teachers.

From the start, inadequate funding has been the most crippling weakness. (Appropriations have not kept up with inflation, and only half of all eligible children are served). But other defects have also surfaced, including wide variations in program quality, ineffective involvement of parents, and burdensome record keeping. In addition, frequent removal of children from their classrooms has caused scheduling complications, distractions, a diffusion of responsibility for the child's learning, and often the peer group branding of children getting special help as "dummies."

In the face of uneven implementation, observers were surprised to learn from careful studies completed in the 1980s that compensatory education appeared to be arresting the steady achievement decline among a population of students who had been falling further and further behind with each year of school. Federally supported compensatory education has succeeded in narrowing the performance gap between disadvantaged and more fortunate children. Even Terrel H. Bell, first Secretary of Education in the Reagan Administration, which had proposed severe cuts in Title I, told Congress in 1981 that the program was working, and that "American education has learned how to educate disadvantaged children." In 1983 Secretary Bell announced new efforts—and new funds—to replicate exemplary Title I programs.

The National Assessment of Educational Progress had found that, between 1970 and 1980, disadvantaged nine-year-olds showed significant improvement in reading ability, with the greatest gains occurring among black children and children in the Southeast, where federal money, particularly under Title I, had been concentrated.

The "Sustaining Effects Study," one of the largest surveys of elementary education ever undertaken, also found a narrowing of the achievement gap in basic skills between historically lower-achieving children and their more affluent counterparts. Title I programs were found to have produced especially significant gains among disadvantaged children in grades one to three in reading, and in grades one to six in math.

These findings did not mean that disadvantaged children had "caught up" with middle-class children. An extra hour a day of instruction could hardly be expected to undo the effects of round-the-clock differences in the environment.

Studies of other individual elements of school change, including the introduction of smaller class size, computer-assisted instruction, cross-age tutoring, and more active, personalized teaching all showed evidence of effectiveness. But effectiveness—though real—is limited, especially in schools with a high concentration of children at risk.

Increasingly, research and experience show that schools that have gone beyond isolated elements of remedial action and made more comprehensive changes have achieved better results—and ultimately at less cost.

CHANGING THE SCHOOL CLIMATE

As early as 1976, an intensive series of case studies of poor black children in Arkansas, Oregon, and New Jersey found that academic success and failure could not be accounted for by the attitudes, attributes, or behavior of "a particular parent, teacher or child, [or by] a particular social setting," but only by the cumulative effects of their multiple interactions. The researchers concluded that "gains are likely to be largest and to be sustained when there is support in the total ecology of the child."

The idea that the full impact of schools on children might be missed by looking only at discrete elements rather than at the whole school environment began to receive increasing attention in the late 1970s.

The first large-scale study to challenge the contention that schools were largely irrelevant to later life outcomes came from the prolific British psychiatrist Michael Rutter. With colleagues at the Institute of Psychiatry in London, he studied twelve inner-city London schools and found enormous differences in children's performance depending on the school they attended. After allowing for variations in social class and ability at school entry, the researchers found differences in academic achievement, attendance, behavior, and extent of delinquency, all of which seemed to be strongly associated with school variables. These variables, which the investigators concluded formed a "school ethos," included emphasis on academics, consistent discipline, and ample rewards for student performance.

A few lone researchers and educators in this country were also convinced that at least some schools were making a difference. George Weber of the Council for Basic Education and Ronald R. Edmonds of the New York City school system set out to identify schools—especially in the inner city—with high levels of achievement and to find out what made effective schools different from ineffective schools. Research on effective schools soon became quite fashionable and a prominent feature of the education literature. Reports on effective schools could even be found in such popular journals as *Consumer Reports* and *Parents' Magazine.*

Remarkably, there was wide agreement on the attributes that various researchers found crucial to making schools effective. The spotlight shifted to the learning environment, the climate in which schoolchildren live, rather than isolated elements of the school or specific learning or teaching techniques. Compared to such controversies as whether reading should be taught by phonics or the look-see method and whether math teaching should emphasize computation or concepts, the issues that emerged were more global and more subtle. The Hispanic Policy Development Project reported that "interpersonal harmony" was the most striking characteristic of effective schools. The students reported that "it was the teachers' caring what they did with their lives that was most important," and observers noted that "caring had been institutionalized as a value in the school and not solely an accidental relationship between a teacher and a lucky student."

The "effective schools" researchers have tried to hone their observations to readily identifiable characteristics, of which the following seem to be central:

- An emphasis on academics; classroom management that maximizes academic learning time; routines that discourage disorder and disruptions.
- A safe, orderly, disciplined—but not rigid—school environment.
- A principal who exercises vigorous instructional leadership; makes clear, consistent, and fair decisions; has a vision of what a good school is and systematically strives to bring that vision to life; and visibly and actively supports a climate of learning and achievement.
- Teachers with high expectations that all their students can and will learn; collegiality among teachers in support of student achievement.
- Regular and frequent review of student progress; modification of instructional practices in light of information about student progress; public ceremonies honoring student achievement.
- Agreement among principals, teachers, students, and parents on the goals, methods, and content of schooling; the belief that each student is capable of making academic progress; and recognition of the importance of a coherent curriculum, of promoting a sense of school tradition and pride, and of protecting school time for learning.

The theme that runs through all these individual attributes, observe historians of education David Tyack and Elisabeth Hansot, is that principals, students, teachers, and parents share a sense of community, a "socially integrating sense of purpose" that allows people to complete a sentence that begins, "What we are proud of around here is . . ." The perception of a common—and special—purpose is also what has made magnet schools so attractive and popular in many communities. Once you have a quality school, observes a New York City school administrator, "If you have kids who've selected your school and their parents selected your school and the teachers selected that school, there's a sense of ownership. And that school's going to do better than a school where you had to go."

The large body of "effective schools" research leaves little doubt that the school environment in its totality has a powerful impact on student outcomes. Increasingly, schools are applying the wealth of new understanding about how children develop and learn and about how teachers, classrooms, and schools function. The schools that are using the new knowledge to raise the odds of school success, especially for disadvantaged children, seem also to emphasize the importance of home-school collaboration to encourage children's learning. Extensive experience, as well as some research, shows not only that the school environment is powerfully influenced by what goes on in the students' homes, but that the school can do much to help parents make the out-of-school influences more supportive of learning.

All children learn best when parents and teachers share similar visions, when there is a "sense of constancy" between home and school, says the discerning sociologist of education, Sara Lawrence Lightfoot. A generation or two ago, schools didn't have to work as deliberately and self-consciously at developing that relationship as they do today. A sense of constancy is harder to achieve than it used to be, and it is much harder to attain in the inner city than in suburbs and small towns, where informal connections are easier to maintain.

Urbanization and increased mobility, greater family stress, and the sapping of family authority by television, have all widened the distance between home and school. That distance is of course greater still for children whose class, race, education, and family income differ most from those of the school staff. When the social network and style of the school are too dissonant from home and neighborhood, and the parents' alienation from the school is communicated to the children, the perception that school is the enemy can effectively destroy the chances that a child will learn.

Parents are not willing accomplices in this process. Poor and minority parents often have an especially high—even passionate—regard for education, and view it as the most promising means to improve their children's futures. Parents may buy books and encyclopedias—and now computers—that they can't afford, in the hope of spurring their children's education. But parents often need help in translating their yearning for their children's educational achievement into useful action.

Rigorous research has assessed some specific forms of home involvement. In one study, children in four inner city London primary schools were asked to take their readers home three or four nights a week, and parents were asked to listen to them read aloud. Over a period of two years, not only did the children's reading improve significantly more than that of a comparison group—even in families where parents could not read or spoke little English— but the experimental group also behaved better and showed "an increased keenness for learning" at school.

When schools make special efforts to bridge cultural and social discontinuities and to enlist parents as allies in teaching their children, there can be high payoffs. There is clear evidence that family concern for education can become practical support for children and for schools, that low educational attainment of a parent need not be a barrier to the parent's providing effective support, and that the more far-reaching the parental involvement—the more roles there are in a school for parents to play—the more effective it will be.

As we shall see in reports from New Haven, from Maryland's Prince Georges County, and from New York City's Harlem, schools that take deliberate action to recognize the critical role of family as educator, and to establish a climate that promotes learning, reap ample—and in these instances, measurable—returns.

"CLIMATE OF ACHIEVEMENT" IN NEW HAVEN

We had been driving for only about ten minutes after leaving the Gothic grandeur of Yale University, and had just passed the New Haven city dump, when we suddenly arrived at our destination. The Katharine Brennan Elementary School is located in the Brookside Public Housing Project, amid a scene of desolation in the middle of nowhere. All one could see was an expanse of uniform two-story buildings, surrounded by bare ground. No trees. At least a quarter of the windows were boarded up. Remnants of signs showed where a public library branch had been, where a convenience store had stood—the victim, my guide said, of too little income and too much vandalism. That meant a two-mile trip if you ran out of milk. And the buses stopped running at six in the evening.

Standing in front of the school, I thought: If James Comer managed to make his model intervention work in a school in this setting, there really are ways to uncouple poverty from its consequences for children.

For years I had read and heard about Dr. Comer's proposals to reform schooling for disadvantaged children and about his success in turning around several New Haven elementary schools. I had come, on this rainy December day, to one of the demonstration schools, and to talk with the famed child psychiatrist, educator, and philosopher at the Yale Child Study Center.

Walking from the car to the school, I steeled myself. I knew things had changed, but in my mind were vivid images from Dr. Comer's book *School Power,* in which he described the elementary school that he had started with. That school drew on a population very much like this one, the children predominantly black and very poor. About the beginnings of the program in September of 1968, Dr. Comer had written:

> On the first day of school, I walked down the hall and was almost attacked by a teacher in trouble. Yelling "Help me! Help me!", she pulled me into her classroom. What I saw was almost unbelievable. Children were yelling and screaming, milling around, hitting each other, calling each other names, and calling the teacher names. When the teacher called for order, she was ignored. When I called for order, I was ignored. That had never happened to me before. We headed for the hall, confused and in despair.

That was not the only classroom in trouble. They all were. Dr. Comer's book quotes from the log of a teacher from the Child Study Center, who had come to help out a first-grade teacher during the second week of school:

> There was constant disarray. It flared into wild disorder many times. There was no quietness, very little listening. There was fighting; there was thumbsucking; there was crying. . . . Every transition, every change during the day, was a disaster. They screamed and yelled and pushed as they lined up at the door to go downstairs. They rushed down the halls, yelling more. It was impossible to get them quiet enough to read a story to them. Even if, by some miracle, everyone was seated, you could not be heard above the din. . . . I cannot describe the physical, mental, and emotional exhaustion we reached by the end of the day, with two of us working every minute at the top of our completely inadequate capacity.

The school I entered that morning seventeen years later bustled with the energy of children and adults who were actively but serenely engaged with their world of learning and teaching. I visited classrooms where children were busy writing, computing, reading, looking things up, comparing impressions. In one room art objects were being devotedly constructed and in another young voices were harmonizing in exuberant song. I saw a gym where a serious basketball drill was under way and a library shown to me by the proud parent in charge. For all the world I could not have distinguished the atmosphere at Brennan from the most prestigious and richly endowed schools I had visited in Washington D.C. in the process of choosing an elementary school for my children.

When I later told Dr. Comer how extraordinary it had seemed to come from those bleak, depressing surroundings into the cheerful, orderly, industrious atmosphere of that school, his eyes laughed, and he said, "I'm always afraid that just when a visitor comes in it's going to be different, but it happens every time, so it must be that way! We really have been able to show that minority kids can learn, that it's possible in low-income areas to create a climate of achievement at school."

But no one need rely on subjective impressions of the effectiveness of Dr. Comer's intervention, because the hard data have been assembled.

The two schools in which the program began in 1968 had the lowest achievement and worst attendance and behavior records in New Haven. They were thirty-second and thirty-third in reading and math achievement of thirty-three New Haven elementary schools. The fourth-graders averaged one and a half years behind the norm. "The people who were working there," said Dr. Comer, "had just given up."

Fifteen years later, without any change in the socioeconomic composition of the student population, the demonstration schools ranked third and fifth among New Haven schools in composite fourth-grade test scores. Graduates of one of the schools, tested three years later, ranked significantly above a comparison group from a nonintervention school in language, math, "school competence," and "perceived total competence." Neither of the demonstration schools has had any serious behavior problems since the program really began to take hold in the early 1970s. Both have superior attendance records—one had had the best attendance record in the city for four of the previous five years. And, Dr. Comer says, "distrust, alienation and conflict have been reduced, and staff energies and expectations of each other and students have been increased."

I asked Dr. Comer how he, a child psychiatrist, had become so deeply involved in reforming elementary schools. He said that after completing his studies he had never been attracted to the private practice of medicine or psychiatry, but wanted to do something to improve the prospects of disadvantaged children.

He explained that he had been one of four black boys in his grade in a working-class neighborhood in East Chicago, Indiana. "My three friends, with whom I started elementary school—one died at an early age from alcoholism; one spent most of his life in jail, and one has been in and out of mental institutions all of his life. I was the only one to survive whole."

Dr. Comer believes that what made things work out for him and his two brothers was that not only had his parents been able to give them support and direction within the family, but they were also able to act on their children's behalf in the world of the school. His father was a steel laborer and church leader. His mother, who had become familiar with middle-class social skills as a domestic, "came to school if there was a problem, and knew how to make sure that people were sensitive and concerned about us. What I've tried to do here in New Haven is to shape the system, the school, so that it becomes the advocate and support for the kid, and a believer in the kid in the same way that my parents were." Schools, he had concluded, were the only thing "that would make a big enough difference—because schools are the final common pathway in our society and are more accessible to systematic change than the family." His focus has been mainly on elementary schools, because he believes that children who succeed in elementary school have a better chance to succeed in high school—and in life.

Dr. Comer told me that the bedlam that he had witnessed on that first day of school back in 1968 was not hard to understand. He believes that children from neighborhoods experiencing social stress enter school "underdeveloped"—socially, emotionally, linguistically, and cognitively—and are thus unable to meet the academic and behavioral expectations of the school. They withdraw, act up, or act out—and don't learn. The school labels them slow learners or behavior problems, when what they need is help with learning of a kind that the schools are not set up to provide.

The intervention that has evolved from Dr. Comer's work with the New Haven school system is disarmingly simple: changing the climate of demoralized schools by paying much more attention to child development and to basic management of the school.

That nonfunctioning schools could be turned around with the application of two ideas which, to an outsider, seem almost pedestrian, is puzzling at first blush. Dr. Comer explains that although teachers work with children all day, most know very little about applied child development and have few child development skills. They may have taken a course that taught them who Freud was but not how kids function, not what a fight in the playground means or what to do in response.

Similarly, Dr. Comer believes that the problems of the basic management of schools have never been adequately taken into account. He is convinced that every school is a special kind of system. Its management must be taken seriously and be based on an understanding of child development.

To translate this theory into practice, the school in Dr. Comer's model establishes a School Planning and Management Team to organize and maintain the school as a setting in which development and learning can take place. The Team is directed by the principal and has twelve to fourteen members, including teachers, teacher's aides, and parents. Its task, bluntly stated, is "to interrupt the forces of confusion and conflict and to establish an orderly, effective process of education in the building." Another group, consisting of the school's social worker, psychologist, special education teacher, and counselor provides child development consultation and skills to support the Planning and Management Team, and also provides direct help to individual children and to teachers.

As Planning and Management Team members, parents collaborate in establishing the school's tone, attitudes, and values. They also serve as teacher's aides, and in a variety of activities to support social and academic programs. Through their presence in the school and their interaction with the faculty, the parents promote a consensus of direction and support which is evident to the children. As Dr. Comer points out, "When the parents become allied with the school, you reduce the dissonance between home and school and you give the kid a long-term supporter for education at home." As an added bonus, it turned out that some parents, their own confidence bolstered by their school activities, went back to school them-

, some took jobs they previously thought they couldn't

,cademic development aspect of the Comer program initially made uneven progress, and took a long time to get going. That may have been because of the complexity of its goals: to raise reading and math achievement, to motivate students to learn for the satisfaction of learning and mastery as well as achievement, to raise occupational aspirations, and to provide children with the basic skills needed to achieve their aspirations. Students identified as at risk for low performance receive special attention but stay in their regular classrooms.

Staff development has a high priority in the Comer program. Because low-income, minority communities tend not to generate optimism and high aspirations naturally, Dr. Comer believes these must be created at school. Not only students but teachers must come to have confidence in their competence and their futures. "Teacher powerlessness," says Dr. Comer, "is more of a problem than ineffective teaching methods."

Dr. Comer wanted to make sure I understood that the essence of his intervention is a *process,* not a package of materials, instructional methods, or techniques. "It is the creation of a sense of community and direction for parents, school staff, and students alike." Although ultimately the motivation to learn comes from within, learning is initially a process of identification with emotionally important people—parents and teachers—that occurs in a supportive climate.

He likens the school's impact on child development to the family's. "They don't have their effect through the specific skills they transmit alone, but through their values, climate, quality of relationships. Especially in the early years, the content is almost, *almost,* incidental. Children learn by internalizing the attitudes, values, and ways of meaningful others. And then, whatever content you expose children to, they learn it."

Dr. Comer's emphasis on process and climate distinguishes his reform proposals from some in current fashion that treat learning more as a mechanical undertaking. "It's no use telling kids who can't produce in the first place that you want more from them. The premises of current fads in school reform, which rely on raising standards and then doing more of the same to get kids to meet the higher standards, are wrong, because they ignore the climate that makes learning possible. You can't simply demand that teachers and principals have higher expectations; you've got to develop a climate that allows people to have high expectations. The same teachers in our schools who, working in chaotic conditions, had low expectations for children, developed high expectations when they began to work in a desirable, supportive climate. And even if you start with high expectations, as many teachers do, you can't sustain them in chaos."

Dr. Comer believes most current attempts at school reform are not sufficiently comprehensive. "People aren't educated in pieces, and kids don't learn in pieces," he says. "That's why it's essential to address the entire social system of the school because of the way the many variables interact and because attitudes, morale, and hope all affect school performance."

Dr. Comer faults his own profession, psychiatry, for fostering the impression that learning is determined entirely from within and that a student who isn't learning just doesn't have what it takes. "Because we lack a theory about the nature and impact of the environment, we ignore it. I would argue that for the vast majority of kids, structuring the environment to facilitate learning and development is going to do more than trying to change the kid."

Dr. Comer also cautions that widespread problems created by poorly functioning institutions cannot be solved through piecemeal psychological intervention with individual youngsters. "When the schools became difficult after the 1940s, psychiatrists, social workers, psychologists, and special education specialists were brought in to deal with behavior problems. Everybody was trained separately, we were never trained to work as a team. And that's what happens —they all come into the school, and each takes a piece of the kid." He recalls that when he first came into the New Haven schools, support personnel were deliberately scheduled never to be in one school at the same time; they couldn't have planned together even if they had wanted to. He remembers one child who was receiving services from nine different people, all of whom "jumped in and out of the classroom, each doing his or her little thing, with the kid pieced up all over the place, with nobody thinking about what the kid needs altogether, and who should address what."

In the Comer model, teachers obtain their increased understanding of child development primarily through on-the-job training and consultation with the support team. Their work with the support team equips them to assist a child in trouble to leave the classroom gracefully, to teach pupils in conflict to learn to negotiate verbally rather than to fight it out, to understand why many parents are uneasy about participation in school programs, and to overcome many previously unreachable impediments to learning.

In his book, Dr. Comer illustrates the approach to a child in trouble taken by the mental health team in one of the demonstration schools:

About six weeks into the semester (of the second year of the program) Matthew Monroe, in a fit of anger, smashed the window in the door of his third grade classroom. Matthew was ten years old, bigger, stronger, older and smarter than his classmates and well-known as a troublemaker. He had never completed a full year in school because his aggressiveness had forced schools to put him on "home-bound status," with a visiting teacher who usually spent an hour a day with him, for a good part of each school year.

Matthew had a minor reading disability, was embarrassed by being two years behind in school, and exploded at the least suggestion that he was deficient. Matthew's parents were separated; his mother was clinically depressed, his father had a serious drinking problem. The mental health team agreed not to focus on Matthew's problems at home, but to concentrate on making school a decent place for him.

A conference of the mental health team and Matthew's teacher began with a discussion of how difficult it is for a child in Matthew's circumstances to channel aggressive energy and develop adequate inner control. This helped Matthew's teacher, who had felt attacked and undermined by Matthew for several weeks, to understand that he was not lashing out at her personally.

The plan the group evolved was designed to provide clear expectations and give Matthew information about how to gain and hold the approval of the important people in his school environment. It called for Matthew to spend an hour a day with the male principal, assisting him in any way that was appropriate. When he could be relatively stable for one hour, he would spend a second hour with the reading teacher. Once this arrangement was working, he would spend gradually increasing amounts of time in the classroom. The step-wise plan was reviewed with Matthew's father, and then with Matthew. He was told how much people at the school wanted him there, and wanted to help him, but could not tolerate his throwing books, attacking other children, or showing disrespect for his teacher. Two months after he had broken the window, Matthew was in class full time, his academic performance had improved, and he finished the year without another incident.

As my visit to Dr. Comer was drawing to a close, he went over to the large pad sitting on an easel in the corner of the room and drew three circles, the largest in the middle.

"There are kids who are going to learn no matter what happens," he said, pointing to the first circle, "because they are particularly bright and curious and have a lot of support at home. But the majority of kids in all school systems are in this second circle— where there is just enough support at home so that with adequate support in school, they would be able to learn. We are losing a lot of kids who would learn if we had a different kind of system at school, kids who would thrive if the schools were set up to facilitate learning. Then there are a small number who really need extra help beyond that, and the school can provide that or it can get help for that student and family from outside the school." But for most, Dr. Comer believes, a change in the school climate, and some help for the teachers in coping with children who have a hard time learning or have other difficulties, can do wonders.

"The most basic problem in education today is the assumption that if the kid doesn't learn, it's the kid's fault. The school doesn't take the responsibility. The classroom teacher may understand what the kid needs, but there's no mechanism for doing anything about it. We've been able to change that in two demonstration schools. Now we're expanding to twelve schools in New Haven. And we hope to be able to show soon that others can put these principles to work with equal success in schools elsewhere."

THE TRANSPLANT THAT TOOK ROOT IN MARYLAND

My curiosity was aroused by Dr. Comer's hint that his work with another school district might soon show whether the principles he had conceived and personally nurtured for two decades in New Haven could indeed be transplanted. At the time of my New Haven visit he was already consulting with school officials in Prince Georges County, Maryland. I was delighted, some time later, to be invited to Prince Georges County to visit Columbia Park Elementary School, one of fourteen schools in the county in which the Comer model was being replicated.

There had been a hint of duress in the county's decision in 1985, to turn to Dr. Comer. Prince Georges, which adjoins the District of Columbia, had been under court order to desegregate its schools for thirteen years and had recently set up several integrated magnet schools. To meet the court's requirements, the school superintendent had also worked out a separate memorandum of understanding to cover fourteen schools which, according to school officials, could not be desegregated because of their distance from predominantly white schools. Known as Milliken schools because their status was defined by a precedent established in the Detroit schools under Michigan's Governor William G. Milliken, the fourteen schools receive supplementary funds for more teachers, teacher training, counseling, and equipment, intended to compensate for the lack of racial integration. (In the superintendent's office, the jargon distinguishes between the schools that have been "magnetized" and those that have been "Millikenized." I wondered how long it would take before "Comerized" would be part of the vocabulary.)

Planning for the use of the Milliken funds, the school system became aware of James Comer's work in New Haven. Attracted by the evidence of his success there, the new superintendent of schools, Dr. John A. Murphy, asked Dr. Comer to serve as consultant to the Prince Georges County school system.

All of the Milliken schools had records of very low test scores and reputations for low teacher expectations. The mother of a child in one of the Milliken schools told a Washington *Post* reporter that the teachers simply assume that parents of poor children are "so busy trying to earn the bread and butter, they don't have time to motivate them," and that teachers therefore ask less of the children —and teach less. The superintendent apparently recognized that more might be needed in those schools than just additional resources and decided to implement the Comer model in an effort to change the school environment in which the funds would be used.

During the next several months, groups of principals, administrators, teachers, counselors, and parents from Prince Georges County traveled to New Haven to meet with Dr. Comer. He described his experiences, discussed their concerns, and urged them, while embracing the essentials of his model, to adapt it to their own situation. "The program will develop differently in Maryland," he told them, "because the needs of each school and school district, and the needs of the students, teachers, and parents, will be unique."

The prediction turned out to be accurate, but as I walked around the classrooms of Columbia Park and talked with its principal, I thought I recognized most of the elements central to Dr. Comer's concept. The "Comer School Development Program," as it is called in Prince Georges County, was in its second year of operation, and the basic components were in place. The School Planning and Management Team meets twice a month to bring the adults in the school community together to make plans that—in the words of the Prince Georges County literature—"give a sense of direction and order to the school . . . will establish trust and mutual respect, and a positive school climate to allow the school to focus its energies on academic achievement, and to meet the developmental needs of its students." The Planning and Management Team has the same composition as its counterpart in New Haven, except that the Prince Georges County schools have added a representative of the nonprofessional support staff. The Student Staff Services Team (principal, counselor, pupil personnel worker, psychologist, and health aide) assists the Planning and Management Team and classroom teachers with both the prevention and the management of problems.

Parents are included in all levels of school activities. Columbia Park, which had had no functioning PTA just two years earlier, now had two hundred fifty families, representing more than half the children, involved. Principal Patricia Green said that the parents feel the warmth of the atmosphere and feel comfortable about calling her and the teachers. "We do a lot of telephoning back and forth, all of us." PTA Vice President Virginia Walker said that not only did Mrs. Green ask for advice from parents, but "she really listens." At another Milliken-Comer elementary school, a teacher commented on "the enthusiasm among parents, who now are regular fixtures at the school" their participation often making school functions "standing room only."

Although it was obviously too early to judge how deeply the changes have gone, many of the effects of the Comer reforms seemed to show up more rapidly in Prince Georges County than they did in New Haven. No one really knows why. Perhaps because the Prince Georges County schools had considerably more resources to deploy than the New Haven schools, perhaps because the infusion of new resources occurred at the same time as the Comer reforms, perhaps because by the time the Comer model was exported it had matured, perhaps because the times were more supportive of efforts to educate disadvantaged children—or perhaps because the Prince Georges schools were operating under court order.

Whatever the reason, Ms. Green said that the atmosphere had changed very rapidly, and now "teachers can teach and kids can learn." At Columbia Park, school suspensions were down from twenty to thirty per year to four in the first "Comer year" and had dropped to one in the second. Test scores were up. At Green Valley, one of the other Milliken-Comer schools, the children—for the first time in memory—exceeded the national average on standardized achievement tests.

Walking through Columbia Park School with its principal was an immersion course in the methods of positive reinforcement. Whenever a child or group of children came into view, she interrupted her explanation to me on the importance to learning of self-esteem and a good self-image, to address the children. "What an orderly line you're all walking in . . . My, but that's a beautiful mushroom you've painted!" In the computer room she looked over small shoulders and complimented fancy designs and imaginative answers as well as correct answers. She moved through classrooms telling students how proud she was of their essays, attendance records, test scores, and behavior on field trips. "Instead of always coming down on what the kids are doing wrong, we try to stress what they're doing right, we try to instill a sense of pride."

Fifth-grade teacher Grace Knox said her experiences of the last year had left her convinced that "students learn more when they believe that they can do it, when they feel good about themselves."

For sixth-grade teacher Peter Westenburger, who had been at Columbia Park for ten years, the big change had been that discipline problems had lessened so dramatically, greatly improving teacher morale. "Teachers can now spend their time teaching," he said.

Back in her office, Patricia Green told me she had just become a principal when, in July of 1985, at a retreat of one hundred seventy-five Prince Georges County principals, she had heard James Comer speak for the first time. "With my own background in child development, it's not surprising that I really liked what I was hearing from him." Other principals, who initially found Dr. Comer's approach more foreign, were now also enthusiastic supporters, Ms. Green said, "because they see that it works."

At first the switch to the Comer model had been hard, she said. "It's hard to do something new, and there were a lot of changes, and that meant a lot of work, a lot of meetings, and it meant a lot of teachers were scared." But Ms. Green said the office of the superintendent had been extremely supportive, offering training, retreats, and seminars—frequently conducted by Dr. Comer—for teachers, administrative staff, parents, and the members of all the School Planning and Management Teams.

One indication that the Comer transplant had taken root seemed to be that credit for the success of the changes was being allocated locally. The teachers at Columbia Park, according to *Washington Post* reporter Sandra Sugawara, called principal Patricia Green "the moving force behind the school's turnaround." And Ms. Green said that it couldn't have been done without the additional resources, the additional personnel, the supportive parents—and most of all, the teachers—who often worked late at night and on weekends, "because they are excited about their work."

Dr. Comer would have been thrilled to hear Ms. Green's parting words to me. "Perhaps the biggest change that I've seen here over the last two years is a shift in focus. I'm hearing less about this or that child having a problem and more about the idea that maybe the system has a problem, that maybe we have to look at the structure and find out whether the school might be doing something that we could change, to make things turn out better for the children."

"RESPECT" SETS THE TONE IN EAST HARLEM

Deborah Meier's vision of a good school is different from James Comer's—but only in the details. The New Haven children sit at straight rows of desks and move through the halls in quiet and orderly lines, while the children of Central Park East are more likely to be found in clumps and corners. The visitor hears more about collaboration and climate from Dr. Comer and about "learning by doing" from Ms. Meier. The one is eager to package his process for adaptation elsewhere, while the other is reluctant to generalize about her success. But the schools that reflect their separate visions have both established an atmosphere where children and learning thrive—whether measured by achievement tests, by how engaged the children seem to be in their activities, or by what happens to the children after elementary school. Respectful, trusting personal relationships among children, teachers, principal, and parents loom large in both. So does attention to the ways that individual children develop and grow.

Central Park East Elementary School (CPE I, because it now has a sister school which is known as CPE II), located in a rundown, seventy-five-year-old building on upper Madison Avenue in New York, is part of School District Four in East Harlem. Half the population of the district have incomes below the poverty line. In 1974, when Deborah Meier founded the school, the district had the worst attendance, highest rate of suspensions, and poorest ranking in reading and math achievement of the thirty-two school districts in New York City. The school system was groping for new ideas. It seemed that things couldn't get any worse, and the district's school board and its superintendent, Anthony Alvarado, took a gamble. They authorized the establishment of schools based on a variety of educational philosophies and teaching styles. Each of the local schools would be permitted unusual flexibility in the use of funds, and parents would be given a choice of which school their children would attend.

Ms. Meier was not out to test any grand design in pedagogy when she responded to this opportunity and turned from teacher (a job she says she often misses) into principal. She wanted the public school children of Harlem to have the same experience of warmth, caring, and creative autonomy at school that she remembered from her own early school days. Her faculty was recruited from the ranks of those who knew her and were anxious to work with her, confident that she would give them the understanding and respect which they, in turn, could give their pupils. When the realization of her vision required that her efforts be shielded from a suffocating school system bureaucracy, Superintendent Anthony Alvarado promised her, "I'll make it possible."

Debbie Meier roams the hallways and classrooms of her school today wearing the placid smile of one who has seen and overcome much, addressing teachers and pupils alike by first name, unsurprised by an unexpected apparition like a huge papier-mâché sculpture. ("I think I see where the nose is.") In the large library, a wall is being knocked out to make room for an addition to house more books. The classrooms are alive with the sounds of learning, from blocks tumbling to Suzuki violin instruction to an occasional murmur in a room where everyone is writing.

Classrooms tend to be organized around themes such as families, Eskimos, the solar system, and skyscrapers, into which the basic learning skills of reading, writing, and arithmetic are integrated. The children are encouraged to venture into unexplored areas and to make their own discoveries. "We believe children learn best when they are treated with courtesy and respect, their interests are encouraged and supported, their friendships and self-discipline valued," says Ms. Meier.

Teachers have enormous independence in the classroom and invest much time and imagination organizing the classroom space and materials so that children can be productive. They move around the room supervising, teaching, coaching, advising, and suggesting. A clear and regular plan for the day for each class is designed by its teacher and posted in the classroom. Firm rules govern how children conduct themselves. Teachers stress cooperative as well as independent learning and believe that children leave CPE I with solid confidence in their personal judgment, as well as a highly developed concern for others.

Heavy emphasis is put on reading—on turning out children who not only can read but want to read and can make sense of the message. Children can go off into schoolroom corners to read, and parents are expected to make sure that reading continues at home. They are asked to read aloud regularly with their children and to let the younger children dictate stories for them to write down. Parents are even encouraged to teach reading—it doesn't matter to Ms. Meier by what method. ("No way they learn to read will harm them.")

A close relationship with home is an important part of the school ethos. Homework is seen not only as providing additional time for learning certain skills, but as a way to "keep family and school in touch with each other, and to give children the opportunity to demonstrate to their families what they have learned." Ms. Meier enthusiastically describes the many ways that school and family work together and has many stories of individual children who are helped when teachers, principal, and social workers (the latter trained and supervised by the Ackerman Institute for Family Therapy) meet and work with parents and child to solve problems that interfere with learning. "It has to be with the family. Teachers cannot be saviors of kids from their families, no matter how many difficulties

THE MYSTERY OF THE VIETNAMESE VALEDICTORIAN

The stories of New Haven, Prince Georges County, and East Harlem all suggest the value of special attention to upgrading the schooling of disadvantaged children by utilizing sound principles of education and child development applied with respect for children, families, and teachers. Despite the formidable returns on such an investment, the idea that schools should be making fundamental changes to assure that all children (or at least a far higher proportion) will emerge properly educated is not always enthusiastically received.

Even after the questions are answered of whether we really know how, whether we can afford it, whether the price of everyone's learning the basics is that of less attention to creativity, to critical thinking skills, and to the gifted—after all those questions have been reasonably answered, one question remains for many of the people I talk to. It is often unspoken, sometimes asked in euphemism, but always there. What it comes down to is some form of: "But *we* made it without all that extra attention, why can't *they?*" Or, "If the Irish and the Italians and the Jews made it, and all the new Asian immigrants are making it, why special efforts (and perhaps new money) so that the people who haven't made it by now can make it too? Even the Vietnamese boat people, for Heaven's sake, who arrive in America penniless and unable to speak English, appear in the headlines a few years later as valedictorians!"

I believe that if more Americans are to become willing to support action to improve schooling for the educationally disadvantaged, it is important to understand what I think of as the Mystery of the Vietnamese Valedictorian.

Hoang Nhu Tran was the Air Force Academy's 1987 valedictorian and one of thirty-two U.S. winners of a Rhodes scholarship to Oxford University—twelve years after leaving Vietnam via leaking boat, Philippine freighter, and refugee camps in Guam and California.

In Austin, Texas, there was Tu Anh Ngac Tran, who fled from Saigon by boat in 1979 and graduated at the top of her high school class two years later, she and two older sisters having worked to support themselves and a younger brother.

In Dallas, there was Nam Danq, class valedictorian in 1981, six years after fleeing Vietnam. He learned his first English from his junior high school French teacher, made straight A's at Dallas's Highland Park High School, and went off to Harvard.

And in New York, the 1984 City College valedictorian was Chi Luu, who came in 1979, via fishing boat and Malaysian refugee camp, and was awarded a fellowship for graduate work at the Massachusetts Institute of Technology.

These stories are not isolated examples, and the Vietnamese are not the only Asian-Americans who have been breaking academic records. In 1986 the top five prizes in the Westinghouse Talent Search, the most prominent science award for U.S. high school students, went to Asian-Americans. Though Asian-Americans make up only 2 percent of the U.S. population, they are 11 percent of the entering class at Harvard and 21 percent of the freshmen at MIT.

So why do these youngsters make it so spectacularly, despite apparent disadvantages? The answers are complicated but reasonably clear. In suggesting some answers by comparing the experiences of recent Asian immigrants with those of other minorities, I do not attempt a comprehensive analysis of the experience of minority populations in American education, but provide some illustrative information in order to dispel at least some of the seeming mystery.

First, today's Asian immigrants are a select group, with a high proportion of well-educated professionals. They are "the cream of their own societies," according to Harvard sociologist Ezra Vogel. Among the parents of the valedictorians described above are two army officers, two pharmacists, a computer programmer, a translator, and a high school principal. Jeanne F. Nidorf, a University of California psychologist who works with young Indochinese refugees in San Diego, points out that a further selection process has occurred: those who survive persecution, refugee camps, and a 50 percent mortality rate among boat people are likely to be the strongest and fittest.

Second, the high value placed on family and education, and the pressures to achieve for the sake of the family which characterize Asian cultures are a tremendous impetus to school success. Katherine Chen, whose physicist father came from Taiwan and who graduated at the top of her class from San Francisco's prestigious Lowell High School, says, "In the Chinese family, education is very important because parents see it as the way to achieve." The studies of Asian refugee success all point to the important role of home, family, and culture; Asian and Asian-American parents seem to be able to instill in their children the motivation to work hard and the idea of education as the road to success. Sociologist William Liu pinpoints the Confucian ethic as the orientation that converts hard work from drudgery to something to be done for the honor of the family.

A third factor seems to be that many of these youngsters feel an overwhelming obligation to do well to justify their parents' sacrifices in begging, borrowing, and taking great risks to rescue them. Jason Tang, a straight-A student at Brighton High School in Boston, says, "My father spent so much to send me here, I am determined to repay him and uphold our family honor."

The family and cultural pressures to learn can be so strong that they can even compensate for inadequate schooling. In an elaborate piece of research involving children with limited English language ability being taught in seventeen different classrooms, linguist Lily Wong Fillmore found that the Hispanic children's progress depended much more on the competence of the teacher than did the Chinese children's progress. Faced with teachers who gave confusing instructions, the Hispanic children's learning suffered, while the Chinese children often became all the more attentive and still performed relatively well.

Last, and perhaps most important, is that both at home and in the neighborhood the child is surrounded by evidence that hard work, respect for authority, and education pay off. The lessons learned outside of school are a perfect fit with the requirements for school success.

It was much the same with Jewish immigrants in an earlier time. The same big-city academic high schools—like Lowell in San Francisco and Stuyvesant in New York—in which Asian-Americans are the majority today had predominantly Jewish student bodies a few decades ago. Among the Jewish immigrant children, as among the Asians, the high value the family placed on education, reading, and respect for authority helped to make the culture of school seem less alien. "The Asian-Americans are very similar to the Jewish immigrants of the 1930s and forties," says the assistant principal of Stuyvesant, "with their emphasis on learning and the family and the sheer energy they get from their new opportunity in America."

Both the Asian-Americans and the Jews, says the principal of Lowell, "see education as a prerequisite to success."

The Irish immigrant route to American success was somewhat different. Irish family values did not put so much emphasis on education, and the children of the Irish did not initially fare so well in American schools. Their own success in school generally began only after their parents had achieved some political and economic success. For most, that happened relatively quickly, for the big Irish immigration occurred while a rapidly expanding economy generated a great demand for workers. The Irish were able to establish themselves and provide for their families, although most arrived here unskilled, illiterate, and extremely poor. They were needed to build the railroads, dig the canals, and work the factories. They tended the machines of New England and soon the machines of big-city politics. Their children could see in their immediate surroundings evidence of reward for hard work and perseverance.

The life experience of blacks in this country provides a dramatic contrast to that of Asian, Jewish, and Irish immigrants. The contrast helps to explain why a significant proportion of black children need something more and something different from schools than most are now receiving, and something more and different than most immigrant children needed.

The contrast begins, of course, with the circumstances of arrival. Blacks came not eagerly, but in chains. They were kept outside the mainstream of American opportunity until long after "emancipation," their exclusion readily maintained by highly visible, indelible color. Unlike other newcomers they could not settle close to family and friends from the "old country" to maintain ties, traditions, and mutual support but lived where the master dictated. For other ethnic groups, language, religion, and cuisine were rallying points and small business opportunities. "But the ethnic identity of black America was the target of cultural genocide."

Destroyed were the strong family traditions of preslavery West Africa, which had emphasized responsibility for even distant kin and had given children a powerful sense of belonging. In America, the white master had total control of food, clothing, shelter, religion, companionship, sex, and work; children were reared for the use of the master, not for the pride of parents or to carry on family traditions.

Education of slaves was seen by whites as a threat to their absolute control, and by 1835 every Southern state had enacted laws which forbade slaves to teach one another and "made the instruction of slaves in reading and writing by whites an indictable offense." Sociologist Sara Lawrence Lightfoot believes that from the days of slavery, in part perhaps because of the repressive laws, blacks attached an almost redemptive, otherworldly quality to education. She cites examples of heroic efforts by blacks to become educated. As black churches and fraternal organizations began to gain in strength in the North, one of their most important functions became the establishment of free schools. But faith in education turned out not to be enough.

When slavery was at last officially abolished, blacks, concentrated in the South, could not readily avail themselves of the expanding industrial opportunities in the North. Blacks were also largely shut out of the labor movement in the early 1900s, and even the skilled trades learned in slavery were lost. In the 1940s, when blacks in large numbers began to migrate northward, the demand for unskilled labor had shrunk. By the time racist obstacles to employment had receded in the 1960s, so had the ample opportunities of the last stage of the industrial revolution. Blacks were hurt more than others by deindustrialization because of their heavy concentration in the auto, rubber, and steel industries. Many black men who had succeeded as agricultural laborers in the South, or briefly as unskilled factory workers in the North, could no longer earn a living wage. As social analyst Michael Harrington put it, just as poor blacks "arrived in the urban labor market ready to climb up the ladder of social mobility, the bottom rungs were being hacked off the ladder."

Although formal segregation had been ended, blacks worked for disproportionately low pay and were out of work in disproportionately high numbers. After World War II, despite diminishing discrimination, large numbers of black men were economically less successful than their fathers had been. The racial division of labor created by centuries of discrimination was reinforced because, in an advanced industrial society, those in the low-wage sector of the economy are more adversely affected by impersonal economic shifts. An economy that had absorbed unprecedented numbers of baby-boomers, women, and immigrants over the last two decades once more left poor blacks behind.

Hispanics, too, came into the U.S. labor market most massively at a time when opportunities for the uneducated and unskilled were shrinking. (The number of Hispanics in the United States has tripled in the last three decades, and 41 per cent of Hispanic adults have only an elementary school education.) As a result, Hispanics face many of the same bleak economic prospects as blacks.

Adults who cannot support their families, who feel excluded, powerless, and alienated, whose own direct experience seems to prove that hard work does not in fact pay off and that education leads nowhere—these adults are not in a good position to imbue their children with the motivation that makes for success at school. Anthropologist John Ogbu found that the parents of the poor black and Hispanic youngsters he studied in California constantly emphasized the need for more education but also taught their children— both verbally and through their own lives—that they were unlikely to "make it." The youngsters' own observations confirmed the negative part of the message. They were convinced their wages were not going to be commensurate with their education. They lost "the desire to perform or compete effectively in their school work," and they stopped trying in school because they saw so few opportunities in their futures.

William J. Bennett, President Reagan's Secretary of Education, has said, quite correctly, that research shows that there is a set of beliefs that contributes to success in school: "Belief in the value of hard work, the importance of personal responsibility, and the importance of education itself." But these beliefs are difficult to maintain in the face of contrary experience. Schools themselves often communicate low expectations for the behavior and achievement of black and Hispanic pupils.

It is a formidable challenge for today's ghetto parent to try to teach a child to go off to school with high expectations, to work hard, to pay attention to the teacher. The lessons that sent other children of the poor scurrying obediently off to school to make something of themselves have little foundation in reality in many inner city schools and neighborhoods today.

There is, of course, another world of black experience in America today, where change has been rapid, where color no longer defines potential, and where young children have bright futures—in school and beyond. *Crisis* magazine used to list every black college graduate—a task no magazine could undertake today. Between 1972 and 1981, the percentage of black accountants, computer programmers, and physicians doubled. Between 1970 and 1987, the number of black elected officials increased by 350 percent. Blacks head major universities, large cities, and influential national organizations.

Many of those who were able to walk through "the doors of opportunity that [the Supreme Court] and the Civil Rights Acts of the 1960s opened" had striking common elements in their background. "The hostility of the outside world which told black children we were not worth much was buffered and countered by our families, schools, churches and mentors who affirmed our worth," writes Marian Wright Edelman in her book *Families in Peril.*

Ms. Edelman, graduate of Spellman College and Yale Law School and the nation's leading advocate for children, grew up in a small Southern town. Her father, a black Mississippi minister, always insisted that there be books in the house and that they be read. As important, "we had teachers and other adult role models who said, 'You can achieve, and we believe in you.' We had a support system that was exceedingly strong."

She contrasts that experience with the ghettos of today, bereft of many of the concrete examples of hope and achievement that help instill a value system in the young, devoid of many of the institutions that were a source of strength to previous generations, robbed of the protective "bonds forged between our education system, our churches and our families."

No one institution can replace that sense of community coherence, especially not in the midst of today's urban decay. But the schools we have described, and others finding their own unique way to educate disadvantaged children, are fashioning new bonds—between schools and families, between children and their futures—that promise a lifeline even to families that have long lived without hope. In collaboration with families and other community institutions, such schools can play an important part in transmitting, even to children growing up at grave risk, a sense of belonging and of hope.

HELPING SCHOOLS FROM OUTSIDE

In recent years, as concern has grown about the difficulties faced by schools in educating disadvantaged youngsters, attempts to help from outside the schools have been initiated by industry and by community organizations. Most of these activities have taken the form of strengthening the links between high school students and the world of work. Some programs, like Cities in Schools, have also provided services directly to individual students.

One particularly dramatic example of outside intervention to help the schools achieve their educational purpose stemmed from the impulsive offer made in 1981 by New York industrialist-philanthropist, Eugene Lang.

As he later told it, Lang had been invited to speak at the commencement of the elementary school from which he had graduated a half-century earlier. Looking down on the fifty-nine black and Hispanic sixth-grade graduates before him, groping for a way to convey his message about the importance of education, he made his dramatic promise: for every one of the students who finished high school, he would pay for a college education!

The generous gesture of the sixty-seven-year-old self-made millionaire captured the imagination of the public—and inspired other individuals to become involved with other groups of disadvantaged sixth-grade students. (By the summer of 1987 a hundred sponsors had made similar commitments to some four thousand children across the country.)

But few observers have appreciated how far beyond a gift of money Lang's involvement went. Discovering by trial and error that a one-shot intervention, even a big one, had its limitations, he ended up by fashioning and funding what amounted to a comprehensive, intensive, and flexible support program.

Soon after the cheering and the hugging had stopped on that sweltering June day in 1981, Lang became aware that few of these youngsters would be able to make use of his pledge of money unless something more were added. A friend who was director of the Youth Action Program, a community action agency serving East Harlem, helped Lang to hire John Rivera, a seventeen-year old student of public administration at John Jay College. Rivera had grown up in East Harlem and had been working at Youth Action as a volunteer. His first assignment from Lang was simply to visit the youngsters at home, to assure them and their families that the offer was for real, and to ask the students to stay in touch with Lang and with him.

It did not take long for Lang, Rivera, and the staff at Youth Action to realize that the students had much greater and more immediate needs, going well beyond the prospect of college tuitions and the trips to New York museums and cultural events that Lang had asked Rivera to arrange. They would need a lot of help in the next six years to make it through school. Rivera found himself with a full-time job.

Lang discovered it was not enough to convey his message about the importance of education just once—or even several times, on the students' occasional visits to his office. It became the mission of trouble-shooter Rivera to carry the message in his frequent encounters with the youngsters. It was the message he conveyed when he showed up at a student's home if he had to be rousted out of bed to get to school. It was the message that came through when Rivera accompanied student and parent to the principal's office after a student had been suspended for fighting. It was the message that he transmitted as he worked with the youngsters to choose the high school they would apply to—exploring alternatives, helping them to think out what interested them, what they were good at, so they could make a good choice of school—and then helping to make sure they got in.

Rivera says, "I was able to help, first, because everybody—the parents, the kids, the schools—welcomed my help because everybody could agree on the focus on education. Second, I could be flexible—I wasn't limited to helping in just one area." So he helped with whatever was needed. ("You just can't imagine the extent of these kids' unmet needs for health and social services.") He helped families with housing. He persuaded the Youth Action Program to set up a writing class for the students. ("At school they were being drilled to perform on achievement tests, but they were already in high school, and none had yet learned to write grammatically.") He worked to make up for what the families and the schools and the community were unable to do to bolster the youngsters' self-esteem and aspirations. He ran support groups to give youngsters the opportunity to talk about what was troubling them. ("Everything, from problems with parents, with teachers, with sexual relationships, but always we returned to a focus on education.")

For six years he stayed with the youngsters, always aware that there was a lot he couldn't do. "Kids walk up and down those buildings, they're afraid of getting mugged and raped. They see things that children ought never to be exposed to. And I can't take them out of those surroundings."

In combination with Eugene Lang's largesse and personal devotion, Johnny Rivera and the Youth Action Program did manage to provide an array of supports that were instrumental in getting a record number of the youngsters through high school. Of the fifty-one students who were still living in New York City six years after Eugene Lang's original promise, thirty completed high school in June 1987, and Rivera expected that forty-eight will have graduated by January of 1988—an unheard-of achievement in a population where the dropout rate is estimated to be anywhere between 40 and 75 percent.

Lang, even as he travels around the country to persuade others to support youngsters in their own communities through his "I Have a Dream" Foundation, recognizes the limitations in these valiant efforts. But he is convinced that he has a contribution to make, not only by his direct involvement in the lives of these youngsters, and by enabling a talented community organizer like John Rivera to work with them for six years. He is also intent on getting the word out that "these kids have to be restored to full membership in the larger community." They have to recognize, and the rest of us have to recognize, he says, "that the resources of the total community are legitimately theirs to take advantage of and contribute to and be a part of."

Rivera believes that efforts to attain these objectives must be undertaken in the closest possible partnership with the schools. Still to be developed is a mechanism whereby schools themselves might generalize from the Lang-Rivera experience in developing new kinds of supports for high-risk students. In the meantime, Eugene Lang and John Rivera, like others who have created model programs described in these pages, have shown that with intensive, comprehensive, and personalized help, the long-term prospects even of children growing up in highly disadvantaged circumstances can be markedly brightened.

· 10 ·

The Lessons
of Successful Programs

At every stage of a child's development, interventions exist that can improve the odds for a favorable long-term outcome. But the programs that have succeeded in changing outcomes for high-risk children are different, in fundamental ways, from prevailing services, and we cannot build on these programs unless we understand the differences.

ATTRIBUTES OF INTERVENTIONS THAT WORK

Programs that are successful in reaching and helping the most disadvantaged children and families typically offer a *broad spectrum of services.* They recognize that social and emotional support and concrete help (with food, housing, income, employment—or anything else that seems to the family to be an insurmountable obstacle) may have to be provided before a family can make use of other interventions, from antibiotics to advice on parenting. A Washington, D.C. agency seeking to provide a high-risk population with prenatal care, for example, reports that unless it responds to the needs that the pregnant women themselves consider more immediate—like housing—then "you just can't get them to pay attention to prenatal care."

Dr. David Rogers, as president of the Robert Wood Johnson Foundation, came to a similar conclusion. The foundation's accumulating experience, he wrote, made him aware that "human misery is generally the result of, or accompanied by, a great untidy basketful of intertwined and interconnected circumstances and happenings" that often all need attention if a problem is to be overcome. Successful programs recognize that they cannot respond to these "untidy basketfuls" of needs without regularly *crossing traditional professional and bureaucratic boundaries.*

Most successful programs find that interventions cannot be routinized or applied uniformly. Staff members and program structures are fundamentally *flexible.* Professionals are able to exercise discretion about meeting individual needs (which new mother needs three home visits every week and which needs only one during the first month), and families are able to decide what services to utilize (whether and when to enroll their child in the available day care program) and how they want to participate (whether to work in their child's school as a library volunteer, a paid aide, or a member of the parent advisory body).

Successful programs *see the child in the context of family and the family in the context of its surroundings.* The successful school mobilizes parents in a collaborative effort to impart a love of reading, and of every other kind of academic learning. The clinician treating an infant for recurrent diarrhea or a child with anemia sees beyond the patient on the examining table to whether a public health nurse or social worker needs to find out what kind of nonmedical help the family may require (qualifying for food stamps or the WIC nutrition program, help with homemaking), or whether something must be done about a contaminated water supply. Successful programs are able to offer services and support to parents who need help with their lives as adults before they can make good use of services for their children.

Successful programs describe their staffs as skilled and highly committed. Often staff become models to parents of effective ways of caring for and teaching children, and models to children of roles they could aspire to. The programs emphasize that their staffs have the training, support, and time to establish solid personal relationships. Professionals in these programs are perceived by those they serve as *people who care about them and respect them, people they can trust.* It is hard to know to what extent these relationships are the product of acquired skills informed by the insights of psychiatry and human development, of the unusual personal attributes of a gifted staff, of the availability of sufficient time—or of some combination of these. But their importance is clear.

Successful programs with a large number of multiproblem families see to it that *services are coherent and easy to use.* Most are convinced that relying too readily on referrals to other agencies interferes with the development of a good working relationship with client or patient and with getting needed services to the individual or family. These programs take special pains to maintain continuity in relationships, especially with high-risk populations and at critical life junctures. They ensure that a nurse who has gotten close to a teenage mother during her pregnancy can continue to see her during the early months of parenthood. The *continuity* does not necessarily have to be provided by a single individual, but often is maintained by a small, committed team.

In these programs someone takes responsibility for assuring that child and family needs are in fact met, regardless of bureaucratic or professional compartments. No one says, "this may be what you need, but helping you get it is not part of my job or outside our jurisdiction." What is perhaps most striking about programs that work for the children and families in the shadows is that all of them find ways to *adapt or circumvent traditional professional and bureaucratic limitations when necessary to meet the needs of those they serve.*

Professionals venture outside their own familiar surroundings to provide services in nontraditional settings, including homes, and often at nontraditional hours. The program does not ask that families surmount formidable barriers unassisted before they can get what they need. It makes sure that payment arrangements and eligibility determinations do not pose insuperable obstacles. It does not set preconditions—such as keeping a series of fixed appointments in faraway places or displaying adequate "motivation"—that may screen out those most in need. On the contrary, successful programs try to reduce the barriers—of money, time, fragmentation, geographic, and psychological remoteness—that make heavy demands on those with limited energy and organizational skills. Rather than wait passively to serve only those who make it through the daunting maze, these programs persevere to reach the perplexed, discouraged, and ambivalent, the hardest to reach, who are often the ones who would benefit most.

In successful programs, *professionals are able to redefine their roles* to respond to severe, but often unarticulated, needs. Recall the Tacoma Homebuilders' therapist who helps the mother to clean house, the neonatologist in Watts who helps run a magnet high school, the pediatrician in Baltimore who founded a Head Start program to work with lead-poisoned children and their mothers, and the child psychiatrist in New Haven who has spent most of several years working in the local school system with teachers, parents, principals, and administrators. These professionals have found a way to escape the constraints of a professional value system that confers highest status on those who deal with issues from which all human complexity has been removed.

In short, the programs that succeed in helping the children and families in the shadows are intensive, comprehensive, and flexible. They also share an extra dimension, more difficult to capture: Their climate is created by skilled, committed professionals who establish respectful and trusting relationships and respond to the individual needs of those they serve. The nature of their services, the terms on which they are offered, the relationships with families, the essence of the programs themselves—all take their shape from the needs of those they serve rather than from the precepts, demands, and boundaries set by professionalism and bureaucracies.

This suggests a fundamental contradiction between the needs of vulnerable children and families and the traditional requirements of professionalism and bureaucracy—a contradiction that future attempts to build on the programs that have been successful in the past must carefully take into account. This contradiction helps to explain why programs that work for populations at risk are so rare, while less effective programs are so much more common.

WHY INEFFECTIVE INTERVENTIONS ARE SO PREVALENT

Prevailing programs have been shaped by powerful political, professional, and administrative forces that are not easily modified by new needs, new opportunities, or even new knowledge.

It is important to understand why lessons of successful models are ignored, while past mistakes are perpetuated; why so many services turn out to be ineffective, sometimes even after financial barriers to access have been removed. Otherwise failures, some of them predictable on the basis of current knowledge, are erroneously interpreted as evidence that high-risk families are beyond help.

Whether it be medical care, social services, or education, when those in greatest need do receive services, they are most likely to be too fragmented and too meager to accomplish their purpose. This is not only wasteful of resources but creates an overwhelming managerial burden for those families who are not yet too discouraged to go on seeking help.

Because these lessons remain unlearned, we pay the price over and over again. Children's advocates succeed in expanding access to medical care, but inside the walls of the doctor's office or clinic the content of care remains unmatched to the needs of the underserved. Recall Gail from Chapter 5, the thirteen-year-old who stabbed a boy on the playground, possibly as a result of a psychomotor seizure which might have been averted with proper medical attention. Gail had been seen at the local hospital more than thirty times. But because of the fragmented, episodic nature of the care that poor families get, Gail had never had a proper workup until after she had killed her schoolmate.

Striving for efficiency by deploying personnel to focus on sharply defined, single problems, bureaucracies fragment services into absurd slivers. New York City's Office of Family Services in 1986 had twenty-two full-time employees working exclusively as "utility disconnect caseworkers," whose task it was to assess a family's utility situation and arrange, in hardship cases, for restoration of gas and electricity, canceled for failure to pay. In April of 1986, these cases represented fully one fifth of the agency's case load. The workers' mandate did not include responding to any family needs except those associated with the inability to pay utility bills. As a result, in the laconic words of a report to the Foundation for Child Development, "these cases tend to reappear in [the agency's] offices with their utilities again disconnected or with other serious problems."

Extreme fragmentation of services and a consistent "pattern of failed connections" were identified as the critical weaknesses in children's mental health services in a broad review by the Children's Defense Fund. The study revealed that children's problems and need for services were often identified early, and sometimes repeatedly. But the services themselves seldom materialized.

A similar finding of "failed connections" emerged from a review of case records of children who had died or been seriously injured as a result of child abuse in Massachusetts during 1984. All the children were known to social agencies. Even children and families with extensive contacts with social agencies were not getting the services they needed. Across the country, case workers with direct responsibility for vulnerable children often experience "impossibly large caseloads, excessive and meaningless paperwork, no time to get to know the children for whom they make decisions, no time to visit families, and no training to deal with complex family problems."

Some services, like traditional psychotherapy, which help many relatively fortunate individuals to live better and richer lives, turn out not to be very useful to individuals in multiproblem families, especially when offered in isolation from other services and supports. When the family's more immediate needs make the quest for internal psychological change seem like an unaffordable luxury, and when the terms for obtaining therapy (such as requirements for various family members to keep appointments at distant places or inconvenient times) exceed the family's organizational resources, psychotherapy is least likely to be helpful. Nevertheless, it is often the only intervention offered to families in distress.

Sister Mary Paul, of Brooklyn's Sunset Park Center for Family Life, says that the most troubled families in her community do not get much help from the local mental health center. The center "can't get involved with the family or the school or the legal system —only the individual client, sitting there in the office." As long as that is true, she says, the mental health center's services will remain largely irrelevant to the families in greatest need.

Conventional parent education, which brings helpful child-rearing information to many middle-class parents, is another intervention that is often quite irrelevant to socially isolated and otherwise seriously disadvantaged parents. The mother who needs the most help with parenting—because she is alcoholic, depressed, or under serious economic stress, or perhaps was profoundly neglected during her own childhood—is unlikely to find the information offered by most parenting classes very useful.

What it comes down to is that, for the children of the shadows, rotten outcomes—even risk factors—cannot be prevented by simplistic, one-pronged approaches of any kind.

But the quest endures. Dr. Jonas Salk, whose vaccine saved millions of children from the ravages of polio, told a 1985 Children's Defense Fund conference that he hoped to see teenage pregnancy eradicated just as polio had been. He said he thought that the peer counseling he had heard so much about might become the needed preventive vaccine.

We cling to the vaccine analogy because identical batches of serum can be mass-produced, a single shot gives years of protection, its efficacy is not dependent on by whom or how it is administered, or on the understanding or motivation of the recipient.

How complex, by comparison, is the problem of protecting a disadvantaged child against too-early childbearing. No standardized dose of essential nurturing interactions can be devised. No booster shot will assure the timely acquisition of school-relevant skills and motivation. No one can send a prepackaged supply of warm, encouraging teachers, an orderly school climate, adequate nutrition, and good health care. Even a good peer counseling program, which can indeed be helpful as part of a broader array of interventions, cannot by itself perform miracles for youngsters in isolated families and depleted neighborhoods.

Some acknowledge the complexity and insist it is so complicated it can't be done at all. Others ignore the complexity and pursue the chimera of a shot in the arm.

Examples abound of the lure of the cheap and easy shortcuts to changing long-term outcomes. A perfectly reasonable observation— that both a mother and her newborn baby seem to thrive when they can spend undisturbed time together soon after birth—was widely regarded for several years as *the* way to a trouble-free future for the whole family. Some professionals and some of the public adopted an "epoxy" theory of attachment, inferring miraculous results from the mother and infant being bonded together before the glue dries, so to speak. (A staff note in one hospital obstetrics ward warned, "Do not remove baby until after bonding has occurred.") Attachment being the product, so far as is known, of a long and complicated process, it is not surprising that several studies have found no positive long-term effects of such mechanistic attempts to promote attachment through early bonding.

The search for shortcuts usually tries to bypass the "messy" psychological and social contaminants of the "real" (i.e., biological) problem. A flurry of excitement was recently aroused by a new technique aimed at reducing premature birth. The process, pioneered in France, consists of identifying high-risk pregnant women, providing them with weekly pelvic exams and education to help them to detect the early signs of premature labor, then promptly administering medication to inhibit uterine activity. The hope was to reduce the incidence of low birthweight without having to reorient obstetrical practice toward greater concern with the living conditions of pregnant women, especially disadvantaged women. A five-site trial of this intervention, supported by the March of Dimes, produced disappointing preliminary results in mid-1987. Whatever small, documented successes occurred were with upper- and middle-income, well-educated women. Once again it was found that the more circumscribed interventions tend to be ineffective for those at greatest risk for nonbiological reasons.

Another example of the futile quest is "child management training," a refined and systematic form of parent education that has attracted considerable attention as a way of preventing delinquency. Child management training, which teaches parents how to use rewards and punishments to control "bratty behavior," was the centerpiece of a popular magazine article by Harvard professor James Q. Wilson on how to reduce violence and crime in America by changing family functioning. Aimed at families whose children are in trouble at home, at school, or with the law, child management training, too, has turned out on further study to be effective primarily in families whose difficulties do not go beyond their "inability to manage child behavior appropriately." The researchers concluded that "a greater range of services are required" for families whose problems are not so circumscribed.

Many interventions have turned out to be ineffective not because seriously disadvantaged families are beyond help, but because we have tried to attack complex, deeply rooted tangles of troubles with isolated fragments of help, with help rendered grudgingly in one-shot forays, with help designed less to meet the needs of beneficiaries than to conform to professional or bureaucratic convenience, with help that may be useful to middle-class families but is often irrelevant to families struggling to survive.

With all the experience now amassed of success and failure in providing high-risk families and children with health and social services, education, child care, and family supports, there is no longer any basis for believing:

- That some single, simple one-shot intervention is bound to work, and produce a quick payoff, if only we could find the right one.
- That whatever works for middle-class people should work for everybody.
- That if only someone were smart enough to devise the right incentives, or the right magical *something,* it could all be done on the cheap—solutions without sacrifice, miracles that change outcomes without cost to the taxpayers.

Disproven premises, all. But much money and much energy have been and are being expended on efforts based on just such illusions. Because they appeal to our yearning for simplicity. Because simple programs and narrowly defined interventions aimed at precisely defined problems make for easy measurement, assessment, and replication. Because it is easiest to mobilize political support to fight one simple evil with one simple remedy. So we are left with a myriad of halfway programs which fail to ameliorate some of our most profound social problems.

Other past failures have their origins in the fact that powerful forces and institutions, far removed from valiant local efforts to establish and maintain effective programs, can decide their fate. Unsupportive policies can threaten the survival of valuable local programs and undermine the chances of successful replication.

Federal and state governments and private health insurers determine what health services will be paid for. If reimbursement methods and definitions of what is paid for do not reflect the complexities of effective interventions, they will undermine the stability of effective programs. If certain services, such as outreach, counseling and support services, are not paid for by Medicaid and private insurers, then hard-pressed health programs are not going to provide them, no matter how essential to the program's purposes. If reimbursement arrangements do not reflect the higher costs of caring for poor, multiproblem families, programs that provide the poor with the care they need cannot survive. That is why there is no correlation between a program's survival and its success in improving outcomes for families at risk.

In the provision of social services, the "extreme and irrational fragmentation" of both tasks and clientele means that attempts to coordinate services at the local agency level and make them available to families in some integrated way are so time-consuming, costly, and difficult that they are unlikely to succeed. Differential reimbursement for different categories of social services often dictates program design and the range of services rendered. When out-of-home placement is better reimbursed than services to preserve families, when more money is available to keep babies in hospitals than in families, the most dedicated individuals and agencies will be frustrated in their efforts to keep families together and place abandoned babies in homes.

MOVING BEYOND ISOLATED MODELS

Having seen that simple, narrow remedies often turn out to be ineffective and that local efforts cannot long survive in the absence of supportive state and federal policies, and having identified the uncommon—even fragile—attributes of programs that succeed in helping high-risk families, we reach the critical question of how effective interventions can be widely implemented.

The most frequent ground for skepticism I encountered while working on this book was on the question of whether model programs, however successful, had any enduring significance, considering the well-known difficulties of large-scale replication. Repeatedly I was asked what purpose it served to describe ten or twenty terrific programs that had been started in unique circumstances by politically influential and charismatic leaders who were in a position to protect their creations against bureaucratic battering and to attract unusually competent and committed staffs.

Starting a program and keeping it afloat in unsupportive surroundings admittedly requires unusually gifted and tenacious individuals. Many of the programs I have described were indeed started with funding put together in strange and ingenious ways by people willing to swim upstream against the currents of prevailing laws, regulations, bureaucracies, and professional traditions.

"A pediatrician working in a program for the underserved needs the virtues and vices of St. Francis of Assissi, Machiavelli and Theodore Roosevelt," wrote Dr. Margaret Heagarty, chief of pediatrics at Harlem Hospital.

It is true that most of the programs described in this book have operated in unusual conditions and with unusually gifted leaders. Almost all were able, for a variety of reasons, to operate free of the normal external constraints. Most were funded at least in part with foundation or government grants that did not flow through the ordinary channels or carry the usual encumbrances. All of their circumstances were somehow idiosyncratic. Several began under the auspices of a university with a mandate to conduct service experiments; two had a specific charge from the federal government that was waging a War on Poverty at the time; one mandate came from a state legislature alarmed about high infant mortality rates and one from a highly unusual state governor; three of the programs began in situations where the special circumstances of the moment allowed effective leaders to insulate the programs from normal pressures; one was begun by a small independent private agency in a particularly benign climate. None of these programs began as part of a large health, social services, or education system under what might be considered ordinary circumstances. Some had as a central part of their activities the objective of modifying an entire system (the Comer program in New Haven, the neighborhood health centers, and the Head Start programs), but not a single one was the product of the normal functioning of a large system—public or private.

But the fact that the programs described in this book are unusual does not make them unimportant—if only because it is essential to understand that there *are* programs that have succeeded in solving difficult problems. Model programs—no matter how special their circumstance—bring home that, even in an imperfect world, something can be done to address certain seemingly intractable social problems. They provide a vision of what can be achieved, a benchmark for judging other efforts, and—at a minimum—a takeoff point in the search for better understanding of the elements of interventions worthy of widespread implementation.

In medical research, discovery of a new technique for splicing a gene or replacing an organ is not dismissed because only one team in the world has assembled the talent and resources to perform the procedure. On the contrary, the initial achievement may stimulate clinicians and investigators everywhere to replicate it. Few are deterred by the prospect that the process will be time-consuming and require unusual skills.

The programs described in this book are performing vital functions and addressing urgent national problems. Yet, with the exception of Head Start, WIC, and Medicaid, which are national in scope (although they still don't reach the majority of their potential beneficiaries), most of these programs are available in only a few isolated places. They owe their existence to idiosyncratic combinations of circumstance, talent, and commitment that have prevailed in the face of the perverse incentives operating to discourage interventions of proven effectiveness. At the most fundamental level, that is poor public policy.

It would be naive to contend that once the nature of successful programs is described and understood, they will speedily be made available to those who most need them. A marvel of our pluralistic system in America is that everything can be tried, but the downside is that even when something works, it is very hard to make it work throughout the land. The difficulties that must be overcome, however, are not insurmountable.

Devising strategies for surmounting obstacles to widespread replication is as difficult as devising a successful intervention in the first place. The development of such strategies is not a task for this book, or indeed for any book. It is a task that involves the sustained give-and-take of many minds, many interests, many disciplines, and many levels of authority and practical experience. It is, however, possible to describe six great challenges that must be addressed if successful programs are to be widely implemented:

- Knowing what works.
- Proving we can afford it.
- Attracting and training enough skilled and committed personnel.
- Resisting the lure of replication through dilution.
- Gentling the heavy hand of bureaucracy.
- Devising a variety of replication strategies.

KNOWING WHAT WORKS

Because of the widely held view that we really know very little about such matters as crime, teenage pregnancy, and school dropouts, reliable evidence about interventions that work has become more important than ever. Twenty years ago, when social policy was being formulated in an atmosphere of boundless optimism, the combination of a little theoretical research, fragments of experience, and a lot of faith and dedication was enough to justify a new social program. Today budget deficits, fears of wasting money and perpetuating dependency, and a gloomy sense of social problems beyond solution have combined to reinforce the demands of the keepers of the purse strings to see tangible evidence of effectiveness as a condition for support of any social program.

Unfortunately, the reasonable demand for evidence that something good is happening as a result of the investment of funds often exerts unreasonable pressures to convert both program input and outcomes into whatever can be readily measured. This rush to quantify, which engages funders, policymakers, academics, policy analysts, and program administrators alike, has had damaging effects on the development of sound interventions aimed at long-term outcomes. Programs are driven into building successes by ducking hard cases. Agencies shy away from high-risk youngsters, who provide scant payoff for effort expended when it comes to bottom-line totals. Energy is diverted into evaluation research that asks trivial questions and sacrifices significance to precision.

Pressures to quantify have crippling effects on the development of the kind of programs most likely to help high-risk families. Current methods of demonstrating effectiveness do not capture the essential extra dimension that characterizes successful programs. Organizations are pressed to shape their objectives and methods of intervening with an eye to easy measurement, and cannot be blamed for choosing to narrow rather than broaden their efforts.

Many of the most effective interventions with high-risk families are inherently unstandardized and idiosyncratic. Many agencies have found a mix of services, adaptable to different sites and responsive to particular family needs, to be an essential component of effective interventions. When a home visitor, for example, responds flexibly to a family's unique problems, the unique outcome may be just what the family needs but what the evaluator dreads. (The young mother worried about the illness of a grandparent seeks the advice of the home visitor, who responds to this concern instead of teaching the mother how to read a thermometer, as planned. Will the evaluator be able to capture the young woman's greater comfort and trust, and their consequences for mother and child?)

Educators working with disadvantaged children find that "these kids can't learn until they learn to trust" and that "sustained intellectual growth depends on the quality of relationships established between parent, teacher and child." Are program objectives like the acquisition of trust or the development of warm personal relationships, found to be essential attributes of virtually all programs serving high-risk families, to be sacrificed because they are so much harder to reduce to quantifiable terms than is performance on multiple-choice or IQ tests?

Some program outcomes, such as the effect of preschool education on increasing the chances of high school completion or the effect of family support on reducing the incidence of delinquency, are difficult and expensive to document because of the distance in time and place between intervention and outcome. Are the interventions whose payoff is difficult to document to receive less support as a result?

For many services, *how* they are delivered is as important as *that* they are delivered. For example, it has been conclusively established that responding to patients' and families' psychological needs has favorable effects on health outcomes, and that the physician's "skillful listening, empathy, warmth and attentive interest" are central to good and appropriate child health care. Yet the subtle "how" eludes us. Policy-making tends to remain on the more solid ground of numbers of children covered by health insurance and numbers who see physicians, even though these numbers tell us little about the adequacy of the health care they receive. Pushed to rely on what is countable, we have come to regard access to health services as an adequate measure of effectiveness. Similarly, the number of dollars spent on education, child care, or social services becomes a proxy measure which is quickly equated with effectiveness—because it is often the only window on what is actually happening.

The rush to quantitative judgment, with its demands for immediate results, also interferes with orderly progress in developing complex programs. Professor Donald Campbell, considered by many the dean of program evaluation, says a new norm is needed to replace the current practice of prematurely evaluating programs not yet working as their staffs intended. The principle he proposes is "Evaluate no program until it is proud." By not insisting on formal evaluations until program personnel have themselves concluded that there is "something special that we know works here and we think others ought to borrow," Dr. Campbell believes the sum total of useful "borrowable" information would be vastly increased.

Professor Campbell also endorses an approach to the use of information that forms a fundamental premise of this book: judgments and decisions should be based on "a cumulation" of wisdom. No single study, no single set of statistics, no single piece of evidence should be the basis of decisions to fund or not to fund, to abandon or to replicate a project. Judgments about what works should be based on a thoughtful appraisal of the many kinds of evidence available. That means relying not only on quantitative but also on qualitative information, not only on evaluations by "objective" outsiders but on the experiences of committed practitioners, not on isolated discoveries but on understanding how consistent the findings are with other knowledge. Relying on common sense, prudence, and understanding in interpreting evidence does not mean sacrificing rigor in assessing information. But applying human intelligence may bring us closer to policy-relevant conclusions than reliance on numbers that have been manipulated in ways that ultimately conceal a basic ignorance of what is really going on.

Proving We Can Afford It

Clearly, successful interventions do not come cheap. Comprehensiveness, intensity, quality of professionals, staff that spends time—none of that comes cheap. The question is not only whether we can afford it, but how to prove that we can.

That the return on the investment far exceeds the cost is true more often than is apparent, because the calculation of true costs and true benefits involves elusive factors not easy to quantify.

First, some benefits are not measurable in dollars at all. The benefits of living in a fair and just society with a shared sense of civility and community cannot be reduced to a dollar figure.

Second, prevention—be it of lung cancer or teenage pregnancy—in its nature means that absolutely nothing happens, its success registered only in later statistical comparisons. The woman who never started smoking will never know how many years she has added to her life and what she has protected her unborn infant from. The school that kept its disadvantaged second-graders on a path toward school success cannot know at the end of the school year how many life trajectories were permanently altered.

However, although they do not tell the whole story, there are solid indicators of economic payoffs from effective interventions.

Substantial money is often saved within the system in which the intervention is provided. For example:

· Good prenatal care reduces low birthweight, which, in turn, reduces requirements for expensive in-hospital and follow-up intensive care. The Institute of Medicine of the National Academy of Sciences calculated the projected saving in medical costs during the first year of life if the low birthweight rate were reduced by two and a half percentage points (an achievement substantially exceeded by all three model prenatal care programs described in Chapter 4): The saving comes out to three and a third times as much as the cost of timely prenatal care to high-risk women.

· Good family supports and social services reduce the need for more expensive out-of-home placement of children. The average cost of the Homebuilders program (Chapter 7) was $2,600 per family (in 1985), compared to $3,600 per capita for foster care, $19,500 for group care, and up to $67,500 for institutional care. Since 90 percent of the children seen by Homebuilders were still with their families at one-year follow-up, and since all would have been removed from their families in the absence of the Homebuilders intervention, the savings were calculated to amount to three to three and a half times the expenditure.

Even more impressive savings result when the impact of the intervention on other systems is taken into account. For example:

· A reduction in teenage parenthood would significantly reduce public assistance costs. An Urban Institute study financed by the National Institutes of Health found that a 50 percent decrease in births to women under the age of eighteen would result, in 1990, in a reduction of $390 million in AFDC payments, $160 million in Medicaid payments, and $170 million in food stamps.

· Nurse home visits during pregnancy and two years after birth in the Elmira program (Chapter 7) cost up to $3,500 per family. The program contributed to higher rates of employment, less public assistance, a lower incidence of child abuse and neglect, a lower use of emergency rooms and neonatal care, and fewer subsequent births. The resultant savings in public costs were particularly significant for the most socially disadvantaged families.

- The day care–family support program run by the Yale Child Study Center in New Haven (Chapter 7) cost $3,000 a year per child, or $7,500 for the full two-and-a-half-year program. At the outset, more than half of the families were receiving public assistance; ten years after the project ended, only two of fifteen were—compared to half the control families. The difference in welfare costs alone totaled more than $60,000 at the ten-year follow-up. In addition, no child had required residential treatment, no child had been in foster care, none had been arrested, and only one child had required psychiatric help.

- Good preschool experiences and a good start in elementary school reduce the need for special education services and improve other outcomes which can be translated into dollar savings. An economic analysis of the Perry Preschool program in Ypsilanti, Michigan (Chapter 8), found that its initial annual cost of $5,000 per child resulted in savings of several times that amount, because of lower crime rates ($3,000), reduced costs of special education ($5,000) and public assistance ($16,000), and the greater amount of taxes participants were expected to pay ($5,000) in comparison to their nonpreschool peers.

These examples of dollar savings hardly exhaust the economic returns society would realize on its investment in improving outcomes for children growing up at risk. One could include the savings to employers, including the armed forces, of being able to draw on a larger pool of skilled, healthy, and motivated young Americans and being able to save on employer-financed compensatory education. One could include savings in budgets for law enforcement and prisons, as well as other economic effects of a reduction in crime. One could include the savings that result when young people are better equipped for parenting—the reduced costs in the next generation of averted dependency, school failure, too-early pregnancy, and crime.

Of course, the decision to invest in decent services and schooling for disadvantaged children should not be dependent on how much the taxpayer saves. Yet the knowledge that costs will be recovered, even if the savings don't show up on the ledger of the same administrator who authorizes the expenditure, must be considered in judging whether a preventive intervention makes economic sense. The significant long-term effects of early and sustained intervention in the lives of disadvantaged children are the basis of the 1987 report of the Committee for Economic Development, which contends that "improving the prospects for disadvantaged children is not an expense but an excellent investment, one that can be postponed only at much greater cost to society."

ATTRACTING AND TRAINING TALENTED PERSONNEL

Effective programs require competent, caring, and flexible professionals. If successful interventions aimed at high-risk populations are to become widely available, the training of professionals and the value systems within which they work must take better account of the special needs of disadvantaged children and their families.

In the hierarchy of values in health, social services, and education, disadvantaged populations rank low, preventive services rank low, and, in medicine, the nontechnological services essential to many successful interventions rank low. When it comes to professional status and economic compensation, the direct provision of basic services to the least powerful has little prestige. The development of better methods to accomplish such important public purposes as reaching hard-to-reach populations with effective services is also not sufficiently prized.

The discovery of a new surgical procedure or a new combination of drugs brings rich rewards. But society may have a far greater stake in assuring a reliable response from school, police, health clinic, or social agency to a mother who asks for help with her chronically truant eight-year-old who comes home drunk or stoned. Nevertheless, if effective new approaches to that problem were devised, they would be unlikely to receive much recognition.

Even at the level of theory and research, the solution of problems with multiple causes, best addressed by combining talents from several disciplines, receives little support in most academic settings. At the level of the practitioner, narrowly drawn boundaries that limit what is expected of a professional are the very essence of professionalism for many. Some professionals work in settings where they see unmet needs so overwhelming that they can only continue functioning by looking away from matters beyond the confines of their own specialties.

The American Academy of Child Psychiatry, in its *Plan for the Coming Decades,* observed that "social forces that effect child psychiatric disorders are beyond the reach of child psychiatry and medicine in general." But should child psychiatry and medicine not be striving constantly to respond to the social forces that affect the children that come to them for help? A psychiatrist in a major children's hospital, after spending two hours with a twelve-year-old girl (the only professional to see her), noted in his evaluation that she was sexually active but did not discuss contraception with her or refer her for family planning services. His sole recommendation was that she should receive treatment to help her deal with her "constriction of feelings, her bonding to and identifying with the aggressor." His strikingly narrow response to the breadth of issues his patient presented suggests a definition of professionalism that meets the provider's needs better than those of the patient.

Social workers react to the low esteem in which work with disadvantaged families is held by moving in ever greater numbers from casework and community work with needy families to the private practice of psychotherapy with patients who can afford to pay. Social agencies serving the poor and disorganized have to make do with shockingly few well-trained and committed professionals.

Like the Vermont pediatrician we met in Chapter 6, physicians who try single-handedly to meet the health needs of large numbers of poor and overwhelmed families are defeated by a combination of counterproductive policies, gaps in their own training, and the lack of support systems that could help with these families' health-related needs.

Teachers are often in the same demoralizing position. Their training has not equipped them to deal with the collection of difficulties that many pupils bring to school—but they can see these problems getting in the way of school learning and are aware that nobody else is dealing with them either.

In most fields, professionals who are trained to work with children are not also trained to work with parents. They are trained to respond to isolated problems but not to a combination of problems. When they encounter difficulties beyond their expertise, they are inclined to retreat to more familiar ground rather than to mobilize the help of others. The limits of their training set the limits of their practice. Both practice and training reflect the low priority assigned to the special needs of the poor.

Dr. John Conger, former dean of the University of Colorado Medical School, says, "We train people for what they like to do, which is related to what is socially valued and well reimbursed, rather than for what needs to be done." On a different occasion, Yale University psychiatrist and researcher Dr. Donald Cohen made the same point: "Professionals go where the money is, where success is most likely, and where it's easy to provide their services. That's why the problem doesn't get defined in terms of family or social needs, but in terms that work for the professionals."

Many more professionals would be willing and able to work more effectively with high-risk children if their training gave them the requisite skills and exposed them to relevant experiences, and if they worked in a setting which assigned higher rewards to doing so.

In addition, in a more encouraging climate many more professionals would be available to work in these programs.

In the early days of the War on Poverty, when the word went out that federal support was available to establish comprehensive health centers in foresaken rural areas and inner city slums, health professionals soon appeared in the hundreds. They left private practices and laboratory benches to respond to the challenge. Child development professionals did the same to launch Head Start. Many times in our history gifted and committed people in all walks of life have responded to articulated human need. With thoughtful planning, inspiring leadership, and serious resolve, that could happen soon again.

RESISTING THE LURE OF REPLICATION THROUGH DILUTION

The temptation to water down a proven model in order to distribute services more widely is ever present. Agonizingly familiar is the story of a successful program which is continued or replicated in a form so diluted that the original concept is destroyed. Dr. Heather Weiss, of the Harvard Family Support Center, has seen it happen many times. She says, "You put a lot of resources into a demonstration, and try and deliver a model program. You show your effectiveness with a strong evaluation, and you think you've succeeded. The program is continued. But either you're asked to do the same thing with sharply reduced funds, or you have the same level of funds and are asked to expand your services."

The pressures to take a successful program and dilute it seem hard to resist. The home visiting program in Elmira (Chapter 7), where the case load of the home visitors was doubled after success had been demonstrated, is a vivid example. So is the Higher Horizons Program in the New York City schools of twenty years earlier, which proved so successful in two schools that, with no increase in funds or staff, it was spread to ten—and swiftly lost its impact.

Especially when funds are scarce, there are powerful pressures to dissect a successful program and select some one part to be continued in isolation, losing sight of the fact that it was the sum of the parts that accounted for the demonstrated success.

Attempts at rigid, cookie-cutter duplication have a similarly sad history. Every program successfully serving high-risk populations has some attributes that are fragile, involve complex human relationships, and do not lend themselves to mass production. Just as "teacher-proof" curricula have not worked, there are no "community-proof" or "people-proof" programs in any field of human services. The most successful practices do not lend themselves to mechanical or even rapid transfer from one setting to another. Communities and institutions differ sufficiently to require adaptation of the most proven techniques to fit new situations. What should be done and how it is best done will vary from place to place. Furthermore, those implementing the program in new settings must be able in fundamental ways to make it their own.

The dangers of dilution and mechanistic duplication were taken into account in the two highly successful efforts at replication described in Chapters 7 and 9. In applying the Homebuilders principles in the Bronx and the Comer principles in Prince Georges County, money was provided (by the Edna McConnell Clark Foundation in the Bronx and the school system in Prince Georges County) to allow for the kind of slow and careful planning that gave those involved with the program in the new setting a full sense of ownership—another seeming luxury that may well be a necessity.

Dilution and mechanistic replication without careful preparation and planning will continue to threaten the spread of successful programs until there is greater understanding that the intensity and comprehensiveness of these programs are almost invariably the very essence of their success, and until enough resources flow to high-risk populations to obviate the need to choose between an elegant program that works for a few and a diluted version that serves many—inadequately.

GENTLING THE HEAVY HAND OF BUREAUCRACY

For sophisticated practitioners and administrators on the human services scene, knowing what should be done is less than half the battle. How actually to make a good program work amid harsh bureaucratic realities may be the greater challenge.

Replication of any initiative on a broad scale obviously involves a certain amount of bureaucratization. Agency boundaries develop willy-nilly. Massive paperwork requirements suddenly appear, along with regulations that discourage the flexibility and creativity central to the program's successful operation. Perhaps the worst part is that these problems are not always the result of small-minded or uncaring people being in charge; rather, they often reflect a legitimate need for accountability and are the understandable consequence of imposing some measure of standardization in order to assure high quality and prevent abuse.

Bureaucratic problems also arise in the attempt to graft new programs to existing systems and institutions, which tend to be inhospitable to change. Robert Halpern, a veteran of helping many kinds of local agencies to bring about incremental social change, points out, "Predominant institutions tend to resist or absorb attempts to improve them. . . . Stability seems more crucial to survival than experimentation."

But the bureaucratization that inevitably accompanies large-scale replication raises the most acute problems for the fragile attributes which characterize effective interventions for high-risk populations. How are they to survive the heavy-handedness of large bureaucracies? How can the most effective tools for breaking the cycle of disadvantage be protected from destruction while being widely deployed?

The first step is to achieve greater recognition and understanding of the problem. Considering all the literature on fragmentation of services and on the tragedies that result when referrals fail and services don't reach those who need them most, it is astonishing to see how many public officials and program administrators seem uninterested in the day-to-day functioning of human services agencies. Professionals, politicians, advocates, and caring citizens must all give greater attention to the detailed questions of how bureaucracies actually deal with people. They must come to recognize that when it comes to health, social services, and education for high-risk families, how individuals are treated is central to whether the service works.

After understanding comes action. As legislators, governors, county executives, and mayors come to realize how poorly agency boundaries correspond to family needs, they must be willing to build bridges across jurisdictional lines. Especially when programs serve primarily the poor and are not only complex but administered by people who believe they are dealing with an "undeserving" clientele and are inclined to be tough and perhaps punitive, outside monitoring is essential. So is training in the skills that allow people in large organizations to continue to see the importance of personal human connections.

Agencies that provide services must be given the funds and in turn must give their staffs the sanction, support, and time to see their role as advocates and brokers as compatible with their professionalism. The advocacy and brokering roles become particularly important when programs are able to meet only a portion of a family's vast collection of urgent needs and when families have to deal with agencies in different service systems and several jurisdictions.

In a climate of greater understanding and support of human service programs, organizations providing systematic information about program models, and technical assistance at state and local levels with the practical details of budgeting, program assessment, and staff training, would all become more potent spurs to the replication of effective programs. A fuller appreciation of what is at stake by all concerned would go far toward creating a climate in which large-scale replication, even of interventions with fragile components, could succeed.

DEVISING A VARIETY OF REPLICATION STRATEGIES

The successful programs recorded in this book are in many different stages of development, and, because they operate in diverse contexts, the best next steps will also be highly diverse. Converting successful local efforts to state or national policy and formulating national policies that will support successful state and local efforts raise different issues in health, social services, and education. Useful action can take many different forms.

Head Start, the WIC nutrition program, and community health centers are the service programs that already come closest to operating on a national scale. In all three of these programs, the structures are there to build on, but the commitment and money are insufficient. All three are far from having reached their full potential.

Head Start, especially in light of the great current interest in child care for preschool children, should be expanded to serve five times as many three- and four-year-olds. Its quality controls, which have grown lax in some areas, must be strengthened. It must also be broadened to include younger children and to provide all-day care. Its successful experiments with Parent and Child Centers must be built on to establish comprehensive programs to serve younger children and put even greater emphasis on incorporating family supports.

Head Start's comprehensive approach can also be built into current efforts by schools, day care centers, and family day care providers to satisfy the adult demand for more child care while simultaneously responding to the golden opportunities to furnish stimulating, safe, coherent, and nurturing environments to vulnerable children during the impressionable preschool years.

An expansion of health care financing through Medicaid and EPSDT and through private insurance, especially to cover the working poor, although not the ideal mechanism for improving health care, would at least put more resources into health services for disadvantaged children and pregnant women. If national health insurance is not a realistic possibility, such an expansion would mean some increased access to care and could help, given thoughtful regulations and administration, to support some of the models of excellent health services we have described.

The greatest weaknesses of the insurance approach to financing health care can be attenuated by a kind of "creative state administration" of health funds, combining Medicaid funds with other federal, state, and local funds into a pool. This pool would be large enough to pay for services to children and pregnant women who are poor but not insured, and to pay for needed services not now specifically covered by third-party payments when they are rendered by community health centers, public health clinics, and hospital outpatient departments serving large numbers of poor children.

School-based health clinics have expanded from a few models to a nationwide movement. Support centers provide expertise and foundations provide grants to ease the way for starting new ones. Funds to continue existing clinics may, however, soon become more problematical, and long-term financing needs attention.

The possibility that schools could also be a base for the provision of a broad range of social services to students and their families deserves considerably more exploration than it has so far received.

The low esteem into which social services have fallen has discouraged investment to support hard-pressed social agencies and dissuades talented people from entering or remaining in the field. However, the enormous interest in current efforts to prevent unnecessary removal of children from the home, and to eliminate some of the most outrageous fragmentation in the provision of social services, suggests that evidence of success in accomplishing these purposes may stimulate a reappraisal. The enthusiasm with which many elements of the Homebuilders program have been put into place around the country indicates that social agencies serving the cause of family preservation have the potential of generating a new surge of public support. The phenomenal growth of grassroots family support groups also deserves close attention. These groups are clearly an important new source of help to families, and while it is hard to predict how more established social agencies will be affected, it is unlikely that they will remain unchanged.

The current ferment in the schools and interest in reform has started to focus more sharply on the education of disadvantaged children. Not only educators themselves, but growing numbers of citizens' groups and the business community, seem to understand the need for better education of all youngsters, even those who start out at a disadvantage. This may make school boards and superintendents particularly receptive to new ideas for making school climates more responsive to the needs of disadvantaged students and families.

Increasing cooperation between the public and private sectors is another hopeful development. It has evolved particularly around schools, with rapidly growing school-industry cooperation, but is now reaching into other domains as well.

In an imaginative departure from tradition, the state of Illinois joined businessman-philanthropist Irving B. Harris to create the Ounce of Prevention Fund to help reduce teenage childbearing, child abuse and neglect, and developmental disabilities among poor and minority families. Harris and officials of the state of Illinois agree that these human tragedies have a disastrous collective impact on the nation and the state. Using a combination of state, federal and, private funds in a remarkably flexible way, the Fund supports services to disadvantaged young people at forty-two locations Its newest endeavor is the uniquely comprehensive "Beethoven Project," described briefly in Chapter 7, which provides intensive support and a full range of services to all pregnant women between 1987 and 1989, and their children until they reach the age of five, in six of the Robert Taylor Homes in South Chicago. Such systematic efforts to reach the families in greatest jeopardy with a critical mass of intensive services may be among the most promising, if difficult, current opportunities to bring about fundamental change.

During the 1980s, with the decline of federal leadership, the importance of the states' role in services for the disadvantaged has been expanding. The New York *Times* reported that activists for the poor say that on a wide range of social issues states are much more responsive to their appeals than the federal government. The legislative counsel to the National Governors' Association declared that governors have become "protectors of the social safety net." Social analyst Sheila Kamerman observed that there is a new political context in which "politically ambitious governors are seriously interested in child care." Former Governor William G. Milliken of Michigan said that states are taking the lead in willingness "to spend more tax money now in ways that would save in the long run."

Soon after the 1986 off-year election, columnist Neal R. Peirce reported that "the issue of children has moved quietly to the top of state agendas." He described state activity to expand child care, prekindergarten programs, especially for disadvantaged children, and teenage pregnancy prevention programs. Even new governors who had scarcely mentioned children in their campaigns were being swayed by the argument that investing in children now would protect against their "dragging down a state's economy in the 1990s."

The increasing competence of state officials has been noted by a number of observers as a reason for optimism about useful action to improve human service programs at the state level.

Federal policies are still highly influential and often decisive. We have seen the importance of federal funds and leadership in Head Start and community health centers, of federal funds in compensatory education, of federal funds and regulations (for better and worse) in the financing of health care. Federal leadership will be essential if the knowledge now available is to be harnessed to change outcomes for the nation's most disadvantaged children.

To make sure that progress in the next decade is based as fully as possible on reliable information and thoughtful analysis, there are additional important roles for researchers, policy analysts, private foundations, and concerned corporations and professional organizations. Well-supported multidisciplinary efforts can help to overcome some of the impediments to large-scale replication of successful interventions. Among the biggest challenges:

- To refine our understanding of realistic ways of reconciling the fragile attributes of programs that successfully serve high-risk populations with the requirements of large-scale implementation within human service bureaucracies.
- To develop improved methods to link populations at risk to needed services.
- To develop better ways to document the effects of complex, multiple, individualized interventions on outcomes of interest to policymakers and program administrators and funders.
- To pursue, imaginatively and persistently, ways of reducing barriers to the most rapid feasible spread of effective interventions.
- To identify the crucial changes in federal and state policies, and in professional practices, that could encourage the spread of effective interventions and maintain the viability of effective programs.

In sum, the arenas for action are far more varied than they were perceived to be twenty years ago. While the federal role remains crucial, state and local governments are increasingly competent and many are becoming more concerned about vulnerable populations. Public-private partnerships are pioneering flexible new approaches towards achieving the common good. No one level of government, and certainly no isolated private efforts, can bring nirvana, and a vast array of people and institutions must be enlisted to make progress. What needs to be done can't be orchestrated by any one group or body—although a President and a few other highly visible leaders who understood, cared, and provided "bully pulpit" leadership on these issues would make a big difference.

But the biggest single need is for a far broader base of understanding among all Americans of what can be done, and what must be done.

Intensive Interventions
for Populations
at Highest Risk

All of us rearing children in America today need more help from outside the family than earlier generations did. Few contemporary families are free of the stresses that come from needing two incomes to maintain the relative standard of living our parents attained with one. Most of us live with the fear that someone in our family will add to the swelling statistics of drug and alcohol abuse, family breakup, AIDS, adolescent suicide, accidental death, or murder.

Virtually every American family raising children is weakened by the absence of family supports, which are provided in other industrialized countries in the form of family allowances, universal health insurance, maternity and infant care leaves, job flexibility, and organized child care.

Cornell Professor Urie Bronfenbrenner, who has spent his professional lifetime studying families, said, "Unless you have the external supports, the internal systems don't work."

Given the universal nature of the need for health care, child care, family support, social services, and schooling, it is tempting to believe that whatever helps most families should be equally helpful to all families. It is easy to overlook the special needs of high-risk populations.

At one end of the continuum of need are the children in families whose own ample resources (financial, social, and psychological) allow them to obtain the outside help they need on whatever terms it is offered. They are able to surmount the barriers of geographical distance, cumbersome procedures, and evidence of ability to pay. Further along on the continuum are children in families who need a little more from the helping systems, such as better access to services through reduced financial barriers, simplified eligibility procedures, and more and better information to help them find the services and institutions they need. At the far end of the continuum are the children who will not be helped with minor adjustments or add-ons to prevailing arrangements. These are the children who are at greatest risk of later damage *and* the children who would benefit most if the kinds of interventions described in this book were available on a vastly wider scale. These are the children whose families need help to provide them with a minimal environment for healthy growth.

Programs that succeed in helping the children and families at highest risk are more intensive, more comprehensive, and sometimes more costly than those typically needed by families living in less disadvantaged circumstances. Health care that is adequate for monitoring the pregnancy of a healthy middle-class woman may totally bypass the most pressing needs of an undernourished, depressed, drug-using pregnant teenager. The parent support component of a preschool program, occasionally helpful to middle-class participants, is often essential for high-risk families.

Throughout this book, we have seen examples of health, social services, and educational institutions that have helped the highest-risk children and families by incorporating an extra dimension beyond what less deprived populations need. They provide intensive, comprehensive, individualized services with aggressive attention to outreach and to maintaining relationships over time—perhaps frills for more fortunate families, but rock-bottom essentials for high-risk populations, whose level of energy and tolerance for frustration may be low, who are likely to have more than one problem at a time, and whose experiences in searching for help are likely to leave them profoundly discouraged and unable to use services as customarily offered.

Justice for disadvantaged populations has traditionally been equated with equitable access to services, assuming equal need and equal efficacy of treatment. It now appears that while equal access is necessary, it is not sufficient. If severely disadvantaged populations are to benefit equally, the content of services needs almost always to be enriched, not only beyond the shabby services typically offered to the most vulnerable but even beyond the standard services offered to most other Americans.

The children in greatest need of intensive interventions to reduce the risk of long-term damage include:

- Children growing up in persistent poverty.
- Children growing up in neighborhoods of concentrated poverty and social dislocation.
- Children growing up in families that are homeless.
- Children growing up with a mentally ill, alcoholic, or drug-addicted parent.
- Children growing up with an isolated parent.

Now that we know there are interventions that can help such children, now that we know how to prevent damage before it occurs, does it really make sense to withhold services until these children or their families exhibit clear signs of pathology?

Services for high-risk groups can be provided as part of a universal program or rendered exclusively to a high-risk population. A home visiting program for high-risk mothers, for example, could be an intensive version of a universal program or could be focused exclusively on poor pregnant teenagers. What is essential is that programs for those with the greatest needs be clearly designed to take their distinct needs into account.

Most social reformers and human service advocates, believing strongly in the superiority of a universal model, have been reluctant to focus sharply on the special needs of society's most disadvantaged families. They fear that concentrating attention on the needs of populations so disadvantaged as to be called an underclass will invite dismissal of this population as beyond help, either because their problems seem so overwhelming or because a significant proportion are members of minorities with whom the dominant majority feels little connection.

Liberal tradition inclines toward dealing with problems of the disadvantaged in a larger framework. Progress has most frequently been made when the middle-class majority has been able to see a very personal connection between their own needs and those lower on the economic scale. ("There, but for the grace of God and a good job, goes my kid.") Permanent social changes that have improved the status of the poor have generally been accomplished by "incorporating the poor through the political back door." (Social Security is a prime example.)

It is hard to rally political support for programs aimed only at the poorest of the poor. Programs aimed exclusively at the most deprived, lacking a broad constituency, have been regarded as hard to protect against deterioration. (As the late Wilbur J. Cohen, former Secretary of Health, Education and Welfare, used to say, "Programs for the poor become poor programs.")

But the determination to avoid a specific focus on the seriously disadvantaged may by now have become counterproductive. Not only has it inhibited the development of programs responding to the distinct needs of multiproblem families, it may also be impeding the flow of resources to children who are at risk because of the circumstances of their environment. The biggest recent expansion of services for very young vulnerable children has targetted children who can be identified as *individually* damaged or at risk, in contrast to children and families who are parts of *populations* at risk.

It is much easier to obtain funding for a home visiting program to serve children with physical or developmental handicaps than for children who are at risk because they have a depressed teenage mother or an alcoholic father or are part of a homeless family. Many states with "early intervention" programs which are authorized to include children at "biological, established, or environmental risk" actually serve primarily children with biological handicaps.

Obviously programs that identify and serve children with individual handicaps should continue, but more resources must flow to population groups at greatest risk.

Policy-making and resource allocation cannot continue to be skewed by uninformed sentiment—symbolized by the heart-warm-ing picture of the smiling child in leg braces sitting on a politician's lap. We now know enough to be able to visualize the equally crippling, if less apparent, effects of failure to provide home visits, other family supports, and comprehensive prenatal care to very young, poor, isolated, and depressed pregnant women. We know the effects of failure to provide enough early help to children in peril of not succeeding at school.

As long as effective services were lacking, it was reasonable to fear that identifying people as needing help because they belonged to population groups at risk would be simply stigmatizing. But the state of current knowledge has changed that. We now know so much more than we did only twenty years ago about interventions that work, and about how to provide services that are not stigmatizing, on terms that families can welcome and exercise some control over. If the finest health, social, and early education services the society can provide cannot yet be made universally available, at least the children at greatest risk must be assured access to them.

In the next decade's efforts to break the cycle of disadvantage and dependence, first priority must go to making intensive, high quality services available early in the life cycle to the populations at highest risk. A broad coalition of citizens and professionals must move the public and private sectors to bring a critical mass of successful programs into the geographical areas with the greatest concentration of persistent poverty and other indicators of disadvantage and disintegration.

Considering the wealth of our knowledge about the dangers of growing up in areas of concentrated poverty—areas now readily identified—and our knowledge about interventions that can change outcomes even for the most disadvantaged children, it becomes unconscionable not to take whatever action is needed to make these interventions available.

Demonstrated individual pathology should not be required as a ticket of admission to first-class services. While effective services must be available on a sustained basis for maximum impact, they are particularly important at periods in the life cycle when families are both vulnerable and unusually receptive to new learning. In the time surrounding pregnancy and birth, for example, good help can be instrumental in getting the relationship between infant and parent off to a good start. Other critical periods in family life occur before a child starts school, again as the child gets established in school, and at the beginning of adolescence. There is no sounder investment in the future than assuring that the best resources and the most appropriate help are available to fragile families at crucial times of life transition.

The best of help must also be available when families in high-risk surroundings come to the attention of helping agencies for reasons that are likely to pose a serious risk to a child's development. Events that signal the need for systematic links to high-quality services for children can now be pinpointed. We know so much about the risks to normal development represented by homelessness or the sudden absence or continuing impairment of a parent; yet we know little about why hospitals admitting mothers of young children for treatment of mental illness or substance abuse rarely make connections with family support services in the communities where the children are left behind. Are these links missing for lack of enough good family support services to make the forging of such connections worthwhile? Or because the personnel and the institutions treating the parent are already stretched too thin? Or because they think in too circumscribed terms? Or, as must be the case with social agencies serving homeless families, are client and professional so overwhelmed by the enormity of the immediate need that the potential for long-term damage to the vagabond children never comes to the fore?

The national stake in getting services to families most in need is now so large, and the potential for effective help so great, that interventions especially designed for the families hardest to help justify a massive new public commitment.

To nurture such a commitment, institutional mechanisms are needed that can embrace a mandate simultaneously broad enough to encompass the full spectrum of effective interventions, and specific enough to assure a sharp focus on the highest-risk populations. To assure that such a commitment is based on the most current knowledge, and continually refreshed by new information and insights, experience gained from interventions aimed at high-risk children and families must be monitored, analyzed, and publicized so that it can be effectively built upon. A great variety of efforts to provide training and technical assistance must give high priority to meeting the needs of the populations that have heretofore been least well served.

Innovative mechanisms must also be developed to assure that

excellent services actually get into the areas that need them most. In the past, discretionary grants gravitated toward relatively better endowed communities, while more universal programs never provided enough resources to meet the greater needs of the most depleted areas. Without explicit attention to this issue, even new funds allocated by the federal government, states, and private funders for the express purpose of aiding high-risk populations are likely to flow to the communities which are relatively better off in resources and services.

Specific measures aimed at areas of the most concentrated poverty and distress must be part of a broad new national commitment, to be discussed in the concluding chapter, to assure that present knowledge is methodically and creatively harnessed to improve outcomes for all children at risk of growing up amid poverty, despair, and family disintegration.

· 12 ·

Breaking the Cycle
of Disadvantage

It lies within our reach, before the end of the twentieth century, to change the futures of disadvantaged children. The children who today are at risk of growing into unskilled, uneducated adults, unable to help their own children to realize the American dream can, instead, become productive participants in a twenty-first-century America whose aspirations they will share. The cycle of disadvantage that has appeared so intractable can be broken.

An essential step has already been taken. More and more Americans have come to recognize that rates of childhood poverty, unmarried teenage childbearing, violent crime, and youth unemployment have reached unacceptable heights.

The crisis has been described by the American Enterprise Institute as threatening to "corrode a free society," by sociologist James S. Coleman as a breakdown of "the process of making human beings human," and by Senator Daniel Patrick Moynihan as "life-threatening to the great cities of the land." The Committee on Economic Development warns that "this nation cannot continue to compete and prosper in the global arena when more than one fifth of our children live in poverty and a third grow up in ignorance." Mayors and governors, individually and collectively, are putting children at the top of their list of concerns, and the *American Agenda,* submitted by former Presidents Gerald Ford and Jimmy Carter to President George Bush at the outset of his Administration, identifies investment in poor children as one of six urgent national priorities.

As concern grows about the number of young people leaving school without the skills and motivation to work, about a shrinking pool of youngsters available for today's hi-tech economy, about the growing costs of prisons and welfare, and about the prospect of a permanent American underclass, it is becoming clear that effective early interventions provide some powerful answers to these concerns, but that many existing schools, health programs, and social services do not seem able to respond to today's critical needs.

The search for better solutions is gaining momentum. Administrators, politicians, professionals, business leaders, and citizens are reexamining outmoded practices and boundaries. Cities and states, often with the support of private funds, are taking unprecedented, if tentative, steps toward a fundamental restructuring of services.

Officials in education are joining forces with their counterparts in health and child welfare to strengthen services for disadvantaged children and their families. State and local administrators in juvenile justice, mental health, and child protection are joining hands to find room within their bureaucracies for intensive, comprehensive, and flexible family-centered services.

Business leaders are putting their influence, their money, and often their personal time into new efforts to help individual children, both directly and through the schools and other community institutions. Making common cause with longtime child advocates, corporate giants are prodding national policy toward greater investment in children. Along with their private contributions, they are reaffirming the role of government in helping the poor and the dispossessed. They recognize, in the words of William S. Woodside, that these efforts "cannot be limited to government, but cannot succeed without government."

There is, then, in the nation, an extraordinary convergence of increased awareness of the problem, new knowledge of what works, and new openness to change the way services are financed, organized, and delivered. We have a historic opportunity to help reverse the growing polarization between the haves and have-nots. Acting on this opportunity means revising public policies in employment, income support, and housing. As important, we must mobilize a great new surge of talent, energy, and resources, in order to systematically extend effective services and supports to vastly more children and families.

First, programs already operating effectively nationwide, like Head Start and WIC, must be extended to all who are or should be eligible.

Second, states and local communities must be helped to extend widely the successful programs that have heretofore operated only on a small scale. The development of concrete strategies to extend successful programs to all those who need them is the challenging new frontier in human services today. Highest priority must go to efforts to combine disparate programs into coherent combinations of services in neighborhoods where persistent poverty and social dislocation are concentrated. Government agencies must review their funding policies and regulations to identify the most important impediments to providing coordinated services and seek their removal. Government at all levels must join with foundations and other private institutions to assure local communities the skilled technical assistance and the additional funds that will be needed to provide effective services to truly disadvantaged populations.

Lastly, everyone concerned—voter and elected official, volunteer and bureaucrat, front-line worker and policy analyst—must recognize that investing in the futures of disadvantaged children means investing in first-class services.

When I reviewed the findings contained in this book for the U.S. House Select Committee on Children, Youth, and Families, the chairman, George Miller of California, remarked, "What you found is what this Committee found, and what we keep finding over and over again: when it comes to services for kids and families in poverty, where it is done in a first-class fashion, it succeeds beyond our wildest dreams. And everywhere we've tried to do it on the cheap, everywhere we've tried to cut a corner, we end up spending money with no appreciable results."

There is no better summary of my findings. The common elements of successful programs—comprehensiveness, intensiveness, family and community orientation, and staff with time and skills to develop relationships of respect and collaboration—add up to first-class services.

Do today's political and budgetary imperatives make a major new commitment to improve the futures of America's most disadvantaged children seem illusory? Do the costs of first-class programs, in dollars and professional resources, preclude elected officials from allocating substantial funds to meet the needs of such a powerless constituency?

Not if enlightened realism prevails. All Americans will benefit from the provision of first-class services to children and families living in adversity. All Americans are burdened by the high cost of *not* making the required investment. Reaching out to the hard-to-reach and helping the hard-to-help are not idle sentiment, but a practical response to an urgent American problem.

The chilling effects of budgetary deficits cannot be allowed to deter action. Dr. Isabel V. Sawhill, senior economist at Washington's Urban Institute, explains it this way: "Large deficits make it difficult to argue for new social spending [because they] lower the rate of economic growth and threaten future standards of living. Unfortunately, a failure to invest in the next generation has precisely these same effects."

Knowing now that effective social interventions *can* reduce the number of children hurt by cruel beginnings and simultaneously promote the national welfare, we must be certain that these newly available tools are put to work. We have the knowledge we need. We know how to organize health programs, family supports, child care, and early education to strengthen families and to prevent casualties in the transition from childhood to adulthood. We know how to intervene to reduce the rotten outcomes of adolescence and to help break the cycle that reaches into succeeding generations. Unshackled from the myth that nothing works, we can assure that children without hope today will have a real chance to become the contributing citizens of tomorrow.

Notes

INTRODUCTION

p. xx. Not all the information we might want: Most research about risk factors, as well as about the effects of efforts to intervene, is helpful in gaining an understanding of opportunities to improve programs and policies for all disadvantaged populations. To the extent that research has been focused on particular ethnic groups, more information is at present available about disadvantaged white and black populations than about Hispanic populations. For this reason there is a comparative scarcity of discussion in these pages about factors which may be uniquely salient for children in Hispanic families.

pp. xx–xxi. Mdyral quote: G. Myrdal, *An American Dilemma,* 1944.

p. xxi. Important guide to action: Others, including the Committee for Economic Development (CED), National Governors' Association (NGA), and the American Psychological Association, have recently also undertaken systematic efforts to identify preventive programs that work. (See especially the CED's *Children in Need: Investment Strategies for the Educationally Disadvantaged,* 1987, and the NGA's *Focus on the First Sixty Months,* 1987.) There is considerable overlap in the programs selected by these three groups and those described in this book, although the processes by which programs were chosen varied considerably. This should reassure the reader that these programs do provide objective indicators of success. Each selection process also identified programs that none of the others found. It seems that no one individual or organization can put between two covers all the promising efforts to respond to the complex needs of families buffeted by changing family structures, increasing poverty, and decreasing employment opportunities.

p. xxiii. Poverty as risk factor: The proportion of children growing up in poverty went down markedly in the 1960s, from 27 percent in 1959 to 15 percent in 1970. It then rose steadily, reaching a high of 22 percent in 1983, and receded to 20 percent in 1985. Poverty rates by race in 1985 were 15.6 percent for white, 43.1 percent for black, and 39.6 percent for Hispanic children. The recent downturn in poverty rates did not include Hispanic children, whose rate of poverty is currently at an all-time high. (See U.S. Congress, House of Representatives, Select Committee on Children, Youth and Families, "U.S. Children and Their Families: Current Conditions and Recent Trends," 1987.

Perhaps as devastating in its effects, the growing inequality in the distribution of the nation's wealth is increasingly isolating the poorest families. The gap between the rich and the poor has reached its widest point in forty years, with the richest fifth of all households receiving 46.1 percent of total income and the poorest fifth receiving 3.8 percent. See U.S. Bureau of the Census, *Current Population Reports,* 1987. Another indication of the fact that poor Americans are getting poorer relative to the rest of the population is that the official U.S. poverty line is further below the average income now than it was in the 1960s. In the mid-1960s, a four-person family at the poverty line had an income that was half that of the average family, but by the mid-eighties it was only a third. As economist Isabel Sawhill puts it, "The standard by which we measure poverty has become increasingly stingy with the passage of time." (I. V. Sawhill, "Anti-Poverty Strategies for the Next Decade," in *Work and Welfare,* 1987.)

p. xxiii. Policies to promote economic growth: Even if the benefits of policies that promote general economic welfare did not trickle down to everyone, even if the rising tide of economic growth did not raise all boats, more people would be working and more of those who work would be earning a living wage.

Policies to promote more jobs and training: In the absence of policies designed specifically to create more jobs and expand job training, the number of jobs continues to shrink relative to the number of people seeking work, a high proportion of young people fail to enter the job market, and chronic poverty and dependency are growing. (See P. B. Edelman, "The Next Century of Our Constitution: Rethinking Our Duty to the Poor," *Hastings Law Journal,* 1987.)

Policies to assure that people who work can earn enough to support a family: Few Americans realize how many working people earn too little to keep them out of poverty. Actually, most poor parents work, and one of every six children who are currently poor lives in a family with a full-time, year-round wage earner. (See report prepared by the Congressional Research Service and Congressional Budget Office, U.S. Congress, *Children in Poverty,* 1985.)

p. xxiii. Effective welfare reform would be more feasible: In a restructured welfare system, work would be a more realistic as well as a more attractive prospect. More young men and women would be helped to obtain the skills they need to become employed and to find and keep jobs. Health coverage and help with child care would not be withdrawn as soon as a poor family gets a foothold on self-sufficiency. High-quality child care and other family supports would be integral components of the reformed system.

For those unable to work or to find jobs, policies to assure a decent level of cash assistance would continue to be essential. The safety net that public assistance was originally designed to provide is so tattered it currently excludes 42 percent of poor children altogether. (See Children's Defense Fund, *A Children's Defense Budget,*

1987.) Those eligible for support typically do not get enough; in not one of the fifty United States does a poor family receive enough cash assistance and food stamps to get out of poverty. (See U.S. House of Representatives, Committee on Ways and Means, "Background Material and Data on Programs within the Jurisdiction of the Committee on Ways and Means," Committee Print, 1986.)

pp. xxiv–xxv. Murray's argument: C. Murray, *Losing Ground: American Social Policy 1950–1980*, 1984.

p. xxv. The evidence countering Murray's argument: The most closely reasoned and persuasive refutations of Murray's entire thesis, as well as of his specific argument that welfare assistance is a cause of teenage unmarried childbearing, are contained in the following books and articles: W. J. Wilson, *The Truly Disadvantaged*, 1987; D. T. Ellwood and L. H. Summers, "Poverty in America," in *Fighting Poverty*, 1986; S. Danziger and P. Gottschalk, "The Poverty of *Losing Ground*," *Challenge*, 1985; R. Greenstein, "Losing Faith in 'Losing Ground,'" *New Republic*, 1985; J. E. Schwarz, *America's Hidden Success*, 1988.

p. xxv. Countries with more generous welfare programs: Government in the United States is far less supportive of children and families than most other Western industrialized countries. [See S. B. Kamerman and A. J. Kahn, "Explaining the Outcomes," in *Changing the Well-Being of Children and the Aged in the U.S.*, (in press).] As Kamerman and Kahn point out elsewhere, "What the Europeans apparently know but what many Americans do not yet perceive is that social services may support, strengthen, enhance the normal family—and that failures in social provision may undermine our most precious institutions and relationships." (A. J. Kahn and S. B. Kamerman, *Not for the Poor Alone*, 1977.)

p. xxv. State-by-state comparisons: D. T. Ellwood and M. J. Bane, "The Impact of AFDC on Family Structure and Living Arrangements," *Research in Labor Economics*, 1984.

p. xxv. Economic stagnation as cause of childhood poverty: The Reagan Administration, in 1983, commissioned a comprehensive assessment of two decades of anti-poverty policies by the University of Wisconsin's Institute for Research on Poverty. The participating scholars and government officials concluded unambiguously that recent increases in childhood poverty and single parent households were the result of economic stagnation and high unemployment. (See S. H. Danziger and D. H. Weinberg, eds., *Fighting Poverty*, 1986.)

p. xxv. Poverty would have been greater: S. H. Danziger et al., "Antipoverty Policy: Effects on the Poor and the Nonpoor," in *Fighting Poverty*, 1986; P. B. Edelman, "The Next Century of Our Constitution," *Hastings Law Journal*, 1987.

p. xxvi. Aged lifted out of poverty: S. H. Danziger et al., "Antipoverty Policy," in *Fighting Poverty*, 1986.

p. xxvi. Children poorest age group: D. P. Moynihan, *Family and Nation*, 1986.

p. xxvi. Poverty rate among preschool children: Congressional Research Service and Congressional Budget Office: *Children in Poverty*, 1985.

p. xxvi. Caring about individual futures and not the common good: In his 1984 presidential address to the Population Association of America, Samuel H. Preston argued that increasing childhood poverty is the political consequence of the facts that the proportion of elderly in the population is growing, children can't vote, and childhood is behind the rest of us. Preston summarizes his argument in "Children and the Elderly in the U.S.," *Scientific American,* 1984. While I do not fully sub-scribe to his explanation for increasing childhood poverty, I entirely share his conclusion: "If we care about our collective future," he says, "we must safeguard the human and material resources represented by children." We cannot "place almost exclusive responsibility for the care of children on the nuclear family." He considers the current tendency to insist that families alone care for the young to "be an evasion of collective responsibility rather than a conscious decision about the best way to provide for the future."

p. xxvii. Help early in the life cycle is more economical: Addressing the leaders of American education about the educational needs of the disadvantaged, the Busi-ness Advisory Commission of the Education Commission of the States made one major recommendation: "Get it right the first time." Early education, they said, is far less costly than remedial education. Preventing students from dropping out is less costly than training dropouts. Preventing damage is far less costly than repair-ing it. (See Education Commission of the States, Reconnecting Youth, 1985.)

p. xxviii. Government role in formation of character: J. Q. Wilson, *Thinking About Crime,* 1975; J. Q. Wilson, "The Rediscovery of Character: Private Virtue and Public Policy," *The Public Interest,* 1985; J. Q. Wilson and R. J. Herrnstein, *Crime and Human Nature,* 1985.

CHAPTER I

p. 2–3. Carrie Eleby: Information about Carrie Eleby comes from visits to her and her family written up in J. Schorr, "The Childhood of the Fuller Murder Convicts," unpublished report, Washington, D.C., 6 June 1986; interview with Jerry S. Goren, Assistant U.S. Attorney, Washington, D.C., 3 Apr. 1986; E. Walsh, "Witness Links Boyfriend to Fuller Murder," *Washington Post,* 13 Nov. 1985; E. Walsh and S. Saperstein, "Fuller Killers Bred by Mean Streets," *Washington Post,* 5 Jan. 1986. Elsa Walsh and Jerry Goren were particularly helpful in sharing their insights about the lives of the young people involved in the Fuller murder.

p. 3. Concern with personal safety: M. Adams, "LQ Survey Finds Safety Top Concern," *USA Today,* 13 Mar. 1985; R. D. McFadden, "Poll Shows 49% of New Yorkers See Crime as City's Top Problem," *New York Times,* 14 Jan. 1985.

p. 4. Spending on personal security: B. J. Wattenberg, *The Good News Is the Bad News Is Wrong,* 1984.

p. 4. Prevention most effective crime control strategy: E. Currie, *Confronting Crime: An American Challenge,* 1985; J. Q. Wilson, "The Rediscovery of Character: Private Virtue and Public Policy," *The Public Interest,* 1985; L. A. Curtis, ed., *American Violence and Public Policy,* 1985; N. Morris, "Crime and Race," Address to Aspen Institute for Humanistic Studies, Aspen, Colo., 18 Aug. 1987.

p. 4. Prison costs: G. Camp and C. Camp, *Corrections Yearbook, 86,* 1986. 1985 construction costs ranged from $29,600 for minimum-security facilities to $70,768 for maximum-security facilities.

p. 4. Numbers in prison: U.S. Department of Justice, "Prisoners in 1985," *Bulle-tin,* 1985; A. Blumstein et al., eds., *Criminal Careers and "Career Criminals,"* 1986; U.S. Department of Justice, "State and Federal Prisoners, 1925–85," *Bulletin,* 1986.

p. 4. International comparisons: U.S. Department of Justice, *Imprisonment in*

Four Countries, 1987; D. Brook, "The Great American Trouble," *The New Republic,* 1986.

p. 4. R. D. White op-ed column: "Uneasy Street," *Washington Post,* 30 Aug. 1985.

p. 4. Spread of crime: J. M. Chaiken and M. R. Chaiken, "Trends and Targets," *Wilson Quarterly,* 1983.

p. 5. Homicide leading cause of death: National Center for Health Statistics, *Health, United States,* 1986.

p. 5. Crime rates: U.S. Department of Justice, *Report to the Nation on Crime and Justice,* 1983; U.S. Department of Justice, *Violent Crime by Strangers,* 1982.

p. 5. Skogan quote: J. M. Chaiken and M. R. Chaiken, "Trends and Targets," *Wilson Quarterly,* 1983.

p. 5. Arrest rates peak early: U.S. Department of Justice, *Report to the Nation on Crime and Justice,* 1983.

p. 5. Violent criminals start young: J. M. Chaiken and M. R. Chaiken, "Trends and Targets," *Wilson Quarterly,* 1983.

p. 5. Most adult criminals start young: J. Q. Wilson and R. J. Herrnstein, *Crime and Human Nature,* 1985; U.S. Department of Justice, *Report to the Nation on Crime and Justice,* 1983.

p. 5. Fear of crime and crime rates: U.S. Department of Justice, *Report to the Nation on Crime and Justice,* 1983. While there has been little overall change in crime rates, the proportion of households touched by crime fell slightly but steadily between 1975 and 1985. (See U.S. Department of Justice, *Households Touched by Crime, 1985,* 1986.)

p. 5. Homicide rates: National Center for Health Statistics, *Health, United States,* 1986.

p. 5. Risk of being a victim of crime: U.S. Department of Justice, *Report to the Nation on Crime and Justice,* 1983.

p. 5–6. International comparisons of crime rates: J. Q. Wilson and R. J. Herrnstein, *Crime and Human Nature,* 1985. The most staggering difference between the United States and other countries is in murders committed with handguns. In the United States in 1983, there were more than 9,000, compared to 35 in Japan, 10 in Australia, 8 in Great Britain, and 6 in Canada. (Handgun Control, Inc., Washington D.C., personal communication, 1987.)

p. 6. Street crime in Japan, Baltimore, and Detroit: C. Haberman, "In Japan, a Crime Wave Is Measured in Drops," *New York Times,* 2 Aug. 1983; S. Schmidt, "Growing Number of Senseless Slayings by Teens Instills Concern," *Washington Post,* 14 Oct. 1985; I. Wilkerson, "Detroit Crime Feeds on Itself and Youth," *New York Times,* 29 Apr. 1987.

p. 6. Wolfgang quote: P. M. Boffey, "Youth Crime Puzzle Defies a Solution," *New York Times,* 5 Mar. 1982.

p. 6. 1970s adolescents commit more serious crimes: N. A. Weiner and M. E. Wolfgang, "The Extent and Character of Violent Crime in America, 1969 to 1982," in *American Violence and Public Policy,* 1985.

p. 6. Street drugs more widespread: The use of illicit drugs increased about twenty-fold during the 1960s and 1970s. (See A. M. Nicholi, "The Nontherapeutic Use of Psychoactive Drugs," *New England Journal of Medicine,* 1983.) Since then, the use of all illegal drugs, except for cocaine and its derivative, crack, has decreased slightly. Illegal drug use causes crime in several ways: Addicts steal to support their habit, turf disputes among dealers result in violence, and some drugs (such as PCP, "speed," and crack) can actually cause violent behavior. About half of those arrested for serious crimes committed in urban areas were using one or more illegal drugs at the time of their arrest. Criminals who are drug abusers commit crimes at least twice as often as other offenders. "The more intense the involvement with drugs, the higher the rate of crime." (A. Blumstein et al., eds., *Criminal Careers and "Career Criminals,"* 1986.)

p. 7. Claude Brown, *Manchild in the Promised Land,* 1965.

p. 7. Brown's description of Harlem today: C. Brown, "Manchild in Harlem," *New York Times Magazine,* 1984.

p. 7. "Any job that can be done by an illiterate": Statement by Labor Secretary William Brock made on the ABC documentary "At a Loss for Words: Illiterate in America," *ABC News,* New York, 3 Sep. 1986.

pp. 7–8. U.S. General Accounting Office, *Labor Market Problems of Teenagers Result Largely from Doing Poorly in School,* 1982.

p. 8. Numbers at risk and cost to nation: Forum of Educational Organization Leaders, "Meeting the Needs of Children and Youth at Risk of School Failure," Statement released in Washington, D.C., 1 June 1987. Committee for Economic Development, *Children in Need: Investment Strategies for the Educationally Disadvantaged,* 1987.

p. 8. Consequences of dropping out of school: G. Berlin, A. Sum, and R. Taggart, "Cutting Through" (in press); U.S. Department of Education, *The Condition of Education,* 1984; U.S. Department of Education, *Digest of Education Statistics,* 1983.

p. 8. Earnings drop: C. Johnson and A. Sum, *Declining Earnings of Young Men,* 1987.

p. 8. Black-white difference in consequences of no high school diploma: U.S. Department of Education, *Digest of Education Statistics,* 1983.

p. 8. Rates of dropping out: U.S. Department of Education, *The Condition of Education,* 1984; U.S. Department of Education, *The Condition of Education,* 1986; Hearings, Senate Caucus on Children, 23 Jan. 1984, held in New York City, as reported by Senator Christopher J. Dodd in the *Congressional Record,* 11 Oct. 1984.

Every year, about 700,000 students at the ninth-grade level or above drop out. Black and Hispanic youth are almost twice as likely to drop out as white teenagers, but this difference is primarily due to the greater extent of poverty in the minority populations. About a quarter of all youngsters from poor families drop out, poor whites at a slightly higher rate (27.1 percent) than poor blacks (24.6 percent). In large public school districts in America's major cities, where the vast majority of students come from poor families, dropout rates often exceed 40 percent. (See Children's Defense Fund, *A Children's Defense Budget,* 1986 and 1987.)

Furthermore, many children who are counted as enrolled are not attending school with any regularity. Truants elude census enumerators and school officials alike, so that many children who do not appear in the dropout statistics are actually out of school more than they are in school.

p. 9. Chicago enrollment and reading figures: *The Bottom Line: Chicago's Failing*

Schools and How to Save Them (Chicago: Designs for Change, 1985), cited in W. J. Wilson, *The Truly Disadvantaged,* 1987.

p. 9. Low expectations of inner-city youngsters: G. Sykes, "The Deal," *Wilson Quarterly,* 1984.

p. 9. Mr. Dashler's statement: "At a Loss for Words: Illiterate in America," *ABC News,* New York, 3 Sep. 1986.

p. 9. Lack of employment skills: Committee for Economic Development, *Investing in Our Children,* 1985.

p. 9. Glazer quote: N. Glazer, "The Problem with Competence," in *Challenge to American Schools,* 1985.

p. 9. Defense Dept. study of competence of U.S. youth: U.S. Department of Defense, *Profile of American Youth,* 1982. Twenty-six percent of all the black youngsters tested and 20 percent of the Hispanics (and 7 percent of the total sample) fell into Category V, ineligible for military service. Forty-six percent of blacks and 39% of Hispanics (and 24 percent of the total) were in Category IV, considered sufficiently risky that the services are allowed by Congress to recruit only a stipulated fraction.

p. 10. Gulf between needed skills and available manpower: Between 1970 and 1984 New York City lost 500,000 jobs in industries where the average job holder has not completed high school and gained 240,000 jobs in industries where most jobs required more than a high school education. But the part of the New York City population which has increased is the part with the fewest skills. Similar shifts have been documented in Philadelphia, Chicago, Detroit, Cleveland, and four other cities. (See J. Kasarda, *The Regional and Urban Redistribution of People and Jobs in the U.S.,* 1986.) The mismatch is further aggravated by the fact that the greatest job losses have occurred in the very industries to which urban minorities have the greatest access. (See W. J. Wilson, *The Truly Disadvantaged,* 1987.)

p. 10. Consequences of lack of basic skills: C. Johnson and A. Sum, *Declining Earnings of Young Men,* 1987.

p. 10. Parents without a high school education pass on handicaps: "At a Loss for Words: Illiterate in America," *ABC News,* New York, 3 Sep. 1986; J. Kozol, *Illiterate America,* 1985.

p. 10. Data General Corporation warning: Quoted by J. R. Munro, Remarks to Children's Defense Fund Strategy Conference, Washington, D.C., 2 Mar. 1984.

p. 10–11. Staggering costs to the economy: J. R. Munro, Remarks to Children's Defense Fund Strategy Conference, 1984. Evidence that his prediction is coming true is accumulating. For example, in 1987, in its first major recruitment effort in more than a decade, the New York Telephone Company found that 84 percent of New York City applicants failed its entry-level examinations. Also in New York, the recruitment manager for Merrill Lynch, Pierce, Fenner and Smith says, "It doesn't appear that schools are providing [young people] with tools that are necessary to come out and move into corporate America." Labor experts are quoted by the New York *Times* as saying that if education does not keep pace with business needs, the city's economic growth could be endangered. The president of the New York Board of Education says, "We will have a group, largely minority, disaffiliated with the rest of society, unconnected with the mainstream economy, (with) frightening potential in terms of increased crime, race relations, how people relate to one another." ("Companies Cite Poor Skills in Entry-Level Applicants," *New York Times,* 4 July 1987.)

p. 11. Low proportion of young people: Calculations and projections by the Metropolitan Life Insurance Company, based on unpublished data of the Bureau of the Census, in *Statistical Bulletin of the Metropolitan Life Insurance Company,* Jan.–Mar. 1984.

p. 11. Coming into adulthood unschooled: "The American work force is running out of qualified people, is the stark way that David T. Kearns, chief executive officer of the Xerox Corporation, put it to the Economic Club of Detroit, 26 Oct. 1987

p. 11. Carnegie Forum on Education and the Economy, *A Nation Prepared: Teachers for the 21st Century,* 1986.

p. 11. Teenage birthrates: National Center for Health Statistics, *Health, United States,* 1986.

p. 11. Pregnancy as reason for dropping out: Twenty-three percent of female high school dropouts in 1980 gave pregnancy as the reason for dropping out. See U.S. Department of Education, *The Condition of Education,* 1986.

p. 12. Dropout because of pregnancy, by race: F. L. Mott and W. Marsiglio, "Early Childbearing and Completion of High School," *Family Planning Perspectives,* 1985.

Early childbearing is a direct cause of truncated schooling, independent of other influences. (See J. Card and L. L. Wise, "Teenage Mothers and Fathers: The Impact of Early Childbearing," *Family Planning Perspectives,* 1978; K. A. Moore and M. R. Burt, *Private Crises, Public Cost,* 1982.) Early childbearing continues to be associated with less schooling, even though an increasing number of school systems try to keep pregnant and parenting teens in school. But the gap between early and later childbearers has not narrowed, probably because the amount of schooling has risen among all women. Among high school students, each year a first birth is delayed means an additional year of schooling completed. (See S. L. Hofferth, "Social and Economic Consequences of Teenage Parenthood," in *Risking the Future,* 1987.)

p. 12. Earnings of teenage mothers: C. M. Suchrindam, *Consequences of Adolescent Pregnancy and Childbearing,* 1978.

p. 12. Work experience and AFDC support of teenage mothers: K. A. Moore and M. R. Burt, *Private Crises, Public Cost,* 1982.

p. 12. Risk of long-term dependency: M. J. Bane and D. T. Ellwood, *Slipping Into and Out of Poverty: The Dynamics of Spells,* 1983.

p. 12. Public expenditures: M. R. Burt and F. Levy, "Measuring Program Costs," in *Risking the Future,* 1987.

p. 12. More children than they want: J. Card and L. L. Wise, "Teenage Mothers and Fathers," *Family Planning Perspectives,* 1978. (Comparisons are to classmates with similar backgrounds.)

p. 12. Outcomes for babies of teenagers: J. Menken, "The Health and Social Consequences of Teenage Childbearing," in *Teenage Sexuality, Pregnancy and Childbearing,* 1981; Institute of Medicine, *Preventing Low Birthweight,* 1985; C. D. Hayes, ed., *Risking the Future,* 1987.

The incidence of fragile health at birth among babies of teenagers has been documented by the National Center for Health Statistics, "Apgar Scores in the United States, 1978," 1981; and National Center for Health Statistics, "Advance Report of Final Natality Statistics, 1984," 1986.

p. 13. Decreased risks through improved prenatal care: See Chapter 4.

p. 13. Proportion of teenage mothers unmarried: National Center for Health Statistics, "Advance Report of Final Natality Statistics, 1984," 1986. (In 1984, among mothers under the age of eighteen, 70 percent were unmarried.)

p. 13. Poverty among children of unmarried teenagers: K. A. Moore, "Teenage Childbirth and Welfare Dependency," *Family Planning Perspectives,* 1978; M. J. Bane and D. T. Ellwood, *Slipping Into and Out of Poverty,* 1983.

p. 13. Small chance of stable marriage: M. O'Connell and C. C. Rogers, "Out-of-Wedlock Births," *Family Planning Perspectives,* 1984. O'Connell and Rogers also point out that women whose first child is conceived or born out of wedlock experience significantly higher rates of marital disruption than do women who are not pregnant or mothers at the time of their first marriage. One of every four women who first marry between the ages of fifteen and seventeen are separated or divorced from their husbands within five years. Furstenberg's study of the marriages of black urban adolescent mothers found that half had broken up within four years, compared with 30 percent of the marriages of their classmates. (See F. F. Furstenberg, Jr., "The Social Consequences of Teenage Parenthood," in *Teenage Sexuality, Pregnancy and Childbearing,* 1981.)

p. 13. In single-parent households: Alan Guttmacher Institute, *Teenage Pregnancy: The Problem That Hasn't Gone Away,* 1981.

p. 13. Between puberty and adulthood: The young person must sort out his or her sense of self, capabilities, values, and goals in the midst of dramatic—and often mystifying—physical changes. (See E. A. McGee, *Too Little, Too Late: Services for Teenage Parents,* 1982.) "For the majority of young persons, the years from 12 to 16 are the most eventful ones of their lives so far as their growth and development is concerned. Admittedly during fetal life and the first year or two after birth developments occurred still faster . . . but the subject himself was not the fascinated, charmed or horrified spectator that watches the developments or lack of developments, of adolescence." (See J. M. Tanner, "Sequence, Tempo and Individual Variation in the Growth and Development of Boys and Girls Aged Twelve to Sixteen," *Daedalus,* 1971.)

p. 13–14. Interruption of adolescent development: The discussion of adolescent development, including the notion of parenthood placing "preemptive demands," comes from B. A. Hamburg, "Developmental Issues in School-Age Pregnancy," in *Aspects of Psychiatric Problems of Childhood and Adolescence,* 1980. It is of some interest to note that childbearing turns out to have less effect on the lives of girls aged 15 and under than it does on the lives of young mothers who are sixteen or seventeen. Hofferth suggests that this may be because very young girls are not expected to make the full transition to adulthood at the same time as they become mothers. The birth is regarded by adults as a mistake, a fluke, and the young girl is expected to stay home with her family and remain in school. The mother who is sixteen or seventeen is more likely to attempt to make the complete transition by leaving school, getting married, and leaving home. (See S. L. Hofferth, "Social and Economic Consequences of Teenage Parenthood," in *Risking the Future,* 1987.)

p. 14. Researchers agree that children of teenagers are likely to be handicapped: C. D. Hayes, ed., *Risking the Future*, 1987; W. Baldwin and V. Cain, "The Children of Teenage Parents," in *Teenage Sexuality, Pregnancy, and Childbearing*, 1981. Adverse effects are most likely to occur when—as is typical—the teenage mother raises her child alone and in poverty. In a study of adolescent children born sixteen years earlier to low-income black teenagers in Baltimore, Furstenberg and Brooks-Gunn found that the children who fared best were in families that were poor but *comparatively economically secure*, or in families where there was a caretaker in addition to the mother. (See F. F. Furstenberg, Jr., and J. Brooks-Gunn, *Adolescent Mothers in Later Life*, 1985.)

Kellam's longitudinal study of 1,242 children and their families in Chicago found that among children born to mothers seventeen years of age and younger, negative effects on school adaptation associated with teenage parenting were ameliorated by the presence of *either* a father *or* a grandmother in the household. (See S. G. Kellam et al., "The Long-term Evolution of the Family Structure of Teenage and Older Mothers," *Journal of Marriage and the Family*, 1982; C. H. Brown, et al., "A Longitudinal Study of Teenage Motherhood and Symptoms of Distress," *Research in Community and Mental Health*, 1981.)

p. 14. Greater risk of neglect: There is disagreement among researchers as to whether teenage mothers are more likely to abuse their children. Elster and colleagues, writing in *Pediatrics*, conclude that while few adolescent mothers seem to abuse their babies during their own adolescence, abusive mothers often were found to have started their childbearing as adolescents. (See A. B. Elster et al., "Parental Behavior of Adolescent Mothers," *Pediatrics*, 1983.) One definitive British study of all children born during one week of April 1970 and followed for five years found that children born to teenagers were more likely to be involved in accidents and injuries and to be hospitalized than children born to older women. The association with early childbearing persisted after the effects of other socioeconomic and biological factors were taken into account. The researchers concluded that the higher morbidity found among these children may reflect maternal inexperience and "defective" maternal supervision. (See B. Taylor et al., "Teenage Mothering, Admission to Hospitals and Accidents During the First Five Years," *Archives of Disease in Childhood*, 1983.)

p. 14. Diversity of outcomes: F. F. Furstenberg, Jr., and J. Brooks-Gunn, *Adolescent Mothers in Later Life*, 1985; K. A. Moore, *Children of Teen Parents: Heterogeneity of Outcomes*, 1986.

p. 14. Adolescent children of teenage mothers: F. F. Furstenberg, Jr., and J. Brooks-Gunn, *Adolescent Mothers*, 1985. Other researchers have also found that the children of younger mothers were more likely to bear children early themselves. (See J. Card and L. L. Wise, "Teenage Mothers and Fathers," *Family Planning Perspectives*, 1978; H. B. Presser, "Early Motherhood: Ignorance or Bliss?" *Family Planning Perspectives*, 1974.)

p. 14. International comparisons: E. F. Jones et al., *Teenage Pregnancy In Developed Countries*, 1987.

p. 14. Numbers of teenage mothers: National Center for Health Statistics, "Advance Report of Final Natality Statistics, 1984," 1986. They include about 167,000 fifteen- to seventeen-year-olds, for whom the gravest consequences accrue. But even the 300,000 or so teenagers who bear children at eighteen or nineteen have elevated risks, especially of long-term poverty and single parenthood.

p. 16. W. J. Wilson: I rely extensively in this section on Professor Wilson's 1987 book, *The Truly Disadvantaged: The Inner City, the Underclass and Public Policy,* a penetrating analysis of inner city poverty, including its historical roots, its current dimensions, and approaches to solutions.

p. 16. Definitions of underclass: These are the elements that appear in definitions of the underclass in E. R. Ricketts and I. V. Sawhill, "Defining and Measuring the Underclass," 1986; W. J. Wilson, *The Truly Disadvantaged,* 1987; and K. B. Clark and R. D. Nathan, "The Urban Underclass," in *Critical Issues for National Urban Policy,* 1982. Of all these definitions, Ricketts and Sawhill's focuses most clearly on the societal burden, such as behavior patterns and norms deviant from those of mainstream populations which "inhibit social mobility, impose costs on the rest of society, or on the children growing up in an environment where such behaviors are commonplace."

p. 16. Estimates of underclass by income: In 1985 persons who were *persistently poor* (and neither elderly or disabled) numbered about 8 million (3.5 percent of the U.S. population and 23.5 percent of the poverty population). (See P. Ruggles and W. P. Marton, "Measuring the Size and Characteristics of the Underclass," 1986.)

In 1979, persons who *lived in areas where more than 40 percent of the population was poor* numbered about 3.7 million (1.6 percent of the U.S. population and 14 percent of the poverty population). (See P. Gottschalk and R. D. Danziger, "Poverty and the Underclass," Testimony before the U.S. Congress, Select Committee on Hunger, Aug. 1986.)

In 1979 persons who were poor and *lived in areas where more than 40 percent of the population was poor* numbered about 1.8 million (0.8 percent of the U.S. population and 7 percent of the poverty population). (See I. V. Sawhill, "Anti-Poverty Strategies for the Next Decade," in *Work and Welfare,* 1987.)

p. 17. More precise definition of underclass by census tract characteristics: E. R. Ricketts and I. V. Sawhill, "Defining and Measuring the Underclass," 1986; revised estimates in E. R. Ricketts and I. V. Sawhill, "Defining and Measuring the Underclass," *Journal of Public Policy Analysis and Management,* forthcoming. (I am indebted to Erol Ricketts and Ron Mincy at the Urban Institute for helping me to make use of the 1980 census tract data developed by Dr. Ricketts and Dr. Isabel Sawhill.)

p. 18. Claude Brown quote: "Today's Native Sons," *Time,* 1 Dec. 1986.

p. 18. Escape from underclass easier in earlier generations: J. V. F. Long and G. E. Vaillant, "Natural History of Male Psychological Health," *American Journal of Psychiatry,* 1984.

p. 18. Earnings and marriage rates of young men: C. Johnson and A. Sum, "Declining Earnings of Young Men," 1987.

p. 18. Number of female-headed families: U.S. Congress, House of Representatives, Select Committee on Children, Youth, and Families, *U.S. Children and Their Families,* 1987.

p. 18. Escaping poverty through marriage: M. J. Bane and D. T. Ellwood, *Slipping Into and Out of Poverty,* 1983.

p. 19. Effect of economy on black families: W. J. Wilson, *The Truly Disadvantaged,* 1987.

p. 19. Black male unemployment: Center for the Study of Social Policy, *The 'Flip Side' of Black Families Headed by Women: The Economic Status of Black Men,* 1984.

p. 19. Black female-headed families: U.S. House of Representatives, Select Committee on Children, Youth, and Families, *U.S. Children and Their Families,* 1987.

p. 19. Projections to the year 2000: Center for the Study of Social Policy, cited in W. J. Wilson and K. M. Neckerman, "Poverty and Family Structure," in *Fighting Poverty,* 1986.

p. 19. Wilson quotes and descriptions of ghetto: W. J. Wilson, *The Truly Disadvantaged,* 1987.

p. 20. Comer quote: D. Whitman and J. Thornton, "A Nation Apart," *U.S. News and World Report,* 1986.

p. 20. Role of drugs: Drug use and drug-related crime increased at an astonishing late between the early 1960s and the late 1970s; the effects of illegal commerce in drugs have had a profound influence on life in urban slums. Drug dealers seduce ever younger children to participate in their trade. For many youngsters, drug dealing seems to offer an attractive alternative to more tedious and less well-compensated work. Police in New York and Detroit report that children as young as ten are using crack and that thirteen-year-olds are not only addicted to crack but selling it for a large profit. (See U.S. House of Representatives, Select Committee on Children, Youth, and Families, Joint Hearing on the Crack-Cocaine Crisis, Washington, D.C., 15 July, 1986.) Almost a third of seventh-grade students in New York State said they had used illegal drugs before they entered seventh grade. (See J. Barnabel, "State Survey Shows Extensive Drug Use Before the 7th Grade," *New York Times,* 18 Oct. 1984.) The use of illicit drugs at increasingly younger ages is particularly alarming in view of the evidence that the age of first use of illegal drugs is a good predictor of later heavy drug involvement. (See L. N. Robins, "The Natural History of Adolescent Drug Use," *American Journal of Public Health,* 1984.)

p. 20. Effect of concentrated poverty on child development: J. P. Comer, "Black Violence and Public Policy," in *American Violence and Public Policy,* 1985.

p. 20. "Community norms": W. J. Wilson, *The Truly Disadvantaged,* 1987.

p. 20. British study of female-headed households: This careful study of London boys found that youngsters who had lost a parent from desertion or divorce were more likely to become delinquent than those who had lost a parent from death or long-term hospitalization. (See D. J. West and D. P. Farrington, *Who Becomes Delinquent?* 1973.)

p. 20. Effects of concentration of female-headed families: S. G. Kellam et al., "Family Structure and the Mental Health of Children," *Archives of General Psychiatry,* 1977.

p. 20. Chicago Housing Authority: T. J. McNulty, "The American Millstone: In a Nation of Riches, A Permanent Underclass," *Chicago Tribune,* 15 Sep. 1985.

p. 21. Mrs. Coleman quote: R. S. Anson, *Best Intentions,* 1987.

p. 21. Increased concentration of poverty: W. J. Wilson, *The Truly Disadvantaged,* 1987.

p. 21. Senator Kennedy quote: Speech to the 1978 Annual Meeting of the NAACP, quoted in K. Auletta, *The Underclass,* 1982.

p. 21. Sviridoff quote: K. Auletta, *The Underclass,* 1982.

pp. 21–22. Professor Norton quote: E. H. Norton, "Restoring the Traditional Black Family," *New York Times Magazine,* 1985.

p. 22. Congressman Gray quote: D. Whitman and J. Thornton, "A Nation Apart," *U.S. News and World Report,* 1986.

p. 22. Professor Morris's statement: Address to the Aspen Institute for Humanistic Studies, Aspen, Colo., 18 Aug. 1987.

CHAPTER 2

p. 23. E. St. Vincent Millay, excerpt from "Upon this age, that never speaks its mind," *Collected Poems,* 1939.

p. 24. Prevention of pellagra: W. H. Sebrell, Jr., "Clinical Nutrition in the United States," *American Journal of Public Health,* 1968.

p. 24. Information for design of social policy: J. W. Gardner, *Excellence,* 1984. I agree also with the conclusion of James Q. Wilson that demands for complete causal explanations, especially in the realm of human behavior, deflect attention from what can be done, draw attention to what cannot be done, and are often a way of deferring any action at all. (See J. Q. Wilson, *Thinking About Crime,* 1975.)

p. 25. Evidence of risk factor interaction from animal studies: S. J. Suomi, "Short- and Long-Term Effects of Repetitive Mother-Infant Separations on Social Development in Rhesus Monkeys," *Developmental Psychology,* 1983.

pp. 25–26. Interaction of constitution and environment in infants: S. K. Escalona, "Babies at Double Hazard: Early Development of Infants at Biologic and Social Risk," *Pediatrics,* 1982.

p. 26. Middle-class status protects: For additional evidence, see P. H. Leiderman, "Social Ecology and Childbirth: The Newborn Nursery as Environmental Stressor," in *Stress, Coping, and Development in Children,* 1983.

p. 26. Biological vulnerability and responsive caregiving: L. Beckwith and A. H. Parmelee, "Infant Sleep States, EEG Patterns, Caregiving and 5 Year IQ's of Preterm Children," Paper presented at the International Conference on Infant Studies, New York, 5–8 Apr. 1984.

p. 26–27. Findings from Kauai longitudinal study: E. E. Werner and R. S. Smith, *Vulnerable but Invincible: A Study of Resilient Children,* 1982; E. E. Werner et al., *The Children of Kauai,* 1971; B. Starfield, "Patients and Populations," *Pediatric Research,* 1981; J. Kagan, *Psychological Research on the Human Infant: An Evaluative Summary,* 1982; L. Eisenberg, "Development as a Unifying Concept in Psychiatry," *British Journal of Psychiatry,* 1977.

p. 27. Interaction of neurological damage and other risk factors: M. D. Levine, "A Study of Risk Factor Complexes In Early Adolescent Delinquency," *American Journal of the Diseases of Childhood,* 1985.

p. 28. Accumulation of risk factors: A. J. Sameroff and S. McDonough, "The Role of Motor Activity in Human Cognitive and Social Development," in *Energy Intake and Activity,* 1984; A. J. Sameroff and R. Seifer, "Sources of Continuity in

Parent-Child Relations," Paper presented at meeting of the Society for Research in Child Development, Detroit, 1983.

p. 28. Multiplication of risk factors: M. Rutter, *Changing Youth in A Changing Society,* 1980. Providing futher corroboration of findings pointing to the interaction of risk factors, Harvard psychiatrist Leon Eisenberg, in a review of research on infants at risk for the National Academy of Sciences, called attention to research showing that very poor nutrition early in life can lead to mental retardation, but apparently only when combined with poor rearing conditions. "In a fashion yet to be understood, appropriate stimulation in the home appears to be able to protect against the deleterious effects of undernutrition on mental development." (See L. Eisenberg, "Conceptual Issues on Biobehavioral Interactions," in *Infants at Risk for Developmental Dysfunction,* 1982.)

p. 30. Middle-class status as a buffer: P. H. Leiderman, "Social Ecology and Childbirth," in *Stress, Coping, and Development in Children,* 1983.

p. 31. Definition of "intervention": A. M. Clarke and A. D. B. Clarke, "Thirty Years of Child Psychology: A Selective Review," *Journal of Child Psychology and Psychiatry,* 1986.

CHAPTER 3

p. 33. Garry Trudeau interview: L. Grove, "The Cartoonist, Rapping About Ronnie, Jane, George and the Four-Panel Smile," *Washington Post,* 10 Nov. 1986.

p. 34. Effects of child being born wanted: Select Panel for the Promotion of Child Health, *Better Health for Our Children: A National Strategy,* 1981; J. C. Kleinman et al., "The Relationship Between Delay in Seeking Prenatal Care and the Wantedness of the Child," Paper presented at the Annual Meeting of the American Public Health Association, Anaheim, Calif., 11–15 Nov. 1984.

p. 34. Consequences of being born unwanted: Institute of Medicine, *Preventing Low Birthweight,* 1985. Czechoslovakian research: H. P. David, "Children Born to Women Denied Abortion: Studies from Prague, Czechoslovakia," Paper presented to the American Psychological Association, Chicago, Aug. 1975; H. P. David, "Unwanted Children," *Family Planning Perspectives,* 1986.

p. 34. Swedish research: H. Forrsman and I. Thuwe, "One-Hundred and Twenty Children Born After Application for Therapeutic Abortions Refused," *Acta Psychiatrica Scandinavica,* 1966; H. Forrsman and I. Thuwe, "Continued Follow-Up Study of 120 Persons Born After Refusal of Application for Therapeutic Abortion," *Acta Psychiatrica Scandinavica,* 1981.

p. 34–35. Too-short interval between births: Institute of Medicine, *Preventing Low Birthweight,* 1985; National Center for Health Statistics, "Interval Between Births: United States, 1970–1977," *Vital and Health Statistics,* 1981.

p. 35. British research on risks of large family size: M. Rutter, *Changing Youth in a Changing Society,* 1980; D. P. Farrington and D. J. West, "The Cambridge Study in Delinquent Development, (United Kingdom)," in *Prospective Longitudinal Research,* 1981.

p. 35. Hawaiian findings: E. E. Werner and R. S. Smith, *Vulnerable but Invincible,* 1982.

p. 35. Risk of late childbearing: Institute of Medicine, *Preventing Low Birth weight*, 1985.

p. 36. Reduction in high-risk childbearing: National Center for Health Statistics, *Health, United States, 1985*, 1985; C. A. Bachrach, "Contraceptive Practice Among American Women, 1973–1982," *Family Planning Perspectives*, 1984.

p. 37. Family planning costs: W. F. Pratt et al., "Understanding U.S. Fertility," *Population Bulletin*, 1984.

p. 37. The meeting with Mr. and Mrs. Shriver: J. A. Kershaw, personal communication, Mar. 1986.

p. 38. The early years of the OEO family planning program: Alan Guttmacher Institute, *Informing Social Change*, 1980; J. A. Kershaw, *Government Against Poverty*, 1970.

p. 39. Reduction in unplanned births: W. F. Pratt et al., "Understanding U.S. Fertility," *Population Bulletin*, 1984. Unwanted births went down from 21 to 7 percent, and earlier-than-wanted births dropped from 45 to 22 percent.

p. 39. Causes of reduced infant mortality: Institute of Medicine, *Preventing Low Birthweight*, 1985.

pp. 39–40. Cutbacks in federal funds: R. B. Gold and J. Macias, "Public Funding of Contraceptive, Sterilization and Abortion Services, 1985," *Family Planning Perspectives*, 1986.

p. 40. Teenagers avoided pregnancy through use of contraception: Alan Guttmacher Institute, "Questions and Answers About Title X and Family Planning," *Issues in Brief*, 1984; M. Chamie et al., "Factors Affecting Adolescents' Use of Family Planning Clinics," *Family Planning Perspectives*, 1982.

p. 40. Documentation of teenagers postponing efforts to obtain family planning services: L. S. Zabin and S. D. Clark, Jr., "Why They Delay," *Family Planning Perspectives*, 1981.

p. 41. International comparisons: E. F. Jones et al., *Teenage Pregnancy in Developed Countries*, 1987.

p. 41. Ketting quote: Editorial, *Family Planning Perspectives*, Mar./Apr. 1985.

p. 41. Majority of teenage pregnancies are unwanted: M. Zelnik and J. F. Kanter, "Sexual Activity, Contraceptive Use and Pregnancy Among Metropolitan-Area Teenagers: 1971–1979," *Family Planning Perspectives*, 1980.

pp. 41–42. Sherita's story: L. Dash, "Motherhood the Hard Way," *Washington Post*, 27 Jan. 1986.

p. 42. Two ends of a blurred spectrum: For an excellent discussion of the complexity of the concept of "wantedness" of pregnancy, see L. Klerman and J. F. Jekel, "Unwanted Pregnancy," in *Perinatal Epidemiology*, 1984.

p. 44. Teenage contraceptive ignorance: M. Zelnik et al., "Sources of Prescription Contraceptives and Subsequent Pregnancy Among Young Women," *Family Planning Perspectives*, 1984.

p. 44. High risk of pregnancy resulting from ignorance: L. S. Zabin et al., "The Risk of Adolescent Pregnancy in the First Few Months of Intercourse," in *Teenage Sexuality, Pregnancy, and Childbearing*, 1981.

p. 44. Fear that parents will find out: L. S. Zabin and S. D. Clark, Jr., "Why They Delay," *Family Planning Perspectives*, 1981.

p. 44. "Unromantic" to prepare: E. E. Kisker, "Teenagers Talk About Sex, Pregnancy and Contraception," *Family Planning Perspectives,* 1985.

p. 44. Available contraceptive methods not well suited to teenagers: F. F. Furstenberg, Jr., et al., "Contraceptive Continuation Among Adolescents," *Family Planning Perspectives,* 1983; E. E. Kisker, "Teenagers Talk About Sex," *Family Planning Perspectives,* 1985.

p. 44. Risks of oral contraceptives: B. Moyers, "The Vanishing Family—Crisis in Black America," Manuscript text from a broadcast produced by Ruth E. Streeter (New York: CBS, 1986); Gallup Organization, "Attitudes Toward Contraception," Unpublished report to the American College of Obstetricians and Gynecologists, Princeton, N.J., 1 Mar. 1985.

p. 45. Disadvantage of diaphragm: E. E. Kisker, "Teenagers Talk About Sex," *Family Planning Perspectives,* 1985.

p. 46. Satisfaction with contraceptive method: J. A. Shea et al., "Factors Associated With Adolescent Use of Family Planning Clinics," *American Journal of Public Health,* 1984.

p. 46. Trust in professional advice: C. A. Nathanson and M. H. Becker, "The Influence of Client-Provider Relationships," *American Journal of Public Health,* 1985.

p. 46. Confidentiality, proximity, and caring: L. S. Zabin and S. D. Clark, "Institutional Factors Affecting Teenagers' Choice and Reasons for Delay," *Family Planning Perspectives,* 1983.

p. 46. Contraceptive services in 37 counties: M. Chamie et al., "Adolescents' Use of Family Planning Clinics," *Family Planning Perspectives,* 1982.

pp. 46–47. Effect of traditional sex education: D. Kirby, *Sexuality Education: An Evaluation of Programs and Their Effects,* 1984.

p. 47. Emphasis on delaying sex: D. Kirby, personal communication, May 1987.

p. 47. Description of Dr. Howard's Atlanta program: J. A. Blamey et al., *Postponing Sexual Involvement,* 1985. The program is based on several successful experiments in reducing adolescent smoking. The assumption of these experiments was that adolescents can get greater control over their health behavior when they have specific skills as well as a sense of their own worth. (See A. L. McAlister, "Tobacco, Alcohol, and Drug Abuse," in *Healthy People: The Surgeon General's Report,* 1979; A. L. McAlister et al., "Adolescent Smoking: Onset and Prevention," *Pediatrics,* 1979.)

pp. 48–49. Description of the St. Paul program: L. E. Edwards et al., "Adolescent Pregnancy Prevention Services in High School Clinics," *Family Planning Perspectives,* 1980; P. J. Porter, "St. Paul: Facing Teen Pregnancy," in *Healthy Children,* 1985; P. J. Porter, personal communication, 1986; L. E. Edwards et al., "Contraceptive Continuation in Adolescents," Paper presented at the Annual Meeting of the American Public Health Association, Las Vegas, 1986; D. Kirby, *Sexuality Education,* 1984; E. A. Brann et al., "Strategies for the Prevention of Pregnancy in Adolescents," *Advances in Planned Parenthood,* 1979; L. E. Edwards et al., "An Experimental Comprehensive High School Clinic," *American Journal of Public Health,* 1977.

pp. 50–53. Description of the Johns Hopkins program and its outcomes: L. S. Zabin et al., "Evaluation of a Pregnancy Prevention Program for Urban Teenagers," *Family Planning Perspectives,* 1986; L. S. Zabin et al., "A School-, Hospital- and University-Based Adolescent Pregnancy Prevention Program," *Journal of Reproductive Medicine,* 1984; interviews with Dr. Zabin, Dr. Hardy, and Ms. Streett, 22 Jan. 1986.

p. 53. Status of school-based clinics: S. Lovick and W. F. Wesson, *School-Based Clinics,* 1986 (updated by personal communication from D. Kirby, Center for Population Options, 24 May 1987); J. Dryfoos, "School-Based Health Clinics: A New Approach to Preventing Adolescent Pregnancy?" *Family Planning Perspectives,* 1985.

p. 54. Support of school-based clinics: C. D. Hayes, ed., *Risking the Future,* 1987; Robert Wood Johnson Foundation, "The School-Based Adolescent Health Care Program," 1986.

p. 54. Dryfoos prediction: J. Dryfoos, "School-Based Health Clinics," *Family Planning Perspectives,* 1985.

p. 54. Funding prospects: D. Kirby, personal communication, 1987.

p. 54. Clinics do not lead to increased sexual activity: This is clear from studies of the experiences of the St. Paul and Baltimore clinics and from preliminary findings of a three-year study of ten school-based clinics. [See Center for Population Options, "A Comprehensive and Comparative Evaluation of the On-Campus Clinic Model for Reducing Adolescent Pregnancy" (in preparation).]

p. 54. DuSable High School: Interviews with John Hockenberry, "All Things Considered," National Public Radio, 16 Oct. 1986; W. Plummer, "A School's RX for Sex," *People,* 28 Oct. 1985.

pp. 55–56. AGI focus on unwanted pregnancy: Alan Guttmacher Institute, *11 Million Teenagers,* 1976; Alan Guttmacher Institute, *Teenage Pregnancy: The Problem That Hasn't Gone Away,* 1981.

p. 56. Marian W. Edelman quote: Children's Defense Fund, *An Anatomy of a Social Problem: In Search of Comprehensive Solutions,* 1987.

p. 56. Increased availability of family planning services: Some three million teenagers (about three fifths of those who are sexually active) annually get medically prescribed contraceptive services through family planning clinics or private physicians. (See A. Torres and J. D. Forrest, "Family Planning Clinic Services in the United States, 1981," *Family Planning Perspectives,* 1983.)

p. 56. Numbers of sexually active youngsters: Between 1971 and 1979, the proportion of fifteen- to nineteen-year-old females who had engaged in premarital intercourse rose from 30 to 50 percent. (See M. Zelnik and F. K. Shah, "First Intercourse Among Young Americans," *Family Planning Perspectives,* 1983.) After 1979, that proportion first leveled off and then in 1982 went down to 45 percent. (See W. F. Pratt and G. E. Hendershot, "The Use of Family Planning Services by Sexually Active Teenage Women," Paper presented at the Annual Meeting of the Population Association of America, Minneapolis, 1984.)

p. 57. Age at first intercourse: M. Zelnik and F. K. Shah, "First Intercourse Among Young Americans," *Family Planning Perspectives,* 1983.

p. 57. J. E. Jones quote: "Comprehensive School-Based Programs: A Pregnancy Prevention Strategy for Disadvantaged Junior High School Students," Proposal submitted to the Carnegie Corporation, New York, 1985.

p. 57. Tauscha Vaughn quote: L. Dash, "When Outcomes Collide with Desires," *Washington Post*, 29 Jan. 1986.

p. 57. Jackson quote: B. Moyers, "The Vanishing Family," CBS, New York, 1986.

p. 57. Sex on TV: J. Kalter, "Let's Run Birth Control Ads During *Dallas* and *Dynasty*," *TV Guide*, 1985; E. A. Rubinstein, "Television as a Sex Educator," in *Sex Education in the Eighties*, 1980.

p. 58. *Time* photographer quote: J. A. Meyers, "A Letter from the Publisher," *Time*, 1985.

p. 58. Child rearing easier than marriage: L. V. Klerman, "Teenage Parents: A Brief Overview of Research," in *Infants at Risk for Developmental Dysfunction*, 1982.

p. 59. Marian W. Edelman quote: Children's Defense Fund, *An Anatomy of a Social Problem*, 1987.

p. 59. Dryfoos conclusions: J. Dryfoos, "Review of Interventions in the Field of Prevention of Adolescent Pregnancy," Oct. 1983, and "Prevention Strategies: A Progress Report," Dec. 1984, Reports to the Rockefeller Foundation, New York. Similar findings come out of other reviews, such as that of E. R. McAnarney and C. Shreider, *Identifying Social and Psychological Antecedents of Adolescent Pregnancy*, 1984.

p. 60. Cross-national studies: E. F. Jones et al., *Teenage Pregnancy in Developed Countries*, 1987.

p. 60. Poverty and race: S. L. Hofferth, "Initiation of Sexual Intercourse," and "Contraceptive Decision Making," both in *Risking the Future*, 1987; D. P. Hogan and E. M. Kitagawa, *The Impact of Social Status, Family Structure, and Neighborhood on the Fertility of Black Adolescents*, 1983; *Indices, a Statistical Index to D.C. Services* (Washington, D. C.: Department of Human Services, 1985).

p. 60. Blacks become sexually active at an earlier age: L. S. Zabin, et al., "The Risk of Adolescent Pregnancy," in *Teenage Sexuality, Pregnancy, and Childbearing*, 1981.

p. 60. Rhode Island study of abortions: Alan Guttmacher Institute, "Teenage Pregnancy: The Problem That Hasn't Gone Away," 1981.

p. 61. Ratio of employed black men: W. J. Wilson, *The Truly Disadvantaged*, 1987.

p. 61. Without seeing eligible black men: Eleanor Holmes Norton, former chairman of the Equal Employment Opportunity Commission, quoted in D. Whitman and J. Thornton, "A Nation Apart," *U.S. News and World Report*, 1986.

p. 61. Slim prospects of marriage to a reliable provider: Children's Defense Fund, *Declining Earnings of Young Men: Their Relation to Poverty, Teen Pregnancy and Family Formation*, 1987; W. J. Wilson and K. M. Neckerman, "Poverty and Family Structure," in *Fighting Poverty*, 1986.

p. 61. School failure a powerful factor in early childbearing: The connection between school failure and early childbearing is the predominant finding of the literature review by S. Phipps-Yonas in "Teenage Pregnancy and Motherhood," *American Journal of Orthopsychiatry*, 1980; and the highlight of Dryfoos's thorough investigation of the pertinent literature and expert opinion. (See J. Dryfoos, "Report to the Rockefeller Foundation," 1983.) In-depth longitudinal studies have found the same phenomenon. Seitz at Yale University found that a substantial majority of girls who became pregnant with their first child had been in academic difficulty at least a year earlier, as indicated by having been retained in grade, receiving failing grades, or having a poor attendance record; only 20 to 30 percent of the girls who became pregnant had had a good educational prognosis a year earlier. (See V. Seitz, N. H. Apfel, and L. E. Rosenbaum, "School Aged Mothers: Infant Development and Maternal Education Outcomes," Paper presented at the Biennial Meeting of the Society for Research and Child Development, Detroit, 1983.)

Furstenberg and Brooks-Gunn's follow-up of disadvantaged black girls born in Baltimore to teenage mothers found that 18 percent of those at grade level got pregnant at the age of sixteen or earlier, compared to 32 percent of those who had repeated a grade. Their findings led them to believe that "despair about the present," especially a present lack of success at school, may be at least as important as a lack of hope for the future as a cause of early childbearing. They point out that adolescents who were behind in school at the time they became pregnant were much less likely to become economically self-sufficient and to postpone having additional children than those who were at grade level. They also found that girls in trouble at school suffer more serious consequences if they become mothers as teenagers. Adolescents who are educationally ambitious and at grade level when they become pregnant have fewer children and a better chance of avoiding economic dependency in adulthood than those who are behind in school and have limited education goals. (See F. F. Furstenberg, Jr., and J. Brooks-Gunn, *Adolescent Mothers in Later Life*, 1985.)

Others who have documented the connection between early problems at school, early initiation of sexual activity, and early parenting are E. R. McAnarney and C. Shreider, *Identifying Social and Psychological Antecedents of Adolescent Pregnancy*, 1984; S. L. Hofferth, "Initiation of Sexual Intercourse," in *Risking the Future*, 1987; and S. H. Fishman, "Delivery or Abortion in Inner-City Adolescents," *American Journal of Orthopsychiatry*, 1977.

p. 61. J. Ladner quote: L. Dash, "At Risk: Chronicles of Teen-age Pregnancy," *Washington Post*, 30 Jan. 1986.

p. 62. School failure and early fatherhood: A. Sum, analyses of data on basic skills levels of teens from the National Longitudinal Survey of Young Adults, Center for Labor Market Studies, Northeastern University, Boston, 1986 (unpublished, made available to the Children's Defense Fund Adolescent Pregnancy Prevention Clearinghouse, Washington, D.C.).

p. 62. McSeed quote: B. Moyers, "The Vanishing Family," CBS, New York, 1986.

p. 62. AFDC ruled out as determinant: Definitive refutations of the contention that AFDC and other family income support programs are a significant causative factor in unmarried and teenage childbearing can be found in W. J. Wilson, *The Truly Disadvantaged*, 1987; S. Danziger and P. Gottschalk, "The Poverty of *Losing Ground*," *Challenge*, 1985; and R. Greenstein, "Losing Faith in 'Losing Ground,'" *New Republic*, 1985.

CHAPTER 4

p. 64. Jamila in the neonatal intensive care unit: J. E. Wideman, *Brothers and Keepers,* 1984.

p. 65. Increased survival as a result of neonatal intensive care: The Robert Wood Johnson Foundation concludes that the high rates of survival have probably not been accompanied by increased rates of disability. "Rather there are decreases in both the number and proportion of children who at age one had congenital anomalies or developmental delays." (Robert Wood Johnson Foundation, *Special Report,* no. 3, 1985.) Others are less sanguine about the consequences of the increasing capacity to save smaller and smaller babies and believe that a general increase in the incidence of cerebral palsy and other handicapping conditions may be linked to increasingly aggressive intervention with frail newborns. (See J. H. Guillemin and L. L. Holmstrom, *Mixed Blessings,* 1986.)

p. 65. Determination to make technologies and skills available to all: Anyone interested in making other kinds of health care, such as prenatal care, more widely available, can learn much from the process of how neonatal care was reorganized. The regionalization of neonatal intensive care, which made it universally available, didn't just happen. It required profound changes in professional and institutional practices, which would never have occurred without the leadership and financial support of the federal government's Division of Maternal and Child Health, the March of Dimes Birth Defects Foundation, and the Robert Wood Johnson Foundation, and the systematic and determined efforts of the American College of Obstetricians and Gynecologists, the American Academy of Pediatrics, and the American Academy of Family Physicians, and the American Medical Association.

p. 65. Prospects of further progress through specialized care: P. H. Wise et al., "Racial and Socioeconomic Disparities in Childhood Mortality in Boston," *New England Journal of Medicine,* 1985.

p. 66. Cost of neonatal versus prenatal care in South Dakota: A. L. Wilson, "Thoughts Following a Congressional Fellowship," *Zero to Three,* 1985.

p. 66. America is number fifteen: Institute of Medicine, *Preventing Low Birthweight,* 1985.

p. 66. Consequences of low birthweight: Institute of Medicine, *Preventing Low Birthweight,* 1985.

p. 67. Later psychosocial problems: M. Rutter, "Prevention of Children's Psychosocial Disorders: Myth and Substance," *Pediatrics,* 1982.

p. 67. Effects on parents: C. M. McCarton, "The Long-Term Impact of a Low Birth Weight Infant on the Family," *Zero to Three,* 1986; Institute of Medicine, *Preventing Low Birthweight,* 1985.

p. 67. Hospitalization and its consequences: M. C. McCormick et al., "Rehospitalization in the First Year of Life for High-Risk Survivors," *Pediatrics,* 1980; also M. C. McCormick, "The Contribution of Low Birthweight to Infant Mortality and Childhood Morbidity," *New England Journal of Medicine,* 1985.

Why repeated childhood hospitalization should have such damaging effects is not well understood. Rutter writes, "The mechanisms involved remain obscure and indeed it is not known whether the effect is due to the admission per se or the altered patterns of parent-child interaction which possibly followed; nor whether the [greater detrimental] effect at the time of the second admission resided in the parent's response or the child's reaction." (M. Rutter, "Stress, Coping and Development," in *Stress, Coping and Development in Children,* 1983.)

p. 67. Learning disorders and behavior problems: Institute of Medicine, *Preventing Low Birthweight,* 1985; C. M. McCarton, "The Long-Term Impact of a Low Birth Weight Infant," 1986.

p. 67. Factors compounding the risks of low birthweight: See Chapter 2. Also see Institute of Medicine, *Preventing Low Birthweight,* 1985.

p. 68. Benefits of prenatal care: Institute of Medicine, *Preventing Low Birthweight,* 1985; B. Starfield, *The Effectiveness of Medical Care,* 1985.

p. 68. Excellent prenatal care for teenagers: Age is not itself a critical factor in accounting for adverse birth outcomes. If biological immaturity is a problem, it appears to be so only at ages fifteen and under—probably while the mother is still growing. Nonbiological factors, especially the quality of prenatal care and family structure, are considerably more powerful determinants of the outcome of teenage pregnancy than age itself. (See B. Zuckerman et al. "Adolescent Pregnancy and Parenthood: An Update," in *Advances in Developmental and Behavioral Pediatrics,* 1987.) How adequate prenatal care can overcome the negative effects of young age was shown by Birgitte Mednick of the University of Southern California, who surveyed all deliveries that took place at the State University Hospital in Copenhagen between 1959 and 1961, among mothers who participated in a system of excellent and comprehensive prenatal care. The babies of teenagers, including those aged ten to fifteen, had more favorable outcomes at birth and at one-year follow-up than the babies of women in their twenties. (See W. Baldwin and V. S. Cain, "The Children of Teenage Parents," in *Teenage Sexuality, Pregnancy, and Childbearing,* 1981.)

p. 68. U.S. approach to prenatal care compared to other countries: C. A. Miller, *Maternal Health and Infant Survival,* 1987.

p. 68. U.S. government contribution to prenatal care: The role of the federal government in the financing, provision, and monitoring of prenatal and maternity care has always been and continues to be modest, especially in comparison to other industrialized countries. Since 1922 the U.S. government has, in one way or another, tried to help states and localities to provide maternity services. Since 1935 it has supported state and local maternal and child health programs through Title V of the Social Security Act. Since 1950 states have been able to obtain additional federal funds to pay for prenatal care for at least some of the poor. With the enactment of Medicaid in 1965 and its subsequent expansion to include more pregnant women and a broader scope of prenatal benefits, Congress attempted to further reduce financial barriers to needed health care—including prenatal care—for the poor. In 1972 the federal government also began to supplement its more broadly available food stamps and other nutrition programs with a program targeted directly at pregnant women and infants, the Special Supplemental Food Program for Women, Infants and Children, known as WIC.

p. 68. Eight hundred thousand pregnant women: National Center for Health Statistics, "Advance Report of Final Natality Statistics, 1984," 1986.

p. 68. Reagan Administration official quote: "Milk for Babies," *New Republic,* 2 Sep. 1985.

p. 68–69. Murray quote: Interview with R. Pear in "Of Babies and Stick," *New York Times,* 11 Apr. 1986.

p. 69. Receipt of prenatal care: The biggest jump in prompt prenatal care occurred in the years immediately following the introduction of Medicaid, the Neighborhood Health Centers, and the Maternal and Infant Care Centers, and the increase was most apparent among the highest-risk women. Among low-income women, the proportion who saw a physician early in pregnancy increased from 58 percent in 1963 to 71 percent in 1970. (See K. Davis and C. Schoen, *Health and the War on Poverty,* 1978.) Among black mothers, the proportion rose from 44 percent in 1970 to 62 percent in 1979, and has not changed much since then. The proportion of all mothers who began their care early rose from 68 percent in 1970 to 77 percent in 1984. (See National Center for Health Statistics, *Health, United States,* 1986.)

p. 69. Relationship between prenatal care and low-birthweight babies: C. A. Miller et al., *Monitoring Children's Health,* 1986; D. Hughes et al., *The Health of America's Children,* 1987.

p. 70. Black-white infant mortality gap: C. A. Miller, "Infant Mortality in the U.S.," *Scientific American,* 1985.

p. 70. The women least likely to obtain prenatal care: Institute of Medicine, *Preventing Low Birthweight,* 1985; S. Gortmaker, "The Effects of Prenatal Care Upon the Health of the Newborn," *American Journal of Public Health,* 1979; W. Lazarus and K. M. West, *Back to Basics,* 1987.

p. 70. Reasons for not receiving timely care: Institute of Medicine, *Preventing Low Birthweight,* 1985; S. Singh et al., "The Need for Prenatal Care in the United States," *Family Planning Perspectives,* 1985; D. Hughes et al., *The Health of America's Children,* 1987.

p. 70. Antismoking efforts during pregnancy are effective: In a randomized, controlled clinical trial, the pregnant women who received information, support, practical advice, and behavioral interventions to help them stop smoking had 25 percent fewer low-birthweight babies than would have been expected. (See M. Sexton and J. R. Hefel, "A Clinical Trial of Change in Maternal Smoking and Its Effects on Birthweight," *Journal of the American Medical Association,* 1984.)

p. 70. Risks of alcohol and drug use: R. Sokol, "A Biological Perspective on Substance Use in Pregnancy," *Infants at Risk for Developmental Dysfunction,* 1982.

p. 70. Reducing substance abuse in pregnant women: Drs. Henry Rosett, Lyn Weiner, and Kenneth Edelin at Boston City Hospital found that they were able to use the problem drinkers' desire to have healthy babies to engage them in successful therapy for heavy drinking as part of their prenatal care. They concluded that "providers who are knowledgeable, interested, and accepting can successfully treat pregnant patients at risk from alcohol" and thereby improve pregnancy outcomes. (See H. L. Rosett et al., "Treatment Experience with Pregnant Problem Drinkers," *Journal of the American Medical Association,* 1983.)

p. 71. Observations by clinicians working with pregnant teenagers: Personal communications with Sarah Brown, M.P.H., on her visit to South Carolina to gather material for this chapter in 1986.

p. 71. Anthropological findings: M. S. Boone, "Social and Cultural Factors in the

Etiology of Low Birthweight Among Disadvantaged Blacks," *Social Science and Medicine*, 1985.

p. 72. "Transmedical" interventions: The president of the Robert Wood Johnson Foundation, David. E. Rogers, M.D., noted in his 1984 Annual Report "that 'health' or 'medical' problems cannot always be neatly dissected away from a myriad of other problems—social, psychologic, or economic—that generally beset those in trouble." He wrote that the foundation's experience with trying to solve "seemingly insoluble or multifaceted problems" through the health route had increased his and his colleagues' awareness of the fact that "human misery is generally the result of, or accompanied by, a great untidy basketful of intertwined and interconnected circumstances and happenings," which often all need attention if a problem is to be overcome. He has also concluded that the health route is frequently the best way to solving complicated problems, and that medical care services are an effective "magnet to attract other human support services so necessary for real programmatic success." (See Robert Wood Johnson Foundation, *Annual Report, 1984.)*

p. 73–77. Description of the California OB Access Project: Based on several interviews with and materials furnished by Lyn Headley, M.D., and an interview with Joseph Klun, both of the California State Department of Health Services, in 1986; and the following reports: M. McManus, "Evaluation of Interventions to Reduce Racial Disparities in Infant Mortality," prepared for the DHHS Infant Mortality Task Force, 1985; M. Gregory et al., *Final Evaluation of the Obstetrical Access Pilot Project, July 1979–June 1982,"* 1984; C. C. Korenbrot, "Risk Reduction in Pregnancies of Low Income Women," *Mobius,* 1984; A. Lennie, J. Klun, and T. Hausner, "Low Birth Weight Reduced by OB Access Project," Paper presented at the 1985 Annual Meeting of the American Public Health Association, Washington, D.C., Nov. 1985.

p. 77–79. Description of the Johns Hopkins prenatal care program: Based on interviews with Dr. Zabin, Dr. Hardy, and Ms. Streett, 22 Jan. 1986, and the report by J. B. Hardy, T. M. King, and J. T. Repke, "The Johns Hopkins Adolescent Pregnancy Program," (revised 16 Jan. 1986) from the Departments of Pediatrics and Gynecology and Obstetrics, the Johns Hopkins University School of Medicine, and the Johns Hopkins University Hospital, Baltimore, Md.

p. 79–83. Description of the South Carolina Resource Mothers program: Based on visits and interviews conducted by Sarah S. Brown, M.P.H., in 1986, and the following reports: D. G. Unger and L. P. Wandersman, "Social Support and Adolescent Mothers," *Journal of Social Issues,* 1985; S. Piechnik and M. A. Corbett, "Reducing Low Birthweight among Socio-Economically High Risk Adolescent Pregnancies," *Journal of Nurse-Midwifery,* 1985.

p. 83. Attributes of successful programs: M. Meglen, "How to Encourage Disadvantaged Women to Enroll in Prenatal Care Early and Remain in Care," Unpublished paper prepared at the request of the Committee to Study the Prevention of Low Birthweight, Institute of Medicine, Washington, D.C., 1984.

p. 83. Content of adequate prenatal care: Additional corroboration of the importance of the *content* of prenatal care comes from Guilford County, N.C., where poor women obtain prenatal care from private obstetricians if they are covered by Medicaid, otherwise from many of the same physicians at health department clinics in Greensboro and High Point. The health department supplements traditional prenatal care with health education, counseling, outreach, and follow-up, help with nutrition, and assurance that the mother will receive a combination of services keyed to individual needs. The care by obstetricians at the health department is supplemented by nurse practitioners, health educators, nutritionists, outreach workers, and case coordinators—people with training and functions hard to incorporate into private office practice. More than seven hundred babies born in 1984 to the two groups of mothers were studied. The findings: Among women who had received "traditional" private care, the proportion of babies born at low birthweight was more than twice as high as among those who had received comprehensive care from the health department. (See P. A. Buescher, *Source of Prenatal Care and Infant Birthweight:* 1986.)

CHAPTER 5

p. 85. Archie's story: Children's Defense Fund, *EPSDT,* 1977.

p. 86. Frequency of middle ear infection: M. I. Gottlieb, "Otitis Media," in *Developmental-Behavioral Pediatrics,* 1983.

p. 86. Poor children have more ear infections: L. Egbuonu and B. Starfield, "Child Health and Social Status," *Pediatrics,* 1982.

p. 86. Consequences of hearing loss: M. I. Gottlieb, "Otitis Media," in *Developmental-Behavioral Pediatrics,* 1983; N. Holmes et al., "Language Development in a Group of Very Low-Birth-Weight Children," *Pediatrics,* 1983.

p. 86. Kenny's story: Children's Defense Fund, *EPSDT,* 1977.

p. 86. Consequences of uncorrected vision problems: P. W. Davidson, "Visual Impairment and Blindness," in *Developmental-Behavioral Pediatrics,* 1983.

p. 86. Incidence of vision defects, extent of treatment: Select Panel for the Promotion of Child Health, *Better Health for Our Children,* 1981; M. I. Erlich et al., "Preschool Vision Screening," *Survey of Ophthalmology,* 1983.

p. 86. T. R. Sizer, *Horace's Compromise,* 1985.

p. 86. The judge's observation was made in the course of a site visit by the Robert Wood Johnson Foundation to a demonstration adolescent health program in Boston in 1984 and repeated to me by Dr. George A. Lamb of the Boston City Health Department.

p. 87. The connection between perceptual problems, early difficulties in learning, and juvenile delinquency was examined by the American Institutes for Research at the request of the U.S. Department of Justice. An extensive literature review and interviews with experts in the field led to the conclusion that learning disabilities per se do not seem to be a "primary cause" of delinquency, but that vision, hearing, perceptual, and integrative disorders can cripple a child's ability to succeed at school and thereby lead to later serious trouble. The report also suggests a "strong possibility" that learning disabilities have more potent adverse effects in an inner city environment. (See C. A. Murray, *The Link Between Learning Disabilities and Juvenile Delinquency,* 1976.)

p. 87. Consequences of learning disabilities: See the excellent summary by the Task Panel on Learning Failure of the President's Commission on Mental Health, "Learning Failure and Unused Learning Potential," 1978.

p. 87. Health problems as risk factors: M. Rutter, *Changing Youth in a Changing Society,* 1980.

p. 87–88. Gail's story, and evidence of the inadequate response of the health system to subtle signs of adverse health conditions: D. O. Lewis and D. A. Balla, *Delinquency and Psychopathology,* 1976; D. O. Lewis and S. Shanok, "A Comparison of the Medical Histories of Incarcerated Delinquent Children," *Child Psychiatry and Human Development,* 1979; D. O. Lewis et al., "Violent Juvenile Delinquents," *Journal of the American Academy of Child Psychiatry,* 1979.

p. 88. Consequences of inadequate immunization: U.S. Department of Health, Education and Welfare, *Healthy People,* 1979.

p. 88. Anemia: L. Egbuonu and B. Starfield, "Child Health and Social Status," *Pediatrics,* 1982; B. Starfield, *The Effectiveness of Medical Care,* 1985.

p. 88. Lead contamination generally comes from environmental sources—fallout from the smelting of 9 million tons of lead annually; soil around old houses and highways; lead-based paint found in deteriorated housing; and fumes from lead-based gasoline, which are at the highest levels in inner city areas with heavy traffic. High levels of lead in the blood can cause anemia, mental retardation, kidney and liver damage, convulsions, coma, and even death. For documentation of consequences of lead poisoning and high blood lead levels, see C. A. Miller et al., *Monitoring Children's Health,* 1986; L. Egbuonu and B. Starfield, "Child Health and Social Status," *Pediatrics,* 1982.

In an imaginatively designed study made possible by the fact that lead is stored in the teeth, pediatrician H. L. Needleman and his colleagues at the Children's Hospital Medical Center in Boston were able to correlate lead concentrations with behavior in school. Deciduous (baby) teeth were collected from 2,146 elementary school pupils in two lower-middle-income communities near Boston. Teachers were asked about the children's classroom behavior and performance. Researchers found an almost perfect correlation between the amount of dentin lead and the degree of negative evaluations—from distractability to low overall functioning. (See H. L. Needleman et al., "Deficits in Psychological and Classroom Performance of Children with Elevated Dentine Lead Level," *New England Journal of Medicine,* 1979.) Children with elevated blood lead levels were also found to perform less well on IQ tests than classroom controls with low lead levels. (See L. Eisenberg, "Prevention: Rhetoric and Reality," *Journal of the Royal Society of Medicine,* 1984.)

p. 88. The consequences of hyperactivity (also referred to as attention deficit disorder): G. Weiss and L. Hechtman, "The Hyperactive Child Syndrome," *Science,* 1979; D. P. Cantwell, "Hyperactive Children Have Grown Up," *Archives of General Psychiatry,* 1985.

p. 91–92. Physician failure to look beyond presenting problems: D. O. Lewis et al., "Race, Health and Delinquency," *Journal of the American Academy of Child Psychiatry,* 1985.

p. 92. Benefits of a much broader approach: See L. B. Schorr, "Environmental Deterrents: Poverty, Affluence, Violence, and Television," in *Developmental-Behavioral Pediatrics,* 1983.

p. 92. School absence and health care in Boston study: L. V. Klerman et al., "School Absence," in *Monitoring Child Health,* 1984.

p. 93–98. Information about the Jackson-Hinds Comprehensive Health Center: Visits on 18 and 19 Oct. 1979; correspondence and interviews with Dr. Aaron Shirley in 1979, 1980, 1984, 1985, and 1986; reports by the center in 1984 and 1986; University of Southern Mississippi School of Social Work–Research Institute, "Report of Evaluation, Jackson-Hinds Comprehensive Care Center: Infant and Child Day Care Program," 1983; M. McPherson, "A Poverty No Program Can Crack," *Washington Post,* 26 Feb. 1978; L. B. Schorr, "Health Services for Mothers and Children: Unmet Needs and Major Issues," Testimony before the U.S. Senate, Committee on Human Resources, Subcommittee on Health and Scientific Research, 1 Mar. 1978.

p. 98–103. Information about the Greenspring Pediatric Associates: Visit and interviews with staff and patients, 19 Dec. 1985; Evan Charney, M.D., personal communications, December 1985 and March 1986; E. Charney, "Critical Issues in Behavioral Pediatric Training," Presentation at the 1985 National Conference on Behavioral Pediatrics, Easton, Md.; E. Charney, "Preparing Physicians in Training," in *Child Health Care Communications,* 1984.

p. 100. Barriers have been removed: Nationally, black children and poor children make substantially less use of nonemergency health services, despite their worse health status. Two careful studies showed that this pattern did not hold for the children using the Greenspring group: S. T. Orr et al., "Differences in Use of Health Services by Children," *Medical Care,* 1984; and S. T. Orr, E. Charney, and J. Straus, "Health Services Utilization by Black Children According to Payment Mechanism," 1986. Typical of the Greenspring approach is the availability of after-hours telephone consultation, a mainstay of middle-class pediatric practice which has often not been available to poor families on the assumption that less educated parents would not use it well. A study by the Greenspring group showed this assumption to be wrong, and that the telephone system is effectively used by all families. (See S. E. Caplan et al., "After-Hours Telephone Use in Urban Pediatric Primary Care Centers," *American Journal of Diseases of Children,* 1983.) Similar findings came out of a study done earlier in Boston, where the effective use of telephone communication by low-income families was also documented. (See M. C. Heagarty et al., "Use of the Telephone by Low-Income Families," *Journal of Pediatrics,* 1968.)

p. 101–103. Information about the Sinai Hospital Department of Pediatrics Head Start program for children with lead poisoning: Visit on 19 Dec. 1985; Barbara Howard, M.D., personal communications regarding outcome findings in 1986 and the summer of 1987; descriptions of the program and outcome data from grant proposals submitted by Dr. Howard in 1986 and 1987.

p. 104–109. Information about the programs of the Department of Pediatrics of the King/Drew Medical Center: Visits on 8 Feb. 1985; Martin Luther King, Jr.–Charles R. Drew Medical School, Los Angeles, Calif., "Data Book of the Department of Pediatrics," 1984, updated by personal communications from Robert J. Schlegel, M.D., in 1984, 1985, and 1986; presentations by Dr. Schlegel, Alice Faye Singleton, M.D., M.P.H., and Vivian Weinstein, M.A., on "Overcoming the 'New Morbidity': Social Pediatrics in Watts," sponsored by the National Health Policy Forum, Washington, D.C., 14 June 1984; R. J. Schlegel, "A Social Hygiene Approach to the New Morbidity," and V. Weinstein, "An Ecological Model for Intervention with Inner-City Poor and/or Minority Handicapped Infants and Their Families: The Community," in *Papers from the Experiences of the Infant-Parent Project,* 1984.

CHAPTER 6

p. 112. Health expenditures: National Center for Health Statistics, *Health, United States,* 1986.

p. 112–113. Gardner quote: Guggenheim Productions, Inc., "The Great Society Remembered," Documentary film, 1985.

p. 113. Effect of insurance on health technology: P. Starr, *The Social Transformation of American Medicine,* 1982.

p. 113. Medicare language: Public Law 89-97 (Title XVIII of the Social Security Act).

p. 113. Operational difficulties in Medicare: Hugh Heclo, of the Department of Government at Harvard University, writes that the concessions made by the Johnson Administration to secure passage of the Economic Opportunity Act played out the familiar story in American public policy of legislative compromises exacted as the price of passage, laying the conditions for later operational failure. His point applies even more tellingly to the Medicare experience. (See H. Heclo, "The Political Foundations of Antipoverty Policy," in *Fighting Poverty,* 1986.)

p. 114. Escalation in health spending: National Center for Health Statistics, *Health, United States,* 1986.

p. 114. "Original sin": P. Starr, "Health Care for the Poor: The Past Twenty Years," in *Fighting Poverty,* 1986. In defense of the original Medicaid concept, it should be noted that a far broader definition of eligibility was anticipated at the time of enactment. New categories of needy children and pregnant women, who do not qualify for AFDC, have been made eligible for Medicaid through amendments enacted more than fifteen years later.

p. 114. Cost containment pressures reduce utilization: The reduction in the number of Americans with public and private insurance that also occurred during the early 1980s came as though under the banner of cost containment, but—as Sara Rosenbaum of the Children's Defense Fund points out in a forthcoming book—"disinsurance" is a separate phenomenon which should not be confused with cost containment efforts. (See S. Rosenbaum, et al. *Maternal and Child Health: Beyond the Reagan Era,* 1988.)

p. 115. The "free market" in health care: R. Fein, "Choosing the Arbiter: The Market or the Government," *New England Journal of Medicine,* 1985.

p. 115. Public hospital closings: *Washington Post,* 30 Jan. 1985. Strain on urban hospitals: J. Feder et al., "Poor People and Poor Hospitals," *Journal of Health Politics, Policy and Law,* 1984; J. Feder et al., "Falling Through the Cracks: Poverty, Insurance Coverage, and Hospitals' Care to the Poor, 1980 and 1982," Working Paper; testimony by L. S. Gage, president of the National Association of Public Hospitals, before the U.S. House of Representatives, Committee on Ways and Means, Subcommittee on Health, 12 Mar. 1987.

p. 115. New pediatric clinics: J. Mervis, "A Quest to Improve the World of Children," *APA Monitor,* Feb. 1985.

p. 116. Cost shifting as fig leaf: U. E. Reinhardt, "Hard Choices in Health Care," in *Health Care: How to Improve It and Pay for It,* 1985.

p. 116. Beaumont hospital: U.S. House of Representatives, Committee on Energy and Commerce, Subcommittee on Health and Environment, Miscellaneous—Part 1, 97th Congress, 1st Session, 1981.

p. 116. Rock Hill pediatrician: "Hospitals in Cost Squeeze 'Dump' More Patients Who Can't Pay Bills," *Wall Street Journal,* 8 Mar. 1985.

p. 116. Relman quote: A. S. Relman, "Economic Considerations in Emergency Care: What Are Hospitals For?" *New England Journal of Medicine,* 1985.

p. 116. Alarming long-term trends: C. A. Miller et al., *Monitoring Children's Health,* 1986; Ezra Davidson, M.D., Chief of the Department of Obstetrics and Gynecology, Charles R. Drew Medical School, Presentation to the National Health Policy Forum, Washington, D.C., 1983.

p. 116–17. Infant mortality statistics: D. Hughes et al., *The Health of America's Children,* 1987. (Based on unpublished data from the National Center for Health Statistics, U.S. Department of Health and Human Services.)

p. 117. "Demarketing" tactics: L. A. Burns, "Hospital Initiatives in Response to Reduction in Medicaid Funding for Ambulatory Care Programs," Paper presented at a symposium on "Changing Roles in Serving the Underserved," Leesburg, Va., 12 Oct. 1981. At the time Ms. Burns presented the paper, she was director, division of ambulatory care, of the American Hospital Association, Chicago, Ill.

p. 117. Debates regarding two-class care: L. C. Thurow, "Medicine versus Economics," *New England Journal of Medicine,* 1985; J. K. Iglehart, "Medical Care of the Poor—A Growing Problem," *New England Journal of Medicine,* 1985; U. E. Reinhardt, "Hard Choices in Health Care," in *Health Care,* 1985.

p. 117. Anlyan quote: J. K. Iglehart, "Report on the Duke University Medical Center Private Sector Conference," *New England Journal of Medicine,* 1982.

p. 118. Berman quote: Robert Wood Johnson Foundation, *Special Report,* no. 2, 1985.

p. 119. Outreach services not reimbursed in Sinai program: E. Charney, personal communication, 1985.

p. 119. Ambulatory services reduced in Denver: Institute of Medicine, *Community Oriented Primary Care,* 1982.

p. 119. "Chilling effect" on mental health services: J. Knitzer, "Mental Health Services to Children and Adolescents," *American Psychologist,* 1984.

p. 120. Institutions close their doors: For a description of the terrible pressures operating on urban hospitals because of the high volume of uncompensated care they furnish, see M. B. Sulvetta and K. Swartz, *The Uninsured and Uncompensated Care,* 1986; J. Feder et al., "Poor People and Poor Hospitals," *Journal of Health Politics, Policy and Law,* 1984.

p. 120. Americans without health insurance: U.S. Bureau of the Census, *Current Population Survey,* 1984.

p. 120. Reasons for fewer people with insurance: S. Rosenbaum, "Children and Private Health Insurance," in *Children in a Changing Health Care System* (in press); D. J. Chollet, "The Changing Pattern of Health Insurance Coverage Among Nonelderly Families," Testimony before the U.S. House of Representatives, Select Committee on Children, Youth and Families, 1 July 1987.

p. 120. Drop in Medicaid coverage: S. Rosenbaum, "Policy Papers on Medical Indigency in America," Report prepared for the National Association of Community Health Centers, Washington, D.C., 1986.

p. 120. Medicaid funds spent on children: U.S. Congress, House of Representatives, Committee on Ways and Means, *Children in Poverty,* 99th Congress, 1st session, 1985.

p. 121. Children eligible for and covered by Medicaid: J. F. Holahan and J. W. Cohen, *Medicaid: The Trade-off between Cost Containment and Access to Care,* 1986; D. Chollet, "The Changing Pattern of Health Insurance Coverage Among Nonelderly Families," Testimony before the U.S. House of Representatives, Select Committee on Children, Youth and Families, 1 July 1987.

p. 121. State Medicaid policies: The "extremely wide variation in Medicaid spending patterns among the states" was termed the most disturbing major finding of a recent Urban Institute study of Medicaid. John F. Holahan and Joel W. Cohen found that in 1984 total per capita spending on Medicaid varied among the states by a factor of ten, and that variations in expenditures per person in poverty were even greater than variations in expenditures per capita. (See J. F. Holahan and J. W. Cohen, *Medicaid: The Trade-off between Cost Containment and Access to Care,* 1986.)

In October 1986 Congress broadened the authority of the states to provide Medicaid coverage to indigent pregnant women and young children. If the states act on their new authority, access to early and continuous prenatal and pediatric care will be significantly expanded. (See S. Rosenbaum, *Medicaid Eligibility for Pregnant Women: Reforms Contained in the Sixth Omnibus Budget Reconciliation Act (SOBRA),* 1987.)

p. 121. Alabama Medicaid: Figures furnished in May 1987 by the state of Alabama to the Children's Defense Fund.

p. 121. Difficulty in maintaining continuity of care: S. Rosenbaum and K. Johnson, "Providing Health Care for Low-income Children," *The Milbank Quarterly,* 1986.

p. 121. Medicaid eligibility for prenatal care: Children's Defense Fund, *Campaign Notes* (Washington, D.C.: Children's Defense Fund, Mar. 1986.)

p. 121. Deposits required for hospital admission: S. Rosenbaum and K. Johnson, *Maternal and Child Health: Exemplary State Initiatives,* Report of the Children's Defense Fund, 1985.

p. 121. Waiting time for prenatal care: W. Lazarus and K. M. West, *Back to Basics: Improving the Health of California's Next Generation,* 1987.

p. 121. Prevailing reimbursement system: Select Panel for the Promotion of Child Health, *Better Health for our Children,* 1981.

p. 122. Methods of paying hospitals: P. Starr, "Health Care for the Poor," in *Fighting Poverty,* 1986.

p. 122. Rewards for high-technology services: G. Easterbrook, "The Revolution in Medicine," *Newsweek,* 1987; Institute of Medicine, *Reforming Physician Payment,* 1984.

p. 123. Narrowness of biomedical approach: Harvard University's Derek Bok devoted his 1982–83 President's Report to current problems in medical education and observed that "thinking like a doctor" means seeing human disease as a scientific phenomenon consisting of deviations from the biomedical norm. Physicians aspire to reach scientifically certain diagnoses by making all the relevant observations and tests (while looking to narrow their ignorance by discovering scientific truths through research); they then hope to be able to cure or alleviate the ailments they have identified through surgery, drugs, or other biomedical intervention. Doctors recognize that environmental, psychological, and behavioral factors influence health, but most of them regard these as unscientific, to be dealt with by lesser professionals such as psychologists, social workers, and public health officials. (See D. Bok, "Needed: A New Way To Train Doctors," *Harvard Magazine,* 1984.)

p. 123. Physician reluctance to care for Medicaid patients: The need of many Medicaid patients for services which may be beyond the skills of many physicians is of course only part of the reason that some physicians do not take care of Medicaid patients. One quarter of all pediatricians and more than a third of obstetricians will not see Medicaid patients at all. Reasons for physician unwillingness to participate in Medicaid identified by physician surveys are Medicaid reimbursement levels, restrictive regulations, cumbersome claims forms and accountability procedures, and the racial composition of the Medicaid clientele. (See J. B. Mitchell and R. Schurman, "Access to Private Ob-Gyn Services Under Medicaid," 1982; S. M. Davidson, "Physician Participation in Medicaid," *Journal of Health Politics, Policy and Law,* 1982.)

In California, New York, and Texas, half the pediatricians surveyed in 1983 saw Medicaid patients only in an emergency, when referred by another physician, if the patient was previously a private patient, or for hospital or acute care only. (See American Academy of Pediatrics, *Trends in Pediatrician Participation in State Medicaid Programs,* 1985.

p. 123. Vermont pediatrician: J. L. Mayer, "Time Out," *New York Times Magazine,* 1986.

p. 124. Studies of health care of low-income children: D. Dutton, "Children's Health Care: The Myth of Equal Access," in *Better Health for Our Children,* 1981; S. T. Orr, E. Charney, J. Strauss, "Health Services Utilization by Black Children According to Payment Mechanism" 1986.

p. 124. Physician utilization by Medicaid recipients: K. Davis and C. Schoen, *Health and the War on Poverty: A Ten Year Appraisal,* 1978; S. T. Orr and C. A. Miller, "Utilization of Health Services by Poor Children Since Advent of Medicaid," *Medical Care,* 1981.

p. 125. Yerby quote: L. B. Schorr, "The Neighborhood Health Center—Background and Current Issues," in *Medicine in a Changing Society,* 1972.

p. 125. Medicaid effects on health status: K. Davis and C. Schoen, *Health and the War on Poverty,* 1978; C. A. Miller, "Infant Mortality in the U.S.," *Scientific American,* 1985: M. Rosenbach, *Insurance Coverage and Ambulatory Medical Care of Low-Income Children: United States, 1980,* 1985; D. E. Rogers et al., "Who Needs Medicaid?" *New England Journal of Medicine,* 1982.

p. 125. Medicaid amendments: S. Rosenbaum, *Medicaid Eligibility for Pregnant Women,* 1987. In this same paper, Ms. Rosenbaum, head of the health division of the Children's Defense Fund, advocates the development of measures whereby the most damaging effects of a pure insurance approach would be attenuated by better reimbursement of community health centers, public health clinics, and hospital outpatient departments serving large numbers of poor children. Under the kind of "creative state administration" Ms. Rosenbaum visualizes, such providers would be reimbursed at higher rates than other providers. These higher levels of Medicaid reimbursement could then be combined with other federal, state, and local funds to provide a pool large enough to cover services not specifically paid for by third-party payments, and to cover children who are poor but not insured. Ms. Rosenbaum believes that by providing generous reimbursement to community-based providers obligated to serve the poor, states could promote greater access and better care for children and pregnant women and more stable funding of comprehensive health programs. These arrangements would also save money by eliminating burdensome individual billing and eligibility procedures.

p. 126. Early choices for EPSDT: A. M. Foltz, "The Development of Ambiguous Federal Policy: EPSDT," *Milbank Memorial Fund Quarterly,* 1975.

p. 127. EPSDT successes: S. Rosenbaum and K. Johnson, "Providing Health Care for Low-income Children," *The Milbank Quarterly,* 1986; W. Keller, "Study of Selected Outcomes of the EPSDT Program in Michigan," *Public Health Reports,* 1984; P. Irwin and R. Conroy-Hughes, "EPSDT Impact on Health Status," *Medical Care,* 1982.

p. 128. Description of WIC: Select Panel for the Promotion of Child Health, *Better Health for Our Children,* 1981.

p. 128. Inadequate funds limit WIC: Children's Defense Fund, *A Children's Defense Budget,* 1987.

p. 128. Early studies of WIC effectiveness: J. C. Endozien, *Medical Evaluation of the Supplemental Food Program for Women, Infants, and Children,* 1976; U.S. Department of Agriculture, Food and Nutrition Service, *CDC Analysis of Nutritional Indices for Selected WIC Participants,* prepared under contract with the U.S. Department of Health, Education, and Welfare, Centers for Disease Control, Atlanta, June 1978; E. T. Kennedy, *Evaluation of the Effects of the WIC Program on Prenatal Patients in Massachusetts,* 1979; M. Bendick, Jr., *Towards Efficiency and Effectiveness in the WIC Delivery System,* 1976.

p. 129. Rush critique of WIC studies: D. Rush, "Is WIC Worthwhile?" *American Journal of Public Health,* 1982.

p. 129. *Times* editorial: "What Happens When Mothers Get Food," *New York Times,* 3 Feb. 1986.

p. 129. WIC study findings: D. Rush et al., "National Evaluation of the Special Supplemental Food Program for Women, Infants and Children (WIC)," Final Report. Five volumes. Department of Agriculture, Office of Analysis and Evaluation, Food and Nutrition Service, 1986.

p. 130. MIC and C&Y centers: The Maternal and Infant Care projects and Children and Youth projects of the Department of Health, Education and Welfare were established to provide more comprehensive and less fragmented prenatal care and child health services. Like the neighborhood health centers of the OEO, they included social services, support services, outreach, and other mechanisms for minimizing barriers to access. Those that were carefully evaluated showed excellent outcomes. For example, a study of a Maternity and Infant Care Project in Cleveland Metropolitan Hospital found that patients receiving more patient education, nutrition counseling, social services, outreach, and follow-up experienced 60 percent less perinatal mortality than a comparison group. (See R. J. Sokol et al., "Risk, Antepartum Care, and Outcome: Impact of a Maternity and Infant Care Project," *Obstetrics and Gynecology*, 1980.)

pp. 130–131. Geiger quote: H. J. Geiger, "A Health Center in Mississippi—A Case Study in Social Medicine," in *Medicine in a Changing Society*, 1972.

p. 131. Stipulations for neighborhood health center grants and other early history: J. T. English and L. B. Schorr, "Background, Context and Significant Issues in Neighborhood Health Center programs," *Milbank Memorial Fund Quarterly*, 1968; L. B. Schorr, "The Neighborhood Health Center—Background and Current Issues," in *Medicine in a Changing Society*, 1972.

p. 132. Early effects of neighborhood health centers: S. S. Bellin et al., "Impact of Ambulatory-Health-Care Services on the Demand for Hospital Beds," *New England Journal of Medicine*, 1969; D. I. Zwick, "Some Accomplishments and Findings of Neighborhood Health Centers," *Milbank Memorial Fund Quarterly*, 1972.

p. 132. Effects of neighborhood health centers on health and costs: K. Davis and C. Schoen, *Health and the War on Poverty*, 1978; A. Chabot, "Improved Infant Mortality in Populations Served By Neighborhood Health Centers," *Pediatrics*, 1971; L. I. Hochheiser et al., "Effect of the Neighborhood Health Center on the Use of Pediatric Emergency Departments in Rochester, New York," *New England Journal of Medicine*, 1971; M. A. Morehead et al., "Comparisons Between OEO Neighborhood Health Centers and Other Health Care Providers," *American Journal of Public Health*, 1971; M. Klein, "The Impact of the Rochester Neighborhood Health Center on Hospitalization of Children, 1968 to 1970," *Pediatrics*, 1973; L. Gordis, "Effectiveness of Comprehensive Care Programs in Preventing Rheumatic Fever," *New England Journal of Medicine*, 1973; J. C. Stewart and L. L. Crafton, *Delivery of Health Care Services to the Poor*, 1975.

p. 133. Starr observations on community health centers: P. Starr, "Health Care for the Poor," in *Fighting Poverty*, 1986.

p. 135. Costly administrative activities: The bulk of these unproductive administrative expenditures result from requiring that individual charges for an annual 1.6 billion hospital admissions and physician visits be attributed to specific patients— and then be individually reimbursed by one or more of an almost infinite number of payors. (See D. U. Himmelstein and S. Woolhandler, "Cost Without Benefit," *New England Journal of Medicine*, 1986.)

pp. 135–136. International comparisons of health spending: U. E. Reinhardt, "Hard Choices in Health Care," in *Health Care*, 1985.

p. 136. Relman on prospects of universal insurance: A. S. Relman, "The United States and Canada: Different Approaches to Health Care," *New England Journal of Medicine*, 1986.

p. 136. Robert Wood Johnson Foundation survey: Robert Wood Johnson Foundation, "Updated Report on Access to Health Care for the American People," *Special Report* no. 1, 1983. Los Angeles *Times* survey: A. Parachini, "Health Care Debate: Who Will Pay The Way?" Los Angeles *Times*, 30 Aug. 1987.

p. 136. Iacocca quote: D. E. Rosenbaum, "Chrysler, Hit Hard by Costs, Studies Health Care System," *New York Times*, 5 Mar. 1984.

p. 136. Starr history: P. Starr, *The Social Transformation of American Medicine*, 1982.

p. **136.** Starr quote: P. Starr, "Health Care for the Poor," in *Fighting Poverty*, 1986.

p. **136.** Others have described: R. Fein, *Medical Care, Medical Costs: The Search for a Health Insurance Policy*, 1986; H. H. Hiatt, *America's Health in the Balance: Choice or Change*, 1987; A. L. Schorr, *Common Decency*, 1986.

p. **137.** Dr. Rothman's observations: D. Rothman, personal communication, 1985.

p. **137.** Ollie Hill's experience with prenatal care: I. Wilkerson, "Infant Mortality: Frightful Odds in Inner City," *New York Times*, 26 June 1987.

p. **138.** Rationing health care: Dr. Saxe's observation is from J. S. Saxe, "How the United States Rations Health Care," *Charlotte Observer*, 13 April 1986. Also see H. J. Aaron and W. B. Schwartz, *The Painful Prescription*, 1984; G. Miller and F. Miller, "The Painful Prescription: A Procrustean Perspective," *New England Journal of Medicine*, 1986; V. R. Fuchs, "The 'Rationing' of Medical Care," *New England Journal of Medicine*, 1984.

p. **138.** Death rates vary by race and income: P. H. Wise et al., "Racial and Socioeconomic Disparities in Childhood Mortality in Boston," *New England Journal of Medicine*, 1985.

p. **139.** The social glue: L. C. Thurow, "Learning to Say 'No,'" *New England Journal of Medicine*, 1984.

CHAPTER 7

p. **140.** Father Harvey's observations and program: From an interview with Marlene Sanders on "Sunday Morning," *CBS News*, 4 May 1986. Father Harvey had been a chaplain at Rikers Island prison. He left because "I couldn't stand the frustration of not helping the kids" and started "Flowers With Care" in 1974. It began as a program to give juvenile offenders and homeless teenagers jobs in florist shops and has gone on to offer a wide range of supplementary services to deeply troubled youngsters. (See K. Teltsch, "A Program Swamps Its Founder," *New York Times*, 14 June 1987.)

p. **141.** Dr. Solnit quote: A. J. Solnit, in the Foreword to S. Provence and A. Naylor, *Working with Disadvantaged Parents and Their Children*, 1983.

p. **141.** George Cadwalader quote: G. Cadwalader, "Why My Reform School Can't Save All Bad Kids," *Washington Post*, 22 June 1986.

p. **141.** Ronald White's experience: R. D. White, "K. Never Clapped," *Washington Post*, 18 Sep. 1985.

pp. **141–142.** Three young adults described by Leon Dash: L. Dash, "Young Black Pregnancies: First Answer is Truth," *Washington Post*, 9 Feb. 1986.

p. **142.** Carson McCullers quote: C. McCullers, *The Ballad of the Sad Cafe and Collected Short Stories*, 1979.

p. **143.** "Once that threshold is crossed": J. Kagan, *The Nature of the Child*, 1984.

pp. **143–144.** Story of Martha: E. L. Bassuk et al., "Characteristics of Sheltered Homeless Families," *American Journal of Public Health*, 1986. (Names are fictional.)

p. 144. Story of Lenore and Dalia: L. Dash, "Children's Children: The Crisis Up Close," *Washington Post,* 26 Jan. 1986. (Names are fictional.)

pp. 144–145. Attachment, a biological survival mechanism: D. A. Hamburg, "Reducing the Casualties of Early Life: A Preventive Orientation," in Carnegie Corporation of New York, *Annual Report,* 1985.

p. 145. Development of trust: M. Rutter, "Maternal Deprivation, 1972–1978: New Findings, New Concepts, New Approaches," *Child Development,* 1979.

p. 145. Infant and mother, "akin to a dance": J. Viorst, *Necessary Losses,* 1986.

p. 145. Secure connection with a caring adult: There is little disagreement about the importance for later outcomes of strong, loving, and dependable relations between young children and those who care for them. The controversy that continues to intrigue child development scholars revolves around the specifics, such as the age by which the foundations for trust, conscience, self-esteem, and willingness to adhere to societal norms are established; the precise extent to which caretaking must be responsive and consistent to have a propitiating effect on development; the number of caretakers to whom most young children can successfully accommodate; the extent to which early experience can be modified by what happens later. None of the disagreements about these issues that engage the passions of researchers calls into question the basic tenets around which interventions for children growing up in adverse environments can be built.

p. 145. Learning "the essential vocabulary of love": S. Fraiberg, *Every Child's Birthright,* 1977.

p. 145. Kauai study findings on early bonds: E. E. Werner and R. S. Smith, *Vulnerable but Invincible,* 1982.

p. 146. Amenability to societal demands: J. Kagan, *The Nature of the Child,* 1984. As Kagan points out, "An attachment to a caregiver creates in the child a special receptivity to being socialized by that caregiver."

p. 146. Child who accepts adult restrictions: D. Baumrind, "Are Authoritative Families Really Harmonious?" *Psychological Bulletin,* 1983.

p. 146. Child buffered against stress: E. E. Maccoby, "Social-Emotional Development and Response to Stressors," in *Stress, Coping, and Development in Children,* 1983.

p. 146. Child who refuses adult restrictions: D. Baumrind, "Are Authoritative Families Really Harmonious?" *Psychological Bulletin,* 1983.

p. 146. "Deviant behavior profile": J. Kagan, *The Nature of the Child,* 1984.

p. 146. "Lack of guilt . . .": M. Rutter, *Maternal Deprivation Reassessed,* 1972.

p. 146. Such a child will withdraw: J. Kagan, *The Nature of the Child,* 1984.

p. 146. Healthy growth is threatened: Psychiatrist Stanley Greenspan's research suggests that children at greatest risk are those growing up in families where the parent or parents are psychiatrically impaired, have poor coping skills, and are experiencing high social and economic stress. If the child in such a family is born with even minor difficulties, the risk of impaired functioning multiplies. (See S. I. Greenspan, "Developmental Morbidity In Infants in Multi-Risk-Factor Families," *Public Health Reports,* 1982; S. I. Greenspan and K. R. White, "Conducting Research with Preventive Intervention Programs," in *Basic Handbook of Child Psychiatry,* 1987; S. I. Greenspan et al., eds., *Infants in Multirisk Families,* 1987.)

Studies which show the widespread negative impact on children of being raised by depressed and isolated mothers include S. G. Kellam et al., "Family Structure and the Mental Health of Children," *Archives of General Psychiatry,* 1977; C. Longfellow, "Stressful Life Conditions and the Mental Health of Mothers," Paper presented at the Annual Meeting of the American Psychological Association, Los Angeles, 1981; M. M. Weissman and E. F. Paykel, *The Depressed Woman,* 1974.

Studies which focus on the opportunities to intervene to improve the life prospects of children when parental impairment comes to professional attention include: S. T. Orr and S. James, "Maternal Depression in an Urban Pediatric Practice: Implications for Health Care Delivery," *American Journal of Public Health,* 1984; E. P. Rice et al., *Children of Mentally Ill Parents,* 1971; J. S. Musick et al., "Maternal Factors Related to Vulnerability and Resiliency in Young Children at Risk," in *The Invulnerable Child,* 1984.

The mechanisms by which impaired parenting can lead to child abuse and neglect are described in N. A. Polansky et al., *Damaged Parents: An Anatomy of Child Neglect,* 1981. A comprehensive literature review of how parental depression and other mental impairments, alcoholism, and immaturity can interfere with normal child development can be found in Office of Technology Assessment, *Children's Mental Health: Problems and Services,* 1986.

The effect on child development of the lack of nurturance, protection, and coherence that accompanies family homelessness has been documented by E. L. Bassuk et al., "Characteristics of Sheltered Homeless Families," *American Journal of Public Health,* 1986.

p. 147. "Nonrewarding patterns" in Kauai: E. E. Werner and R. S. Smith, *Kauai's Children Come of Age,* 1977.

p. 147. Temperamental mismatch: G. E. Vaillant, "The Longitudinal Study of Behavioral Disorders," *American Journal of Psychiatry,* 1984. See also A. Thomas and S. Chess, "Genesis and Evolution of Behavioral Disorders: From Infancy to Early Adult Life," *American Journal of Psychiatry,* 1984.

p. 147. Large cast of caretakers: M. Rutter, "Separation Experiences: A New Look at an Old Topic," *Pediatrics,* 1979.

p. 147. "Lack of early emotional bonds": M. Rutter, "Separation Experiences," *Pediatrics,* 1979. See also W. Dennis, *Children of the Creche,* 1973.

p. 147. Family discord and chaos: M. Rutter, "Maternal Deprivation, 1972–1978," *Child Development,* 1979. Comparing homes broken by divorce or separation with homes with stable marriages or where a parent had died, Rutter found that the delinquency rate was twice as high for boys from the homes broken by divorce or separation. He concluded, "it may be the discord and disharmony, rather than the breakup of the family as such, which lead to antisocial behavior." (M. Rutter, "Separation Experiences: A New Look at an Old Topic," *Pediatrics,* 1979.)

p. 148. Sense of coherence in Kauai: E. E. Werner and R. S. Smith, *Vulnerable but Invincible,* 1982.

p. 148. Changing effects of parental impairment: Psychiatrist Stanley Greenspan describes how parents with marginal coping capacities may have difficulty in setting limits or be made anxious by a toddler's rapid and unpredictable shifts between needing maternal comfort at one moment and independence at another. (See S. I. Greenspan, *Psychopathology and Adaptation in Infancy and Early Childhood,* 1981.)

Psychoanalyst Judith Kestenberg makes the same point with regard to a later stage of development: "Each transition from one phase to the next presents a challenge to both parents and children to give up outdated forms of interaction and to adopt a new system of coexistence." (J. Kestenberg, "The Effects on Parents of the Child's Transition Into and Out of Latency," in *Parenthood: Its Psychology and Psychopathology,* 1970.)

p. 148. Response to disequilibrium: E. E. Maccoby, "Social-Emotional Development and Response to Stressors," in *Stress, Coping, and Development in Children,* 1983.

If the child is surrounded by chaos at home and in the neighborhood and cared for by adults who are overwhelmed by economic and other exterior stresses, whose own coping abilities are marginal, and who have little support in their own lives, the child is unlikely to receive help in dealing with increasing complexity. No one will regulate his exposure to those elements of experience that are initially beyond the child's capacity to understand and deal with. The impaired or overwhelmed parent cannot respond empathically and cannot read a child's cues, and will therefore offer too much or too little stimulation, provide insufficient buffering, and expect the child to perform tasks or meet challenges beyond its capacities. If a parent's lack of empathy is pervasive and expectations are profoundly unrealistic, the child's development of self-esteem may be severely compromised. (See H. Kohut, *The Restoration of the Self,* 1977; J. S. Musick et al., "Maternal Factors Related to Vulnerability and Resiliency in Young Children at Risk," in *The Invulnerable Child,* 1984; S. Chess and A. Thomas, "Individuality," in *Developmental-Behavioral Pediatrics,* 1983.)

p. 149. Importance of structure: Dr. Kathryn Barnard, personal communication, 1985.

p. 150. Wilson question: J. Q. Wilson, *Thinking About Crime,* 1975. It should be noted that in his more recent writings Wilson no longer seems to believe that there is no role for public policy in the prevention of crime and other antisocial behavior. See Note to p. xxvii.

p. 151. Effects of stress: K. A. Crnic et al., "Effects of Stress and Social Support on Mothers and Premature Full-Term Infants," *Child Development,* 1983; K. A. Crnic et al., "Early Stress and Social Support Influences on Mothers' and High-Risk Infants' Functioning in Late Infancy," *Infant Mental Health Journal,* 1986.

p. 151. Whether the stress stems . . . : Professor Jerome Kagan cautions that stress, no matter how external its source, affects individuals differently depending on their own interpretation of its meaning. He suggests, for example, that the poverty experienced by inner city families today has different consequences than the poverty of the 1930s depression because the affected individuals have such different interpretations of its meaning and causes. (See J. Kagan, "Stress and Coping in Early Development," in *Stress, Coping and Development in Children,* 1983.)

p. 152. High rates of child abuse: J. Garbarino and D. Sherman, "High-Risk Neighborhoods and High-Risk Families: The Human Ecology of Child Maltreatment," *Child Development,* 1980.

p. 152. High rates of delinquency: J. Garbarino, "Child Abuse and Juvenile

Delinquency: The Developmental Impact of Social Isolation," in *Exploring the Relationship Between Child Abuse and Juvenile Delinquency,* 1978.

p. 152. Importance of support for adolescent mothers: N. Colletta, "Social Support and the Risk of Maternal Rejection by Adolescent Mothers," *Journal of Psychology,* 1981.

p. 152. Support during pregnancy: B. Starfield, "Social Factors in Child Health," in *Ambulatory Pediatrics,* 1984.

p. 152. Support for families of irritable infants: S. Crockenberg, "Infant Irritability," *Child Development,* 1981.

p. 152. Brought up by an isolated mother: S. G. Kellam et al., "Family Structure and the Mental Health of Children," *Archives of General Psychiatry,* 1977; F. F. Furstenberg, Jr., and J. Brooks-Gunn, *Adolescent Mothers in Later Life,* 1985.

p. 152. Animal stress in isolation: G. R. Patterson, "Stress: A Change Agent for Family Process," in *Stress, Coping, and Development in Children,* 1983.

p. 152. Blum observation regarding concrete help: Barbara Blum, personal communication, 1985.

p. 153. How support operates: J. P. Shonkoff, "Social Support and the Development of Vulnerable Children," *American Journal of Public Health,* 1984.

p. 153. Informal support as buffer: H. B. Weiss, Testimony before the U.S. House of Representatives, Select Committee on Children, Youth and Families, Hearings on Family Strength, 25 Feb. 1986; S. Kamerman, *Parenting in an Unresponsive Society:* 1980; C. B. Stack, *All Our Kin,* 1974; H. P. McAdoo, "Factors Related to Stability in Upwardly Mobile Black Families," *Journal of Marriage and the Family,* 1978.

p. 153. Children of isolated teenage mothers: F. F. Furstenberg, Jr., and J. Brooks-Gunn, *Adolescent Mothers in Later Life,* 1985; S. G. Kellam et al., "Family Structure and the Mental Health of Children," *Archives of General Psychiatry,* 1977.

p. 153. Network of kin: E. E. Werner and R. S. Smith, *Vulnerable but Invincible,* 1982.

p. 153. "World crowded with supportive kin": A. S. Rossi, "A Biosocial Perspective on Parenting," *Daedalus,* 1977.

p. 154. Scarcity of people "free from drain": J. Garbarino and D. Sherman, "High-Risk Neighborhoods and High-Risk Families," *Child Development,* 1980.

p. 155. Protection from variety of pathological states: S. Cobb, "Social Support as a Moderator of Life Stress," *Psychosomatic Medicine,* 1976; L. Eisenberg, "Conceptual Issues in Biobehavioral Interactions," in *Infants at Risk for Developmental Dysfunction,* 1982.

p. 155. Family support programs have mushroomed: B. Weissbourd, "History of Family Support Programs," in *America's Family Support Programs,* 1987.

p. 155. Description of support programs: S. Cobb, "Social Support as a Moderator of Life Stress," *Psychosomatic Medicine,* 1976; N. Colletta, "Social Support and the Risk of Maternal Rejection by Adolescent Mothers," *Journal of Psychology,* 1981; B. Weissbourd, "History of Family Support Programs," in *America's Family Support Programs,* 1987; V. Seitz, "Preschool Intervention," Paper presented at the meeting of the American Association for the Advancement of Science, Toronto, Jan. 1981.

p. 155. Informal support least available: Garbarino richly documents the need for increased social support to reduce social isolation, especially in order to prevent both child abuse and juvenile delinquency. He stresses that the social isolation that is so damaging to children extends beyond the family to the neighborhood, and suggests that this kind of social isolation will not be relieved without the most vigorous intervention efforts. (See, for example, J. Garbarino and D. Sherman, "High-Risk Neighborhoods and High-Risk Families," *Child Development,* 1980.)

p. 155. Mothers with relatively little stress: S. Crockenberg, "Infant Irritability," *Child Development,* 1981.

p. 155. Informal support as source of stress: D. Belle, "Social Ties and Social Support," in *Lives in Stress,* 1982.

p. 156. Traditional services don't work for neglectful families: N. Polansky, "Isolation of the Neglectful Family," *American Journal of Orthopsychiatry,* 1979.

pp. 156–160. Description of the Tacoma Homebuilders: J. M. Kinney et al., "Homebuilders: Keeping Families Together," *Journal of Consulting and Clinical Psychology,* 1977; J. M. Kinney, "Homebuilders: An In-Home Crisis Intervention Program," *Children Today,* 1978; D. A. Haapala and J. M. Kinney, "Homebuilders Approach to the Training of In-Home Therapists," in *Home-Based Services for Children and Families,* 1979; materials furnished by Behavioral Sciences Institute, Federal Way, Wash.; Edna McConnell Clark Foundation, *Keeping Families Together: The Case for Family Preservation,* 1985; interviews in 1986 and 1987 with Peter Forsythe, Director, Program for Children, and Peter D. Bell, President, Edna McConnell Clark Foundation.

p. 161. Inadequacy of foster care, child placement, and length of time in foster care: D. Fanshel, "Decision-Making Under Uncertainty," *American Journal of Public Health,* 1981.

p. 161. Child removal a costly system norm: P. W. Forsythe, Report to Children's Program Advisory Committee, Edna McConnell Clark Foundation, New York, 10 Dec. 1986.

p. 161. Recent rises in number of children removed from home: In September, 1987, the foster care crisis in New York City had escalated to the point where children were being kept in welfare offices during the day, and moved to a series of temporary beds at night. A federal judge ruled that the constitutional rights of hundreds of foster children were being violated, declaring that the city had "effectively turned a portion of the city's foster children into homeless children." (M. Oreskes, "New York Faulted for Rights Lapses in Its Foster Care," *New York Times,* 26 Sep. 1987.)

pp. 161–163. Information about the replication of the Homebuilders program in the Bronx: Conversations with Mr. Forsythe and Mr. Bell; David Tobis, Senior Associate, Welfare Research, Inc., in 1987; Kathleen Feely, New York City Department of Juvenile Justice, in 1987; and materials prepared by Mr. Tobis.

pp. 163–169. Description of the Yale Child Welfare Research Program: This draws heavily on the detailed description of the project by its founder, Dr. Sally Provence, and her associate, Audrey Naylor, in S. Provence and A. Naylor, *Working with Disadvantaged Parents and Their Children,* 1983; supplemented by personal conversations with Dr. Provence in 1985 and 1986; a report of the five-year follow-up in P. K. Trickett et al., "A Five Year Follow-Up of Participants in the

Yale Child Welfare Research Program," in *Day Care,* 1981; and a report of the ten-year follow-up in V. Seitz et al., "Effects of Family Support Intervention: A Ten-Year Follow-Up," *Child Development,* 1985.

p. 166. Comparison group: The comparison group was composed of mothers who met the original criteria for the project and whose children matched the participants on the basis of sex, family income, number of parents in the home, and ethnicity of the mother. A careful analysis of the study design concluded that the control group seems to have been somewhat more advantaged than the intervention families, thus providing a conservative test of the effects of the intervention. (See V. Seitz et al., "Effects of Family Support Intervention," *Child Development,* 1985.) This makes the results from the ten-year follow-up even more impressive.

p. 167. School problems: The difference in school attendance is particularly important because of the relationship between poor school attendance and later delinquency and school-age pregnancy. The project children missed an average of 7.3 days per year, compared to 13.3 among the control group; over a quarter of the control children missed more than twenty days of school during the year—a level of absenteeism considered seriously damaging to learning.

p. 168. Dr. Solnit's observation: From his Foreword to S. Provence and A. Naylor, *Working with Disadvantaged Parents and Their Children,* 1983.

pp. 169–175. Description of the Elmira nurse home visiting program: Based on a visit to the program on 30 May 1985, which included interviews with the original project director, Dr. David L. Olds, the original nursing staff, the staff at the time of the visit, and officials of the Chemung County Health Department; also, the following materials: D. L. Olds, "Improving Formal Services for Mothers and Children," in *Protecting Children from Abuse and Neglect,* 1981; D. L. Olds, "The Prenatal/Early Infancy Project," in *In the Beginning,* 1982; D. L. Olds et al., "Improving the Delivery of Prenatal Care and Outcomes of Pregnancy," *Pediatrics,* 1986; D. L. Olds, C. R. Henderson, R. Tatelbaum, and R. Chamberlin, "Improving the Life-Course Development of Socially Disadvantaged Parents," unpublished report, 1986; D. L. Olds et al., "Preventing Child Abuse and Neglect," *Pediatrics,* 1986. Outcome data are from the latter three reports.

p. 173. Fewer kidney infections: The lower rate of kidney infections was probably the result of the home-visited mothers seeking and receiving treatment more promptly, and possibly because—as a result of greater social support and less stress—they had greater resistance to infection.

p. 176. Maine official: Sally Buckwalter, Family Support Specialist, Maine Department of Human Services, Address at Conference on Infants at Risk, Portland, Maine, 18 Oct. 1984.

p. 176. Dr. Greenspan's observation: Dr. Greenspan, personal communications and visits to his program during 1984 and 1985.

p. 176. Dr. Barnard's observation: Dr. Barnard, personal communication, 3 Oct. 1984.

pp. 176–177. Sr. Mary Paul's observation: Interview with Sister Mary Paul, Brooklyn, N.Y., 2 Apr. 1985.

p. 177. Beethoven Project: I. B. Harris address to the National Governors' Association Committee on Human Resources, Conference on "Focus on the First 60 Months," 6 Feb. 1986; K. Teltsch, "A Cradle-To-Kindergarten Aid Plan in Chicago," *New York Times,* 13 Jan. 1987; "Head Start on Head Start," *New York Times,* 13 Jan. 1987; L. Baldacci, " 'Beethoven' Aims to Break Poverty Cycle," *Chicago Sun-Times,* 4 Jan. 1987.

CHAPTER 8

p. 179. Provisions for the care and education of children under five: The inseparability of the education and care of young children is so fundamental to the development of sound policy that Professor Bettye M. Caldwell of the University of Arkansas, distinguished child developmentalist, believes a new term, such as "educare," may have to be coined to clarify the importance of combining these two essential aspects of arrangements for preschool children.

p. 179. Data on working mothers: Select Committee on Children, Youth and Families, *U.S. Children and Their Families,* 1987.

p. 179. Economic reasons that mothers work: The Joint Economic Committee of the U.S. Congress has shown that the real income of most American families has declined significantly between 1974 and 1985. The chairman of the Committee, Congressman David R. Obey of Wisconsin, in releasing the Committee's studies stated that "We have changed from a society in which families could expect steady financial advancement to one in which it is difficult to hold your own." (Press release, November 28, 1985.) Economist Frank Levy concluded from his recent study on American income distribution, *Dollars and Dreams,* "You have to be a two-earner family today to qualify for the middle class."

p. 178. Daily experiences teach . . . cause and effect: P. B. Neubauer, *Process of Child Development,* 1976.

p. 178. Class differences in language development: B. Tizard and M. Hughes, *Young Children Learning,* 1984; R. D. Hess and V. Shipman, "Maternal Influences Upon Early Learning," in *Early Education,* 1968; H. L. Bee et al., "Social Class Differences in Maternal Teaching Strategies and Speech Patterns," *Developmental Psychology,* 1969; M. L. Kohn, *Class and Conformity,* 1969; J. Segal and H. Yahraes, *A Child's Journey,* 1979.

pp. 181–182. Aja's story: J. Schorr, "The Childhood of the Fuller Murder Convicts," unpublished report, 6 July 1986. (Aja is a fictional name.)

p. 182. The Rossis' story: L. S. Bandler, "Family Functioning," in *The Drifters,* 1967.

p. 182. "Culture of literacy": Testimony of Dr. James Garbarino, President, Erikson Institute for Advanced Study in Child Development, Chicago, Ill., before the U.S. House of Representatives, Select Committee on Children, Youth and Families, 28 Apr. 1987.

pp. 182–183. A bright school future: Julius B. Richmond, M.D., estimated in 1970 that "one third of our children are being reared in environments that virtually insure failure in society's major institutions for all children, the schools." (See J. B. Richmond, "Disadvantaged Children," *Yale Journal of Biology and Medicine,* 1970.)

p. 183. When lower- class children enter school: J. Kagan, *The Nature of the Child,* 1984.

p. 184–192. Early history of Project Head Start: I draw in part on my own recollections and extensively on the excellent book, E. Zigler and J. Valentine, eds., *Project Head Start,* 1979.

p. 184. President Johnson's speech: E. Zigler and J. Valentine, *Project Head Start,* 1979.

p. 185. Role of economists in antipoverty program: Those most active in urging President Kennedy, and then President Johnson, to undertake a war on poverty were all economists: Walter Heller, chairman of the Council of Economic Advisers, and staff members Robert Lampman, William Capron, Burton Weisbrod, and Rashi Fein. (See S. A. Levitan, *The Great Society's Poor Law,* 1969.)

p. 185. Shriver's recollections: R. S. Shriver, "Head Start, A Retrospective View: The Founders," in *Project Head Start,* 1979. Shriver was initially influenced particularly by the work of Susan Gray, later published in S. W. Gray et al., *Before First Grade,* 1966.

p. 186. Evidence from child development research: H. M. Skeels and H. Dye, "A Study of the Effects of Differential Stimulation on Mentally Retarded Children," *Proceedings of the American Association of Mental Deficiency,* 1939; H. M. Skeels, "A Study of the Effects of Differential Stimulation on Mentally Retarded Children: Follow-up Report," *American Journal of Mental Deficiency,* 1942; J. M. Hunt, *Intelligence and Experience,* 1961; H. Wortis, "Child-rearing Practices in a Low Socioeconomic Group," *Pediatrics,* 1963; B. S. Bloom, *Stability and Change in Human Characteristics,* 1964; M. Deutsch, "The Role of Social Class in Language," *American Journal of Orthopsychiatry,* 1965; J. B. Richmond and B. M. Caldwell, "Mental Retardation—Cultural and Social Considerations," in *Child Care in Health and Disease,* 1968. (The findings from Dr. Richmond and Dr. Caldwell's direct experience, like others on which Project Head Start was based, became widely influential before they were published.) Also see, R. A. Klaus and S. W. Gray, "The Early Training Project for Disadvantaged Children," *Monographs of the Society for Research in Child Development,* 1968; U. Bronfenbrenner, *The Ecology of Human Development,* 1979. (Professor Bronfenbrenner's conviction that children's development could be understood only in the context of their environment was just beginning to be accepted in the mid-1960s. He synthesized and published his approach much later.)

p. 186. Bronfenbrenner's role: Described in S. A. Levitan, *The Great Society's Poor Law,* 1969; U. Bronfenbrenner, "Head Start, A Retrospective View," in *Project Head Start,* 1979.

p. 187. "Across the face of this nation": R. S. Shriver, "Head Start, A Retrospective View," in *Project Head Start,* 1979,

p. 188. A few firm federal requirements: E. Zigler and K. Anderson, "An Idea Whose Time Had Come," in *Project Head Start,* 1979.

p. 188. At work in Washington: Unable to relinquish his responsibilities in Syracuse, Dr. Richmond was at once department head and dean of the College of Medicine at the Upstate Medical Center there, and director of Project Head Start in Washington, D.C. Shriver held Richmond in such high esteem that as the health activities of the OEO became increasingly significant, Shriver persuaded Richmond in June 1966 to take on yet a fourth position—director of OEO's Office of Health Affairs.

pp. 188–189. Teacher/pupil ratio: J. B. Richmond, "Head Start, A Retrospective View," in *Project Head Start,* 1979.

p. 190. Sugarman recollections: J. M. Sugarman, "Head Start, A Retrospective View," in *Project Head Start,* 1979. Jule Sugarman's published reminiscences were supplemented for me by those of Polly Greenberg, Sylvia Pechman, Marie Ritter, and Miriam Bazelon in personal communications during 1986 and 1987.

p. 190. 600,000 in summer programs: J. B. Richmond et al., "A Decade of Head Start," in *Project Head Start,* 1979.

p. 190. Head Start appropriations: Children's Defense Fund, *A Children's Defense Budget,* 1987; U.S. Congress, House of Representatives, Select Committee on Children, Youth and Families, *U.S. Children and Their Families,* 1987.

p. 191. Westinghouse Learning Corporation evaluation of Head Start: J. B. Richmond et al., "A Decade of Head Start," in *Project Head Start,* 1979.

p. 192. Children "enter school healthier": New York City, Early Childhood Commission, *Take a Giant Step,* 1986.

pp. 192–193. Tennessee's Early Training project: S. W. Gray et al., "The Early Training Project 1962–1980," in *As the Twig Is Bent,* 1983.

p. 193. Michigan's Perry Preschool Program: L. J. Schweinhart and D. P. Weikart, *Young Children Grow Up,* 1980; J. R. Berrueta-Clement et al., *Changed Lives,* 1984; L. J. Schweinhart and D. Weikart, "The Effects of The Perry Preschool Program on Youths Through Age 15," in *As the Twig Is Bent,* 1983.

p. 194. Harlem's IDS Project: M. Deutsch, et al., "The IDS Program," in *As the Twig Is Bent,* 1983.

p. 195. Long-term impact of Early Training Project: S. W. Gray et al., "The Early Training Project 1962–1980," in *As the Twig Is Bent,* 1983.

p. 195. Long-term impact of Perry Preschool: J. R. Berrueta-Clement et al., *Changed Lives,* 1984.

p. 195. Long-term impact of IDS Harlem Project: M. Deutsch, "Long-Term Effects of Early Intervention: Summary of Selected Findings," Report from the Institute for Developmental Studies, New York University, 1985.

p. 195. Consortium for Longitudinal Studies: Fifteen projects met the criteria, and all but one agreed to participate. The Consortium's findings were published in Consortium for Longitudinal Studies, *Lasting Effects after Preschool,* 1978; I. Lazar et al., "Lasting Effects of Early Education," *Monographs of the Society for Research in Child Development,* 1982; and Consortium for Longitudinal Studies, *As the Twig Is Bent,* 1983.

p. 196. Gains that disappear by third or fourth grade: The existence of a slump in achievement around third or fourth grade among children who have participated in successful preschool programs has been confirmed by several studies. Hypothesized explanations for this phenomenon include developmental factors in the children, changes in the nature of the educational task, the waning of the effect of the original intervention, and failures in the educational environments of elementary schools. (See B. M. Caldwell, J. Fitzgerald, and D. T. Campbell, "The Third Grade Slump: Fact or Artifact," final report submitted to the Foundation for Child Development, New York, 1 Mar. 1985; M. Kotelchuck and J. B. Richmond, "Head Start," *Pediatrics,* 1987.

p. 196. Consortium findings: Consortium for Longitudinal Studies, *As the Twig Is Bent,* 1983.

p. 196. Dr. Deutsch quote: Larry Rohter, "Study Stresses Preschool Benefits," *New York Times,* 9 Apr. 1985.

p. 196. From rhetoric to documented fact: L. Schweinhart and D. Weikart, "Evidence that Good Early Childhood Programs Work," *Phi Delta Kappan,* 1985.

p. 196. CED quote: Committee for Economic Development, *Investing in Our Children,* 1985.

p. 196. Gov. Collins quote: E. B. Fiske, "Early Schooling Is Now the Rage," *New York Times Educational Supplement,* 1986.

p. 197. Indications of Head Start deterioration: E. Zigler, "Assessing Head Start at 20," *American Journal of Orthopsychiatry,* 1985; Office of Human Development Services, *Head Start in the 1980s, Review and Recommendations,* (Washington, D.C.: U.S. Department of Health and Human Services, 1980).

p. 197. Head Start serving 450,000 children: U.S. House of Representatives, Select Committee on Children, Youth and Families, *U.S. Children and Their Families,* 1987.

pp. 197–200. Head Start program in Fairfax County, Virginia: Based on visits and interviews on 6 Nov. 1986 and material furnished by Ms. Glynne.

p. 201. Fastest-growing type of child care: K. T. Young and E. Zigler, "Infant and Toddler Day Care," *American Journal of Orthopsychiatry,* 1986.

p. 201. Effects of early out-of-home care: See, for example, J. Belsky, "Infant Day Care: A Cause for Concern?" *Zero to Three,* 1986; D. Phillips et al., "Selective Review of Infant Day Care Research," *Zero to Three,* 1987; T. J. Gamble and E. Zigler, "Effects of Infant Day Care," *American Journal of Orthopsychiatry,* 1986.

p. 201. Standards for good out-of-home care: In 1980 the federal government presided over laborious and lengthy negotiations which culminated in the Federal Interagency Day Care Requirements, which have never been enforced. The guidelines they established for staff-child ratios were one to three for infants and one to four for toddlers in day care centers, and one to five in a family day care if no more than two of the children are under two years of age. The proposed group size for all types of day care is six for infants and twelve for toddlers. (See K. T. Young and E. Zigler, "Infant and Toddler Day Care," *American Journal of Orthopsychiatry,* 1986.

p. 201. Damage from poor infant day care for disadvantaged children: "A socially impoverished day care center poses [increased risks to the infant who] also comes from a highly stressed home environment." (T. J. Gamble and E. Zigler, "Effects of Infant Day Care," *American Journal of Orthopsychiatry,* 1986.)

p. 202. Children's needs from day care: K. T. Young and E. Zigler, "Infant and Toddler Day Care," *American Journal of Orthopsychiatry,* 1986.

p. 202. Children from less educated families benefited only from intensive interventions: D. E. Pierson et al., "A School-Based Program from Infancy to Kindergarten," *The Personnel and Guidance Journal,* 1984.

p. 202. "A social worker to work with the most disadvantaged families": Dr. Deborah K. Walker, personal communication, 1987.

pp. 203–205. Family Learning Center in Leslie, Michigan: Information comes from a telephone interview with its director, Jean Ekins, on 20 June 1987; and materials about the program provided by Ms. Ekins, the Children's Defense Fund, and the Ford Foundation.

p. 205. Infant care leave recommendations: N. Brozan, "Infant Care Leaves: Panel Urges Policy," *New York Times,* 28 Nov. 1985.

p. 205. "Unique position of the United States," and "Almost every civilized country,": S. B. Kamerman et al., *Maternity Policies and Working Women,* 1983; A. J. Kahn and S. B. Kamerman, *Not for the Poor Alone: European Social Services,* 1977.

p. 206. Susan Montgomery's story: Children's Defense Fund, *The Child Care Handbook,* 1982.

p. 206. Washington State survey: A. B. Wicks and C. M. Caro, *Factors Affecting the Employability of Welfare Recipients,* 1986.

p. 206. Child care and self-sufficiency: Children's Defense Fund, *A Children's Defense Budget,* 1987.

p. 206. Dr. Howard's story: Children's Defense Fund, *The Child Care Handbook,* 1982.

p. 206. Child care that guarantees adverse outcomes: Statement made by Bernice Weissbourd at a meeting of the Board of the National Center for Clinical Infant Programs, 5 Dec. 1986.

pp. 206–207. Washington, D.C., parent's story: D. Fallows, *A Mother's Work,* 1985.

p. 207. Children on Florida day care waiting list: P. Ward and M. Ward, "Dade's Child Care Tragedy," *Miami News,* 19 Nov. 1986.

p. 207. Survey of day care by National Council of Jewish Women: M. D. Keyserling, *Windows on Day Care,* 1972.

p. 208. Deborah Fallows' observations of day care: D. Fallows, *A Mother's Work,* 1985. Fallows' observations are confirmed by the most knowledgeable child care professionals. "Too many of us are visiting too many settings where children are being damaged," said Yale University's Dr. Edward Zigler at the December 1986 board meeting of the National Center for Clinical Infant Programs in Washington, D.C.

p. 208. Little data on family day care; quality varies: R. Klein, "Caregiving Arrangements by Employed Women with Children Under One Year of Age," *Developmental Psychology,* 1985; E. Zigler, Testimony before the U.S. House of Representatives, Select Committee on Children, Youth and Families, 4 Apr. 1984; elsewhere Professor Zigler described family day care as "a cosmic crapshoot for America's parents."

p. 209. Problems and potential of family day care: J. S. Sale, "Family Day Care —Potential Child Development Service," *American Journal of Public Health,* 1972; J. S. Sale, "Family Day Care: One Alternative in the Delivery of Developmental Services in Early Childhood," *American Journal of Orthopsychiatry,* 1973.

p. 209. Standards not promulgated or enforced: S. Kamerman, Testimony before the U.S. House of Representatives, Select Committee on Children, Youth and Families, 4 Apr. 1984.

p. 209. Training requirements for day care workers: K. T. Young and E. Zigler, "Infant and Toddler Day Care," *American Journal of Orthopsychiatry,* 1986; D. S.

Wittmer, "Model Versus Modal Child Care for Children From Low-Income Families," *Zero to Three,* 1986.

p. 209. Earnings of child care workers: D. Phillips, "The Federal Model Child Care Standards Act of 1985," *American Journal of Orthopsychiatry,* 1986; and Children's Defense Fund, *A Children's Defense Budget,* 1987.

p. 209. Jerel's story: D. E. Wittmer, "Model Versus Modal Child Care," *Zero to Three,* 1986.

p. 209. Turnover among child care workers: "New Occupation Separation Data," *Monthly Labor Review,* 1984.

pp. 209–210. No special funds for training; Jayne's story: D. S. Wittmer, "Model Versus Modal Child Care," *Zero to Three,* 1986.

p. 211. Preschool less crucial for middle-class children: D. E. Pierson et al., "A School-based Program From Infancy to Kindergarten," *Personnel and Guidance Journal,* 1984.

p. 211. Preschool participation by income: M. Chorvinsky, "Preprimary Enrollment, 1980," 1982; S. Kamerman, Testimony before the U.S. House of Representatives, Select Committee on Children, Youth and Families, 4 Apr. 1984.

p. 211. Preschool participation and minority status: U.S. Bureau of the Census, *Who's Minding the Kids?,* 1987.

p. 211. Low-income children priced out of high-quality preschools: Unpublished report of Carnegie Foundation for the Advancement of Teaching cited in E. B. Fiske, "Early Schooling Is Now the Rage," *New York Times Educational Supplement,* 13 Apr. 1986.

CHAPTER 9

p. 215. H. Mann, "Report to the Massachusetts State Board of Education, 1848," in *Documents of American History,* 1948.

p. 216. M. Sadler, "Impressions of American Education," *Educational Review,* 1903.

p. 216. *Public Papers of the Presidents of the U.S., L. B. Johnson, 1965.* Washington, D.C.: U.S. Government Printing Office, 1966.

p. 216. C. Brown, *Manchild in the Promised Land,* 1965.

p. 217. Eliot quote: M. Lazerson and W. N. Grubb, eds. *American Education and Vocationalism,* 1974.

p. 217. Graham quote: P. Graham, "Schools: Cacaphony About Practice, Silence About Purpose," 1984.

p. 217. Schools reinforced social inequality: D. Tyack and E. Hansot, "Hard Times, Then and Now," *Harvard Education Review,* 1984.

p. 217. President Johnson quote: B. D. Stickney and L. R. Marcus, "Education and the Disadvantaged 20 Years Later," *Phi Delta Kappan,* 1985.

p. 217. Some children pushed aside: P. Graham, "Schools," *Daedalus,* 1984.

p. 218. Effects of school desegregation: The literature on the long-term effects on educational outcomes of court-ordered school desegregation is not extensive, in part because the objectives of school desegregation were of course far broader than improved educational achievement. The findings most relevant for our purposes are the following: 318 black Hartford, Ct., students who were sent to predominantly white schools beginning in 1966 were more likely to have graduated from high school, were involved in fewer incidents with the police, and were less likely to have had a child before they were eighteen years old than a comparison group that remained in predominantly black schools. (See R. Crain and J. Strauss, *School Desegregation and Black Educational Attainments,* 1985.)

A Rand Corporation review of seventy-three studies of desegregation and black achievement found a significant rise in the academic achievement levels of minority students as a result of desegregation, while those of white students had risen slightly or stayed the same. (See R. Crain and R. Mahard, "Desegregation and Black Achievement," *Law and Contemporary Problems,* 1978.)

p. 218. NDEA as response to Sputnik: In retrospect it appears that the Soviet triumph in launching Sputnik was not so much the product of tougher-minded Soviet education as of a tougher-minded Soviet allocation of budget resources to military objectives. (See H. Smith, *The Russians,* 1976; S. Jacoby, *Inside Soviet Schools,* 1975.)

p. 218. Congress sees income and school outcomes related: V. R. L. Plunkett, "From Title I to Chapter I," *Phi Delta Kappan,* 1985.

p. 218. Coalition for federal aid to education: B. D. Stickney and L. R. Marcus, "Education and the Disadvantaged 20 Years Later," *Phi Delta Kappan,* 1985.

p. 218. ESEA, 1965: U.S. House of Representatives, Committee on Education and Labor, *Report to Accompany H.R. 2362,* (Washington, D.C.: U.S. Government Printing Office, Report No. 143, 1965).

p. 219. "The most important bill . . .": W. Manchester, *The Glory and the Dream,* 1974.

p. 219. "Schools make no difference": G. Hodgson, "Do Schools Make a Difference?" *Atlantic Monthly,* 1973. Coleman's massive study had concluded that "schools bring little influence to bear on a child's achievement that is independent of his background and general social context." (See J. S. Coleman et al., *Equality of Educational Opportunity,* 1966.) Just three years later Jensen wrote, "Compensatory education has been tried, and it apparently has failed." (See A. Jensen, "How Much Can We Boost I.Q. and Scholastic Achievement?" *Harvard Education Review,* 1969.) Jencks and colleagues seemed to have struck the knockout blow when their elaborate study concluded, "Schools seem to have very little effect on any measurable attribute of those who attend them." (C. Jencks et al., *Inequality,* 1972.)

p. 219. Educators and public receptive to negative findings: L. Eisenberg, "Social Context of Child Development," *Pediatrics,* 1981. The futility of trying to change school outcomes by changing schools, implied or stated in the work of Coleman, Jensen, Jencks (see note above), and other educators, psychologists, and sociologists, provided the foundations on which a new, discouraged conventional wisdom was built. (See, for example, M. Frankel, "A Subtle but Sweeping Reversal," *New York Times,* 8 Mar. 1972; R. Reinhold, "School Role in Poverty Contested," *New York Times,* 8 Jan. 1973.)

p. 220. The most influential of the commission reports: E. Boyer, *High School,* 1983; J. S. Coleman et al., *High School Achievement,* 1982; J. I. Goodlad, *A Place Called School,* 1983; National Commission on Excellence in Education, *A Nation at Risk, 1983;* Task Force on Education for Economic Growth, *Action for Excellence,* 1983.

p. 220. State responses: H. M. Levin, "The Educationally Disadvantaged," *The State Youth Initiatives Project,* 1985; Children's Defense Fund, *A Children's Defense Budget,* 1987.

p. 220. "1983 reports did not change the system": R. Reinhold, "School Reform: Four Years of Tumult, Mixed Results," *New York Times,* 10 Aug. 1987.

p. 220. Similar set of core competencies: National Academy of Sciences, *High Schools and the Changing Workplace,* 1984.

p. 220. "Provide to the many the same quality of education . . .": Carnegie Forum on Education and the Economy, Task Force on Teaching as a Profession, *A Nation Prepared,* 1986.

p. 220. "The most ominous question of all": G. Holton, *"A Nation at Risk* Revisited," *Daedalus,* 1984.

p. 220. Bell quote: R. Reinhold, "School Reform: Four Years of Tumult, Mixed Results," *New York Times,* 10 Aug. 1987.

pp. 220–221. Boyer quote: Associated Press, "Warning of Urban School Decline," *New York Times,* 7 Sept. 1986.

p. 221. CED report: Committee on Economic Development, *Children in Need: Investment Strategies for the Educationally Disadvantaged,* 1987.

p. 221. Levin fears for disadvantaged: H. M. Levin, "The Educationally Disadvantaged," *The State Youth Initiatives Project,* 1985.

p. 221. Early difficulties at school: Early school problems have been linked to long-term damage generally, and to delinquency, dropping out, and early child-bearing specifically, by an impressive collection of research and literature reviews, including: R. Loeber and T. Dishion, "Early Predictors of Male Delinquency," *Psychological Bulletin,* 1983; L. N. Robins, "Sturdy Childhood Predictors of Adult Antisocial Behavior," *Psychological Medicine,* 1978; J. G. Bachman et al., *Adolescence to Adulthood,* 1978; D. S. Elliot et al., "An Integrated Theoretical Perspective on Delinquent Behavior," *Journal of Research in Crime and Delinquency,* 1979; J. G. Dryfoos, "Review of Interventions in the Field of Prevention of Adolescent Pregnancy," Preliminary report to the Rockefeller Foundation, Oct. 1983; A. L. Stroup and L. N. Robins, "Elementary School Predictors of High School Dropout Among Black Males," *Sociology of Education,* 1972; J. L. Kaplan and E. C. Luck, "The Dropout Phenomenon," *Educational Forum,* 1977; L. V. Klerman et al., "School Absence," in *Monitoring Child Health,* 1984, (showing that high absence rates in elementary school are predictive of future school dropouts); S. Phipps-Yonas, "Teenage Pregnancy and Motherhood," *American Journal of Orthopsychiatry,* 1980; F. F. Furstenberg, Jr., and J. Brooks-Gunn, *Adolescent Mothers in Later Life,* 1985; V. Seitz, N. H. Apfel, and L. E. Rosenbaum, "Schoolaged Mothers: Infant Development and Maternal Education Outcomes," Paper presented at the biennial meeting of the Society for Research and Child Development, Detroit, 1983.

p. 222. Encouraging school environment as protector: N. Garmezy, "Stressors of Childhood," in *Stress, Coping and Development in Children,* 1983.

p. 222. Teacher judgments made in first few days: R. C. Rist, "Student Social Class and Teacher Expectations," *Harvard Educational Review,* 1970.

p. 222. Benefits of supportive teachers: V. C. Shipman, *Disadvantaged Children and Their First School Experiences,* 1976.

p. 222. Teachers less nurturing, other changes at third grade: B. M. Caldwell, J.

Fitzgerald, and D. T. Campbell, "The Third Grade Slump: Fact or Artifact," Final Report submitted to the Foundation for Child Development, New York, 1 Mar. 1985. When Professor Caldwell went from being an early childhood educator to become an elementary school principal, she noted that it is in third and fourth grades that many disciplinary and behavior problems start and achievement levels of disadvantaged children diverge more markedly from the norm. The relative drop in scores is especially noticeable among children who have participated in Head Start or some other preschool intervention and who had been doing better than equally disadvantaged children without preschool intervention in the first grade but not by the time they got to third or fourth grade.

p. 223. Changing demands in learning to read: J. S. Chall, *Stages of Reading Development*, 1983; J. S. Chall and V. A. Jacobs, "Writing and Reading in the Elementary Grades," *Language Arts*, 1983.

p. 223. Contrast between acquiring math and reading skills: L. F. Carter, "The Sustaining Effects of Compensatory and Elementary Education," *Educational Researcher*, 1984.

p. 223. Having concluded he won't make it: J. Kagan, *The Nature of the Child*, 1984.

p. 224. Question whether Title I funds going to most disadvantaged: Children's Defense Fund of the Washington Research Project, *Title I of ESEA*, 1966.

p. 224. Chapter I money for instructional services: T. W. Hartle and A. Bilson, "Increasing the Educational Achievement of Disadvantaged Children: Do Federal Programs Make a Difference?" Paper prepared for Working Seminar on the Family and American Welfare Policy, American Enterprise Institute, Washington, D.C., 1986.

p. 224. Compensatory education inadequately funded: V. R. L. Plunkett, "From Title I to Chapter I," *Phi Delta Kappan*, 1985.

p. 224. Problems with compensatory education: D. U. Levine, "Successful Approaches for Improving Academic Achievement in Inner-City Elementary Schools," *Phi Delta Kappan*, 1982.

p. 224. Bell statement that America knows how to educate disadvantaged: U.S. House of Representatives, Committee on Education and Labor, Hearing on H.R. 3645, 97th Congress, 15th Session, 28 May 1981.

pp. 224-225. New funds for compensatory education: V. R. L. Plunkett, "From Title I to Chapter I," *Phi Delta Kappan*, 1985.

p. 225. Improved reading: R. H. Forbes, "Academic Achievement of Historically Lower-Achieving Students During the Seventies," *Phi Delta Kappan*, 1982; U.S. House of Representatives, Subcommittee on Elementary, Secondary, and Vocational Education, Oversight Hearing on Reading and Writing Achievement, 97th Congress, First Session, 7 May 1981; "Scores Up Because of Hard Work, Big City School Administrators Say," *Education USA* (6 July 1981).

p. 225. Effectiveness of Title I: U.S. House of Representatives Subcommittee on Elementary, Secondary, and Vocational Education, Oversight Hearing on Title I, 97th Congress, Second Session, 23-25 Mar. 1982. The Sustaining Effects Study was conducted under contract with the Department of Education and reported on in L. F. Carter, "The Sustaining Effects Study of Compensatory and Elementary Education," *Educational Researcher*, 1984; L. F. Carter, "A Study of Compensatory and Elementary Education: The Sustaining Effects Study," Report prepared by the System Development Corporation for the U.S. Department of Education, Jan. 1983.

p. 225. Effectiveness of single elements of school change: U.S. Department of Education, *What Works: Research About Teaching And Learning*, 1986; U.S. Department of Education, *What Works: Schools That Work, Educating Disadvantaged Children*, 1987; H. M. Levin, G. V. Glass, and G. R. Meister, "Cost-Effectiveness of Four Educational Interventions," Report prepared for the U.S. Department of Education by the Institute for Research on Educational Finance and Governance, Stanford University, Palo Alto, Calif., 1984; J. Brophy, "Successful Teaching Strategies for the Inner-City Child," *Phi Delta Kappan*, 1982.

p. 225. "Support in the total ecology": This conclusion was based on a study by Dr. Shipman and colleagues at the Educational Testing Service of children who in third grade performed exceptionally well or exceptionally poorly in reading and math in comparison with other children of similar ethnic and economic background, and in comparison with predictions based on their own performance at age four. (See V. C. Shipman, *Disadvantaged Children and Their First School Experiences*, 1976.)

p. 226. Importance of "school ethos": M. Rutter et al., *Fifteen Thousand Hours*, 1979.

p. 226. Research on effective schools: R. Edmonds, "Effective Schools for the Urban Poor," *Educational Leadership*, 1979; G. Weber, *Inner-City Children Can be Taught to Read*, 1971; L. Cuban, "Transforming the Frog into a Prince," *Harvard Educational Review*, 1984.

p. 226. Importance of "interpersonal harmony": Hispanic Policy Development Project, *Make Something Happen*, 1984.

p. 227. Attributes of effective schools: Drawn from R. Edmonds, "Effective Schools for the Urban Poor," *Educational Leadership*, 1979; G. Weber, *Inner-City Children Can Be Taught to Read*, 1971; S. Bossert, "Effective Elementary Schools," in *Reaching for Excellence*, 1985; S. C. Purkey and M. S. Smith, "Effective Schools: A Review," *Elementary School Journal*, 1983.

p. 227. "Socially integrating sense of purpose": D. Tyack and E. Hansot, "Hard Times, Hard Choices," *Phi Delta Kappan*, 1982. Tyack and Hansot borrow this concept from sociologist Philip Selznick's *Leadership in Administration: A Sociological Perspective*, 1957.

p. 227. Selecting schools: Sy Fliegel, New York City Schools District Administrator in East Harlem, interviewed by John Merrow for the *MacNeil, Lehrer News Hour*, Corporation for Public Broadcasting, 23 Mar. 1987.

p. 228. Constancy between home and school: S. L. Lightfoot, *Worlds Apart*, 1978; J. P. Comer, "Home-School Relationships," *Education and Urban Society*, 1984.

p. 228. Parents' yearning for children's education: S. L. Lightfoot, *Worlds Apart*, 1978; F. Montalvo, "Making Good Schools from Bad," in *Make Something Happen*, 1984.

p. 229. Effectiveness of parent reading: J. Tizard et al., "Collaboration Between Teachers and Parents," *British Journal of Educational Psychology*, 1982.

p. 229. Effectiveness of parent involvement: D. Rich, *The Forgotten Factor in School Success—The Family*, 1985.

pp. 229-237. Description of the New Haven program: Based on a visit to the Brennan Elementary School on 11 Dec. 1985; interview with Dr. Comer on 11 Dec. 1985; Dr. Comer's remarks to the 1987 Annual Conference of the Children's Defense Fund, 13 Mar. 1987; J. P. Comer, *School Power*, 1980; J. P. Comer, "The Yale-New Haven Primary Prevention Project," *Journal of the American Academy of Child Psychiatry*, 1985; J. P. Comer, "Home-School Relationships," *Education and Urban Society*, 1984.

pp. 237-241. Description of the Columbia Park Elementary School: Based on interviews with the principal, Patricia Green, and the representative of the superintendent's office, Jan Stocklinski; a visit to the school on 31 Mar. 1987; and materials provided by the Prince Georges County Public Schools.

pp. 241-245. Description of the Central Park East Elementary School in East Harlem: Based on visits in June 1986 and April 1987, including interviews with the principal, Deborah Meier, and tours of the school on both occasions; and materials provided by the school. Also, an evaluation of the school, "Central Park East: Quality Education in the Inner City," by David Bensman, May 1986; and Deidre Carmody, "New York's New School Chief Suggests an End to Alienation," *New York Times*, 26 Mar. 1987.

p. 246. Vietnamese valedictorians: G. C. Wilson, "From Vietnam to Top of the Class," *Washington Post*, 25 May 1987; Associated Press, "Former 'Boat Person' Graduates at Top of the Class," 28 May 1981; United Press International, "Refugees Earn High Honors," 29 May 1981; C. Burke, "Vietnamese to Graduate as Valedictorian," United Press International, 20 May 1984.

pp. 247-248. Reasons for Asian achievement: F. Butterfield, "Why Asians Are Going to the Head of the Class," *New York Times Education Supplement*, 1986.

p. 248. Research comparing Hispanic and Chinese learning styles: L. W. Fillmore, "Equity or Excellence?" *Language Arts*, 1986.

p. 248. Principal of Stuyvesant: F. Butterfield, "Why Asians Are Going to the Head of the Class," *New York Times Education Supplement*, 1986.

p. 249. Principal of Lowell: C. Rafferty, "New Academic Elite Keeps Up Old Tradition," *New York Times*, 15 Apr. 1984.

p. 249. Political and economic success of Irish: S. M. Miller, "Dropouts—A Political Problem," in *The School Dropout*, 1964; M. Harrington, *The New American Poverty*, 1984; J. M. Blum et al., *The National Experience*, 1984.

p. 249. Early black experience in America: J. P. Comer, "Black Violence and Public Policy," in *American Violence and Public Policy*, 1985; M. Harrington, *The New American Poverty*, 1984; Joint Center for Political Studies, *A Policy Framework for Racial Justice*, 1983. Also very helpful were several conversations, in July 1985, with Lawrence H. Fuchs, chairman of American Studies at Brandeis University, about his work in progress on the contrasting American experience of blacks and other ethnic groups.

pp. 249-250. Education during slavery: S. L. Lightfoot, *Worlds Apart*, 1978.

p. 250. Blacks hurt by deindustrialization: W. J. Wilson, *The Truly Disadvantaged*, 1987; J. P. Comer, "Black Violence and Public Policy," in *American Violence and Public Policy*, 1985; M. Harrington, *The New American Poverty*, 1984.

p. 250. Economic shifts left blacks and Hispanics behind: W. J. Wilson, *The Truly Disadvantaged*, 1987; "The Family Crisis and What We Can Do About It: An

Interview with Marian Wright Edelman," *The Harvard Education Letter,* 1987; Hispanic Policy Development Project, *Make Something Happen,* 1984.

p. 251. Blacks and Hispanics see few opportunities: J. U. Ogbu, *The Next Generation,* 1974.

p. 251. Bennett re belief in hard work: U.S. Department of Education, *What Works: Research About Teaching and Learning,* 1986.

p. 251. Schools convey low expectations: A task force in Champaign, Ill., found that many school staff in that community communicated their low expectations to minority students. (See National Coalition of Advocates for Students, *Barriers to Excellence,* 1985.) W. J. Wilson cites a study by Bowles and Gintis which demonstrates that attitudes toward students in ghetto schools typically do not foster the levels of self-esteem or styles of presentation which make for success in employment. (See W. J. Wilson, *The Truly Disadvantaged,* 1987.)

p. 252. Marian Wright Edelman's observations: M. W. Edelman, *Families in Peril,* 1987.

pp. 253–255. Information about Eugene Lang's program: Based on interviews with John Rivera in May and June 1987, and Bruce A. Jones, Director of Support Services, "I Have a Dream Foundation," May 1987; material supplied by the foundation; J. Perlez, "In Harlem, Millionaire's Promise Still Inspires," *New York Times,* 20 June 1987.

CHAPTER 10

p. 257. "To pay attention to prenatal care": Personal communication from Joan Maxwell, President, The Better Babies Project, Washington, D.C., 1985.

p. 257. Dr. Rogers re "human misery": Robert Wood Johnson Foundation, *Annual Report, 1984.*

p. 258. Continuity: The importance of continuity of supportive relationships from the time of the mother's pregnancy into the early months of parenting has emerged as a major factor from the experience and research of K. Barnard, et al., "Caring for High-Risk Infants and Their Families," in *The Psychosocial Aspects of the Family,* 1985; V. Seitz, N. H. Apfel, and L. K. Rosenbaum, "Schoolaged Mothers: Infant Development and Maternal Educational Outcomes," Paper delivered at the Biennial Meeting of the Society for Research in Child Development, Detroit, 21 Apr. 1983; J. Hardy, "A Comprehensive Approach to Adolescent Pregnancy," in *Teenage Parents and Their Offspring,* 1981.

p. 259. "Issues from which human complexity has been removed": A. Abbott, "Status and Status Strain in the Professions," *American Journal of Sociology,* 1981.

p. 260. "The overwhelming managerial burden": Identified by Dr. Jane Knitzer as a major problem for multiproblem users of conventional social services when Dr. Knitzer met with a committee of the Foundation for Child Development in New York City in 1985. Also see J. Knitzer, *Unclaimed Children,* 1982.

p. 261. "These cases tend to reappear": D. Tobis, "Restructuring the Human Resources Administration: The Implementation of the Beattie Commission Report," Report to the Foundation for Child Development by Welfare Research, Inc., New York, Oct. 1986.

p. 261. "Pattern of failed connections": J. Knitzer, "Mental Health Services to

Children and Adolescents," *American Psychologist,* 1984; J. Knitzer, *Unclaimed Children,* 1982; J. Knitzer, Report to a meeting of the Working Group on Early Life, Harvard Division of Health Policy Research and Education, Boston, 20 Nov. 1984.

p. 261. "Impossibly large caseloads": J. Knitzer et al., *Children Without Homes,* 1978. Citing this report in its 1985 publication, *Keeping Families Together,* the Edna McConnell Clark Foundation stated that "too little" had changed in the intervening years.

p. 261. Traditional psychotherapy helps many: Psychotherapy has been shown to be effective in relieving suffering under many different circumstances. (For a review of the evidence, see M. L. Smith and G. V. Glass, "Meta-Analysis of Psychotherapy Outcome Studies," *American Psychologist,* 1977.)

p. 261. Psychotherapy alone is often not helpful to multiproblem families: M. Rutter, "Psychological Therapies in Child Psychiatry," *Psychological Medicine,* 1982. The major study of long-term outcomes of psychotherapy provided to poor inner city youngsters was done in St. Louis, by Cass and Thomas, who followed the troublesome lower-class eight- to eleven-year-olds referred to the Child Guidance Clinic at the Washington University School of Medicine for conventional psychotherapy in the 1950s and assessed them again in their twenties. Their treatment had made no difference in any measurable outcome. (See L. K. Cass and C. B. Thomas, *Childhood Pathology and Later Adjustment,* 1979.)

p. 261. Mental health center "can't get involved": Interview with Sister Mary Paul, Brooklyn, N.Y., 2 Apr. 1985.

p. 261. Conventional parent education irrelevant to socially isolated: N. A. Polansky, "Isolation of the Neglectful Family," *American Journal of Orthopsychiatry,* 1979; N. A. Polansky et al., *Damaged Parents: An Anatomy of Child Neglect,* 1981.

p. 263. "Until bonding has occurred": R. B. McCall, "A Hard Look at Stimulating and Predicting Development," *Pediatrics in Review,* 1982.

p. 263. Attachment a long process: M. E. Lamb, "Early Contact and Maternal-Infant Bonding," *Pediatrics,* 1982. Pediatricians Klaus and Kennell, who first described the process, themselves stated that early contact is neither necessary nor sufficient for attachment to occur. (See M. H. Klaus and J. H. Kennell, *Maternal-Infant Bonding,* 1976.) Claims made for bonding include improvements in mothering, breast feeding, and child development and the prevention of abuse and neglect. Most of these claims did not stand up under rigorous examination. (For example, see E. Siegel et al., "Hospital and Home Support During Infancy," *Pediatrics,* 1980.) However, there is some evidence that *for poor mothers with few social supports,* the opportunity for greater contact between mother and baby during the first hours and days of life may have some lasting effect. (See R. B. McCall, "A Hard Look," *Pediatrics,* 1982.) It may well be that in chaotic surroundings, the structure and intense intimacy of this early contact help tip a delicate balance toward greater positive involvement between mother and baby.

p. 263. New technique seems ineffective for those at nonbiological risk: Robert Goldenberg, M.D., and Arthur Salisbury, M.D., personal communications, Apr. 1987.

p. 263. "Child management training": J. Q. Wilson, "Raising Kids," *Atlantic,* 1983.

p. 263. "Greater range of services required": S. A. Szykula and M. J. Fleischman, "Reducing Out-of-Home Placements of Abused Children," *Child Abuse and Neglect,* 1985.

"Child management training" was pioneered by Gerald Patterson, family therapist and research scientist at the Oregon Learning Center in Eugene. The Patterson approach has attracted considerable attention, probably because the skills it teaches have been refined into a clear-cut and well-defined technology. Also, both its design and evaluation are based on unusually careful and systematic observations. The fundamental weakness of this approach lies in its limited usefulness to the families that need help the most, as even its admirers are coming to recognize.

The task of persuading parents to adopt its techniques seems to be far from simple. As James Q. Wilson wrote, "Teaching these common sense methods was difficult, but not nearly as difficult as motivating the parents to put them to use. Both instruction and motivation required extraordinary clinical skills and patience, neither of which was easy to sustain." (J. Q. Wilson and R. J. Herrnstein, *Crime and Human Nature,* 1985.)

An even greater difficulty is that the circumscribed skills that are taught do not take account of the complex, stressful world in which the highest-risk families live. Patterson himself acknowledges that "Child rearing practices can be severely disrupted by marital conflict and by crises external to the family . . . Consistent success requires the use of both a parent training technology and a set of skills for dealing with client resistance, marital conflict, and familial crises." (See G. R. Patterson et al., "A Comparative Evaluation of a Parent-Training Program," *Behavior Therapy,* 1982.) Three years later he was writing again about the need to help parents cope with their own crises, "for crises and antisocial families seem intimately related." (See G. R. Patterson, "Stress: A Change Agent for Family Process," in *Stress, Coping, and Development in Children,* 1983.)

Other studies have found that the more isolated the mother, the less effective is treatment aimed at helping parents to improve their child-rearing techniques. (See. R. G. Wahler, "The Insular Mother: Her Problems in Parent-Child Treatment," *Journal of Applied Behavior Analysis,* 1980.)

Evaluations of other "social learning treatment" programs based on the Patterson model also suggest that the Patterson model would be more effective as part of a more comprehensive set of interventions to provide families with both practical and psychological supports. (See S. A. Szykula and M. J. Fleischman, "Reducing Out-of-Home Placements of Abused Children," *Child Abuse and Neglect,* 1985.)

p. 265. No correlation between program success and survival: A classic study of the factors that accounted for financial survival of rural health clinics found that the more laboratory tests a clinic provided as a proportion of total services, the more likely it was to become self-sufficient. The more outreach services it provided, the more likely it was to shut down when grant funding came to an end. (See R. Feldman et al., "The Financial Viability of Rural Primary Health Care Centers," *American Journal of Public Health,* 1978.)

Social welfare researchers Sheila B. Kamerman and Alfred J. Kahn arrived at the same conclusion with regard to social services: "There is no relation between survival of agencies and either need or impact." (See S. B. Kamerman and A. J.

Kahn, "Social Services for Children, Youth and Families," A proposal to the Annie E. Casey Foundation, New York, Nov. 1986.

p. 265. "Extreme and irrational fragmentation": This is the phrase used by Professors Kamerman and Kahn of the Columbia University School of Social Work, in describing the current state of social services in the document prepared for the Casey Foundation in 1986.

pp. 265–266. "Virtues and vices": M. Heagarty, "Providing Health Services to the Underserved," in *Ambulatory Pediatrics, III,* 1984.

p. 267. Poor public policy: "The development and survival of local programs during the past decade is nothing less than phenomenal considering the obstacles they face . . . They stand as a testimony to the vibrancy, resourcefulness and responsiveness of local efforts," observed Weatherley and colleagues after surveying comprehensive service programs for pregnant and parenting adolescents. This group recognized that the exemplary programs and excellent services they found were exceptions and "must inevitably remain so in the absence of basic policy changes." The difficulties at the local level which must be overcome to succeed in developing and operating good programs, and the cumbersome strategies that must be devised to overcome prevailing constraints, "favor the development of services in a relatively few fortunate (resource-rich and better-served) localities." They conclude, as we do, by asking whether "the encouragement of a cottage industry is an appropriate response to . . . a serious, widespread social problem." (See R. A. Weatherley, S. B. Perlman, M. Levine, L. V. Klerman, *Patchwork Programs: Comprehensive Services for Pregnant and Parenting Adolescents,* Report prepared by the Center for Social Research, University of Washington, for the U.S. Public Health Service, Office of Population Affairs, U.S. Department of Health and Human Services, 1985.)

p. 268. Whatever can be readily measured: Like the drunk looking for his house keys under the street light where he can see, rather than in the dark empty lot where he dropped them, evaluation researchers tend to measure the measurable and count the countable, even if this means concentrating on narrow and even trivial interventions. Many evaluation researchers are baffled and discouraged by the ingeniously individualized, multifaceted services which are a boon to families and children with multiple needs but hard to quantify.

p. 268. Sacrifices significance for precision: That the orthodoxy of evaluation research tends to push researchers into asking easier, less important questions was one of the conclusions of a study by Professor Linda Borque at the University of California at Los Angeles of three hundred consecutive federally funded evaluation studies of services for children. (See L. Borque, "Does Evaluation Research Have Utility for Children's Advocates?" Report presented at the annual meeting of the Pacific Sociological Association, San Francisco, Apr. 1980.) There is also an increasing trend to collect data about *processes* (such as user satisfaction with the program, number of professional encounters, and fidelity of program attendance) which can be helpful to program managers in understanding and monitoring what is going on but is less useful to policymakers who want to know what the program is accomplishing in terms that matter to them (e.g., is it preventing delinquency, school dropouts, school-age birth, unemployment, and welfare dependency?). While it is unrealistic and uneconomical to expect every service program to collect long-term, policy-relevant outcome information, it is also a mistake to think that information about program processes can be substituted for information about outcomes.

p. 268. The essential extra dimension: Donald T. Campbell of Lehigh University, considered by many to be the academic guru of program evaluation, warns that "The dominant ideology of program evaluation . . . needs to be modified so as to avoid harmful side effects and pseudo-science." (See his thoughtful essay, "Problems for the Experimenting Society," in *America's Family Support Programs*, 1987.) Similarly, Robert Halpern notes that unique outcomes, desirable from the service provider's perspective, "wreak havoc on research designs seeking group differences in central tendency scores." (See R. Halpern, "Home-Based Early Intervention," *International Mental Health Journal*, 1984).

p. 269. "Until they learn to trust": Personal communication from Judith Tolmach, Executive Director of City Lights, Washington, D.C., 1986.

p. 269. "Quality of relationships": V. C. Shipman, *Disadvantaged Children and Their First School Experiences*, 1976.

p. 269. Effects on health outcomes: H. J. Schlesinger et al., "The Effects of Psychological Intervention on Recovery from Surgery," in *Emotional and Psychological Responses to Anesthesia and Surgery*, 1980.

p. 269. "Skillful listening, empathy": M. Green, "The Pediatric Interview and History," in *Pediatric Diagnosis*, 1986.

pp. 269–270. "Evaluate no program until it is proud," base judgments on "a cumulation" of wisdom: D. T. Campbell, "Problems for the Experimenting Society," in *America's Family Support Programs*, 1987.

p. 271. Savings from prenatal care: Institute of Medicine, *Preventing Low Birthweight*, 1985. Calculations of cost savings resulting from providing comprehensive care to high-risk pregnant women have also been made by several states, including Michigan, Virginia, California, and Oregon. For example, Michigan officials estimate that for every dollar the state spends on prenatal care for uninsured women, it saves six dollars in neonatal intensive care expenditures. (See M. B. Petchek and S. Adams-Taylor, "Prenatal Care Initiatives: Moving Toward Universal Prenatal Care in the United States," Report of the Center for Population and Family Health, Columbia University, and the Child Health Outcomes Project, University of North Carolina.)

p. 271. Savings from family supports: Cost estimates of Homebuilders intervention and of alternative out-of-home placements come from the organization which now sponsors Homebuilders, the Behavioral Sciences Institute, Federal Way, Wash., 1987. The state of Oregon studied 261 families served over a two-year period by its Intensive Family Services Unit and found that the cost of providing intensive family services averaged $1,132 per year, less than one fifth the placement cost. (See W. Showell, *Biennial Report of CSD's Intensive Family Services*, 1985.)

p. 271. Savings from reduction in teenage parenthood: K. A. Moore and R. F. Werthheimer, "Teenage Childbearing and Welfare," *Family Planning Perspectives*, 1984. (Calculations are in 1982 dollars.)

p. 271. Savings from nurse home visits: D. Olds et al. "Prenatal/Early Intervention Project. A Follow-Up Evaluation at the Third and Fourth Years of Life." Final Report to the Robert Wood Johnson Foundation, 1986.

p. 272. Savings from Yale day care–family support: V. Seitz et al., "Effects of Family Support Intervention," *Child Development,* 1985; A. Naylor, "Child Day Care," *Journal of Preventive Psychiatry,* 1982.

p. 272. Savings from preschool: C. U. Weber et al., *An Economic Analysis of the Ypsilanti Perry Preschool Project,* 1978. Most participants were in the Perry Preschool program for two years. However, one year of participation had almost the same long term effects.

The National Coalition of Advocates for Students calculated that every dollar spent on a full Head Start program for a preschool child from a low-income family would save $7 in social service costs. (See National Coalition of Advocates for Students, *Barriers to Excellence,* 1985.)

p. 273. "Not an expense but an excellent investment": Committee on Economic Development, *Children in Need: Investment Strategies for the Educationally Disadvantaged,* 1987.

p. 274. "Beyond the reach of child psychiatry": American Academy of Child Psychiatry, *Child Psychiatry,* 1983.

p. 274. Narrow definition of professionalism: The hospital's director of community services, when asked about the psychiatrist's circumscribed approach, added to the impression of pervasive tunnel vision. He said that even had the psychiatrist thought of it, there was probably no source of family planning services—in his very big city—to which such a troubled youngster might have been referred for appropriate services.

p. 275. Conger comments: Made at a meeting of the Board on Mental Health of the Institute of Medicine, National Academy of Sciences, Washington, D.C., 16 May 1986.

p. 275. Cohen comments: Made at a meeting of the Panel on Mental Health of Children and Adolescents, Institute of Medicine, National Academy of Sciences, Washington, D.C., 15 Jan. 1985.

pp. 275–276. Dilution of successful programs: Dr. Heather Weiss, personal communication, Apr. 1987.

p. 277. "Institutions tend to resist": R. Halpern, "Action Research for the Late 1980s," *Journal of Community Psychology,* (in press).

p. 279. Expanding Head Start: See E. Zigler and W. Berman, "Discerning the Future of Early Childhood Intervention," *American Psychologist,* 1983.

p. 279. "Creative state administration": See S. Rosenbaum, *Medicaid Eligibility for Pregnant Women,* 1987.

p. 280. Public-private collaboration: See I. B. Harris, address to the National Governors' Association Committee on Human Resources, Conference on "Focus on the First 60 Months," 6 Feb. 1986.

p. 281. "Protectors of the safety net": R. Pear, "States Are Found More Responsive on Social Issues," *New York Times,* 19 May 1985.

p. 281. Governors taking the lead: J. Herbers, "10 Agencies Win Grants For Innovative Projects," *New York Times,* 26 Sep. 1986.

p. 281. Children at top of state agendas: N. R. Peirce, "State Investments in Children," *Boston Globe,* 24 Nov. 1986.

CHAPTER II

p. 286. Services for high-risk populations can be part of universal programs: Minnesota's Early Childhood Family Education Program provides one example, in the view of Dr. Heather Weiss of the Harvard Family Research Project, of how the tension between universal and targeted services can be reconciled. Under the umbrella of a statewide, community-based effort to help parents promote healthy child development, the program provides parenting education and support for everyone but also offers specific services that are more intensive and comprehensive, targeted toward very high-risk groups.

p. 287. "Incorporating the poor through the back door": H. Heclo, "The Political Foundations of Antipoverty Policy," in *Fighting Poverty: What Works and What Doesn't,* 1986.

p. 287. Expansion of services for children individually damaged or at risk: As one example, in the state of Massachusetts, which has a very active program of Early Childhood Developmental Services, only 21 percent of the children were in the program as a result of being classified as "environmentally at risk." (Data for 1986, provided by Karl P. Kastorf, Director, October 1987). There are several reasons that resources flow more easily to children with individual handicaps than to children and families at environmental risk. Program administrators fear escalating and unpredictable costs of real efforts to identify an unknown number of children at environmental risk and provide them with "early intervention" services. They can gamble on not making the effort, because these children lack the parent lobbies that speak for handicapped children.

Furthermore, the health and mental health systems are geared to respond to diagnostic entities, not to risks, especially not to environmental risks, and most especially not to psychosocial risks in the environment. Medical professionals are the most prestigious of the helping professions, and the poor relations emulate the lifestyles of the rich. Individual assessment, diagnosis, and prescription, the foundation of the medical approach, has been transferred, through the Education for the Handicapped legislation, for medical practice into the schools. Within medicine, identified pathology brings in the fees. Child psychiatrists complain of being unable to collect third-party reimbursement for seeing the child of a mentally ill parent until the child himself shows signs of illness.

Because biological aberrations rank highest among diagnostic entities, professionals feel more comfortable applying the criteria of biological handicap or risk than environmental risk. Most professionals are trained to identify handicaps in the child but not risks in the environment or in the interaction of the two. Many sensitive professionals worry that they may seem prejudiced against people who are poor, or who have backgrounds or lifestyles different from their own; they fear stigmatizing a family by labeling it "environmentally at risk." It may seem preferable to ignore even such strong risk factors as a mother who is depressed or socially isolated and hope that everyone really has the same life chances—even though the alternative is often that the isolated mother must wait for disaster to strike her youngster so the family can quality for remedial help.

Research funds are also easier to obtain for work on individual, biological handicaps. Although it is well established that most mental illness is in fact the result of an interplay of biology and environment, a group of eminent psychiatrists I met with in 1986 took very seriously the news that at the Office of Management and Budget "they don't believe that mental illness is real." They decided they would do well, at least in the near term, to heed the advice of the director of the National Institute of Mental Health and concentrate their research and clinical efforts on the biological components of mental illness.

p. 288. Demonstrated pathology should not be ticket of admission: Head Start has certainly succeeded in serving a high-risk population without requiring individual demonstrations of pathology. As Dr. Julius B. Richmond, its first director, recently wrote, Head Start "was established fundamentally not to remove pathology but to encourage inherent capacities . . . It was not a screening program, but a program which was based on empirical data that the inherent capacities for development in the child and the family were present but not emerging because of environmental circumstances characterized by a lack of opportunity." (See J. B. Richmond and W. R. Beardslee, "Resiliency: Research and Practical Implications for Pediatricians," Lectureship in Developmental and Behavioral Pediatrics, Society for Behavioral Pediatrics, presented in Anaheim, Calif., 27 Apr. 1987.)

p. 290. Grants gravitate to better endowed communities: In one of the few systematic studies of this phenomenon, Weatherley and colleagues found that the conditions associated with the successful development of comprehensive programs "tend to be clustered in states and communities with greater-than-average affluence." They describe a "distressing bias in the distribution of services," and show that competitive grants tend to be awarded to "resource-rich, better-served" localities that need them the least. (See R. A. Weatherley, et al., "Comprehensive Programs for Pregnant Teenagers and Teenage Parents: How Successful Have They Been?" *Family Planning Perspectives,* 1986.)

CHAPTER 12

p. 292. "Corrode a free society": M. Novak et al., *The New Consensus on Family and Welfare,* 1987.

p. 292. "The process of making human beings human": James L. Coleman's statement, made in 1982, cited in D. P. Moynihan, *Family and Nation,* 1986.

p. 292. "Life-threatening to the great cities": Senator Moynihan quoted in E. M. Yoder, Jr., "Listen to Moynihan on Kids in Poverty," *Washington Post,* 28 July 1987.

p. 292. "This nation cannot continue to compete": Committee for Economic Development, *Children in Need,* 1987.

p. 292. *American Agenda, Report to the Forty-First President of the United States,* President Gerald R. Ford, President Jimmy Carter, Chairmen, 1988. The *American Agenda Report* called the expansion of programs of proven effectiveness for poor children its "top domestic priority," and advocated federal "child development grants" targeted on low-income communities, to "build on what we know about the most successful interventions to date."

p. 293. "Cannot be limited to government": From "Investing in Prevention,"

Remarks by William S. Woodside, President, Primerica Foundation, delivered to Center for National Policy, Washington, D.C., June 29, 1988.

p. 293. Congressman George Miller on first-class services: U.S. House of Representatives, Select Committee on Children, Youth, and Families, Hearing on "A Domestic Priority: Overcoming Family Poverty," Washington, D.C., September 22, 1988.

p. 294. Dr. Isabel Sawhill on deficits: From "Poverty and the Underclass" by Isabel V. Sawhill, in *American Agenda, Report to the Forty-First President of the United States*, 1988.

Bibliography

Aaron, H. J., and W. B. Schwartz. *The Painful Prescription: Rationing Health Care*. Washington, D.C.: Brookings Institution, 1984.

Abbott, A. "Status and Status Strain in the Professions." *American Journal of Sociology* 86 (1981): 819–35.

Alan Guttmacher Institute. *11 Million Teenagers*. New York: Alan Guttmacher Institute, 1976.

———. *Informing Social Change*. New York: Alan Guttmacher Institute, 1980.

———. *Teenage Pregnancy: The Problem That Hasn't Gone Away*. New York: Alan Guttmacher Institute, 1981.

———. "Questions and Answers About Title X and Family Planning." *Issues in Brief* 4, no. 1, Mar. 1984.

American Academy of Child Psychiatry. *Child Psychiatry: A Plan for the Coming Decades*. Washington, D.C.: American Academy of Child Psychiatry, 1983.

American Academy of Pediatrics. *Trends in Pediatrician Participation in State Medicaid Programs*. Elk Grove, Ill.: American Academy of Pediatrics, 1985.

Anson, R. S. *Best Intentions: The Education and Killing of Edmund Perry*. New York: Random House, 1987.

Auletta, K. *The Underclass*. New York: Vintage Books, 1982.

Bachman, J. G., P. M. O'Malley, and J. Johnston. *Adolescence to Adulthood: Change and Stability in the Lives of Young Men*. Ann Arbor, Mich.: University of Michigan Institute for Social Research, 1978.

Bachrach, C. A. "Contraceptive Practice Among American Women, 1973–1982." *Family Planning Perspectives* 16, no. 6 (Nov.–Dec. 1984): 253–59.

Baldwin, W., and V. Cain. "The Children of Teenage Parents." In *Teenage Sexual-*

ity, Pregnancy, and Childbearing, F. F. Furstenberg, Jr., R. Lincoln, and J. Menken, eds. Philadelphia: University of Pennsylvania Press, 1981, pp. 265–79.

Bandler, L. S. "Family Functioning: A Psychosocial Perspective." In *The Drifters: Children of Disorganized Lower Class Families,* E. Pavenstedt, ed. Boston: Little, Brown, 1967, pp. 225–54.

Bane, M. J., and D. T. Ellwood. *Slipping Into and Out of Poverty: The Dynamics of Spells.* Cambridge, Mass.: National Bureau of Economic Research, 1983 (working paper 1199).

Barnard, K., M. Hammond, S. K. Mitchell, C. L. Booth, A. Spietz, C. Snyder, and T. Elsas. "Caring for High-Risk Infants and Their Families." In *The Psychosocial Aspects of the Family: The New Pediatrics,* M. Green, ed. Lexington, Mass.: D.C. Heath, 1985, pp. 245–59.

Bassuk, E. L., L. Rubin, and A. S. Lauriat. "Characteristics of Sheltered Homeless Families." *American Journal of Public Health* 76, no. 9 (Sept. 1986): 1097–1101.

Baumrind, D. "Rejoinder to Lewis's Reinterpretation of Parental Firm Control Effects: Are Authoritative Families Really Harmonious?" *Psychological Bulletin* 94 (1983): 132–42.

Bee, H. L., L. F. Van Egeren, A. P. Streissguth, B. A. Nyman, and M. S. Leckie. "Social Class Differences in Maternal Teaching Strategies and Speech Patterns." *Developmental Psychology* 1, no. 6 (1969): 726–34.

Belle, D. "Social Ties and Social Support." In *Lives in Stress: Women and Depression,* D. Belle, ed. Beverly Hills: Sage, 1982, pp. 133–44.

Bellin, S. S., H. S. Geiger, and C. D. Gibson. "Impact of Ambulatory-Health-Care Services on the Demand for Hospital Beds." *New England Journal of Medicine* 280, no. 15 (10 Apr. 1969): 808–12.

Belsky, J. "Infant Day Care: A Cause for Concern?" *Zero to Three* 4, no. 5 (Sep. 1986): 1–7.

Bendick, M., Jr. *Towards Efficiency and Effectiveness in the WIC Delivery System.* Washington, D.C.: Urban Institute, 1976.

Berrueta-Clement, J. R., L. J. Schweinhart, W. S. Barnett, A. E. Epstein, and D. P. Weikart. *Changed Lives: The Effects of the Perry Preschool Programs on Youths Through Age 19.* Ypsilanti, Mich.: High/Scope Press, 1984.

Blamey, J. A., M. Howard, and W. Pollard. *Postponing Sexual Involvement: Progress Report on the Educational Series.* Atlanta: Emory University, School of Medicine, Department of Gynecology and Obstetrics, 1985.

Bloom, B. S. *Stability and Change in Human Characteristics.* New York: John Wiley & Sons, 1964.

Blum, J. M., E. S. Morgan, W. L. Rose, A. M. Schlesinger, Jr., K. M. Stampp, and C. V. Woodward. *The National Experience: A History of the United States.* New York: Harcourt Brace Jovanovich, 1984.

Blumstein, A., J. Cohen, J. Roth, and C. A. Visher, eds. *Criminal Careers and "Career Criminals."* Panel on Research on Criminal Careers, Commission on Behavioral and Social Sciences and Education. Washington, D.C.: National Academy Press, 1986.

Bok, D. "Needed: A New Way to Train Doctors." *Harvard Magazine* (May–June 1984): 32–43, 70–72.

Boone, M. S. "Social and Cultural Factors in the Etiology of Low Birthweight Among Disadvantaged Blacks." *Social Science and Medicine*, 20 (1985): 1001–11.

Bossert, S. "Effective Elementary Schools." In *Reaching for Excellence: An Effective Schools Sourcebook*, R. Kyle, ed. Washington, D.C.: U.S. Government Printing Office, 1985, pp. 39–53.

Boyer, E. *High School: A Report on Secondary Education in America*. Princeton, N.J.: Carnegie Foundation for the Advancement of Teaching, 1983.

Brann, E. A., L. Edward, T. Callicott, E. S. Story, P. A. Berg, J. A. Mahoney, J. L. Stine, and A. Hixson. "Strategies for the Prevention of Pregnancy in Adolescents." *Advances in Planned Parenthood* 14 (1979) 68–76.

Bronfenbrenner, U. *The Ecology of Human Development: Experiments by Nature and Design*. Cambridge, Mass.: Harvard University Press, 1979.

————. "Head Start, A Retrospective View." In *Project Head Start*, E. Zigler and J. Valentine, eds. New York: Free Press, 1979, pp. 77–88.

Brook, D. "The Great American Trouble." Review of *Crime and Human Nature* by J. Q. Wilson and R. J. Herrnstein, and *Confronting Crime* by E. Currie. *The New Republic* (20 Jan., 1986): 27–32.

Brophy, J. "Successful Teaching Strategies for the Inner-City Child." *Phi Delta Kappan* (Apr. 1982): 527–30.

Brown, C. "Manchild in Harlem." *New York Times Magazine* (16 Sept. 1984).

————. *Manchild in the Promised Land*. New York: Macmillan, 1965.

Brown, C. H., R. G. Adams, and S. G. Kellam. "A Longitudinal Study of Teenage Motherhood and Symptoms of Distress: The Woodlawn Community Epidemiological Project." *Research in Community and Mental Health* 2 (1981): 183–213.

Buescher, P. A. *Source of Prenatal Care and Infant Birthweight: The Case of a North Carolina County*. No. 39 (Mar. 1986). (Part of a Special Report Series by the North Carolina Department of Human Resources, Division of Health Services, State Center for Health Statistics, Raleigh, N.C.)

Burt, M. R., and F. Levy. "Estimates of Public Costs for Teenage Childbearing." In *Risking the Future: Adolescent Sexuality, Pregnancy and Childbearing*. Vol. 2, Working Papers, C. D. Hayes, ed. Washington, D.C.: National Academy Press, 1987, pp. 264–93.

Butterfield, F. "Why Asians Are Going to the Head of the Class." *New York Times Education Supplement* (Fall 1986): 18–23.

Camp, G., and C. Camp. *Corrections Yearbook, 86*. New York: Criminal Justice Institute, 1986.

Campbell, D. T. "Problems for the Experimenting Society in the Interface between Evaluation and Service Providers." In *America's Family Support Programs: Perspectives and Prospects*, S. L. Kagan, D. R. Powell, B. Weissbourd, and E. Zigler, eds. New Haven: Yale University Press, in press.

Cantwell, D. P. "Hyperactive Children Have Grown Up." *Archives of General Psychiatry* 42 (1985): 1026–8.

Caplan, S. E., S. T. Orr, J. R. Skulstad, and E. Charney. "After-Hours Telephone Use in Urban Pediatric Primary Care Centers." *American Journal of Diseases of Children* 137 (Sep. 1983): 879–82.

Card, J., and L. L. Wise. "Teenage Mothers and Fathers: The Impact of Early

Childbearing on the Parents' Personal and Professional Lives." *Family Planning Perspectives* 10 (1978): 199–207.

Carnegie Forum on Education and the Economy, Task Force on Teaching as a Profession. *A Nation Prepared: Teachers for the 21st Century.* New York: Carnegie Forum on Education and the Economy, 1986.

Carter, L. F. "The Sustaining Effects Study of Compensatory and Elementary Education." *Educational Researcher* 13, no. 7 (Aug.-Sep. 1984): 4–13.

Cass, L. K., and C. B. Thomas. *Childhood Pathology and Later Adjustment: The Question of Prediction.* New York: Wiley, 1979.

Center for the Study of Social Policy. *The 'Flip Side' of Black Families Headed by Women: The Economic Status of Black Men.* Washington, D.C.: Center for the Study of Social Policy, 1984.

Chabot, A. "Improved Infant Mortality in Populations Served by Neighborhood Health Centers." *Pediatrics* 47, no. 6 (June 1971): 989–94.

Chaiken, J. M., and M. R. Chaiken. "Trends and Targets." *Wilson Quarterly* (Spring 1983): 103–15.

Chall, J. S. *Stages of Reading Development.* New York: McGraw-Hill, 1983.

Chall, J. S., and V. A. Jacobs. "Writing and Reading in the Elementary Grades: Development Trends Among Low SES Children." *Language Arts* 60, no. 5 (May 1983): 617–26.

Chamie, M., S. Eisman, J. D. Forrest, M. Orr, and A. Torres. "Factors Affecting Adolescents' Use of Family Planning Clinics." *Family Planning Perspectives* 14, no. 3 (May–June 1982): 126–39.

Charney, E. "Preparing Physicians in Training for Child Health Care Communication." In *Child Health Care Communications,* W. K. Frankenburg and S. M. Thornton, eds. (The Johnson and Johnson Pediatric Round Table VIII). New York: Praeger, 1984, pp. 203–16.

Chess, S., and A. Thomas. "Individuality." In *Developmental-Behavioral Pediatrics,* M. D. Levine, W. B. Carey, A. C. Crocker, and R. T. Gross, eds. Philadelphia: W. B. Saunders, 1983, pp. 158–74.

Children's Defense Fund. *An Anatomy of a Social Problem: In Search of Comprehensive Solutions.* Washington D.C.: Children's Defense Fund Adolescent Pregnancy Prevention Clearinghouse, 1987.

———. *The Child Care Handbook.* Washington, D.C.: Children's Defense Fund, 1982.

———. *A Children's Defense Budget.* Washington, D.C.: Children's Defense Fund, 1986.

———. *A Children's Defense Budget.* Washington, D.C.: Children's Defense Fund, 1987.

———. *Declining Earnings of Young Men: Their Relation to Poverty, Teen Pregnancy and Family Formation,* Washington, D.C.: Children's Defense Fund Adolescent Pregnancy Prevention Clearinghouse, 1987.

Children's Defense Fund of the Washington Research Project. *EPSDT: Does It Spell Health Care For Poor Children?* Washington, D.C.: Children's Defense Fund, 1977.

———. *Title I of ESEA: Is It Helping Poor Children?* Washington, D.C.: Washington Research Project, 1966.

Chorvinsky, M. *Preprimary Enrollment, 1980.* Washington, D.C.: National Center for Educational Statistics, 1982.

Clark, K. B., and R. D. Nathan. "The Urban Underclass." In *Critical Issues for National Urban Policy: A Reconnaissance and Agenda for Further Study.* Washington, D.C.: National Research Council, 1982, pp. 33–53.

Clarke, A. M., and A. D. B. Clarke. "Thirty Years of Child Psychology: A Selective Review." *Journal of Child Psychology and Psychiatry* 27, no. 6 (1986): 719–59.

Cobb, S. "Social Support as a Moderator of Life Stress." *Psychosomatic Medicine* 38 (1976): 300–14.

Coleman, J. S., E. Q. Campbell, C. J. Hobson, J. McPartland, A. M. Mood, F. D. Weinfeld, and R. L. York. *Equality of Educational Opportunity.* Washington, D.C.: U.S. Government Printing Office, 1966.

———, T. Hoffer, and S. Kilgore. *High School Achievement: Public, Catholic and Private Schools Compared.* New York: Basic Books, 1982.

Colletta, N. "Social Support and the Risk of Maternal Rejection by Adolescent Mothers." *Journal of Psychology* 109 (1981): 191–97.

Comer, J. P. "Black Violence and Public Policy." In *American Violence and Public Policy,* L. A. Curtis, ed. New Haven: Yale University Press, 1985, pp. 63–86.

———. *School Power.* New York: Free Press, 1980.

———. "Home-School Relationships As They Affect the Academic Success of Children." *Education and Urban Society* 16, no. 3 (May 1984): 323–37.

———. "The Yale–New Haven Primary Prevention Project: A Follow-up Study." *Journal of the American Academy of Child Psychiatry* 24, no. 2 (1985): 154–60.

Committee for Economic Development. *Children in Need: Investment Strategies for the Educationally Disadvantaged.* New York: Committee for Economic Development, 1987.

———. *Investing in our Children.* New York: Committee for Economic Development, 1985.

Congressional Research Service and Congressional Budget Office. *Children in Poverty.* Washington, D.C.: U.S. Government Printing Office, 1985.

Consortium for Longitudinal Studies. *As the Twig Is Bent . . . Lasting Effects of Preschool Programs.* Hillsdale, N.J.: Lawrence Erlbaum Associates, 1983.

———. *Lasting Effects after Preschool: Summary Report.* Washington, D.C.: U.S. Government Printing Office. 1978.

Crain, R., and R. Mahard. "Desegregation and Black Achievement: A Review of the Research." *Law and Contemporary Problems* 42, no. 3 (Summer 1978): 35–45.

Crain, R., and J. Strauss. *School Desegregation and Black Educational Attainments.* Center for Social Organization of Schools, report no. 359. Baltimore: Johns Hopkins University Press, 1985.

Crnic, K. A., M. Greenburg, A. Ragozin, N. Robinson, and R. Basham. "Effects of Stress and Social Support on Mothers and Premature Full-Term Infants." *Child Development* 54 (1983): 209–17.

Crnic, K.A., M. T. Greenberg, and N. M. Slough. "Early Stress and Social Support Influences on Mothers' and High-Risk Infants' Functioning in Late Infancy." *Infant Mental Health Journal* 7, no. 1 (Spring 1986): 19–33.

Crockenberg, S. "Infant Irritability, Mother Responsiveness, and Social Support

Influences on the Security of Infant-Mother Attachment." *Child Development* 52 (1981): 656–65.

Cuban, L. "Transforming the Frog into a Prince: Effective Schools Research, Policy and Practice at the District Level." *Harvard Educational Review* 54, no. 2 (1984): 129–51.

Currie, E. *Confronting Crime: An American Challenge.* New York: Pantheon Books, 1985.

Curtis, L. A., ed. *American Violence and Public Policy.* New Haven: Yale University Press, 1985.

Danziger, S. H., and P. Gottschalk. "The Poverty of *Losing Ground.*" *Challenge* (May–June 1985): 32–38.

Danziger, S. H., R. H. Haveman, and R. D. Plotnik. "Antipoverty Policy: Effects on the Poor and the Nonpoor." In *Fighting Poverty.* S. H. Danziger and D. H. Weinberg, eds. Cambridge, Mass.: Harvard University Press, 1986, pp. 50–77.

Danziger, S. H., and D. H. Weinberg, eds. *Fighting Poverty: What Works and What Doesn't.* Cambridge, Mass.: Harvard University Press, 1986.

David, H. P. "Unwanted Children: A Follow Up from Prague." *Family Planning Perspectives* 18, no. 3 (June 1986): 143–44.

Davidson, P. W. "Visual Impairment and Blindness." In *Developmental-Behavioral Pediatrics,* M. D. Levine, W. B. Carey, A. C. Crocker, and R. T. Gross, eds. Philadelphia: W. B. Saunders, 1983.

Davidson, S. M. "Physician Participation in Medicaid, Background and Issues." *Journal of Health Politics, Policy and Law* 6, no. 4 (Winter 1982): 703–17.

Davis, K., and C. Schoen. *Health and the War on Poverty: A Ten Year Appraisal.* Studies in Social Economics. Washington, D.C.: Brookings Institution, 1978.

Dennis, W. *Children of the Creche.* New York: Appleton-Century-Crofts, 1973.

Deutsch, M. "The Role of Social Class in Language: Development and Cognition." *American Journal of Orthopsychiatry* 35, no. 1 (1965): 78–88.

Deutsch, M., C. P. Deutsch, T. J. Jordan, and R. Grallo. "The IDS Program: An Experiment in Early and Sustained Enrichment." In *As the Twig Is Bent . . . Lasting Effects of Preschool Programs,* Consortium for Longitudinal Studies. Hillsdale, N.J.: Lawrence Erlbaum Associates, 1983, pp. 377–410.

Dryfoos, J. "School-Based Health Clinics: A New Approach to Preventing Adolescent Pregnancy?" *Family Planning Perspectives* 17, no. 2 (Mar.–Apr. 1985): 70–75.

Dutton, D. "Children's Health Care: The Myth of Equal Access." In *Better Health for Our Children: A National Strategy.* Vol. IV, Report of the Select Panel for the Promotion of Child Health. Washington, D.C.: U.S. Department of Health and Human Services, 1981, pp. 357–440.

Easterbrook, G. "The Revolution in Medicine." *Newsweek* (26 Jan. 1987).

Edelman, M. W. *Families in Peril.* Cambridge, Mass.: Harvard University Press, 1987.

Edelman, P. B. "The Next Century of Our Constitution: Rethinking Our Duty to the Poor" *Hastings Law Journal* 39, no. 1 (November 1987): 1–61.

Edmonds, R. "Effective Schools for the Urban Poor." *Educational Leadership* 37 (1979): 15–27.

Edna McConnell Clark Foundation. *Keeping Families Together: The Case for Family Preservation.* New York: Edna McConnell Clark Foundation, 1985.

Edwards, L. E., M. E. Steinman, and E. Y. Hakanson. "An Experimental Comprehensive High School Clinic." *American Journal of Public Health* 8 (1977): 765–76.

Edwards, L. E., M. E. Steinman, K. Arnold, and E. Y. Hakanson. "Adolescent Pregnancy Prevention Services in High School Clinics." *Family Planning Perspectives* 12, no. 1 (Jan.–Feb. 1980): 6–14.

Egbuonu, L., and B. Starfield. "Child Health and Social Status." *Pediatrics* 69 (1982): 550–57.

Eisenberg, L. "Conceptual Issues in Biobehavioral Interactions." In *Infants at Risk for Developmental Dysfunction,* D. L. Parron and L. Eisenberg, eds. Washington, D.C.: Institute of Medicine, National Academy of Sciences, 1982, pp. 57–68.

———. "Development as a Unifying Concept in Psychiatry." *British Journal of Psychiatry* 131 (1977): 225–37.

———. "Prevention: Rhetoric and Reality." *Journal of the Royal Society of Medicine* 77 (Apr. 1984): 268–80.

———. "Social Context of Child Development." *Pediatrics* 68, no. 5 (Nov. 1981): 705–12.

Elliot, D. S., S. S. Ageton, and R. J. Canter. "An Integrated Theoretical Perspective on Delinquent Behavior." *Journal of Research in Crime and Delinquency* 16, no. 1 (1979): 3–27.

Ellwood, D. T., and M. J. Bane. "The Impact of AFDC on Family Structure and Living Arrangements." *Research in Labor Economics* 7 (1984): 137–207.

Ellwood, D. T., and L. H. Summers. "Poverty in America: Is Welfare the Answer or the Problem?" In *Fighting Poverty, What Works and What Doesn't,* S. H. Danziger and D. H. Weinberg, eds. Cambridge, Mass.: Harvard University Press, 1986, pp. 78–105.

Elster, A. B., E. R. McAnarney, and M. E. Lamb. "Parental Behavior of Adolescent Mothers." *Pediatrics* 71 (1983): 494–503.

English, J. T., and L. B. Schorr. "Background, Context and Significant Issues in Neighborhood Health Center Programs." *Milbank Memorial Fund Quarterly* 46 (1968): 289–96.

Erlich, M. I., R. D. Reinecke, and K. Simmons. "Preschool Vision Screening for Amblyopia and Strabismus. Programs, Methods, Guidelines 1983." *Survey of Ophthalmology* 28 (Nov.–Dec. 1983): 145–63.

Escalona, S. K. "Babies at Double Hazard: Early Development of Infants at Biologic and Social Risk." *Pediatrics* 70, no. 5 (Nov. 1982): 670–76.

Fallows, D. *A Mother's Work.* Boston: Houghton Mifflin Co., 1985.

"The Family Crisis and What We Can Do About It: An Interview with Marian Wright Edelman." *The Harvard Education Letter* 3, no. 3 (May 1987): 4–6.

Fanshel, D. "Decision-Making Under Uncertainty: Foster Care for Abused or Neglected Children?" *American Journal of Public Health* 71, no. 7 (July 1981): 685–86.

Farrington, D. P., and D. J. West. "The Cambridge Study in Delinquent Development (United Kingdom)." In *Prospective Longitudinal Research: An Empirical*

Basis for the Primary Prevention of Psychosocial Disorders, S. A. Mednick and A. E. Baert, eds. Oxford: Oxford University Press, 1981, pp. 137–45.

Feder, J., J. Hadley, and R. Mullner. *Falling Through the Cracks: Poverty, Insurance Coverage, and Hospitals' Care to the Poor, 1980 and 1982.* Working Paper. Washington, D.C.: Urban Institute, 1984.

———. "Poor People and Poor Hospitals." *Journal of Health Politics, Policy, and Law* 9 (1984): 237–50.

Fein, R. "Choosing the Arbiter: The Market or the Government." *New England Journal of Medicine* 313, no. 2 (11 July 1985): 113–5.

———. *Medical Care, Medical Costs: The Search for a Health Insurance Policy.* Cambridge, Mass.: Harvard University Press, 1986.

Feldman, R., D. M. Deitz, and E. F. Brooks. "The Financial Viability of Rural Primary Health Care Centers." *American Journal of Public Health* 68, no. 10 (Oct. 1978): 981–7.

Fillmore, L. W. "Equity or Excellence?" *Language Arts* 63, no. 5 (Sep. 1986): 475–481.

Fishman, S. H. "Delivery or Abortion in Inner-City Adolescents." *American Journal of Orthopsychiatry* 47 (1977): 127–33.

Fiske, E. B. "Early Schooling Is Now the Rage." *New York Times Educational Supplement* (13 Apr. 1986).

Foltz, A. M. "The Development of Ambiguous Federal Policy: EPSDT." *Milbank Memorial Fund Quarterly. Health and Society* 53 (Winter 1975): 35–64.

Forbes, R. H. "Academic Achievement of Historically Lower-Achieving Students During the Seventies." *Phi Delta Kappan* (Apr. 1982): 542–44.

Forrsman, H., and I. Thuwe. "Continued Follow-Up Study of 120 Persons Born After Refusal of Application for Therapeutic Abortion." *Acta Psychiatrica Scandinavica* 64 (1981): 142.

———. "One Hundred and Twenty Children Born After Application for Therapeutic Abortions Refused." *Acta Psychiatrica Scandinavica* 42 (1966): 71.

Fraiberg, S. *Every Child's Birthright.* New York: Basic Books, 1977.

Fuchs, V. R. "The 'Rationing' of Medical Care." *New England Journal of Medicine* 311, no. 24 (13 Dec. 1984): 1572–73.

Furstenberg, F. F., Jr. "The Social Consequences of Teenage Parenthood." In *Teenage Sexuality, Pregnancy and Childbearing,* F. F. Furstenberg, Jr., F. Lincoln, and J. Menken, eds. Philadelphia: University of Pennsylvania Press, 1981, pp. 184–210.

Furstenberg, F. F., Jr., and J. Brooks-Gunn. *Adolescent Mothers in Later Life.* New York: Commonwealth Fund, 1985.

Furstenberg, F. F., Jr., J. Shea, P. Allison, R. Herceg-Baron, and D. Webb. "Contraceptive Continuation Among Adolescents Attending Family Planning Clinics." *Family Planning Perspectives* 15, no. 5 (Sept.–Oct. 1983): 211–17.

Gamble, T. J., and E. Zigler. "Effects of Infant Day Care: Another Look at the Evidence." *American Journal of Orthopsychiatry* 56, no. 1 (Jan. 1986): 26–42.

Garbarino, J. "Child Abuse and Juvenile Delinquency: The Developmental Impact of Social Isolation." In *Exploring the Relationship Between Child Abuse and Juvenile Delinquency,* Y. Walker, ed. Seattle: Northwest Institute for Human Services, 1978, pp. 115–27.

Garbarino, J., and D. Sherman. "High-Risk Neighborhoods and High-Risk Families: The Human Ecology of Child Maltreatment." *Child Development* 51 (1980): 188–98.

Gardner, J. *Excellence.* New York: W. W. Norton, 1984.

Garmezy, N. "Stressors of Childhood." In *Stress, Coping and Development in Children,* N. Garmezy and M. Rutter, eds. New York: McGraw-Hill, 1983, pp. 43–84.

Geiger, H. J. "A Health Center in Mississippi—A Case Study in Social Medicine." In *Medicine in a Changing Society,* L. Corey, S. E. Saltman, and M. F. Epstein, eds. Saint Louis: C. V. Mosby, 1972, pp. 157–67.

Glazer, N. "The Problem with Competence." In *Challenge to American Schools,* J. H. Bunzel, ed. New York: Oxford University Press, 1985, pp. 216–31.

Gold, R. B., and J. Macias. "Public Funding of Contraceptive, Sterilization and Abortion Services, 1985." *Family Planning Perspectives* 18, no. 6 (Nov.–Dec. 1986): 259–64.

Goodlad, J. I. *A Place Called School: Prospects for the Future.* New York: McGraw-Hill, 1983.

Gordis, L. "Effectiveness of Comprehensive Care Programs in Preventing Rheumatic Fever." *New England Journal of Medicine* 239, no. 7 (16 Aug. 1973): 331–35.

Gortmaker, S. "The Effects of Prenatal Care Upon the Health of the Newborn." *American Journal of Public Health* 69, no. 7 (1979): 653–60.

Gottlieb, M. I. "Otitis Media." In *Developmental-Behavioral Pediatrics,* M. D. Levine, W. B. Carey, A. C. Crocker, and R. T. Gross, eds. Philadelphia: W. B. Saunders, 1983, pp. 463–73.

Graham, P. "Schools: Cacophony about Practice, Silence about Purpose." *Daedalus* 113, no. 4 (Fall 1984): 29–57.

Gray, S. W., R. A. Klaus, J. O. Miller, and F. J. Forrester. *Before First Grade, The Early Training Project for Disadvantaged Children.* New York: Teachers College Press, 1966.

Gray, S. W., B. K. Ramsey, and R. A. Klaus. "The Early Training Project 1962–1980." In *As the Twig Is Bent . . . Lasting Effects of Preschool Programs,* Consortium for Longitudinal Studies. Hillsdale, N.J.: Lawrence Erlbaum Associates, 1983, pp. 33–69.

Green, M. "The Pediatric Interview and History." In *Pediatric Diagnosis,* 4th ed., M. Green and J. B. Richmond, eds. Philadelphia: W. J. Saunders, 1986, pp. 191–203.

Greenspan, S. I. "Developmental Morbidity In Infants in Multi-Risk-Factor Families: Clinical Perspectives." *Public Health Reports* 97, no. 1 (Jan.–Feb. 1982): 16–23.

————. *Psychopathology and Adaptation in Infancy and Early Childhood: Principles of Clinical Diagnosis and Preventive Intervention.* Clinical Infant Reports, no. 1. New York: International Universities Press, 1981.

Greenspan, S. I., and K. R. White. "Conducting Research with Preventive Intervention Programs." In *Basic Handbook of Child Psychiatry: Advances and New Directions,* vol. 5, J. D. Noshpitz, ed. New York: Basic Books, 1987, pp. 554–65.

Greenspan, S. I., S. Wieder, A. F. Lieberman, R. A. Norer, R. S. Lourie, and M. E.

Robinson, eds. *Infants in Multirisk Families: Case Studies in Preventive Intervention.* Clinical Infant Reports, no. 3. Madison, Conn.: International Universities Press, 1987.

Greenstein, R. "Losing Faith in 'Losing Ground.' " *New Republic* 192 (25 Mar. 1985): 12–17.

Gregory, M., T. Hausner, and A. Solarz, *Final Evaluation of the Obstetrical Access Pilot Project, July 1979–June 1982.* Sacramento: State of California Department of Health Services, 1984.

Guillemin, J. H., and L. L. Holmstrom. *Mixed Blessings.* New York: Oxford University Press, 1986.

Haapala, D. A., and J. M. Kinney. "Homebuilders Approach to the Training of In-Home Therapists." In *Home-Based Services for Children and Families,* S. Maybanks and M. Bryce, eds. Springfield, Ill.: Charles C. Thomas, 1979, pp. 248–52.

Halpern, R. "Action Research for the Late 1980s." *Journal of Community Psychology* (in press).

———. "Home-Based Early Intervention: Emerging Purposes, Intervention Approaches and Evaluation Strategies." *International Mental Health Journal* 5, no. 4 (Winter 1984): 206–20.

Hamburg, B. A. "Developmental Issues in School-Age Pregnancy." In *Aspects of Psychiatric Problems of Childhood and Adolescence,* E. Purcell, ed. New York: Josiah Macy, Jr. Foundation, 1980, pp. 299–325.

Hamburg, D. A. "Reducing the Casualties of Early Life: A Preventive Orientation." In *Carnegie Corporation of New York, Annual Report 1985.* New York: Carnegie Corporation, 1985, pp. 3–19.

Hardy, J. "A Comprehensive Approach to Adolescent Pregnancy." In *Teenage Parents and Their Offspring,* K. G. Scott, T. Field, and E. Robertson, eds. New York: Grune & Stratton, 1981.

Harrington, M. *The New American Poverty.* New York: Holt, Rinehart and Winston, 1984.

Hart, J. T. "The Inverse Care Law." *Lancet* 1 (1971): 405–12.

Hayes, C. D., ed. *Risking the Future: Adolescent Sexuality, Pregnancy, and Childbearing.* Working Papers. Washington, D.C.: National Academy Press, 1987.

Heagarty, M. C. "Providing Health Services to the Underserved." In *Ambulatory Pediatrics, III,* M. Green and R. J. Haggerty, eds. Philadelphia: W. B. Saunders, 1984, pp. 23–26.

Heagarty, M. C., L. Robertson, J. Kosa, and J. J. Alpert. "Use of the Telephone by Low-Income Families." *Journal of Pediatrics* 73 (Nov. 1968): 740.

Heclo, H. "The Political Foundations of Antipoverty Policy." In *Fighting Poverty: What Works and What Doesn't,* S. H. Danziger and D. H. Weinberg, eds. Cambridge, Mass.: Harvard University Press, 1986, pp. 312–40.

Hess, R. D., and V. Shipman. "Maternal Influences upon Early Learning: The Cognitive Environments of Urban Pre-School Children." In *Early Education,* R. D. Hess and R. M. Bear, eds. Chicago: Aldine, 1968, pp. 91–103.

Hiatt, H. H. *America's Health in the Balance: Choice or Change.* New York: Harper & Row, 1987.

Himmelstein, D. U., and S. Woolhandler. "Cost Without Benefit." *New England Journal of Medicine* 314, no. 7 (14 Feb. 1986): 441–5.

Hispanic Policy Development Project. *Make Something Happen*. Vol. 2. New York: Hispanic Policy Development Project, 1984.

Hochheiser, L. I., K. Woodward, and E. Charney. "Effect of the Neighborhood Health Center on the Use of Pediatric Emergency Departments in Rochester, New York." *New England Journal of Medicine* 285, no. 3 (15 July 1971): 148–52.

Hodgson, G. "Do Schools Make a Difference?" *Atlantic Monthly* (Mar. 1973): 35–46.

Hofferth, S. L. "Contraceptive Decision Making Among Adolescents." In *Risking the Future: Adolescent Sexuality, Pregnancy, and Childbearing*. Vol. 2, Working Papers, C. D. Hayes, ed. Washington, D.C.: National Academy Press, 1987, pp. 56–77.

———. "Factors Affecting Initiation of Sexual Intercourse." In *Risking the Future: Adolescent Sexuality, Pregnancy, and Childbearing*. Vol. 2, Working Papers, C. D. Hayes, ed. Washington, D.C.: National Academy Press, 1987, pp. 7–35.

———. "Social and Economic Consequences of Teenage Childbearing." In *Risking the Future: Adolescent Sexuality, Pregnancy and Childbearing*. Vol. 2, Working Papers, C. D. Hayes, ed. Washington, D.C.: National Academy Press, 1987, pp. 123–44.

Hogan, D. P., and E. M. Kitagawa. *The Impact of Social Status, Family Structure, and Neighborhood on the Fertility of Black Adolescents*. Chicago: Population Research Center, University of Chicago, 1983.

Holahan, J. F., and J. W. Cohen. *Medicaid: The Trade-off between Cost Containment and Access to Care*. Washington, D.C.: Urban Institute Press, 1986.

Holmes, N., M. J. Conway, L. Flood, J. G. Fraser, and A. Stewart. "Language Development in a Group of Very Low-Birth-Weight Children Whose Post-Auricular Myogenic Response Was Tested in Infancy." *Pediatrics* 71 (1983): 257.

Holton, G. "*A Nation at Risk* Revisited." *Daedalus* (Fall 1984): 1–27.

Hughes, D., K. Johnson, S. Rosenbaum, J. Simons, and E. Butler. *The Health of America's Children: Maternal and Child Health Data Book*. Washington, D.C.: Children's Defense Fund, 1987.

Hunt, J. M. *Intelligence and Experience*. New York: Ronald Press, 1961.

Iglehart, J. K. "Medical Care of the Poor—A Growing Problem." *New England Journal of Medicine* 313, no. 1 (4 July 1985): 59–63.

———. "Report on the Duke University Medical Center: Private Sector Conference." *New England Journal of Medicine* 307, no. 1 (1 July 1982): 68–71.

Institute of Medicine, Committee to Study the Prevention of Low Birthweight, Division of Health Promotion and Disease Prevention. *Preventing Low Birthweight*. Washington, D.C.: National Academy Press, 1985.

Institute of Medicine, Division of Health Care Services. *Community Oriented Primary Care: Conference Proceedings*, E. Connor and F. Mullan, eds. Washington, D.C.: National Academy Press, 1982.

———. *Reforming Physician Payment*. Washington, D.C.: National Academy Press, 1984.

Irwin, P., and R. Conroy-Hughes. "EPSDT Impact on Health Status: Estimates

Based on Secondary Analysis of Administratively Generated Data." *Medical Care* 10 (1982): 216–34.

Jacoby, S. *Inside Soviet Schools.* New York: Schocken, 1975.

Jencks, C., M. Smith, H. Acland, M. J. Bane, D. Cohen, H. Gintis, B. Heyns, and S. Michelson. *Inequality: A Reassessment of the Effect of Family and Schooling in America.* New York: Basic Books, 1972.

Jensen, A. "How Much Can We Boost I.Q. and Scholastic Achievement?" *Harvard Education Review* 39, no. 1 (Winter 1969): 1–123.

Johnson, C., and A. Sum. *Declining Earnings of Young Men: Their Relation to Poverty, Teen Pregnancy and Family Formation.* Washington, D.C.: Children's Defense Fund, Adolescent Pregnancy Prevention Clearinghouse, May 1987.

Joint Center for Political Studies. *A Policy Framework for Racial Justice.* Washington, D.C.: Joint Center for Political Studies, 1983.

Jones, E. F., J. D. Forrest, N. Goldman, S. K. Henshaw, R. Lincoln, J. I. Rosoff, C. F. Westoff, and D. Wulf. *Teenage Pregnancy in Developed Countries.* New Haven: Yale University Press, 1987.

Kagan, J. *The Nature of the Child.* New York: Basic Books, 1984.

———. *Psychological Research on the Human Infant: An Evaluative Summary.* New York: William T. Grant Foundation, 1982.

———. "Stress and Coping in Early Development." In *Stress, Coping and Development in Children,* N. Garmezy and M. Rutter, eds. New York: McGraw-Hill, 1983, pp. 191–216.

Kahn, A. J., and S. B. Kamerman. *Not for the Poor Alone: European Social Services.* New York: Harper and Row, 1977.

Kalter, J. "Let's Run Birth Control Ads During *Dallas* and *Dynasty.*" *TV Guide* (23 Nov. 1985): 30–36.

Kamerman, S. B. *Parenting in an Unresponsive Society: Managing Work and Family.* New York: Free Press, 1980.

Kamerman, S. B., and A. J. Kahn. "Explaining the Outcomes: Social Policy and Children in the U.S. and Europe." In *Changing the Well-Being of Children and the Aged in the U.S.: International and Intertemporal Perspectives,* J. L. Palmer, T. S. Smeeding, and B. B. Torrey, eds. Washington, D.C.: Urban Institute (in press).

Kamerman, S. B., A. J. Kahn, and P. Kingston. *Maternity Policies and Working Women.* New York, Columbia University Press, 1983.

Kaplan, J. L., and E. C. Luck. "The Dropout Phenomenon as a Social Problem." *Educational Forum* 42 (1977): 41–56.

Kasarda, J. *The Regional and Urban Redistribution of People and Jobs in the U.S.* Washington, D.C.: National Research Council Committee on National Urban Policy, 1986.

Kellam, S. G., R. G. Adams, C. H. Brown, and M. E. Ensminger. "The Long-Term Evolution of the Family Structure of Teenage and Older Mothers." *Journal of Marriage and the Family* (Aug. 1982): 539–54.

Kellam, S. G., M. E. Ensminger, and R. J. Turner. "Family Structure and the Mental Health of Children." *Archives of General Psychiatry* 34 (Sep. 1977): 1012–22.

Keller, W. "Study of Selected Outcomes of the EPSDT Program in Michigan." *Public Health Reports* 28 (1984): 110–18.

Kennedy, E. T. *Evaluation of the Effects of the WIC Program on Prenatal Patients in Massachusetts.* Cambridge, Mass.: Harvard University, School of Public Health, 1979.

Kershaw, J. A. *Government Against Poverty.* Washington, D.C.: Brookings Institution, 1970.

Kestenberg, J. "The Effects on Parents of the Child's Transition Into and Out of Latency." In *Parenthood: Its Psychology and Psychopathology,* E. J. Anthony and T. Benedek, eds. Boston: Little, Brown, 1970, pp. 289–306.

Keyserling, M. D. *Windows on Day Care.* New York: National Council of Jewish Women, 1972.

Kinney, J. M. "Homebuilders: An In-Home Crisis Intervention Program." *Children Today* 7, no. 1 (Jan.–Feb. 1978): 15–35.

Kinney, J. M., B. Madsen, T. Fleming, and D. A. Haapala. "Homebuilders: Keeping Families Together." *Journal of Consulting and Clinical Psychology* 45, no. 4 (1977): 667–73.

Kirby, D. *Sexuality Education: An Evaluation of Programs and Their Effects: An Executive Summary.* Santa Cruz, Calif.: Network Publications, 1984.

Kisker, E. E. "Teenagers Talk About Sex, Pregnancy and Contraception." *Family Planning Perspectives* 17, no. 2 (Mar.–Apr. 1985): 83–90.

Klaus, M. H., and J. H. Kennell. *Maternal-Infant Bonding: The Impact of Early Separation or Loss on Family Development.* St. Louis: Mosby, 1976.

Klaus, R. A., and S. W. Gray. "The Early Training Project for Disadvantaged Children: A Report After Five Years." *Monographs of the Society for Research in Child Development* 33, no. 4 (1968).

Klein, M. "The Impact of the Rochester Neighborhood Health Center on Hospitalization of Children, 1968 to 1970." *Pediatrics* 51, no. 5 (May 1973): 833–39.

Klein, R. "Caregiving Arrangements by Employed Women with Children Under One Year of Age." *Developmental Psychology* 21 (1985): 403–6.

Klerman, L. V. "Teenage Parents: A Brief Review of Research." In *Infants at Risk for Developmental Dysfunction,* D. L. Parron and L. Eisenberg, eds. Washington, D.C.: National Academy Press, 1982, pp. 125–32.

Klerman, L. V., and J. F. Jekel, "Unwanted Pregnancy." In *Perinatal Epidemiology,* M. B. Bracken, ed. New York: Oxford University Press, 1984, pp. 283–300.

Klerman, L. V., M. Weitzman, J. J. Alpert, and G. A. Lamb. "School Absence: Can It Be Used to Monitor Child Health?" In *Monitoring Child Health in the United States: Selected Issues and Policies,* D. K. Walker and J. B. Richmond, eds. Cambridge, Mass.: Harvard University Press, 1984, pp. 143–52.

Knitzer, J. "Mental Health Services to Children and Adolescents: A National View of Public Policies." *American Psychologist* 39, no. 8 (Aug. 1984): 905–11.

———. *Unclaimed Children: The Failure of Public Responsibility to Children and Adolescents in Need of Mental Health Services.* Washington, D.C.: The Children's Defense Fund, 1982.

Knitzer, J., B. McGowan, and M. L. Allen. *Children Without Homes: An Examination of Public Responsibility to Children in Out-of-Home Care.* Washington, D.C.: Children's Defense Fund, 1978.

Kohn, M. L. *Class and Conformity.* Homewood, Ill.: Dorsey, 1969.

Kohut, H. *The Restoration of the Self.* New York: International Universities Press, 1977.

Korenbrot, C. C. "Risk Reduction in Pregnancies of Low Income Women: Comprehensive Prenatal Care Through the OB Access Project." *Mobius* 4 (1984): 34–43.

Kotelchuck, M., and J. B. Richmond. "Head Start: Evolution of a Successful Comprehensive Child Development Program." *Pediatrics* 79, no. 3 (Mar. 1987): 441–5.

Kozol, J. *Illiterate America.* Garden City, N.Y.: Anchor Press, 1985.

Lamar, J. V. "Today's Native Sons." *Time* (1 Dec. 1986): 26–9.

Lamb, M. E. "Early Contact and Maternal-Infant Bonding: One Decade Later." *Pediatrics* 70, no. 5 (Nov. 1982): 763–8.

Lazar, I., R. B. Darlington, H. Murray, J. Royce, and A. Snipper. "Lasting Effects of Early Education." *Monographs of the Society for Research in Child Development* 47 (1982).

Lazarus, W., and K. M. West. *Back to Basics: Improving the Health of California's Next Generation.* Santa Monica, Calif.: Southern California Child Health Network, 1987.

Lazerson, M., and W. N. Grubb, eds. *American Education and Vocationalism.* New York: Teachers College Press, 1974.

Leiderman, P. H. "Social Ecology and Childbirth: The Newborn Nursery as Environmental Stressor." In *Stress, Coping, and Development in Children.* N. Garmezy and M. Rutter, eds. New York: McGraw-Hill, 1983, pp. 133–59.

Levin, H. M. "The Educationally Disadvantaged: A National Crisis." *The State Youth Initiatives Project, Working Paper No. 6.* Philadelphia: Public/Private Ventures, 1985.

Levine, D. U. "Successful Approaches for Improving Academic Achievement in Inner-City Elementary Schools." *Phi Delta Kappan* (Apr. 1982): 523–26.

Levine, M. D. "A Study of Risk Factor Complexes in Early Adolescent Delinquency." *American Journal of the Diseases of Childhood* 139 (Jan. 1985): 50–56.

Levitan, S. A. *The Great Society's Poor Law: A New Approach to Poverty.* Baltimore: Johns Hopkins University Press, 1969.

Levy, F. *Dollars and Dreams: The Changing American Income Distribution.* New York: Russell Sage, 1987.

Lewis, D. O., and D. A. Balla. *Delinquency and Psychopathology.* New York: Grune and Stratton, 1976.

Lewis, D. O., and S. Shanok. "A Comparison of the Medical Histories of Incarcerated Delinquent Children and a Matched Sample of Nondelinquent Children." *Child Psychiatry and Human Development* 9 (1979): 210–14.

Lewis, D. O., M. Feldman, and A. Barrengos. "Race, Health and Delinquency." *Journal of the American Academy of Child Psychiatry* 24 (1985): 161–67.

———. "Violent Juvenile Delinquents: Psychiatric, Neurological, Psychological and Abuse Factors." *Journal of the American Academy of Child Psychiatry* 18 (1979): 307–19.

Lightfoot, S. L. *Worlds Apart.* New York: Basic Books, 1978.

Loeber, R., and T. Dishion. "Early Predictors of Male Delinquency: A Review." *Psychological Bulletin* 94, no. 1 (1983): 68–99.

Long, J. V. F., and G. E. Vaillant. "Natural History of Male Psychological Health, XI: Escape From the Underclass." *American Journal of Psychiatry* 141, no. 3 (Mar. 1984): 341–46.

Lovick, S., and W. F. Wesson. *School-Based Clinics: Update 1986.* Washington, D.C.: Center for Population Options, 1986.

Maccoby, E. E. "Social-Emotional Development and Response to Stressors." In *Stress, Coping, and Development in Children.* N. Garmezy and M. Rutter, eds. New York: McGraw-Hill, 1983, pp. 217–34.

Manchester, W. *The Glory and the Dream.* Boston: Little, Brown, 1974.

Mann, H. "Report to the Massachusetts State Board of Education, 1848." In *Documents of American History,* H. S. Commanger, ed. New York: Appleton-Century-Crofts, 1948.

Mayer, J. L. "Time Out." *New York Times Magazine* (19 Oct. 1986): 96.

McAdoo, H. P. "Factors Related to Stability in Upwardly Mobile Black Families." *Journal of Marriage and the Family* 40 (1978): 761–78.

McAlister, A. L. "Tobacco, Alcohol, and Drug Abuse: Onset and Prevention." In *Healthy People: The Surgeon General's Report on Health Promotion and Disease Prevention.* Vol. 2. Washington, D.C.: U.S. Department of Health, Education and Welfare, Public Health Service, 1979, pp. 197–206.

McAlister, A. L., C. Perry, and N. Maccoby. "Adolescent Smoking: Onset and Prevention." *Pediatrics* 63 (1979): 650–58.

McAnarney, E. R., and C. Shreider. *Identifying Social and Psychological Antecedents of Adolescent Pregnancy: The Contributions of Research to Concepts of Prevention.* New York: William T. Grant Foundation, 1984.

McCall, R. B. "A Hard Look at Stimulating and Predicting Development: The Cases of Bonding and Screening." *Pediatrics in Review* 3, no. 7 (Jan. 1982): 203–8.

McCarton, C. M. "The Long-Term Impact of a Low Birth Weight Infant on the Family." *Zero to Three* 6, no. 4 (Apr. 1986): 6–10.

McCormick, M. C. "The Contribution of Low Birthweight to Infant Mortality and Childhood Morbidity." *New England Journal of Medicine* 312 (1985): 82–90.

McCormick, M. C., S. Shapiro, and B. H. Starfield. "Rehospitalization in the First Year of Life for High-Risk Survivors." *Pediatrics* 66 (1980): 991–99.

McCullers, C. *The Ballad of the Sad Cafe and Collected Short Stories.* Boston: Houghton Mifflin, 1979.

McGee, E. A. *Too Little, Too Late: Services for Teenage Parents.* New York: Ford Foundation, 1982.

Menken, J. "The Health and Social Consequences of Teenage Childbearing." In *Teenage Sexuality, Pregnancy and Childbearing,* F. F. Furstenberg, Jr., R. Lincoln, and J. Menken, eds. Philadelphia: University of Pennsylvania Press, 1981, pp. 167–83.

Meyers, J. A. "A Letter from the Publisher." *Time* (9 Dec. 1985): 4.

Miller, C. A. "Infant Mortality in the U.S." *Scientific American* 231, no. 1 (1985): 31–37.

———. *Maternal Health and Infant Survival: An Analysis of Medical and Social*

Services to Pregnant Women, Newborns and Their Families in Ten European Countries. Washington, D.C.: National Center for Clinical Infant Programs, 1987.

Miller, C. A., A. Fine, S. Adams-Taylor, and L. B. Schorr. *Monitoring Children's Health: Key Indicators.* Washington, D.C.: American Public Health Association, 1986.

Miller, G., and F. Miller. "The Painful Prescription: A Procrustean Perspective." *New England Journal of Medicine* 314, no. 21 (22 May 1986): 1380–84.

Miller, S. M. "Dropouts—A Political Problem." In *Profile of the School Dropout,* D. Schreiber, ed. Washington, D.C.: National Education Association, 1964, pp. 11–24.

Montalvo, F. "Making Good Schools from Bad." In *Make Something Happen.* Vol. 2. New York: Hispanic Policy Development Project, 1984, pp. 71–74.

Moore, K. A. *Children of Teen Parents: Heterogeneity of Outcomes.* Final Report to the National Institute of Child Health and Human Development. Washington, D.C.: Child Trends, 1986.

————. "Teenage Childbirth and Welfare Dependency." *Family Planning Perspectives* 10 (1978): 233–35.

Moore, K. A., and M. R. Burt. *Private Crises, Public Cost: Policy Perspectives on Teenage Childbearing.* Washington, D.C.: Urban Institute Press, 1982.

Moore, K. A., and R. F. Werthheimer. "Teenage Childbearing and Welfare: Preventive and Ameliorative Strategies." *Family Planning Perspectives* 16, no. 6 (Nov.–Dec. 1984): 285–89.

Morehead, M. A., R. S. Donaldson, and M. R. Seravalli. "Comparisons Between OEO Neighborhood Health Centers and Other Health Care Providers of Ratings of the Quality of Health Care." *American Journal of Public Health* 61, no. 7 (July 1971): 1294–1306.

Mott, F. L., and W. Marsiglio. "Early Childbearing and Completion of High School." *Family Planning Perspectives* 17, no. 5 (Sep.–Oct. 1985): 234–7.

Moynihan, D. P. *Family and Nation.* San Diego: Harcourt Brace Jovanovich, 1986.

Murray, C. *Losing Ground: American Social Policy 1950–1980.* New York: Basic Books, 1984.

Murray, C. A. *The Link Between Learning Disabilities and Juvenile Delinquency, Current Theory and Knowledge.* Washington, D.C.: National Institute for Juvenile Justice and Delinquency Prevention, 1976.

Musick, J. S., F. M. Stott, K. K. Spencer, J. Goldman, and B. J. Cohler. "Maternal Factors Related to Vulnerability and Resiliency in Young Children at Risk." In *The Invulnerable Child,* E. J. Anthony and B. Cohler, eds. New York: Guilford, 1984.

Myrdal, G. *An American Dilemma.* New York: Harper and Row, 1944.

Nathanson, C. A., and M. H. Becker. "The Influence of Client-Provider Relationships on Teenage Women's Subsequent Use of Contraception." *American Journal of Public Health* 75, no. 75 (Jan. 1985): 33–38.

National Academy of Sciences. *High Schools and the Changing Workplace: The Employers' View.* Washington, D.C.: National Academy of Sciences, 1984.

National Center for Health Statistics. "Advance Report of Final Natality Statistics, 1984." *Monthly Vital Statistics Report* 35, no. 4. Hyattsville, Md.: U.S. Public Health Service, 1986.

———. "Apgar Scores in the United States, 1978." *Monthly Vital Statistics Report* 30, no. 1 (1981).

———. *Health, United States, 1985.* DHHS pub. no. (PHS) 86-1232. Washington, D.C.: U.S. Government Printing Office, 1985.

———. *Health, United States, 1986.* DHHS pub. no. (PHS) 87-1232. Washington, D.C.: U.S. Government Printing Office, 1986.

———. "Interval Between Births: United States, 1970–1977." *Vital and Health Statistics,* ser. 21, no. 39 (1981).

National Coalition of Advocates for Students. *Barriers to Excellence: Our Children at Risk.* Boston, Mass.: The National Coalition of Advocates for Students, 1985.

National Commission on Excellence in Education. *A Nation at Risk: The Imperative for Educational Reform.* Washington, D.C.: U.S. Department of Education, 1983.

National Governors' Association. *The First Sixty Months.* Washington, D.C.: National Governors' Association, 1987.

Naylor, A. "Child Day Care: Threat to Family Life or Primary Prevention?" *Journal of Preventive Psychiatry* 1, no. 4 (1982): 431–41.

Needleman, H. L., C. Nunnoe, A. Leviton, R. Reed, H. Peresie, C. Maher, and P. Barrett. "Deficits in Psychological and Classroom Performance of Children with Elevated Dentine Lead Level." *New England Journal of Medicine* 300 (1979): 689.

Neubauer, P. B. *Process of Child Development.* New York: New American Library, 1976.

New York City, Early Childhood Commission. *Take a Giant Step: An Equal Start in Education for All New York City Four-Year-Olds.* New York: Early Childhood Commission, 1986.

Nicholi, A. M. "The Nontherapeutic Use of Psychoactive Drugs." *New England Journal of Medicine* 308, no. 16 (21 Apr. 1983): 925–33.

Norton, E. H. "Restoring the Traditional Black Family." *New York Times Magazine* (2 June 1985): 43.

Novak, M. *The New Consensus on Family and Welfare.* Washington, D.C.: American Enterprise Institute for Public Policy Research, 1987.

O'Connell, M., and C. C. Rogers. "Out-of-Wedlock Births, Premarital Pregnancies and Their Effect on Family Formation and Dissolution." *Family Planning Perspectives* 16, no. 4 (July–Aug. 1984): 157–62.

Office of Technology Assessment. *Children's Mental Health: Problems and Services.* Washington, D.C.: U.S. Government Printing Office, 1986.

Ogbu, J. U. *The Next Generation: An Ethnography of Education in an Urban Neighborhood.* New York: Academic Press, 1974.

Olds, D. L. "Improving Formal Services for Mothers and Children." In *Protecting Children from Abuse and Neglect,* J. Garbarino and S. H. Stocking, eds. San Francisco: Jossey-Bass, 1981, pp. 173–97.

———. "The Prenatal/Early Infancy Project." In *In the Beginning,* J. Belsky, ed. New York: Columbia University Press, 1982, pp. 270–85.

Olds, D. L., C. R. Henderson, R. Chamberlin, and R. Tatelbaum. "Preventing

Child Abuse and Neglect: A Randomized Trial of Nurse Home Visitation."
Pediatrics 78 (July 1986): 65–78.

Olds, D. L., C. R. Henderson, R. Tatelbaum, and R. Chamberlin. "Improving the
Delivery of Prenatal Care and Outcomes of Pregnancy: A Randomized Trial of
Nurse Home Visitation." *Pediatrics* 77, no. 1 (Jan. 1986): 16–28.

Orr, S. T., and S. James. "Maternal Depression in an Urban Pediatric Practice:
Implications for Health Care Delivery." *American Journal of Public Health* 74,
no. 4 (Apr. 1984): 363–65.

Orr, S. T., and C. A. Miller. "Utilization of Health Services by Poor Children
Since Advent of Medicaid." *Medical Care* 19, no. 6 (June 1981): 583–90.

Orr, S. T., C. A. Miller, and S. A. James. "Differences in Use of Health Services by
Children According to Race: Relative Importance of Cultural and System-re-
lated Factors." *Medical Care* 22, no. 9 (Sep. 1984): 848–53.

Patterson, G. R. "Stress: A Change Agent for Family Process." In *Stress, Coping,
and Development in Children.* N. Garmezy and M. Rutter, eds. New York:
McGraw-Hill, 1983, pp. 235–64.

Patterson, G. R., P. Chamberlain, and J. B. Reid. "A Comparative Evaluation of a
Parent-Training Program." *Behavior Therapy* 13 (1982): 638–50.

Phillips, D. "The Federal Model Child Care Standards Act of 1985: Step in the
Right Direction or Hollow Gesture." *American Journal of Orthopsychiatry* 56,
no. 5 (Jan. 1986): 56–63.

Phillips, D., K. McCartney, S. Scarr, and C. Howes. "Selective Review of Infant
Day Care Research: A Cause for Concern!" *Zero to Three* 7, no. 3 (Feb. 1987):
18–21.

Phipps-Yonas, S. "Teenage Pregnancy and Motherhood: A Review of the Literature." *American Journal of Orthopsychiatry* 50, no. 3 (July 1980): 403–31.

Piechnik, S., and M. A. Corbett. "Reducing Low Birthweight among Socio-Economically High Risk Adolescent Pregnancies." *Journal of Nurse-Midwifery* 30
(Mar.–Apr. 1985): 88.

Pierson, D. E., D. K. Walker, and T. Tivnan. "A School-Based Program from
Infancy to Kindergarten for Children and Their Parents." *Personnel and Guidance Journal* 62, no. 8 (Apr. 1984): 448–55.

Plunkett, V. R. L. "From Title I to Chapter I: The Evolution of Compensatory
Education." *Phi Delta Kappan* (Apr. 1985): 533–37.

Polansky, N. A. "Isolation of the Neglectful Family." *American Journal of Orthopsychiatry* 49, no. 1 (Jan. 1979): 149–52.

Polansky, N. A., M. A. Chambers, E. Buttenwieser, and D. P. Williams. *Damaged
Parents: An Anatomy of Child Neglect.* Chicago: University of Chicago Press,
1981.

Porter, P. J. "St. Paul: Facing Teen Pregnancy." In *Healthy Children.* Boston:
Harvard University, Division of Health Policy, 1985, pp. 4–11.

Pratt, W. F., W. D. Mosher, C. A. Bachrach, and M. C. Horn. "Understanding
U.S. Fertility: Findings from the National Survey of Family Growth, Cycle III."
Population Bulletin 39, no. 5 (Dec. 1984): 1–42.

President's Commission on Mental Health. *Learning Failure and Unused Learning
Potential.* Report of the Task Panel on Learning Failure and Unused Learning
Potential, Task Panel Reports Submitted to the President's Commission on

Mental Health. Vol. 3. Washington, D.C.: U.S. Government Printing Office. 1978.

Presser, H. B. "Early Motherhood: Ignorance or Bliss?" *Family Planning Perspectives* 6 (1974): 8–14.

Preston, S. H. "Children and the Elderly in the U.S." *Scientific American* 251, no. 6 (Dec. 1984): 44–48.

Provence, S., and A. Naylor. *Working with Disadvantaged Parents and Their Children.* New Haven: Yale University Press, 1983.

Public Papers of the Presidents of the U.S., L. B. Johnson, 1965. Washington, D.C.: U.S. Government Printing Office, 1966.

Purkey, S. C., and M. S. Smith. "Effective Schools: A Review." *Elementary School Journal* 83, no. 4 (1983): 427–52.

Reinhardt, U. E. "Hard Choices in Health Care: A Matter of Ethics." In *Health Care: How to Improve It and Pay For It.* Washington, D.C.: Center for National Policy, 1985, pp. 19–32.

Relman, A. S. "Economic Considerations in Emergency Care: What Are Hospitals For?" *New England Journal of Medicine* 312, no. 6 (7 Feb. 1985): 372.

———. "The United States and Canada: Different Approaches to Health Care." *New England Journal of Medicine* 315, no. 25 (18 Dec. 1986): 1608–10.

Rice, E. P., M. C. Ekdahl, and L. Miller. *Children of Mentally Ill Parents.* New York: Behavioral Publications, 1971.

Rich, D. *The Forgotten Factor in School Success—The Family.* Washington, D.C.: Home and School Institute, 1985.

Richmond, J. B. "Head Start, A Retrospective View: The Founders." In *Project Head Start: A Legacy of the War on Poverty,* E. Zigler and J. Valentine, eds. New York: The Free Press, 1979, pp. 120–28.

———. "Disadvantaged Children: What Have They Compelled Us to Learn?" *Yale Journal of Biology and Medicine* 43 (Dec. 1970): 127–44.

Richmond, J. B., and B. M. Caldwell. "Mental Retardation—Cultural and Social Considerations: A Day Care Program for Disadvantaged Infants and Young Children." In *Child Care in Health and Disease,* A. Dorfman, ed. Chicago: Yearbook Publishers, 1968, pp. 126–39.

Richmond, J. B., D. J. Stipek, and E. Zigler. "A Decade of Head Start." In *Project Head Start,* E. Zigler and J. Valentine, eds. New York: Free Press, 1979, pp. 135–52.

Ricketts, E. R., and I. V. Sawhill. "Defining and Measuring the Underclass." Discussion Paper. Washington, D.C.: Urban Institute, 1986.

Rist, R. C. "Student Social Class and Teacher Expectations: The Self-Fulfilling Prophecy in Ghetto Education." *Harvard Educational Review* 40 (1970):411–51.

Robert Wood Johnson Foundation. *Annual Report, 1984.* Princeton, N.J.: Robert Wood Johnson Foundation, 1984.

———. *Special Report.* No. 2. Princeton, N.J.: Robert Wood Johnson Foundation, 1985.

———. *Special Report.* No. 3. Princeton, N.J.: Robert Wood Johnson Foundation, 1985.

———. "Updated Report on Access to Health Care for the American People," *Special Report.* No. 1. Princeton, N.J.: Robert Wood Johnson Foundation, 1983.

Robins, L. N. "The Natural History of Adolescent Drug Use." *American Journal of Public Health* 74, no. 7 (July 1984): 656–57.

———. "Sturdy Childhood Predictors of Adult Antisocial Behavior: Replications from Longitudinal Studies." *Psychological Medicine* 6 (1978): 611–22.

Rogers, D. E., R. J. Blendon, and T. W. Moloney. "Who Needs Medicaid?" *New England Journal of Medicine* 301, no. 1 (1 July 1982): 13–18.

Rosenbach, M. *Insurance Coverage and Ambulatory Medical Care of Low-Income Children: United States, 1980.* National Medical Care Utilization and Expenditure Survey, Series C. Washington, D.C.: National Center for Health Statistics, 1985.

Rosenbaum, S. "Children and Private Health Insurance." In *Children in a Changing Health Care System.* M. Schlesinger and L. Eisenberg, eds. Baltimore: Johns Hopkins University Press (in press).

———. *Medicaid Eligibility for Pregnant Women.* Washington, D.C.: Children's Defense Fund, 1987.

Rosenbaum, S., and K. Johnson. *Maternal and Child Health: Exemplary State Initiatives.* Washington, D.C.: Children's Defense Fund, 1985.

———. "Providing Health Care for Low-income Children: Reconciling Child Health Goals with Child Health Financing Realities." *Milbank Quarterly* 64, no. 3 (1986) 442–78.

Rosenbaum, S., K. Johnson, and D. Hughes. *Maternal and Child Health: Beyond the Reagan Era.* Washington, D.C.: Children's Defense Fund, 1988.

Rosett, H. L., L. Werner, and K. Edelin. "Treatment Experience with Pregnant Problem Drinkers." *Journal of the American Medical Association* 249, no. 15 (15 Apr. 1983): 2029–33.

Rossi, A. S. "A Biosocial Perspective on Parenting." *Daedalus* (Spring 1977): 1–31.

Rubinstein, E. A. "Television as a Sex Educator." In *Sex Education in the Eighties: The Challenge of Healthy Sexual Evolution.* L. Brown, ed. New York: Plenum, 1980, pp. 115–26.

Ruggles, P., and W. P. Marton. "Measuring the Size and Characteristics of the Underclass: How Much Do We Know?" Washington, D.C.: Urban Institute, 1986.

Rush, D. "Is WIC Worthwhile?" *American Journal of Public Health* 72, no. 10 (Oct. 1982): 1101.

Rutter, M. *Changing Youth in a Changing Society: Patterns of Adolescent Development and Disorder.* Cambridge, Mass.: Harvard University Press, 1980.

———. "Maternal Deprivation, 1972–1978: New Findings, New Concepts, New Approaches." *Child Development* 50 (1979): 283–305.

———. *Maternal Deprivation Reassessed.* New York: Penguin, 1972.

———. "Prevention of Children's Psychosocial Disorders: Myth and Substance." *Pediatrics* 6 (1982): 883–94.

———. "Psychological Therapies in Child Psychiatry: Issues and Prospects." *Psychological Medicine* 12 (1982): 723–40.

———. "Separation Experiences: A New Look at an Old Topic." *Pediatrics* 95 (1979): 147–54.

———. "Stress, Coping and Development: Some Issues and Some Questions." In

Stress, Coping and Development in Children. N. Garmezy and M. Rutter, eds. New York: McGraw-Hill, 1983, pp. 1–41.

Rutter, M., B. Maughan, P. Mortimore, and J. Ouston. *Fifteen Thousand Hours: Secondary Schools and Their Effects on Children.* Cambridge, Mass.: Harvard University Press, 1979.

Sadler, M. "Impressions of American Education." *Educational Review* 25 (1903).

St. Vincent Millay, E. *Collected Poems.* New York: Harper & Row, 1939.

Sale, J. S. "Family Day Care: One Alternative in the Delivery of Developmental Services in Early Childhood." *American Journal of Orthopsychiatry* 43, no. 1 (Jan. 1973): 37–45.

———. "Family Day Care—Potential Child Development Service." *American Journal of Public Health* 62, no. 5 (May 1972): 668–70.

Sameroff, A. J., and S. McDonough. "The Role of Motor Activity in Human Cognitive and Social Development." In *Energy Intake and Activity,* E. Pollitt and P. Amante, eds. New York: Alan R. Liss, 1984, pp. 331–53.

Sawhill, I. V. "Anti-Poverty Strategies for the Next Decade." In *Work and Welfare: The Case for New Directions in National Policy.* Washington, D.C.: Center for National Policy, 1987, pp. 21–34.

Schlesinger, H. J., E. Mumford, and G. V. Glass. "The Effects of Psychological Intervention on Recovery from Surgery." In *Emotional and Psychological Responses to Anesthesia and Surgery,* F. Guerra and J. A. Aldrete, eds. New York: Grune and Stratton, 1980, pp. 9–18.

Schorr, A. L. *Common Decency: Domestic Policies after Reagan.* New Haven: Yale University Press, 1986.

Schorr, L. B. "The Neighborhood Health Center—Background and Current Issues." In *Medicine in a Changing Society,* L. Corey, S. E. Saltman, and M. F. Epstein, eds. Saint Louis: C. V. Mosby, 1972, pp. 138–47.

———. "Environmental Deterrents: Poverty, Affluence, Violence and Television." In *Developmental-Behavioral Pediatrics,* M. D. Levine, W. B. Carey, A. C. Crocket, and R. T. Gross, eds. Philadelphia: W. B. Saunders, 1983, 293–312.

Schwarz, J. E. *America's Hidden Success: A Reassessment of Public Policy from Kennedy to Reagan.* New York: W. W. Norton, 1988.

Schweinhart, L. J., and D. P. Weikart. "The Effects of the Perry Preschool Program on Youths Through Age 15." In *As the Twig is Bent . . . Lasting Effects of Preschool Programs,* Consortium for Longitudinal Studies. Hillsdale, N.J.: Lawrence Erlbaum Associates, 1983, pp. 71–101.

———. "Evidence that Good Early Childhood Programs Work." *Phi Delta Kappan* (Apr. 1985): 545–51.

———. *Young Children Grow Up: The Effects of the Perry Preschool on Youths Through Age 15.* Ypsilanti, Mich.: High/Scope Press, 1980.

Sebrell, W. H., Jr. "Clinical Nutrition in the United States." *American Journal of Public Health* 59, no. 11 (1968) 2035–42.

Segal, J., and H. Yahraes. *A Child's Journey.* New York: McGraw-Hill, 1979.

Seitz, V., L. K. Rosenbaum, and N. H. Apfel. "Effects of Family Support Intervention: A Ten-Year Follow-Up." *Child Development* 53 (1985): 376–91.

Select Panel for the Promotion of Child Health. *Better Health for Our Children: A*

National Strategy. 4 vols. Washington, D.C.: U.S. Department of Health and Human Services, 1981.

Selznick, P. *Leadership in Administration: A Sociological Perspective.* New York: Harper & Row, 1957.

Sexton, M., and J. R. Hebel. "A Clinical Trial of Change in Maternal Smoking and Its Effects on Birthweight." *Journal of the American Medical Association* 251 (1984): 911–15.

Shea, J. A., R. Herceg-Baron, and F. F. Furstenberg, Jr. "Factors Associated with Adolescent Use of Family Planning Clinics." *American Journal of Public Health* 74, no. 11 (Nov. 1984): 1227–30.

Shipman, V. C. *Disadvantaged Children and Their First School Experiences.* Princeton, N. J.: Educational Testing Service, 1976.

Shonkoff, J. P. "Social Support and the Development of Vulnerable Children." *American Journal of Public Health* 74, no. 4 (Apr. 1984): 310–12.

Showell, W. *Biennial Report of CSD's Intensive Family Services.* Salem, Oreg.: State of Oregon Intensive Family Services Unit, 1985.

Shriver, R. S. "Head Start, A Retrospective View: The Founders." In *Project Head Start: A Legacy of the War on Poverty,* E. Zigler and J. Valentine, eds. New York: The Free Press, 1979, pp. 49–67.

Siegel, E., K. Bauman, E. Schaefer, M. Saunders, and D. Ingram. "Hospital and Home Support During Infancy: Impact on Maternal Attachment, Child Abuse and Neglect, and Health Care Utilization." *Pediatrics* 66, no. 2 (Aug. 1980): 183–90.

Singh, S., A. Torres, and J. D. Forrest. "The Need for Prenatal Care in the United States: Evidence from the 1980 National Natality Survey." *Family Planning Perspectives* 17, no. 3 (May–June 1985): 118–24.

Sizer, T. R. *Horace's Compromise: The Dilemma of the American High School.* Boston: Houghton Mifflin, 1985.

Skeels, H. M. "A Study of the Effects of Differential Stimulation on Mentally Retarded Children: Follow-up Report." *American Journal of Mental Deficiency* 46 (1942): 340–50.

Skeels, H. M., and H. Dye. "A Study of the Effects of Differential Stimulation on Mentally Retarded Children." *Proceedings of the American Association of Mental Deficiency* 44 (1939): 114–36.

Smith, H. *The Russians.* New York: Ballentine, 1976.

Smith, M. L., and G. V. Glass. "Meta-Analysis of Psychotherapy Outcome Studies." *American Psychologist* 32 (1977): 752–60.

Sokol, R. J. "A Biological Perspective on Substance Use in Pregnancy: Alcohol as a Paradigm for Possible Effects of Drugs on the Offspring." In *Infants at Risk for Developmental Dysfunction,* D. Parran and L. Eisenberg, eds. Washington, D.C.: National Academy of Sciences, 1982, pp. 93–104.

Sokol, R. J., R. Woolf, M. Rosen, and K. Weingarten. "Risk, Antepartum Care, and Outcome: Impact of a Maternity and Infant Care Project." *Obstetrics and Gynecology* 56, no. 2 (Aug. 1980): 150–6.

Solnit, A. J. Foreword to S. Provence and A. Naylor, *Working with Disadvantaged Parents and Their Children.* New Haven: Yale University Press, 1983.

Stack, C. B. *All Our Kin: Strategies for Survival in the Black Community*. New York: Harper & Row, 1974.

Starfield, B. *The Effectiveness of Medical Care: Validating Clinical Wisdom*. Baltimore: Johns Hopkins University Press, 1985.

———. "Patients and Populations: Necessary Links Between the Two Approaches to Pediatric Research." *Pediatric Research* 15 (1981): 1–5.

———. "Social Factors in Child Health." In *Ambulatory Pediatrics III*, M. Green and R. Haggerty, eds. Philadelphia: W. B. Saunders, 1984.

Starr, P. "Health Care for the Poor: The Past Twenty Years." In *Fighting Poverty: What Works and What Doesn't*, S. H. Danziger and D. H. Weinberg, eds. Cambridge, Mass.: Harvard University Press, 1986, pp. 106–32.

———. *The Social Transformation of American Medicine*. New York: Basic Books, 1982.

Stewart, J. C., and L. L. Crafton. *Delivery of Health Care Services to the Poor: Findings from a Review of the Current Periodical Literature*. Human Services Monograph Series, no. 1 Austin, Tex.: University of Texas at Austin, Center for Social Work Research, 1975.

Stickney, B. D., and L. R. Marcus. "Education and the Disadvantaged 20 Years Later." *Phi Delta Kappan* (Apr. 1985): 559–67.

Stroup, A. L., and L. N. Robins. "Elementary School Predictors of High School Dropout Among Black Males." *Sociology of Education* 25 (Spring 1972): 212–22.

Suchrindam, C. M. *Consequences of Adolescent Pregnancy and Childbearing*. Washington, D.C.: National Institute of Child Health and Human Development, Department of Health, Education and Welfare, 1978.

Sugarman, J. M. "Head Start, A Retrospective View: The Founders." In *Project Head Start: A Legacy of the War on Poverty*, E. Zigler and J. Valentine, eds. New York: The Free Press, 1979, pp. 114–20.

Sulvetta, M. B., and K. Swartz. *The Uninsured and Uncompensated Care: A Chartbook*. Washington, D.C.: National Health Policy Forum, 1986.

Suomi, S. J. "Short- and Long-Term Effects of Repetitive Mother-Infant Separations on Social Development in Rhesus Monkeys." *Developmental Psychology* 19, no. 5 (Sep. 1983): 770–86.

Sykes, G. "The Deal." *Wilson Quarterly* (New Year's 1984): 59–77.

Szykula, S. A., and M. J. Fleischman. "Reducing Out-of-Home Placements of Abused Children: Two Controlled Field Studies." *Child Abuse and Neglect* 9 (1985): 277–83.

Tanner, J. M. "Sequence, Tempo and Individual Variation in the Growth and Development of Boys and Girls Aged Twelve to Sixteen." *Daedalus* (Fall 1971): 907–30.

Task Force on Education for Economic Growth. *Action for Excellence: A Comprehensive Plan to Improve our Nation's Schools*. Denver: Education Commission of the States, 1983.

Taylor, B., J. Wadsworth, and N. R. Butler. "Teenage Mothering, Admission to Hospitals and Accidents During the First Five Years." *Archives of Disease in Childhood* 58, no. 1 (1983):6–11.

Thomas, A., and S. Chess. "Genesis and Evolution of Behavioral Disorders: From

Infancy to Early Adult Life." *American Journal of Psychiatry* 141, no. 1 (Jan. 1984): 1–9.

Thurow, L. C. "Learning to Say 'No.' " *New England Journal of Medicine* 311, no. 24 (13 Dec. 1984): 1569–72.

———. "Medicine versus Economics." *New England Journal of Medicine* 313, no. 10 (5 Sep. 1985): 611–14.

Tizard, B., and M. Hughes. *Young Children Learning.* Cambridge, Mass.: Harvard University Press, 1984.

Tizard, J., W. N. Schofield, and J. Hewison. "Collaboration Between Teachers and Parents in Assisting Children's Reading." *British Journal of Educational Psychology* 52, part 1 (1982): 1–15.

Torres, A., and J. D. Forrest. "Family Planning Clinic Services in the United States, 1981." *Family Planning Perspectives* 15, no. 6 (Nov.–Dec. 1983): 272–78.

Trickett, P. K., N. H. Apfel, L. K. Rosenbaum, and E. F. Zigler. "A Five Year Follow-Up of Participants in the Yale Child Welfare Research Program." In *Day Care: Scientific and Social Policy Issues,* E. F. Zigler and E. W. Gordon, eds. Boston: Auburn House, 1981, pp. 200–22.

Tyack, D., and E. Hansot. "Hard Times, Hard Choices: The Case for Coherence in Public School Leadership." *Phi Delta Kappan* (Apr. 1982): 511–15.

———. "Hard Times, Then and Now: Public Schools in the 1930s and 1980s." *Harvard Education Review* 54 (Feb. 1984): 33–66.

Unger, D. G., and L. P. Wandersman. "Social Support and Adolescent Mothers: Action Research Contributions to Theory and Application." *Journal of Social Issues* 41, no. 1 (1985): 29–45.

U.S. Bureau of the Census. *Current Population Reports.* ser. P-60, no. 157. (Advance Report). Washington, D.C.: U.S. Government Printing Office, 1987.

———. *Who's Minding the Kids? Child Care Arrangements: Winter 1984–85.* Current Population Report, ser. P-70, no. 9. Washington, D.C.: U.S. Government Printing Office, 1987.

U.S. Congress, House of Representatives, Committee on Ways and Means. *Children in Poverty.* Washington, D.C.: U.S. Government Printing Office, 1985.

U.S. Congress, House of Representatives, Select Committee on Children, Youth and Families. *U.S. Children and their Families: Current Conditions and Recent Trends, 1987.* Washington, D.C.: U.S. Government Printing Office, 1987.

U.S. Department of Defense, Office of the Assistant Secretary of Defense. *Profile of American Youth.* Washington, D.C.: U.S. Department of Defense, 1982.

U.S. Department of Education. *The Condition of Education.* Washington, D.C.: U.S. Government Printing Office, 1984.

———. *The Condition of Education.* Washington, D.C.: U.S. Government Printing Office, 1986.

———. *Digest of Education Statistics, 1983–84.* Washington, D.C.: U.S. Government Printing Office, 1983.

———. *What Works: Research About Teaching and Learning.* Washington, D.C.: U.S. Department of Education, 1986.

———. *What Works: Schools That Work, Educating Disadvantaged Children.* Washington, D.C.: U.S. Department of Education, 1987.

U.S. Department of Health, Education and Welfare. *Healthy People, The Surgeon*

General's Report on Health Promotion and Disease Prevention. Washington, D.C.: U.S. Government Printing Office, 1979.

U.S. Department of Justice, Bureau of Justice Statistics. *Households Touched by Crime, 1985.* Washington, D.C.: U.S. Department of Justice, 1986.

———. *Imprisonment in Four Countries, Special Report.* Washington, D.C.: U.S. Department of Justice, 1987.

———. *Prisoners in 1985.* Washington, D.C.: U.S. Department of Justice, 1985.

———. *Report to the Nation on Crime and Justice: The Data.* Washington, D.C.: U.S. Department of Justice, 1983.

———. *State and Federal Prisoners, 1925–85.* Washington, D.C.: U.S. Department of Justice, 1986.

———. *Violent Crime by Strangers.* Washington, D.C.: U.S. Department of Justice, 1982.

U.S. General Accounting Office. *Labor Market Problems of Teenagers Result Largely from Doing Poorly in School.* Washington, D.C.: U.S. Government Printing Office, 1982.

Vaillant, G. E. "The Longitudinal Study of Behavioral Disorders." *American Journal of Psychiatry* 141, no. 1 (Jan. 1984): 61–62.

Viorst, J. *Necessary Losses: The Loves, Illusions, Dependencies and Impossible Expectations That All of Us Have to Give Up in Order to Grow.* New York: Simon and Schuster, 1986.

Wahler, R. G. "The Insular Mother: Her Problems in Parent-Child Treatment." *Journal of Applied Behavior Analysis* 13, no. 2 (Summer 1980): 207–19.

Wattenberg, B. J. *The Good News Is the Bad News Is Wrong.* New York: Simon and Schuster, 1984.

Weatherley, R. A., S. B. Perlman, M. H. Levine, and L. V. Klerman. "Comprehensive Programs for Pregnant Teenagers and Teenage Parents: How Successful Have They Been?" *Family Planning Perspectives* 18, no. 6 (Mar.–Apr. 1986): 73–78.

Weber, C. U., P. W. Foster, and D. P. Weikart. *An Economic Analysis of the Ypsilanti Perry Preschool Project.* Monographs of the High/Scope Educational Research Foundation, no. 5. Ypsilanti, Mich.: High/Scope Educational Research Foundation, 1978.

Weber, G. *Inner-City Children Can Be Taught to Read: Four Successful Schools.* Washington, D.C.: Council for Basic Education, 1971.

Weiner, N. A., and M. E. Wolfgang. "The Extent and Character of Violent Crime in America, 1969 to 1982." In *American Violence and Public Policy.* L. A. Curtis, ed. New Haven: Yale University Press, 1985, pp. 17–39.

Weiss, G., and L. Hechtman. "The Hyperactive Child Syndrome." *Science* 205 (1979): 1348–54.

Weissbourd, B. "History of Family Support Programs." In *America's Family Support Programs: Perspectives and Prospects,* S. L. Kagan, D. R. Powell, B. Weissbourd, and E. Zigler, eds. New Haven: Yale University Press, in press.

Weissman, M. M., and E. F. Paykel. *The Depressed Woman.* Chicago: University of Chicago Press, 1974.

Werner, E. E., J. M. Bierman, and F. E. French. *The Children of Kauai.* Honolulu: University Press of Hawaii, 1971.

Werner, E. E., and R. S. Smith. *Kauai's Children Come of Age.* Honolulu: University Press of Hawaii, 1977.

———. *Vulnerable but Invincible: A Longitudinal Study of Resilient Children and Youth.* New York: McGraw-Hill, 1982.

West, D. J., and D. P. Farrington. *Who Becomes Delinquent?* London: Heinemann Educational Books, 1973.

Whitman, D., and J. Thornton. "A Nation Apart." *U.S. News & World Report* (17 Mar. 1986): 18–21.

Wicks, A. B., and C. M. Caro. *Factors Affecting the Employability of Welfare Recipients.* Washington, D.C.: National Science and Law Center, 1986.

Wideman, J. E. *Brothers and Keepers.* New York: Holt, Rinehart and Winston, 1984.

Wilson, A. L. "Thoughts Following a Congressional Fellowship." *Zero to Three* 5, no. 4 (Apr. 1985): 12–15.

Wilson, J. Q. "Raising Kids." *Atlantic* (Oct. 1983): 45–56.

———. "The Rediscovery of Character: Private Virtue and Public Policy." *The Public Interest* 81 (Fall 1985): 3–16.

———. *Thinking About Crime.* New York: Basic Books, 1975.

Wilson, J. Q., and R. J. Herrnstein. *Crime and Human Nature.* New York: Simon and Schuster, 1985.

Wilson, W. J. *The Truly Disadvantaged: The Inner City, the Underclass and Public Policy.* Chicago: University of Chicago Press, 1987.

Wilson, W. J., and K. M. Neckerman. "Poverty and Family Structure: The Widening Gap between Evidence and Public Policy Issues." In *Fighting Poverty,* S. H. Danziger and D. H. Weinberg, eds. Cambridge, Mass.: Harvard University Press, 1986, pp. 232–59.

Wise, P. H., M. Kotelchuck, M. L. Wilson, and M. Mills. "Racial and Socioeconomic Disparities in Childhood Mortality in Boston." *New England Journal of Medicine* 313 (1985): 360–66.

Wittmer, D. S. "Model Versus Modal Child Care for Children from Low-Income Families." *Zero to Three* 6, no. 5 (Sep. 1986): 8–10.

Wortis, H. "Child-rearing Practices in a Low Socioeconomic Group." *Pediatrics* 32 (1963): 298–307.

Young, K. T., and E. Zigler. "Infant and Toddler Day Care: Regulations and Policy Implications." *American Journal of Orthopsychiatry* 56, no. 1 (Jan. 1986): 43–55.

Zabin, L. S., and S. D. Clark, Jr. "Why They Delay: A Study of Teenage Family Planning Clinic Patients." *Family Planning Perspectives* 13, no. 5 (Sep.–Oct. 1981): 205–17.

———. "Institutional Factors Affecting Teenagers' Choice and Reasons for Delay in Attending a Family Planning Clinic." *Family Planning Perspectives* 15, no. 1 (Jan.–Feb. 1983): 25–29.

Zabin, L. S., M. B. Hirsch, E. A. Smith, R. Streett, and J. B. Hardy. "Evaluation of a Pregnancy Prevention Program for Urban Teenagers." *Family Planing Perspectives* 18, no. 3 (May–June 1986): 119–26.

Zabin, L. S., J. F. Kanter, and M. Zelnik. "The Risk of Adolescent Pregnancy in the First Few Months of Intercourse." In *Teenage Sexuality, Pregnancy, and*

Childbearing, F. F. Furstenberg, Jr., R. Lincoln, and J. Menken, eds. Philadelphia, University of Pennsylvania Press, 1981, pp. 136–48.

Zabin, L. S., R. Streett, J. B. Hardy, and T. M. King. "A School-, Hospital- and University-Based Adolescent Pregnancy Prevention Program." *Journal of Reproductive Medicine* 29, no. 6 (June 1984): 421–26.

Zelnik, M., and J. F. Kanter. "Sexual Activity, Contraceptive Use and Pregnancy Among Metropolitan-Area Teenagers: 1971–1979." *Family Planning Perspectives* 12, no. 5 (Sep.–Oct. 1980): 230–37.

Zelnik, M., M. A. Koening, and Y. J. Kim. "Sources of Prescription Contraceptives and Subsequent Pregnancy Among Young Women." *Family Planning Perspectives* 16, no. 1 (Jan.–Feb. 1984): 6–13.

Zelnik, M., and F. K. Shah. "First Intercourse Among Young Americans." *Family Planning Perspectives* 15, no. 2 (Mar.–Apr. 1983): 64–70.

Zigler, E. "Assessing Head Start at 20: An Invited Commentary." *American Journal of Orthopsychiatry* 55, no. 4 (Oct. 1985): 603–9.

Zigler, E., and K. Anderson. "An Idea Whose Time Had Come: The Intellectual and Political Climate for Head Start." In *Project Head Start,* E. Zigler and J. Valentine, eds. New York: Free Press, 1979, pp. 3–20.

Zigler, E., and W. Berman. "Discerning the Future of Early Childhood Intervention." *American Psychologist* 38 (Aug. 1983): 894–906.

Zigler, E., and J. Valentine, eds. *Project Head Start: A Legacy of the War on Poverty.* New York: Free Press, 1979.

Zuckerman, B., D. K. Walker, D. A. Frank, and C. Chase. "Adolescent Pregnancy and Parenthood: An Update." In *Advances in Developmental and Behavioral Pediatrics,* vol. 7, M. Wolraich and D. K. Routh, eds. Greenwich, Conn.: JAI Press, 1986, pp. s275–311.

Zwick, D. I. "Some Accomplishments and Findings of Neighborhood Health Centers." *Milbank Memorial Fund Quarterly* 50, pt. 1, (Oct. 1972).

Index